T0205852

Lecture Notes in Artificial Intelligence 13101

Subseries of Lecture Notes in Computer Science

Series Editors

Randy Goebel
University of Alberta, Edmonton, Canada

Yuzuru Tanaka
Hokkaido University, Sapporo, Japan

Wolfgang Wahlster
DFKI and Saarland University, Saarbrücken, Germany

Founding Editor

Jörg Siekmann
DFKI and Saarland University, Saarbrücken, Germany

More information about this subseries at http://www.springer.com/series/1244

Max Bramer · Richard Ellis (Eds.)

Artificial Intelligence XXXVIII

41st SGAI International Conference
on Artificial Intelligence, AI 2021
Cambridge, UK, December 14–16, 2021
Proceedings

Editors
Max Bramer
University of Portsmouth
Portsmouth, UK

Richard Ellis
RKE Consulting
Micheldever, UK

ISSN 0302-9743   ISSN 1611-3349 (electronic)
Lecture Notes in Artificial Intelligence
ISBN 978-3-030-91099-0   ISBN 978-3-030-91100-3 (eBook)
https://doi.org/10.1007/978-3-030-91100-3

LNCS Sublibrary: SL7 – Artificial Intelligence

This Springer imprint is published by the registered company Springer Nature Switzerland AG
The registered company address is: Gewerbestrasse 11, 6330 Cham, Switzerland

Preface

This volume, entitled Artificial Intelligence XXXVIII, comprises the refereed papers presented at the 41st SGAI International Conference on Innovative Techniques and Applications of Artificial Intelligence, held in December 2021, in both the technical and the application streams. The conference was organised by SGAI, the British Computer Society Specialist Group on Artificial Intelligence. Because of the COVID-19 pandemic the event was held as a virtual conference using video-conferencing software.

The technical papers included present new and innovative developments in the field, divided into sections on machine learning and AI techniques. This year's Donald Michie Memorial Award for the best refereed technical paper was won by a paper entitled 'On the Generalization Abilities of Fine-Tuned Commonsense Language Representation Models' by Ke Shen and Mayank Kejriwal (University of Southern California, USA).

The application papers included present innovative applications of AI techniques in a number of subject domains. This year, the papers are divided into sections on applications of machine learning, AI for medicine and advances in applied AI. This year's Rob Milne Memorial Award for the best refereed application paper was won by a paper entitled 'Patients Forecasting in Emergency Services by using Machine Learning and Exogenous Variables' by Hugo Álvarez Chaves, David F. Barrero, Maria D. R-Moreno, and Mario Cobos (Universidad de Alcalá, Spain).

The volume also includes the text of short papers in both streams presented as posters at the conference.

On behalf of the conference Organising Committee, we would like to thank all those who contributed to the organisation of this year's programme, in particular the Program Committee members, the Executive Program Committees, and our administrators Mandy Bauer and Bryony Bramer.

September 2021   Max Bramer
                                                                        Richard Ellis

Organization

Conference Committee

Conference Chair

Max Bramer   University of Portsmouth, UK

Technical Program Chair

Max Bramer   University of Portsmouth, UK

Deputy Technical Program Chair

Jixin Ma   University of Greenwich, UK

Application Program Chair

Richard Ellis   RKE Consulting, UK

Workshop Organiser

Adrian Hopgood   University of Portsmouth, UK

Treasurer

Rosemary Gilligan   SGAI, UK

Poster Session Organiser

Richard Ellis   RKE Consulting, UK

AI Open Mic and Panel Session Organiser

Andrew Lea   University of Brighton, UK

Publicity Organiser

Frederic Stahl   DFKI - German Research Center for Artificial
                                    Intelligence, Germany

UK CBR Organiser

Stelios Kapetanakis   University of Brighton, UK

Conference Administrator

Mandy Bauer   BCS, UK

Paper Administrator

Bryony Bramer   SGAI, UK

Technical Executive Program Committee

Max Bramer (Chair)   University of Portsmouth, UK
Frans Coenen   University of Liverpool, UK
Adrian Hopgood   University of Portsmouth, UK
John Kingston   Nottingham Trent University, UK
Jixin Ma (Deputy Chair)   University of Greenwich, UK
Gilbert Owusu   BT, UK

Application Executive Program Committee

Richard Ellis (Chair)   RKE Consulting, UK
Nadia Abouayoub   SGAI, UK
Rosemary Gilligan   SGAI, UK
Andrew Lea   Amplify Life, UK
Lars Nolle   Jade University of Applied Sciences, Germany
Richard Wheeler   University of Edinburgh, UK

Technical Program Committee

Per-Arne Andersen   University of Agder, Norway
Juan Augusto   Middlesex University London, UK
Farshad Badie   Aalborg University, Denmark
Raed Sabri Hameed Batbooti   Southern Technical University and Basra
                                 Engineering Technical College, Iraq
Yaxin Bi   Ulster University, UK
Soufiane Boulehouache   University of 20 August 1955 of Skikda, Algeria
Max Bramer   University of Portsmouth, UK
Krysia Broda   Imperial College London, UK
Ken Brown   University College Cork, Ireland
Marcos Bueno   TU Eindhoven, The Netherlands
Nikolay Burlutskiy   ContextVision AB, Sweden
Philippe Chassy   University of Liverpool, UK

Darren Chitty	Aston University, UK
Frans Coenen	University of Liverpool, UK
Bertrand Cuissart	Université de Caen, France
Ireneusz Czarnowski	Gdynia Maritime University, Poland
Nicolas Durand	Aix-Marseille University, France
Frank Eichinger	DATEV eG, Germany
Hossein Ghodrati Noushahr	University of Leicester, UK
Chris Headleand	University of Lincoln UK
Adrian Hopgood	University of Portsmouth, UK
Joanna Jedrzejowicz	University of Gdansk, Poland
Stelios Kapetanakis	University of Brighton, UK
Navneet Kesher	Facebook, USA
John Kingston	Nottingham Trent University, UK
Ivan Koychev	University of Sofia, Bulgaria
Nicole Lee	University of Hong Kong, SAR China
Fernando Lopes	LNEG - National Laboratory of Energy and Geology, Portugal
Jixin Ma	University of Greenwich, UK
Fady Medhat	University of York, UK
Silja Meyer-Nieberg	Universität der Bundeswehr München, Germany
Roberto Micalizio	Università di Torino, Italy
Daniel Neagu	University of Bradford, UK
Lars Nolle	Jade University of Applied Sciences, Germany
Joanna Isabelle Olszewska	University of the West of Scotland, UK
Daniel O'Leary	University of Southern California, USA
Fernando Saenz-Perez	Universidad Complutense de Madrid, Spain
Miguel A. Salido	Universitat Politècnica de València, Spain
Sadiq Sani	BT Applied Research, UK
Rainer Schmidt	Rostock University Medical Center, Germany
Sid Shakya	BT TSO, UK
Frederic Stahl	DFKI - German Research Center for Artificial Intelligence, Germany
Simon Thompson	GFT Technology, UK
M. R. C. van Dongen	University College Cork, Ireland
Martin Wheatman	Yagadi Ltd, UK
Nirmalie Wiratunga	Robert Gordon University, UK

Application Program Committee

Hatem Ahriz	Robert Gordon University, UK
Ines Arana	Robert Gordon University, UK
Mercedes Arguello Casteleiro	University of Manchester, UK
Juan Carlos Augusto	Middlesex University London, UK
Ken Brown	University College Cork, Ireland
Nikolay Burlutskiy	ContextVision AB, Sweden
Xiaochun Cheng	Middlesex University London, UK

Contents

Short Technical Stream Papers

Application Papers

Applications of Machine Learning

AI for Medicine

Advances in Applied AI

Short Application Stream Papers

Technical Papers

On the Generalization Abilities of Fine-Tuned Commonsense Language Representation Models

Ke Shen and Mayank Kejriwal(✉)🄳

Information Sciences Institute, University of Southern California,
Marina del Rey, CA 90292, USA
kejriwal@isi.edu
https://usc-isi-i2.github.io/kejriwal/

Abstract. Recently, transformer-based methods such as RoBERTa and GPT-3 have led to significant experimental advances in natural language processing tasks such as question answering and commonsense reasoning. The latter is typically evaluated through multiple benchmarks framed as multiple-choice instances of the former. According to influential leaderboards hosted by the Allen Institute (evaluating state-of-the-art performance on commonsense reasoning benchmarks), models based on such transformer methods are approaching human-like performance and have average accuracy well over 80% on many benchmarks. Since these are *commonsense* benchmarks, a model that *generalizes* on commonsense reasoning should not experience much performance loss across multiple commonsense benchmarks. In this paper, we study the generalization issue in detail by designing and conducting a rigorous scientific study. Using five common benchmarks, multiple controls and statistical analysis, we find clear evidence that fine-tuned commonsense language models still do not generalize well, even with moderate changes to the experimental setup, and may, in fact, be susceptible to dataset bias.

Keywords: Commonsense reasoning · Language representation model · Generalization

1 Introduction

Commonsense reasoning has become a resurgent area of research in both the NLP and broader AI communities[1] [12,47,50], despite having been introduced as an early AI challenge more than 50 years ago, in the context of machine translation [3]. Traditionally, it was believed that the problem could only be solved through a combination of techniques, including Web mining, logical reasoning, handcrafted knowledge bases and crowdsourcing [14,29,36]. More recently, the advent of powerful 'transformer' neural networks, especially in NLP [15,31], suggests that the time is right to build commonsense reasoners that generalize to a

---

[1] Two other example domains include computer vision [51] and social networks [16].

© Springer Nature Switzerland AG 2021
M. Bramer and R. Ellis (Eds.): SGAI-AI 2021, LNAI 13101, pp. 3–16, 2021.
https://doi.org/10.1007/978-3-030-91100-3_1

wide variety of situations, including those involving social and physical reasoning [7,44]. There are several related reasons why commonsense reasoning is such an important topic in AI. Commonsense reasoning is an innately human ability that machines have (thus far) not proven adept at 'conquering' unlike other task-specific domains such as face recognition [30]. Perhaps for that reason, it has always presented an enticing challenge to many AI researchers throughout the decades [11,27,33,46]. There is also the widely held belief that, for a 'general AI' to truly emerge, commonsense reasoning is one problem, among others, that will need to be solved in a sufficiently robust manner [4]. A more functional reason for increased interest in commonsense reasoning is the rise of chatbots and other such 'conversational AI' services (e.g., Siri and Alexa) that represent an important area of innovation in industry [5,17,41,49]. Recently, the US Department of Defense also launched a machine common sense (MCS) program in which a diverse set of researchers and organizations, including the Allen Institute of Artificial Intelligence, is involved [43].

Despite the success of these models, there is some evidence, not necessarily all quantitative, to suggest that the models are still superficial i.e. do not have the same commonsense abilities as humans, despite what the performance numbers suggest. [14] suggested in a seminal review article that, for truly human-level, performance 'knowledge of the commonsense world– time, space, physical interactions, people, and so on-will be necessary.' While we do not deny the theoretical possibility that a language representation model such as BERT, RoBERTa or GPT-3 may have learned these different aspects of the real world purely by 'reading' large corpora of natural language [9,15,31], we do claim that such possibilities can, and must, be tested through rigorous evaluation. Unfortunately, as we cover in the *Related Work*, there has been little to no work by way of conducting such a systematic and focused analysis, with the central goal of evaluating generalization of a system on commonsense reasoning, using a publicly available and replicable system, although there is plenty of precedent for this type of study, as discussed in the *Related Work*.

In this paper, we attempt to address this gap by carefully designing and conducting an empirical study with the specific intent of answering the question of whether fine-tuned commonsense language models generalize in robust ways. Our goal is not to attack either a model or a particular benchmark, or a set of benchmarks, but to present clear and cautionary evidence that the current set of evaluations and reported results, as well as evaluation practices, need to be considered with more skepticism by the community. Considering the pace at which research on commonsense reasoning continues, we posit that this is a timely study and could serve as a methodology for future such studies assessing the generalization of commonsense AI.

2   Related Work

As noted in the *Introduction*, commonsense reasoning has recently experienced a resurgence in the AI research community. Central references that attest to this resurgence include [12,13,45,48,50,51]. We also noted that commonsense reasoning has also been an ambitious agenda in the past. It is not feasible to cite all relevant work herein; instead, we refer the reader both to the review article by [14], as well as more recent surveys on commonsense reasoning tasks and benchmarks [47].

Much progress has been made on specific *kinds* of commonsense reasoning, especially in reasoning about time and internal relations [25,39], reasoning about actions and change [37], and the sign calculus [14]. Semantics have played an important role in some of these successes [40] including 'semantic networks' and other structured sources, important ones of which include ConceptNet [19]. WordNet [35] and Cyc [26]. These resources have been frequently applied in multiple reasoning systems [2,8,28]. In contrast with WordNet and ConceptNet, Cyc focuses on designing a universal schema (a higher-order logic) to represent commonsense assertions, which also supports reasoning systems [38,42] conduct richer logical inference.

In the last decade, in particular, as more accurate but also more 'non-interpretable' (or explainable) models like neural networks have become more prevalent, a relevant line of research has developed in 'adversarially attacking' these models to understand their weaknesses in a variety of domains [1,23,53]. Other problems, that require more precise inputs and prompts, include bias in the data and also in the model [24,32]. This line of work is valuable precedent for our own work, and there has been some early work already on conducting such robustness tests on transformer-based language representation models [10,22,34]. However, this paper significantly departs in at least one respect from these lines of work–namely, we do not adversarially or selectively modify the input or the model in any way. Our results show, in fact, that sophisticated adversarial modifications are not necessary for concluding that generalization is a concern for transformer-based QA models.

Theoretical work on commonsense reasoning along the lines of cognitive science and computational commonsense paradigms should also be noted [18,20,21]. We note this line of work because it could potentially be used for designing better evaluations, as well as for diagnosing why some transformer-based models are not generalizing better, despite (individually) good performance across the board on many benchmark datasets.

3 Background and Preliminaries

3.1 Commonsense Question Answering (QA) Benchmarks

As noted in both the introduction and the related work, commonsense reasoning has emerged as an important and challenging research agenda in the last several years. The usual way to evaluate systems (with the state-of-the-art systems being based, in some significant way, on the transformer-based models described in the next section) purporting to be capable of commonsense reasoning in the natural language setting is to use *question answering* benchmarks with multiple choices per 'question' from which exactly one correct answer must be selected by the

	Example
aNLI	obs1: 'Jim was working on a project.' obs2: 'Luckily, he found it on a nearby shelf.' hyp1: 'Jim found he was missing an item.' hyp2: 'Jim needed a certain animal for it.'
HellaSwag	ctx a: 'Two men are on a platform, fencing.' ctx b: 'they' opt1: 'jab at each other with their swords.' opt2: 'are in a par four olympics match.' opt3: 'are slipping and sliding between two beams.' opt4: 'pick up sticks and start the match, alternating back and forth.'
PIQA	goal: 'Remove soap scum from shower door.' sol1: 'Rub hard with bed sheets, then rinse.' sol2: 'Rub hard with dryer sheets, then rinse.'
Social IQA	context: 'Carson was excited to wake up to attend school.' question: 'Why did Carson do this?' answerA: 'Take the big test.' answerB: 'Just say hello to friends.' answerC: 'Go to bed early.'
Cyc	question: 'Rob honoured Will. Cliff maligned Will. Who made Will feel happy?' answer option0: 'Joy' answer option1: 'Rob' answer option2: 'Cliff' answer option3: 'Daisy' answer option4: 'Charity'

Fig. 1. Question-answer instances from five commonsense benchmark datasets used for the evaluations in this paper. The question-like 'prompt' is highlighted in light gray, and the correct answer in dark gray.

system. The NLP (and broader AI) community has developed numerous such benchmarks, especially in the last 3–5 years, using a range of methodologies both for acquiring the questions and for devising the answers. We describe the five benchmarks used in the research study in this paper below, with references for further reading. Examples are provided in Fig. 1.

1. **aNLI (Abductive Natural Language Inference):** Abductive Natural Language Inference (aNLI)[2] [6] is a new commonsense benchmark dataset designed to test an AI system's capability to apply abductive reasoning and common sense to form possible explanations for a given set of observations. Formulated as a binary-classification task, the goal is to pick the most plausible explanatory hypothesis given two observations from narrative contexts.
2. **HellaSwag:** HellaSWAG[3] [52] is a dataset for studying grounded commonsense inference. It consists of 70,000 multiple choice questions about 'grounded situations': each question comes from one of two domains–Activity Net or wikiHow–with four answer choices about what might happen next in the scene. The correct answer is the (real) sentence for the next event; the three incorrect answers are adversarially generated and human-verified, ensuring a non-trivial probability of 'fooling' machines but not (most) humans.

---

[2] https://storage.googleapis.com/ai2-mosaic/public/alphanli/alphanli-train-dev.zip.
[3] https://storage.googleapis.com/ai2-mosaic/public/hellaswag/hellaswag-train-dev.zip.

3. **PIQA:** Physical Interaction QA (PIQA)[4] [7] is a novel commonsense QA benchmark for naive physics reasoning, primarily concerned with testing machines on how we interact with everyday objects in common situations. It tests, for example, what actions a physical object 'affords' (e.g., it is possible to use a cup as a doorstop), and also what physical interactions a group of objects afford (e.g., it is possible to place an computer on top of a table, but not the other way around). The dataset requires reasoning about both the prototypical use of objects (e.g., glasses are used for drinking) but also non-prototypical (but practically plausible) uses of objects.

4. **Social IQA:** Social Interaction QA[5] [44] is a QA benchmark for testing social common sense. In contrast with prior benchmarks focusing primarily on physical or taxonomic knowledge, Social IQA is mainly concerned with testing a machine's reasoning capabilities about people's actions and their social implications. Actions in Social IQA span many social situations, and answer-candidates contain both human-curated answers and ('adversarially-filtered') machine-generated candidates.

5. **CycIC:** Cyc Intelligence Challenge dataset (Cyc)[6] is a set of multiple choice and true/false questions requiring general common sense knowledge and reasoning in a very broad variety of areas, including simple reasoning about time, place, everyday objects, events, and situations. Some questions may require some logic to get the correct answer. Here, we only use the multiple-choice questions (and not true/false questions) for experiments.

One important aspect to note about these benchmarks is that, while all offer multiple-choice answer formats, the 'prompt' is not always a question. For example, in the case of the aNLI benchmark, the 'prompt' is a set of two observations, and the 'choices' are two hypotheses (of which the one that best fits these observations should be selected). For this reason, we refer to each question and corresponding answer choices as an *instance*. The instance formats of the benchmarks described above are stated in Table 1.

3.2 Transformer-Based Models and RoBERTa

As covered in the *Related Work*, transformer-based models have rapidly emerged as state-of-the-art in the natural language processing community, both for specific tasks like question answering, but also for deriving 'contextual embeddings' (for more details, we refer the reader to the citations in that section). RoBERTa has been a particularly successful model, and is (in essence), a highly optimized and better-trained version of BERT. Unlike the most recent model (GPT-3), a pre-trained version of RoBERTa is fully available for researchers to use and can

---

[4] https://storage.googleapis.com/ai2-mosaic/public/physicaliqa/physicaliqa-train-dev.zip.

[5] https://storage.googleapis.com/ai2-mosaic/public/socialiqa/socialiqa-train-dev.zip.

[6] https://storage.googleapis.com/ai2-mosaic/public/cycic/CycIC-train-dev.zip.

Table 1. 'Instance formats' of commonsense QA benchmarks. The -> is used to separate what is given (e.g., obs1, obs2 for aNLI) and the answer choices (hypo1, hypo2). Here, 'obs', 'hypo', 'opt', 'ans', 'sol' and 'ctx' stand for *observation, hypothesis, option, answer, solution* and *context* respectively.

	Format
aNLI	obs1, obs2->hypo1, hypo2
HellaSwag	ctx_a, ctx_b->opt1, opt2, opt3, opt4
PIQA	goal->sol1, sol2
Social IQA	context, question-> ans1, ans2, ans3
Cyc	question->ans0, ans1, ans2, ans3, ans4

be 'fine-tuned' for specific tasks [31]. Unsurprisingly, many of the systems occupying the top-5 leaderboard positions[7] for the commonsense reasoning benchmarks described earlier are based on RoBERTa in some significant manner. The experiments in this paper, described next, use a publicly available *RoBERTa Ensemble* model[8] that was not developed by any the authors, either in principle or practice, can be downloaded and replicated very precisely, and on average, achieves over 80% on the five benchmarks when fine-tuned on the benchmark without any change to the model itself.

4   Experiments

We design and conduct a rigorous series of experiments (with full statistical analyses) to study the question noted in the title of this paper itself. While the data and system have already been described in the previous section, we use the next section to provide some relevant technical and methodological details, followed by the results.

4.1   Data and Methodology

We use the five benchmarks described earlier for our evaluation datasets. Each of these benchmarks is publicly available, and even has a leaderboard dedicated to it. Many researchers have used these benchmarks for evaluating commonsense reasoning models [47]. Note that the 'test' partition of these benchmarks is not available publicly; hence, for research purposes, the development or 'dev.' set is used as the test set. To ensure replication, we do the same. Our goal here is not to develop a superior algorithm that may do better on the unknown test set, but to explore the capabilities of a popular language model-based solution to this problem. Details on the benchmarks' training and development set partitions, as well as current state-of-the-art (SOTA) performance by a highly optimized RoBERTa system on the leaderboard (designed and fine-tuned on just that specific task

---

[7] https://leaderboard.allenai.org/.

[8] https://github.com/isi-nlp/ai2/tree/base.

or benchmark) are shown[9] in Table 2. As described in the previous section, we used the *RoBERTa Ensemble* model for our experiments, which achieves over 80% performance (on average) over the five benchmarks and is not substantially different from the SOTA model. While some formatting was necessary in order to ensure that the *RoBERTa Ensemble* system, when trained on one dataset (say Cyc), could be applied to instances from another dataset (say Social IQA), we did not modify any of the information content within the instances (either in the questions/prompts or in the answers).

Table 2. State-of-the-art (SOTA) accuracy performance and number (num.) of instances in training (train.) and development (dev.) partitions of the five commonsense QA benchmarks.

Benchmark	Num. train./dev. set instances	SOTA accuracy
aNLI	169,654/1,532	0.873
HellaSwag	39,905/10,042	0.939
PIQa	16,113/1,838	0.901
Social IQA	33,410/1,954	0.832
Cyc	6,570/947	0.913

Furthermore, since one of our goals is to test the generalization ability of precisely such models (i.e. a 'commonsense QA' model that has been trained on one kind of commonsense data, but evaluated on another), we define a *performance loss metric (PL)* as:

$$PL = \frac{Acc_{indomain} - Acc_{outdomain}}{Acc_{indomain}}. \tag{1}$$

Here, $Acc_{indomain}$ is the 'in-domain' prediction accuracy achieved on the benchmark when we train the model on that benchmark's training set partition and evaluate on the development set from the *same* benchmark; $Acc_{outdomain}$ is the 'out-domain' prediction accuracy achieved when one benchmark is used for training and another benchmark's *dev.* set partition is used for evaluation. Since there are four training options (the other four benchmarks) once the dev. benchmark has been fixed, it is possible to compute four separate $Acc_{outdomain}$ metrics for any given benchmark. The PL has an intuitive interpretation: how much of the 'in-domain' performance (in percentage terms) does the model 'lose' when the evaluation benchmark is changed? Given the descriptions of the five benchmarks used in this paper in the previous section, we would *expect* that the PL would be greatest for the benchmarks that are highly narrow in their domains (e.g., if we train on Social IQA and test on PIQA) as opposed to cases when the training benchmark is broad (such as when the training benchmark is aNLI, HellaSwag

---

[9] These numbers were acquired from the Allen Institute's leaderboards in late August, and may have shifted slightly.

and Cyc). In the next section, we assess the validity of this hypothesis. Note that a high PL implies that the model is generalizing less. A negative PL is theoretically possible (and potentially unbounded from below, as $Acc_{indomain}$ tends to 0), but not observed. The PL can never be greater than 100% (when $Acc_{outdomain} = 0$).

Statistical significance is an important part of such studies. To ensure that results are valid, we conduct two kinds of significance testing for each 'out-domain' experiment. Both tests use the 'base' or in-domain setting (*train.* and *dev.* partitions come from the same benchmark during testing) as the 'reference' distribution against which we test for equality of means. Specifically, we conduct the *paired* Student's t-test between the in-domain accuracy data and the out-domain accuracy data when the *dev.* set of the reference and the test distribution coincide (but the *train.* does not). For example, for the experiment where we train on aNLI, but test on HellaSwag, we conduct the paired Student's t-test between the out-domain accuracy data on HellaSwag and the in-domain accuracy data on HellaSwag (since the same *dev.* set was used for collecting both sets of data). Since the results are 'aligned',[10] the paired Student's t-test is applicable.

The second test (the unpaired Student's t-test) is the converse of the above– namely, when the training sets coincide but the *dev.* sets are different. Since the *dev.* sets are different, we can only test for equality of means in the unpaired setting, since data points are not aligned across systems. Taking again the above example, we would conduct the unpaired Student's t-test between the out-domain result (trained on aNLI, but tested on HellaSwag) and the in-domain result achieved on aNLI (trained on aNLI, tested on aNLI). Note that both tests are complementary and necessary in this kind of experiment, since both the training and test settings can change. The first test evaluates significance of results holding the *dev.* set fixed, while the second test keeps the training set fixed.

4.2 Results and Analysis

Table 3. Accuracy (fraction of questions of which the answers are correctly predicted) of the *Roberta Ensemble* model in different evaluation settings. The row represent the benchmark of which the training set partition is used to train, while the column name represents the benchmark of which the development (dev.) set partition is used to test.

	aNLI	Hella Swag	PIQA	Social IQA	Cyc
aNLI	0.819	0.611	0.702	0.531	0.442
HellaSwag	0.681	0.835	0.699	0.515	0.351
PIQA	0.68	0.564	0.756	0.51	0.371
Social IQA	0.688	0.604	0.687	0.769	0.508
Cyc	0.628	0.49	0.628	0.493	0.811

---

[10] The reason being that the 'reference' (the model trained on HellaSwag) and the out-domain system (the model trained on aNLI) are both tested on the same questions, namely the dev. partition of HellaSwag.

Table 4. The performance loss (PL; Eq. 1) of the *Roberta Ensemble* model when evaluated on a different benchmark ('out-domain') than it was trained on ('in-domain'). The row represent the benchmark of which the training set partition is used to train, while the column name represents the benchmark of which the development (dev.) set partition is used to test.

	aNLI	Hella Swag	PIQA	Social IQA	Cyc
aNLI	0	0.268	0.071	0.309	0.455
HellaSwag	0.168	0	0.075	0.330	0.567
PIQa	0.169	0.325	0	0.336	0.543
Social IQA	0.159	0.276	0.09	0	0.374
Cyc	0.233	0.413	0.169	0.358	0

The absolute accuracy results of the *RoBERTa Ensemble* model when trained on one benchmark and tested on another are tabulated in Table 3. Overall, we see very clear evidence that, regardless of the *train.* dataset used, out-domain performance inevitably declines, sometimes by significant margins. It is telling that these declines occur, regardless of whether we train on a 'broader' commonsense benchmark (like HellaSwag) or whether we test on a broad or narrow benchmark (e.g., PIQA). For better analysis of relative differences, we tabulate the performance loss (PL) metric in Table 4. The diagonals are all 0, since the performance loss is 0 when the training and testing benchmark are the same (per Eq. 1). The numbers correspond closely to those in Table 3, but generally tend in the opposite direction (i.e. PL is lower when the absolute accuracy is higher for a test benchmark, all else being the same.).

Recall that, in the previous section, we stated a hypothesis that we expect test benchmarks that are too 'narrow' (such as PIQA or Social IQA) to exhibit more PL than benchmarks which are broader, except (possibly) when the training set is also broad. Table 4 shows that the data on this question is surprisingly mixed. In particular, PL on PIQA is always low when it is used as a test set, despite the fact that it covers such a narrow domain. In contrast, the PL on Social IQA is high (usually, the second highest after Cyc). Similarly, with respect to testing on the 'broader' benchmarks, PL is low on aNLI but higher on HellaSwag. When training on aNLI or HellaSwag, and comparing to training on either PIQA or Social IQA, we find that the difference is not considerable e.g., the system trained on HellaSwag achieves PL of 16.8%, 33% and 56.7% respectively on aNLI, Social IQA and Cyc, and the system trained on PIQA achieves PL of 16.9%, 33.6% and 54.4% respectively on the same three test sets. Therefore, it is simply not true that performance loss is observed simply because the 'domains are different' (though by definition, they are all commonsense benchmarks), which is sometimes the cause in similarly designed (and more traditional) transfer learning and weak supervision experiments.

Interestingly, based both on the data in Tables 3 and 4, we find clear evidence that Cyc is the most 'different' benchmark, since the PL is markedly higher with

Cyc used as the training (and also the testing) dataset. Namely, the PLs observed in the Cyc 'column' are the highest among the values in the corresponding training dataset's 'row' e.g., when PIQA is used as the training dataset, the PL of 54.3% observed for Cyc is the highest in that row.

Significance Analysis. The paired Student's t-test methodology (the 'first' significance test mentioned in the previous section) was first applied to all values in Table 3, and compared against the 'diagonal' value. For example, the results obtained when training (respectively) on HellaSwag, PIQA, Social IQA and Cyc, and testing on aNLI, are tested individually using the test statistic from a paired Student's t-test analysis against the the in-domain aNLI setting (the diagonal accuracy value of 81.9% in Table 3). We find that the null hypothesis can be rejected at the 99% level for all such paired tests, for all test benchmarks. The differences in accuracy are therefore significant, as are the PLs in Table 4, which is just a scaled, affine transformation of Table 3.

We also conducted the unpaired Student's t-test (the 'second' significance test mentioned in the previous section). For example, we compared the *dev.* set results on HellaSwag, PIQA, Social IQA and Cyc (individually), when trained on aNLI, against the (*dev.* set) results obtained on aNLI for the same model. Therefore, the training set (and hence, the model) is identical in all settings, but the *dev.* set is different. The results for the unpaired Student's t-test showed that the majority of results are significant at the 99% level; however, for the models trained on Social IQA and Cyc, we found that the (respective) results obtained when aNLI's *dev.* set is used, are significant only at the 95% level against the 'reference' results obtained when the *dev.* set of Social IQA and Cyc is used, respectively. A lone insignificant result (even at the 90% level) is when we train on HellaSwag and test on aNLI, and compare it to the results of the same model tested on HellaSwag.

Discussion on Observed Differences. The previous results clearly illustrate that the choice of the training benchmark matters, often in surprising (but statistically significant) ways. One hypothetical reason why this behavior is observed is that PIQA may just be an 'easier' dataset, and Cyc may just be a 'harder' dataset (hence leading to lower and higher PLs respectively). However, if this were the case, then the 'diagonal' values in Table 3 would reflect it. The observed values in Table 3 tell a different story; all results are clustered in the range of 75–83%, and the in-domain result for PIQA is similar to that of Social IQA, suggesting that the two are of reasonably equal difficulty. Yet, one proves to be more 'generalizable' than another in out-domain settings. Another hypothetical reason could be the number of answer choices available per prompt. The hypothesis is that, once there is a mismatch between the training and testing setting, the performance becomes more random. While this hypothesis may explain why Cyc has the highest PL (it has five answer choices, generally, for every question; see Table 1), it does not explain why Social IQA (which has three answer choices per question) has higher PL than HellaSwag (which has four). Furthermore, the large differences in accuracy observed in the out-domain settings in Table 3 cannot be explained only by differences in the number of answer choices available in the different benchmarks. Finally, if the model had become more random, expected accuracy on Cyc and aNLI would be around 20% and 50% respectively (assuming relatively equal distribution of answer choices); however, the accuracies are significantly higher, according to Table 3.

Colloquially, the model is clearly learning 'something'. Furthermore, given the relatively large sizes and broad domains covered by some of these datasets (see Table 2; even Cyc, the smallest 'training' dataset has more than 6,000 questions in its training partition), it is unlikely that the fault lies purely with the data. The most plausible explanation that remains is that the fine-tuned RoBERTa model is subject to some degree of dataset bias, and that leaderboard performance numbers on individual benchmarks should not necessarily be assumed to be a reflection of advances in human-like 'commonsense reasoning' without significantly more qualification.

5   Conclusion

Language representation models such as BERT, RoBERTa and (more recently) GPT-3 have received prolific academic and media attention due to their ability to achieve near-human performance on a range of individual benchmarks, including on several commonsense benchmarks. In this paper, we showed that there is still a significant performance drop when one such competitive model is trained on one kind of commonsense dataset but tested on another. It is important to remember that all datasets considered in this work were supposed to test 'commonsense reasoning', although some are more diverse and broader than others. The breadth of either the training or testing dataset is not found to significantly impact the overall conclusions. At minimum, our analyses suggest a potential source of dataset bias when evaluating commonsense reasoning. The large values of performance loss observed in several settings strongly suggest that these commonsense models are not generalizing, and that more research is required before 'human-like' commonsense reasoning performance can be confidently said to be within reach of these systems.

References

1. Akhtar, N., Mian, A.: Threat of adversarial attacks on deep learning in computer vision: A survey. IEEE Access **6**, 14410–14430 (2018)
2. Angeli, G., Manning, C.: Naturalli: Natural logic inference for common sense reasoning, pp. 534–545 (2014). https://doi.org/10.3115/v1/D14-1059
3. Bar-Hillel, Y.: The present status of automatic translation of languages. In: Advances in Computers, vol. 1, pp. 91–163. Elsevier (1960)
4. Baroni, M., et al.: Commai: Evaluating the first steps towards a useful general ai (2017). arXiv preprint arXiv:1701.08954
5. Basu, K.: Conversational ai: open domain question answering and commonsense reasoning (2019). arXiv preprint arXiv:1909.08258

6. Bhagavatula, C., et al.: Abductive commonsense reasoning. In: International Conference on Learning Representations (2020). https://openreview.net/forum?id=Byg1v1HKDB
7. Bisk, Y., Zellers, R., Bras, R.L., Gao, J., Choi, Y.: Piqa: reasoning about physical commonsense in natural language. In: Thirty-Fourth AAAI Conference on Artificial Intelligence (2020)
8. Botschen, T., Sorokin, D., Gurevych, I.: Frame- and entity-based knowledge for common-sense argumentative reasoning. In: Proceedings of the 5th Workshop on Argument Mining, pp. 90–96. Association for Computational Linguistics, Brussels, Belgium (2018). https://doi.org/10.18653/v1/W18-5211, https://www.aclweb.org/anthology/W18-5211
9. Brown, T.B., et al.: Language models are few-shot learners (2020). arXiv preprint arXiv:2005.14165
10. Cheng, M., Yi, J., Chen, P.Y., Zhang, H., Hsieh, C.J.: Seq2sick: evaluating the robustness of sequence-to-sequence models with adversarial examples. In: AAAI, pp. 3601–3608 (2020)
11. Chklovski, T.: Learner: a system for acquiring commonsense knowledge by analogy. In: Proceedings of the 2nd International Conference on Knowledge Capture, pp. 4–12 (2003)
12. Davis, E.: Representations of Commonsense Knowledge. Morgan Kaufmann, Burlington (2014)
13. Davis, E.: Logical formalizations of commonsense reasoning: a survey. J. Artif. Intell. Res. **59**, 651–723 (2017)
14. Davis, E., Marcus, G.: Commonsense reasoning and commonsense knowledge in artificial intelligence. Commun. ACM **58**(9), 92–103 (2015)
15. Devlin, J., Chang, M.W., Lee, K., Toutanova, K.: Bert: Pre-training of deep bidirectional transformers for language understanding (2018). arXiv preprint arXiv:1810.04805
16. Dinakar, K., Jones, B., Havasi, C., Lieberman, H., Picard, R.: Common sense reasoning for detection, prevention, and mitigation of cyberbullying. ACM Trans. Interact. Intell. Syst. (TiiS) **2**(3), 1–30 (2012)
17. Gao, J., Galley, M., Li, L.: Neural approaches to conversational ai. In: The 41st International ACM SIGIR Conference on Research & Development in Information Retrieval, pp. 1371–1374 (2018)
18. Gordon, A.S., Hobbs, J.R.: A Formal Theory of Commonsense Psychology: How People Think People Think. Cambridge University Press, Cambridge (2017)
19. Havasi, C., Speer, R., Alonso, J.: Conceptnet 3: a flexible, multilingual semantic network for common sense knowledge. In: Recent Advances in Natural Language Processing, pp. 27–29. Citeseer (2007)
20. Hobbs, J., Croft, W., Davies, T., Edwards, D., Laws, K.: Commonsense metaphysics and lexical semantics. Comput. Linguist. **13**(3–4), 241–250 (1987)
21. Hobbs, J.R., Kreinovich, V.: Optimal choice of granularity in commonsense estimation: why half-orders of magnitude. In: Proceedings Joint 9th IFSA World Congress and 20th NAFIPS International Conference (Cat. No. 01TH8569), vol. 3, pp. 1343–1348. IEEE (2001)
22. Hsieh, Y.L., Cheng, M., Juan, D.C., Wei, W., Hsu, W.L., Hsieh, C.J.: On the robustness of self-attentive models. In: Proceedings of the 57th Annual Meeting of the Association for Computational Linguistics, pp. 1520–1529 (2019)
23. Ilyas, A., Engstrom, L., Athalye, A., Lin, J.: Black-box adversarial attacks with limited queries and information (2018). arXiv preprint arXiv:1804.08598

24. Kim, B., Kim, H., Kim, K., Kim, S., Kim, J.: Learning not to learn: training deep neural networks with biased data. In: Proceedings of the IEEE Conference on Computer Vision and Pattern Recognition, pp. 9012–9020 (2019)
25. Ladkin, P.B.: Time representation: a taxonomy of internal relations. In: AAAI, pp. 360–366 (1986)
26. Lenat, D.B.: CYC: a large-scale investment in knowledge infrastructure. Commun. ACM **38**(11), 33–38 (1995). https://doi.org/10.1145/219717.219745
27. Lenat, D.B., Prakash, M., Shepherd, M.: CYC: using common sense knowledge to overcome brittleness and knowledge acquisition bottlenecks. AI Mag. **6**(4), 65–65 (1985)
28. Lin, H., Sun, L., Han, X.: Reasoning with heterogeneous knowledge for commonsense machine comprehension. In: EMNLP (2017)
29. Liu, H., Singh, P.: Conceptnet? a practical commonsense reasoning tool-kit. BT Technol. J. **22**(4), 211–226 (2004)
30. Liu, W., Wen, Y., Yu, Z., Li, M., Raj, B., Song, L.: Sphereface: deep hypersphere embedding for face recognition. In: Proceedings of the IEEE Conference on Computer Vision and Pattern Recognition, pp. 212–220 (2017)
31. Liu, Y., et al.: Roberta: a robustly optimized bert pretraining approach (2019). arXiv preprint arXiv:1907.11692
32. Lu, K., Mardziel, P., Wu, F., Amancharla, P., Datta, A.: Gender bias in neural natural language processing (2018). arXiv preprint arXiv:1807.11714
33. Marcus, G.F.: Rethinking eliminative connectionism. Cogn. Psychol **37**(3), 243–282 (1998)
34. Michel, P., Li, X., Neubig, G., Pino, J.M.: On evaluation of adversarial perturbations for sequence-to-sequence models (2019). arXiv preprint arXiv:1903.06620
35. Miller, G.A.: Wordnet: a lexical database for english. **38**(11), 39–41 (1995). https://doi.org/10.1145/219717.219748
36. Moore, R.C.: The role of logic in knowledge representation and commonsense reasoning. SRI International, Artificial Intelligence Center (1982)
37. Narayanan, S.: Reasoning about actions in narrative understanding. In: Proceedings of the 16th International Joint Conference on Artificial Intelligence (2000)
38. Panton, K., et al.: Common sense reasoning ? from Cyc to intelligent assistant, vol. 3864, pp. 1–31 (2006)
39. Pinto, J., Reiter, R.: Reasoning about time in the situation calculus. Ann. Math. Artif. Intell **14**, 251–268 (1995)
40. Rajagopal, D., Cambria, E., Olsher, D., Kwok, K.: A graph-based approach to commonsense concept extraction and semantic similarity detection. In: Proceedings of the 22nd International Conference on World Wide Web, pp. 565–570 (2013)
41. Ram, A., et al.: Conversational ai: the science behind the alexa prize (2018). arXiv preprint arXiv:1801.03604
42. Ramachandran, D., Reagan, P., Goolsbey, K.: First-orderized researchcyc: expressivity and efficiency in a common-sense ontology (2005)
43. Sap, M., et al.: Atomic: an atlas of machine commonsense for if-then reasoning. In: Proceedings of the AAAI Conference on Artificial Intelligence, vol. 33, pp. 3027–3035 (2019)
44. Sap, M., Rashkin, H., Chen, D., Bras, R.L., Choi, Y.: Social iqa: commonsense reasoning about social interactions. In: EMNLP 2019 (2019)
45. Sap, M., Shwartz, V., Bosselut, A., Choi, Y., Roth, D.: Commonsense reasoning for natural language processing. In: Proceedings of the 58th Annual Meeting of the Association for Computational Linguistics: Tutorial Abstracts, pp. 27–33 (2020)

46. Singh, P.: The open mind common sense project. KurzweilAI. net (2002)
47. Storks, S., Gao, Q., Chai, J.Y.: Commonsense reasoning for natural language understanding: A survey of benchmarks, resources, and approaches, pp. 1–60 (2019). arXiv preprint arXiv:1904.01172
48. Tandon, N., Varde, A.S., de Melo, G.: Commonsense knowledge in machine intelligence. ACM SIGMOD Rec. 46(4), 49–52 (2018)
49. Young, T., Cambria, E., Chaturvedi, I., Huang, M., Zhou, H., Biswas, S.: Augmenting end-to-end dialog systems with commonsense knowledge (2017). arXiv preprint arXiv:1709.05453
50. Zang, L.J., Cao, C., Cao, Y.N., Wu, Y.M., Cun-Gen, C.: A survey of commonsense knowledge acquisition. J. Comput. Sci. Technol 28(4), 689–719 (2013)
51. Zellers, R., Bisk, Y., Farhadi, A., Choi, Y.: From recognition to cognition: visual commonsense reasoning. In: Proceedings of the IEEE Conference on Computer Vision and Pattern Recognition, pp. 6720–6731 (2019)
52. Zellers, R., Holtzman, A., Bisk, Y., Farhadi, A., Choi, Y.: Hellaswag: can a machine really finish your sentence? In: Proceedings of the 57th Annual Meeting of the Association for Computational Linguistics (2019)
53. Zügner, D., Akbarnejad, A., Günnemann, S.: Adversarial attacks on neural networks for graph data. In: Proceedings of the 24th ACM SIGKDD International Conference on Knowledge Discovery & Data Mining, pp. 2847–2856 (2018)

Machine Learning

Generation of Human-Aware Navigation Maps Using Graph Neural Networks

Daniel Rodriguez-Criado[1]([⊠]) ⓘ, Pilar Bachiller[2]ⓘ, and Luis J. Manso[1]ⓘ

[1] College of Engineering and Physical Sciences, Aston University,
B4 7ET Birmingham, UK
{190229717,l.manso}@aston.ac.uk
[2] Robotics and Artificial Vision Laboratory, University of Extremadura,
Badajoz, Extremadura, Spain
pilarb@unex.es

Abstract. Minimising the discomfort caused by robots when navigating in social situations is crucial for them to be accepted. Graph Neural Networks can process representations including arbitrarily complex relationships between entities such as human interactions. This is particularly interesting in the context of social navigation, where relational information should be considered. This paper presents a model combining Graph Neural Network (GNN) and Convolutional Neural Network (CNN) layers to produce cost maps for human-aware navigation in real-time. The model leverages the relational inductive bias of GNNs to generate scenario representations that can be efficiently exploited using CNNs. In addition, a framework to bootstrap existing zero-dimensional models to generate cost map datasets is proposed. The model is evaluated against the original zero-dimensional dataset and in simulated navigation tasks. The results outperform similar state-of-the-art-methods considering the accuracy for the dataset and the navigation metrics used. The applications of the proposed framework are not limited to human-aware navigation, it could be applied to other fields where cost map generation is needed.

1 Introduction

Mobile and assistive robots will become widely used in our society as both our companions and assistive aids to older and disabled people with activities of daily living [6,10]. These robots will be required to follow social conventions to avoid being disruptive, to be predictable for humans and to increase their acceptability amongst people [14]. To follow these conventions, robots need to be aware of their surroundings, the people nearby and their activities. Surveys of the extensive research completed on Human-Aware Navigation (HAN) and its impact can be found in [14,22] and [4].

Human-aware navigation can be seen as a motion planning problem where the robot has to consider many variables. These variables include the environment, the original robot's pose and its final destination, but also humans, their

© Springer Nature Switzerland AG 2021
M. Bramer and R. Ellis (Eds.): SGAI-AI 2021, LNAI 13101, pp. 19–32, 2021.
https://doi.org/10.1007/978-3-030-91100-3_2

activity and preferences. Most approaches use a cost function and a variant of A^* [19] or Rapidly-exploring Random Trees (RRT) [15] to search for optimal paths. Factoring in the power of current computers, the main challenge lies in modelling the aforementioned cost function, one which ideally would consider proxemics, human preferences, activities, emotions and aims. These functions can be hand-crafted algorithms, Machine Learning (ML) models, or a combination of both. Hand-crafted algorithms require a considerable amount of resources to develop, are difficult to debug and even domain experts often overlook meaningful variables. These solutions often disregard interactions or make simplistic assumptions, whilst ML can consider factors that go beyond expert intuition. The available ML-based approaches also present limitations. Specifically, they require performing a large number of queries when searching for pathways, making the process prohibitively time consuming (see Sect. 2).

HAN can also be approached using Reinforcement Learning (RL) [8] techniques, which do not necessarily rely on test-time state-space search. Despite having appealing characteristics, RL-based HAN algorithms still require reward functions whose development is arguably as challenging as that of cost functions, especially in HRI settings. End-to-end RL approaches that do not explicitly search at run time provide no obvious cost function that can be plotted, which means they essentially operate as a black box. This makes these RL approaches more difficult to integrate with other algorithms, complicates the inclusion of hard-coded conditions (*e.g.*, arbitrary boundaries) and reduces their explainability.

The paper at hand aims to provide a model for robot disruption in human comfortability that can efficiently generate two-dimensional cost maps for HAN considering interactions, an area that has been overlooked until recently. Although a number of recent works (see Sect. 2) address interactions, they perform arbitrary decisions or have serious efficiency limitations when applied to path planning.

The **contributions** of the paper are two-fold: **a)** a technique to bootstrap two-dimensional datasets from point-wise datasets; and **b)** **SNGNN-2D** (Social Navigation Graph Neural Network with 2-dimensional output), an architecture that combines Graph Neural Networks (GNN) and Convolutional Neural Networks (CNN) to generate two dimensional cost maps based on the data available to the robot. After training, the resulting ML architecture can efficiently generate cost maps that can be used as a cost function for Human-Aware Navigation. The experiments performed in Sect. 4 provides the accuracy of the model, time efficiency and statistical information of the trajectories used by the robot when using SNGNN-2D and a reference Gaussian Mixture Model-based (GMM) algorithm. The software to bootstrap the two-dimensional dataset and SNGNN-2D has been released as open-source in a public repository, with all the data required to replicate the experiments[1].

The base model used in this work to generate the two-dimensional dataset was trained with static information, taking static frames of the simulation.

---

[1] https://github.com/gnns4hri/sngnn2d.

Nevertheless, the same strategy can be followed using a dataset with dynamic scenarios and a model to generate a score for them as the one in [1]. In this case, the graph fed to the GNN encodes the dynamics of the scenario (e.g. relative motion of the humans and the robot) besides the static information.

2   Related Work

Much of the current literature addressing the problem of robot navigation has focused on the avoidance of collisions with objects, humans and walls, with people being viewed as dynamic obstacles. Human-Aware Navigation (HAN) aims to go a step further by considering the underlying social interactions as well as respecting personal and interpersonal spaces. In this regard, there have been two major trends. On the one hand, proxemics and its psychological and sociological studies [11,22]. According to [14], there are three main requirements for a robot to navigate socially: comfort, naturalness, and sociability. Comfort requires respecting interpersonal space, collision avoidance and not interfering with peoples' paths. Naturalness pursuits to mimic human motion and behaviour. This requirement is important to reduce the chance of collisions and use the space efficiently [14]. Finally, sociability implies adherence to social conventions. For instance, when two people interact, it is expected that the robot will not interfere.

Social Force Models (SFM) are the second trend. The concept was introduced in [13] and continued in [25] and [20]. SFMs and their derivative architectures [9] model humans as repulsive forces, making robots keep a distance. These approaches have been used to model the movement of pedestrians so that it can be mimicked by robots.

The main limitation of these trends is that they are hand-crafted approaches. As mentioned in the introduction, the high number of variables to consider and the difficulty to estimate their importance make the modelling process especially challenging [12].

The approach followed by this paper and other works covered in this section is to create models using ML or a combination of hard-coded models and ML. CNNs have been used to gather information about the environment, fed with raw images of the scenario. An example of this kind of approaches can be found in [21], where a Fully Convolutional Network (FCN) learns from expert path demonstrations and is integrated with an RRT* planner. Their work, although promising, presents some limitations. The dataset is relatively small due to the time-consuming task of generating trajectories by humans for each sample. More importantly, it does not encode significant features for social rules such as human-human and human-object interactions. This is a key aspect in the context of HAN.

Among learning-based models, Deep Reinforcement Learning (DRL) has been used effectively for navigation in crowds. A policy that allows a robot to navigate through an environment with many pedestrians while respecting the social norms is presented in [8]. In this case, social conventions are modelled using a reward function based on geometric features. Hence, some of the previously mentioned limitations in hand-crafted methods can also be applied to this approach. It is important to highlight the difficulty of generating reward functions that encourage social behaviour.

Conversely, Inverse Reinforcement Learning (IRL) [18] allows agents to learn from human's experience. In contrast to reinforcement learning, IRL learns reward functions from human demonstration. A recent example is [24], which uses a combination of A* and IRL for social navigation taking just the robot's sensors as input. IRL has also been used to generate social cost maps for robot navigation in [26]. Despite IRL-based models achieving outstanding results in HAN, the relations and interactions among humans and human-object are learned implicitly, which can lead to poor performance when there is a dense population. To solve this problem, [7] and [5] propose the combination of Graph Neural Networks (GNNs) and reinforcement learning for crowd navigation. They present an end-to-end approach where the model directly outputs the robot control signals. Thanks to the use of GNNs, the dynamics of crowds are better represented and captured. However, the reward function is not learned but hand-crafted and only considers the distance to the closest human. Additionally, these works do not take into account explicit interactions among people.

Using RL or IRL end-to-end approaches allows for directly producing the final signals controlling the robot. Any information about the environment that may affect the control of the robot has to be initially considered as there is no possibility to include that information at a later stage in end-to-end approaches. This means that not only information about the people and their relations with the environment is important, but also other factors such as the size and shape of the objects. An alternative is to build a cost map that can be used by a planner to generate a minimum cost path. Cost maps can combine information from different sources and are more easily explainable than final control signals which, may be helpful during the development of the system.

SNGNN-2D, the model presented in this paper, is an ML-based approach that aims to generate cost maps for social aware navigation, overcoming some of the aforementioned limitations related to the ability to incorporate symbolic information that cannot be naturally represented using a single vector or grid, such as interactions. Specifically, SNGNN-2D combines GNNs and CNNs to generate a cost map from a graph representing the different elements of a room as well as the relationships between them. Pure CNN models are not designed to capture the relational information among the elements in the scene [3], which is crucial in HAN. In addition, CNNs fed with raw images of a scenario would be dependent on specific features of the environment (e.g. the textures of the floor and the walls). This would prevent from obtaining a general model that could be applicable in other scenarios. The combination of GNN and CNN layers provides a general solution to the generation of maps for social navigation that integrates both geometrical and relational data. An interesting feature of SNGNN-2D is that the model is trained using a map-like 2D dataset bootstrapped from a single-point model developed in a previous work [17]. In such a model (SNGNN), for any given graph describing a scenario, the network generates a single scalar estimation of how disruptive the robot is overall for the people in the scenario. To generate a cost map from these single scores, it would be necessary to query the model for each of the elements in the cost map. The time required for generating the cost map this way makes this solution unsuitable for real-time applications. SNGNN-2D uses a generated dataset that contains scenario-maps tuples which are computed by sampling the output of SNGNN for every robot position. The bootstrapped dataset is used to train a neural network that produces a final real-time cost map from a given scenario description.

3   Method

This section presents the main contributions of our proposal: a) the technique employed to generate the dataset; b) the scenario-to-graph transformation; and c) the architecture of the proposed SNGNN-2D model.

3.1   2D Dataset Generation

The acquisition of two-dimensional cost or *disruption* maps to create datasets for learning purposes generates a number of challenges. First, asking people contributing to the datasets to provide a cost map instead of a single score per scenario would be more time-consuming. Another factor to consider is the precision of the answer is being dependent on the subjects' capability to represent their preferences graphically. Their inclination and motivation to stay engaged in the task would also be a challenge.

From an ML perspective, when factoring in an approximately equal time commitment and effort when generating answers, providing a single scalar for each scenario would yield answers for a higher number of scenarios. This would, in turn, generate a higher variability in the input scenarios that would make the model less prone to overfitting.

A dataset containing scalars as output data cannot directly be used to train a model which provides a two-dimensional output, so the approach followed in this case is to use a model which provides single value estimations (SNGNN [16]) and sample its output shifting the robot's position, bootstrapping this way a two-dimensional dataset. The process, depicted in Fig. 1, is as follows. Given a scenario and a given position of the robot, SNGNN estimates the disruption caused by the robot to the humans in it. To generate a map from this model, multiple queries to SNGNN are made for each scenario, modifying only the position of the robot. This process generates a two-dimensional output representing a cost map per scenario. For each scenario in the bootstrapped dataset a matrix of 73×73 samples is generated. A total of 37131 scenarios were randomly generated following the same strategy of SocNav1 [17]. The dataset split for training, development and test is of 31191, 2970 and 2970 scenarios, respectively. Given the relatively high number of samples and the randomness of the selection process, each set in this split can be considered sufficiently representative of the whole set.

3.2 Scenario to Graph Translation

Considering that the input data is not presented in the form of a graph, its conversion to a graph-like structure is one of the most relevant steps if GNNs are to be used. This process follows the same steps as [16], with the exception that there is an additional grid of 18×18 nodes whose values are passed to the CNN layers of the architecture and decoded into the final output. The first part of the graph (scenario graph), which coincides with [16] represents the entities in the room and their relations, using a node per entity (room, humans, walls and objects). The walls are split into segments, creating a node for each of these segments. A global *room* node connects to every other node in the graph to facilitate the use of global information in the room using fewer layers. The human-to-human and human-to-object interactions (if they exist) are represented as edges among the respective nodes. The scenario graph can be seen on the top half of Fig. 2.

The grid is a lattice of interconnected nodes, structured to represent the area of the room surrounding the robot by associating them to 2D coordinates. The number of nodes of this grid and the area they cover are hyperparameters that can be tuned to reach a trade-off between performance, computation time, and area coverage. The x, y coordinates of a grid node in row i and column j from the robot's perspective are computed as in Eq. 1, where N is the width and height of the lattice and W is the side of the squared area covered by the grid.

$$
\begin{aligned}
x &= \frac{W \left(\lfloor (N-1)/2 \rfloor - i \right)}{N-1} \\
y &= \frac{W \left(j - \lfloor (N-1)/2 \rfloor \right)}{N-1}
\end{aligned}
\tag{1}
$$

Once both sub-graphs have been generated, the elements in the scenario graph are grounded into the grid using additional edges whose coordinates are the closest spatially. This generates a single and final graph that can be fed into the model. Figure 2 provides a representation of what the final graph for the scenario depicted in Fig. 1a looks like.

The GNN layer model used for training allows for labelled edges. Therefore, each edge is associated with a specific edge type corresponding to the nodes it connects to and their direction. For instance, a connection from a *human* node to an *object* node will differ that of an *object*-to-*human* connection. This also applies to the edges between the scenario graph and the grid graph. However, the edges in the grid are labelled based on the direction of the connection to properly account for their relative positions (*i.e.*, up, down, left, right).

Each node on the graph is endowed with a feature vector of 21 dimensions. The feature vector $h_i^{(0)}$ for the i-th node is built by concatenating a one-hot encoding and type-specific metric information as in Eq. 2, where t_i is a one-hot encoding to differentiate the 5 types of nodes: human, object, room, wall and grid.

$$
h_i^{(0)} = (t_i \, \| \, p_i \, \| \, o_i \, \| \, r_i \, \| \, w_i \, \| \, g_i)
\tag{2}
$$

The sub-vectors p_i, o_i and w_i store metric information for human, object and wall nodes, respectively. These metric sub-vectors have 4 dimensions, corresponding

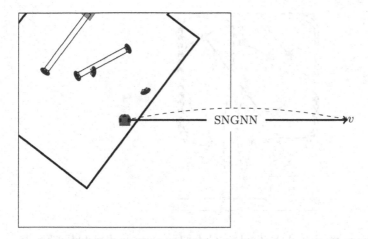

(a) SNGNN can be used to estimate the disruption caused by the robot given a particular scenario. In the scenario on the left, humans are shown as ellipses, objects as squares and interactions as parallel lines. The value V represents the response of SNGNN to the presence of the robot.

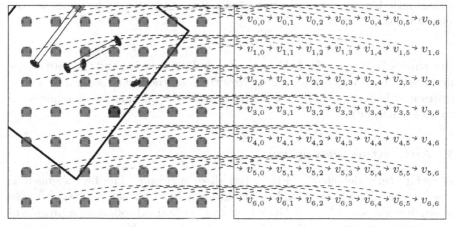

(b) The expected 2D outputs are generated performing multiple queries to SNGNN, shifting the scenario around the robot.

Fig. 1. The process used to bootstrap the two-dimensional dataset: a) how a single SNGNN query works; b) how to generate two-dimensional outputs.

to the 2D coordinates of the entity, and the cosine and sine of its orientation. The sub-vectors r_i and g_i refer to metric properties of the room and grid nodes, respectively. Room feature vectors store the number of humans in the room. The grid vector stores the 2D coordinates of the corresponding node. Metric vectors which do not correspond to the type of the node are filled with zeros. The metric features of the different types of entities could be merged into a single metric

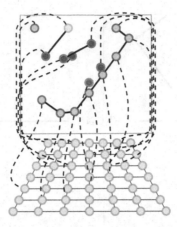

Fig. 2. Graphical representation of the final graph for the scenario depicted in Fig. 1a. The nodes for the room, humans, objects and walls are drawn within the square in the top of the figure. Grid nodes (in lighter grey) are connected among them and form a squared mesh area. The nodes in the scenario graph connect to the closest node of the grid (see dashed arrows). All nodes in the graph are bidirectionally connected to the room node but are not drawn to facilitate the visualisation. Edge types are not displayed to avoid clutter.

vector since all of them refer to the same kind of information and the entity type is described in the one-hot encoding. Nevertheless, the use of separated metric features may help the neural network to combine the information as required to obtain the final output.

3.3   Architecture Description

The architecture, depicted in Fig. 3, has three segments. The first segment is a sequence of 8 Relational Graph Convolutional Network layers (R-GCN) [23]. The number and size of the R-GCN layers were obtained following a process of hyperparameter tuning (see Sect. 4.1). Its output is a graph with the same nodes and structure as the input graph, whose feature vectors are converted from 21 into 7 dimensions. The second segment filters out the nodes which are not part of the grid in order to connect the output of the last GNN layer to the input of the first CNN layer. Specifically, a grid composed of 18×18 nodes is considered in the model, which produces an $18 \times 18 \times 7$ tensor that is used as input of the third segment of the architecture. This third and last segment consists of a sequence of two transposed convolutional layers that generate the final 73×73 output as found in the bootstrapped dataset. The combination of R-GCN and CNN layers, connected through a layer that filters out non-grid nodes to generate cost maps, is the second contribution of the paper.

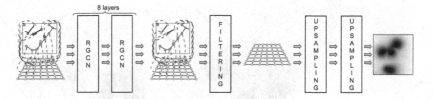

Fig. 3. Architecture of the SNGNN-2D model.

4 Experiments

To validate our proposal, this section includes experimental results regarding the accuracy of the proposed model, its time performance and a comparison to other approaches.

4.1 Training Results

The model was trained as a regression model using MSE (Mean Square Error) as the loss function where the expected output are the bootstrapped cost maps. After running 150 training tasks to optimise the hyperparameters of the architecture, the best model achieved an MSE of 0.00071, 0.00112 and 0.00114 for the training, development and test splits of the bootstrapped dataset, respectively. The model reached the best performance on the development dataset after 35 epochs. The 8 R-GCN layers transform the input feature vectors from 21 into 7 dimensions. The 2 transposed CNN layers of the model with the lowest test MSE have kernel sizes of 5 and 3, with a stride of 2 and a padding of 1. The non-linearity of the best performing model was ELU. Figure 4 depicts three scenarios and the corresponding output of the SNGNN (sampled) and SNGNN-2D models.

4.2 Comparison Against the Reference Dataset (SocNav1)

Given that the bootstrapped dataset does not contain information gathered directly from users but from the output of a zero-dimensional GNN model (one single value as output), comparing SNGNN-2D against the test data of the bootstrapped dataset could lead to unrealistic results. To provide a realistic evaluation of our model with the previous zero-dimensional model, the original SocNav1/test dataset was used. Given that SNGNN-2D provides a whole frame, in this section, the MSE was computed using only its central pixel, which corresponds to the position of the robot, the data that the users assessed in the SocNav1 dataset. Based on user assessed data only, the MSE of SNGNN-2D computed for the SocNav1/test set was 0.01873. The SNGNN version used to generate the bootstrapped dataset performed slightly better than the one reported in the original paper, with an MSE on the SocNav1/test set of 0.0198. SNGNN-2D not only achieves better time efficiency but also achieves slightly

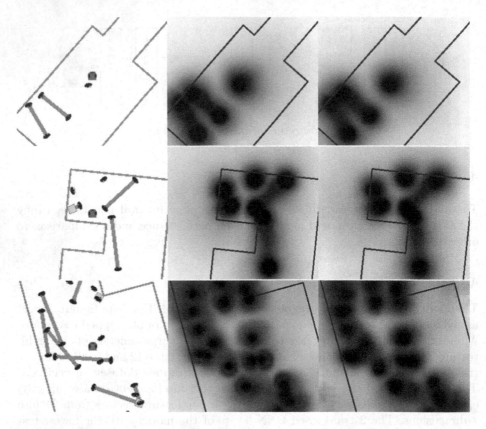

Fig. 4. Results obtained for 3 different scenarios. On the left, representations of the rooms. The central images correspond to the bootstrapped labels used as ground-truth. On the right, the output generated by SNGNN-2D.

better accuracy on the test set when compared to SNGNN. This accuracy is in turn noticeably superior than the one obtained by the non-ML based approach in [27] (0.12965 as reported in [16]), which is used as reference method in Sect. 4.4 to evaluate navigation results. This indicates that the cost maps generated using SNGNN-2D reflect more precisely how people would feel in different situations.

4.3   Real-Time Evaluation

The time required by SNGNN to generate a 73×73 frame in a 6th generation Intel i7 computer with a Geforce GTX 950M is 37.55 s (it requires 5329 SNGNN queries). The time required by SNGNN-2D to generate a similar output is 0.045 s, with just one query (three orders of magnitude difference).

4.4   Comparison Against GMM-based Methods

To assess the effectiveness of SNGNN-2D, this section presents simulated navigation results and a comparison with the social aware navigation approach proposed in [27], which is based on Gaussian Mixture Models (GMMs).

The experiments were conducted under simulated environments using the SONATA [2] toolkit. The walls delimiting a room are also randomly generated considering rectangular and L-shaped rooms. SONATA also provides real-time access to the information of the elements in the environment and their properties. This information is used by the two tested methods to generate a cost map, which is integrated into a control system in charge of planning a minimum cost path (using $A*$) and moving the robot towards the goal position.

The simulation provides all the necessary information to create the graphs. In a non-simulated environment, the robot would operate in a sensorised environment. Data from the different sensors (RGBD cameras, microphones, lasers...) would be preprocessed by other models yielding the needed global knowledge to generate the graphs (position of entities, relations, global information...).

According to the number of humans in the room, three different types of scenarios were tested: rooms with 2 standing humans and 1 walking human (S_A), rooms with 4 standing humans and 2 walking humans (S_B) and rooms with 5 standing humans and 3 walking humans (S_C). All the scenarios included a randomly generated number of objects, room shape and wall length. The number of interactions between humans or humans and objects was also randomly generated. For each type of scenario, each method was executed in 50 different simulations to cover a wide range of situations. The results of applying each method were evaluated according to the following metrics: τ (navigation time), d_t (travelled distance), CHC (cumulative heading changes), d_{min} (minimum distance to a human), si_i (number of intrusions into the intimate space of humans -closer than 0.45 m), si_p (number of intrusions into the personal space of humans -closer than 1.2 m-) and si_r (number of intrusions into an interaction -closer than 0.5 m).

Table 1 shows the mean and the standard deviation of these metrics using the GMM-based method and SNGNN-2D, considering separately each group of scenarios. The best value of every metric for each type of scenario has been highlighted in bold. For the first two types of scenarios (S_A and S_B) the mean values of most of the metrics can be considered comparable, although SNGNN-2D produces better results according to the travelled distance (d_t) and the cumulative heading changes (CHC). More variability is observed in the GMM-based approach as can be seen by the standard deviation of each parameter. In addition, for complex scenarios (S_C) greater differences can be observed between the two methods, showing that the proposed model behaves in a more socially acceptable way in crowded environments. Another important result is that the time required to generate a cost map using GMM substantially increases with the number of people and relations, whereas the impact of the complexity of the scenario in the proposed model is negligible.

Table 1. Mean and Standard Deviation $(M \pm SD)$ of the navigation metrics for each group of scenarios using GMM and SNGNN-2D.

	GMM			SNGNN-2D		
	S_A	S_B	S_C	S_A	S_B	S_C
$\tau(s)$	12.16 ± 7.0	$\mathbf{13.12 \pm 6.7}$	18.9 ± 10.2	$\mathbf{12.11 \pm 4.7}$	13.75 ± 5.2	$\mathbf{15.99 \pm 6.2}$
$d_t(m)$	4.92 ± 2.5	4.88 ± 2.8	5.7 ± 3.1	$\mathbf{4.14 \pm 1.2}$	$\mathbf{4.53 \pm 2.2}$	$\mathbf{4.67 \pm 1.9}$
$CHC(rads)$	4.36 ± 2.9	4.44 ± 2.1	5.99 ± 3.3	$\mathbf{2.87 \pm 1.4}$	$\mathbf{3.18 \pm 1.3}$	$\mathbf{3.64 \pm 1.6}$
$d_{min}(m)$	$\mathbf{1.53 \pm 0.7}$	$\mathbf{1.24 \pm 0.5}$	0.98 ± 0.4	1.48 ± 0.7	1.12 ± 0.5	1.01 ± 0.4
$si_i(\%)$	0 ± 0	$\mathbf{0 \pm 0}$	0.2 ± 0.91	0 ± 0	0.11 ± 0.73	$\mathbf{0 \pm 0}$
$si_p(\%)$	12.0 ± 27.2	$\mathbf{18.1 \pm 27.2}$	$\mathbf{30.2 \pm 32.4}$	$\mathbf{11.2 \pm 16.5}$	22.6 ± 25.8	30.3 ± 25.4
$si_r(\%)$	0.37 ± 1.6	$\mathbf{0.18 \pm 0.9}$	1.66 ± 5.9	$\mathbf{0 \pm 0}$	0.39 ± 1.7	$\mathbf{0.55 \pm 2.4}$

5   Conclusions

As shown in Sect. 4, the combination of arbitrarily structured and grid nodes in a two-staged architecture integrating GNN and CNN layers achieved good results considering both MSE and the properties measured in the navigation simulations. The reduction in time in comparison to SNGNN is also remarkable, allowing the model to be used in real-time applications.

The main limitation when applying SNGNN-2D is the absence of dynamic properties (*i.e.*, movement) in the input data. This limitation can be tackled by gathering a dataset that considers the velocity of the robot and humans instead of SocNav1, the one used to bootstrap the 2D dataset. Another aspect that will be considered for improvement is to train the models to estimate interactions based on previous human behaviour and movements instead of relying on third-party models to detect interactions (which are considered given in this work).

We have presented navigation results in comparison with a Gaussian Mixture Model showing better performance of SNGNN-2D, specially when the number of people in the scenario increases. A comparison against a pure CNN model was not carried out since such a comparison can be considered unbalanced for several reasons. First and foremost, the CNN is not able to encode the explicit relations as the GNN. Besides, the GNN is provided with explicit information extracted from other sources as the position of the entities in the room while the CNN would have to implicitly extract this information from the raw data. Finally, the training of the CNN would be scenario-specific since it depends on the position of the cameras and the textures of the environment (floor and walls). The GNN is agnostic to these details and can be deployed in environments with similar sensors.

It is worth noting that the method followed in this paper can be used to generate other kinds of maps with completely unrelated applications by applying the process to other datasets.

References

1. Bachiller, P., Rodriguez-Criado, D., Jorvekar, R.R., Bustos, P., Faria, D.R., Manso, L.J.: A graph neural network to model disruption in human-aware robot navigation. Multimedia Tools Appl. (2021). https://doi.org/10.1007/s11042-021-11113-6
2. Baghel, R., Kapoor, A., Bachiller, P., Jorvekar, R.R., Rodriguez-Criado, D., Manso, L.J.: A toolkit to generate social navigation datasets (2020). arXiv preprint arXiv:2009.05345
3. Battaglia, P.W., et al.: Relational inductive biases, deep learning, and graph networks, pp. 1–40 (2018). arXiv: 1806.01261
4. Charalampous, K., Kostavelis, I., Gasteratos, A.: Recent trends in social aware robot navigation: a survey. Rob. Auton. Syst. **93**, 85–104 (2017)
5. Chen, C., Hu, S., Nikdel, P., Mori, G., Savva, M.: Relational graph learning for crowd navigation (2019). arXiv preprint arXiv:1909.13165
6. Chen, T.L., et al.: Robots for humanity: using assistive robotics to empower people with disabilities. IEEE Rob. Autom. Mag. **20**(1), 30–39 (2013)
7. Chen, Y., Liu, C., Shi, B.E., Liu, M.: Robot navigation in crowds by graph convolutional networks with attention learned from human gaze. IEEE Rob. Autom. Lett **5**(2), 2754–2761 (2020)
8. Chen, Y.F., Everett, M., Liu, M., How, J.P.: Socially aware motion planning with deep reinforcement learning. In: IEEE International Conference on Intelligent Robots and Systems 2017-September, pp. 1343–1350 (2017)
9. Ferrer, G., Sanfeliu, A.: Proactive kinodynamic planning using the Extended Social Force Model and human motion prediction in urban environments. In: IEEE International Conference on Intelligent Robots and Systems, pp. 1730–1735 (2014)
10. Gross, H.M., Scheidig, A., Müller, S., Schütz, B., Fricke, C., Meyer, S.: Living with a mobile companion robot in your own apartment - final implementation and results of a 20-weeks field study with 20 seniors. In: Proceedings - IEEE International Conference on Robotics and Automation 2019-May, pp. 2253–2259 (2019)
11. Hall, E.T.: The hidden Dimension: Man's Use of Space in Public and Private. The Bodley Head Ltd., London (1966)
12. van der Heiden, T., Weiss, C., Shankar, N.N., van Hoof, H.: Social navigation with human empowerment driven reinforcement learning (2020). arXiv preprint arXiv:2003.08158
13. Helbing, D., Molnár, P.: Social force model for pedestrian dynamics. Phys. Rev. E **51**(5), 4282–4286 (1995)
14. Kruse, T., Pandey, A.K., Alami, R., Kirsch, A.: Human-aware robot navigation: a survey. Rob. Auton. Syst. **61**(12), 1726–1743 (2013)
15. LaValle, S.M., Kuffner, J.J.: Rapidly-exploring random trees: Progress and prospects. Algorithmic Comput. Rob. Direct. **5**, 293–308 (2001)
16. Manso, L.J., Jorvekar, R.R., Faria, D.R., Bustos, P., Bachiller, P.: Graph Neural Networks for Human-aware Social Navigation, pp. 1–6 (2019). arXiv preprint arXiv:1909.09003
17. Manso, L.J., Nuñez, P., Calderita, L.V., Faria, D.R., Bachiller, P.: Socnav1: a dataset to benchmark and learn social navigation conventions. Data **5**(1) (2020). https://www.mdpi.com/2306-5729/5/1/7
18. Ng, A.Y., Russell, S.J., et al.: Algorithms for inverse reinforcement learning. In: ICML, vol. 1, p. 2 (2000)
19. Nilsson, N.J.: Principles of Artificial Intelligence. Morgan Kaufmann, Burlington (2014)

20. Patompak, P., Jeong, S., Nilkhamhang, I., Chong, N.Y.: Learning proxemics for personalized human-robot social interaction. Int. J. Soc. Rob. **12**, 267–280 (2019)
21. Pérez-Higueras, N., Caballero, F., Merino, L.: Learning human-aware path planning with fully convolutional networks. In: Proceedings - IEEE International Conference on Robotics and Automation, pp. 5897–5902 (2018)
22. Rios-Martinez, J., Spalanzani, A., Laugier, C.: From proxemics theory to socially-aware navigation: a survey. Int. J. Soc. Rob. **7**(2), 137–153 (2014). https://doi.org/10.1007/s12369-014-0251-1
23. Schlichtkrull, M., Kipf, T.N., Bloem, P., van den Berg, R., Titov, I., Welling, M., et al.: Modeling relational data with graph convolutional networks. In: Gangemi, A. (ed.) ESWC 2018. LNCS, vol. 10843, pp. 593–607. Springer, Cham (2018). https://doi.org/10.1007/978-3-319-93417-4_38
24. Sun, S., Zhao, X., Li, Q., Tan, M.: Inverse reinforcement learning-based time-dependent A* planner for human-aware robot navigation with local vision. Adv. Rob. **34**(13), 888–901 (2020)
25. Truong, X., Ngo, T.D.: Toward socially aware robot navigation in dynamic and crowded environments: a proactive social motion model. IEEE Trans. Autom. Sci. Eng. **14**(4), 1743–1760 (2017)
26. Vasquez, D., Okal, B., Arras, K.O.: Inverse reinforcement learning algorithms and features for robot navigation in crowds: an experimental comparison. In: IEEE International Conference on Intelligent Robots and Systems, pp. 1341–1346 (2014)
27. Vega, A., Manso, L.J., Macharet, D.G., Bustos, P., Núñez, P.: Socially aware robot navigation system in human-populated and interactive environments based on an adaptive spatial density function and space affordances. Pattern Recogn. Lett. **118**, 72–84 (2019)

Extended Category Learning with Spiking Nets and Spike Timing Dependent Plasticity

Christian Huyck(✉) and Carlos Samey

Middlesex University, London NW4 4BT, UK
c.huyck@mdx.ac.uk
http://www.cwa.mdx.ac.uk/chris/chrisroot.html

Abstract. Neuroscience makes use of models of neurons, synapases, and learning rules that modify the efficiency of synapses in stimulating neurons. These models can be used to simulate spiking neural networks, and the standard learning rule is based on the timing of the spikes of the pre and post-synaptic neurons. This paper describes the use of these models to categorise documents by translating this Spike Timing Dependent Plasticity into an unsupervised learning rule by representing documents and categories in neurons and presenting them in specific fashion for learning and categorisation. The resulting system is comparable to other unsupervised machine learning systems. This presentation mechanism is extended to combine input feature value pairs to resolve the exclusive or problem. It is further refined to approximate co-variance of features to an arbitrary degree of precision.

Keywords: Spiking neurons · Spike timing dependent plasticity · Categorisation · Document classification

1 Introduction

Human's think using the neurons in their brains. Since our performance is superior to machines on many and probably most tasks, exploring brain behaviour may help with machine learning. While systems, like deep nets, may surpass human performance on some tasks [23], these large machine learning tasks can be computationally expensive and neuromorphic systems [8] using model neuron may solve the problem using substantially less energy. So exploring learning in systems closely adhering to biological neural behaviour provide several avenues to advance the state of the art in machine learning.

There is a long history of simulating biological neurons as models for biological behaviour [22]. While many basic assumptions are widely held, the neural processes that lead to intelligent behaviour are not well understood [19]. Two islands of confidence in computational neuroscience are Hebbian learning [13] and integrate and fire (IF) neurons [20]. There is ongoing debate about the precise

© Springer Nature Switzerland AG 2021
M. Bramer and R. Ellis (Eds.): SGAI-AI 2021, LNAI 13101, pp. 33–43, 2021.
https://doi.org/10.1007/978-3-030-91100-3_3

nature of these models in academic circles, but the general nature of these models is widely accepted. That is, neurons integrate activity from other neurons, and if they get enough, they fire (IF); and if a neuron frequently assists another neuron to fire, the synaptic weight will tend to increase (Hebbian learning).

This paper describes two different sets of simulations using biologically accurate leaky integrate and fire neurons (a variant of IF) and biologically accurate Spike Timing Dependent Plasticity (STDP). That is, they use spiking neural networks (SNNs) with Hebbian learning rules. These simulations learn categories. The first of these (see Sect. 4) categorises documents and the simulations use a two layer feedforward topology extending prior work [14] into new categorisation tasks. The second set of simulations (see Sect. 5) explore simple benchmarks that require the combination of two input feature values; it provides two mechanisms to combine feature values; this extends the basic categorisation method from the prior work.

2   Literature Review

The work reported in this paper makes use of commonly used computational neuroscience platforms. In particular, one commonly used mechanism is to use PyNN [5] as middleware to specify the neural topology, synaptic modification rules, neural stimulation, and recording. This acts as middleware between the developer and existing neural simulators; there are many simulators, and the simulations below have made use of the NEST [9] simulator. The code from these simulations is available[1] with an explanation of how to run the simulations to reproduce the data reported below. While NEST and PyNN support the use of user specified neural and synaptic modification models, this work has made use of existing, commonly used models.

In this paper, the leaky integrate and fire neural models are from Brette and Gerstner [3] (IF cond exp in PyNN). The neural model is based on voltage and is described by Eq. 1.

$$\frac{dV_M}{dt} = \frac{(-I_{Leak} + I_{Ex}^{syn} - I_{In}^{syn} + I_{Ext})}{C_M} \tag{1}$$

The voltage V_m, changes each time step, with some leaking away I_{Leak}, increasing from excitatory input from other neurons I_{Ex}^{syn}, decreasing from inhibitory input from other neurons I_{In}^{syn}, and changing from external sources I_{Ext}. This is all modulated by the size of the neuron C_M. When the voltage reaches the threshold, there is a spike and the voltage is reset. No current is transferred during the refractory period. This is a standard model and all default parameters are used. The time step is 1 ms.

In the brain, most if not all learning is Hebbian [13]. If the pre synaptic neuron tends to cause the post synaptic neuron to fire, the weight will tend to increase. There are many variations of this rule, but a great deal of biological

---

[1] The code can be found on http://www.cwa.mdx.ac.uk/spikeLearn/spikeLearn.html.

evidence supports Spike Timing Dependent Plasticity [2]. Bi and Poo [2] have perhaps the first published example that shows the performance of the changing efficiency of biological synapses. Song et al. [24] have developed an idealised curve that fits the biological data, though it is a curve fitting exercise.

The simulations below use the standard spike pair STDP rule described by Eq. 2. The presynaptic neuron fires at t_r and the post-synaptic neuron fires at t_o. If the presynaptic neuron fires first, the weight is increased (modulated by a constant c_+) otherwise it decreases (modulated by the constant c_-).

$$\Delta_w = \begin{cases} c_+ * e^{t_r - t_o} & t_r <= t_o \\ c_- * e^{t_o - t_r} & t_o > t_r \end{cases} \tag{2}$$

The first set of simulations use the additive version of the rule, where the weight change is independent of the current weight. The simulations from Sect. 5 use the multiplicative rule, where the existing synaptic weight changes less as the weight approaches specified maximum and minimum weight parameters. This relates to Oja's rule [21] and is more stable.

Interest in the use of various forms of SNNs learning via STDP for standard machine learning tasks is growing. There are several different forms of STDP that are used (for a review see [26]), though many forms of the rule are not consistent with biological evidence. A widely used form (called classical STDP [26]) is consistent with standard biological evidence and Eq. 2. In these rules, if the presynaptic neuron fires before the postsynaptic neuron, the synaptic weight increases, and if the order is reversed, the weight decreases. The closer the two times are, the more the weight changes. This is the type of rule used in the simulations below.

Prior work [14] showed that data can be categorised using standard neural models and STDP with a simple presentation mechanism. This work is extended below.

3   Methods

Biologically plausible SNNs and standard STDP effectively categorised benchmark data [14]. Biological neuron simulations run for a period of simulated time with the neuron behaving throughout the period. When a neuron fires, activation spreads from it to other neurons that have synapses from it. In this work, *input* neurons representing data feature values are caused to fire, and activation spreads to neurons that represent categories. These weights change via STDP. After training, depending on the firing behaviour of the *category* neurons, the test data items are categorised.

In the simulations below a layer of neurons represent the data items, and a layer of neurons represent the output categories. Each data item feature value pair is represented by a neuron, and each category is represented by a neuron.

The input layer is connected to the categorisation layer by synapses that learned via STDP. (In part of Sect. 5, an extra layer of neurons represents the combination of features.) Data is presented to the system using the PyNN spike source mechanism connected to the appropriate neuron with a weight that causes the neuron to spike once at a precise time. The time step of the simulation is 1 ms.

During training, the spike sources cause the *input* neurons to fire shortly before the *category* neurons. As the weights increase when the presynaptic neurons fire shortly before the postsynaptic neurons, the spike sources were timed in this manner. This meant that features that supported particular categories had high synaptic weights to these categories after learning. So, when test data is presented, category neurons fire, and based on this firing behaviour, the data is categorised.

The input neurons are well connected to the output neurons using plastic synapses. The plasticity rule is a variant of Hebbian STDP consistent with Song et al. [24], described in Sect. 2.

During training, the input neuron is spiked first, followed by the correct category output neuron. The simulation is ongoing. During training for simulations in Sect. 4, data items are presented (followed by their category) one after another, with a 50 ms. gap between the items. In many cases the incorrect category neuron from the prior item will fire before the data items, and this allows the weights to decrease using STDP. This leads to a weight that roughly reflects the covariance of the input feature value with the output category. An improved presentation mechanism is used and described in Sect. 5.

At the end of training, the synaptic matrix is stored. It is read in for testing, but the synapses are now static.

Testing is performed by presenting inputs, and measuring the firing behaviour of the output neuron. Typically, the category neuron that fires most also fires first, so the input is categorised as an element of the category whose neuron fires first.

4   Document Classification with SNNs

This model explored the use of SNNs to build a text classifier. The model was built using the AG News Topic Classification Dataset[2]. It has more than 100,000 news articles alongside their title, description and the category of the article (either world, sport, business or science). For the purpose of this experiment, only a 1000 articles of the data are used for training and 200 articles for testing. The task is to be able to build a classifier able to successfully retrieve the category of each document.

Computers do not currently effectively ground words [12], so they do not really understand text. In this simulation, natural semantics are approximated using distributional semantics; the data is encoded using a bag of words technique. To do that, the text was translated to a vector representation using Word2Vec [10], a word embedding technique. Word2Vec creates a vector representation of words based on the documents in which they occur. The Word2Vec

---

[2] https://www.kaggle.com/amananandrai/ag-news-classification-dataset.

model was trained on the whole AG News Topic dataset (more than 100,000 articles), transforming each document into a sequence vector. Then two samples of 1000 and 200 articles respectively are selected to train and test the SNN model.

As all documents do not have the same size, the sequences do not have the same size. To regularize the document size, two approaches are implemented. The first is the average of each column of the word vectors to have a new vector of the same size [18]. The second is the use of both Word2Vec and TF-IDF (Term Frequency-Inverse Document Frequency) to compute vectors. This is done by creating a weighted sum of the word vectors and the TF-IDF. Word vectors are normalized to have values ranging between 0 and 1. Normalized values are multiplied so that the input data has values between 0 and 100. The final input data is 100 features with values between 0 and 100.

4.1   SNN Model

As described in Sect. 3, the neural network is a feedforward SNN with two layers: the input and the output layer. Spiking neurons take binary input unlike classical neural networks. The dataset has 100 columns with each column having values ranging from 0 to 100, so the input layer has 10000 neurons. The output layer has 4 neurons, one for each class.

SNN models rely on spike representation of data (spike trains), thus each input has been converted into spike trains using an approach consistent with the method used by Hao et al. [11]. Each input, now a document represented by 100 values, is presented to the network followed by the neuron representing the category. Each of the document category presentations are presented in sequence, and the presentation of all the documents is called an epoch. Stimulation has been applied not only to the neuron corresponding to the input value but also to neighbour neurons with a defined windows size. In this case, the window size is three providing some generalisation. If for instance, a training set item has a feature value of 52, but 53 never occurs, this window of three will generalise the training item to include 53 and 51.

The model is trained for five epochs with 50 ms between each example. This led to a total training duration of 260000 ms. of simulated time. As mentioned above, the training is performed twice, one for each of the two preprocessing methods. The preprocessing method leading to the best result was the average of word vectors approach with an accuracy of 81% on the test set.

4.2   Results

The data is split into two sets: the training and the test set containing respectively 1000 and 200 articles. For each set, the data was selected randomly from the AG's News Topic Classification Dataset so that each class is represented evenly. Below, the result of the model on the test set is compared with different models evaluated on the same dataset.

The AG News Topic Classification Dataset is a popular dataset and to explore text classification. However, most have used classical machine learning (such as Decision Trees and Multinomial Naive Bayes) and deep learning algorithms (such as LSTM). The authors are not aware of any other categorisation model in SNNs.

The SNN models are compared to five different algorithms: Naive Bayes, Decision Trees, Stochastic Gradient Descent (SGD), and Light Gradient Boosting Machine (LGBM) [17], and on LSTM [16]. All use the same dataset, but training and testing sets vary.

Table 1 summarizes the SNN model accuracy alongside the other approaches.

Table 1. Model Accuracy

Algorithm	Accuracy
SNN (Average)	81%
SNN (TF-IDF)	74%
LSTM	91%
Naive Bayes	88.1%
Decision trees	77.1%
SGD	88.7%
LGBM	86.22%

Overall, the accuracy of the model was fairly good considering that algorithms such as SGD, LGBM and LSTM are supervised, and the SNN models described in this paper are unsupervised. This shows that SNN models can make use of high dimensional input, and perform document classification relatively well.

5   Combining Features

The systems and presentation mechanism described above lead to a categoriser based strictly on feature value co-occurrence with category. A well known version of a categorisation problem that cannot be solved by feature value co-occurence alone is the exclusive or category. If the category is A or B, but not both, the features contribute equally to the *in* category and the *out* category.

Fortunately, a simple modification to the presentation can overcome this problem. This mechanism takes advantage of the timing variance of STDP. In the standard rule, if a neuron fires and two post-synaptic neurons fire shortly thereafter, the synapse that connects to the post-synaptic neuron that fires first will have the greatest increase in synaptic strength.

The topology is represented in Fig. 1. There are four input neurons and four output category neurons.

The key change is the addition of two neurons for each category. This extended by the modification of the input times. In a given cycle of 50 ms, two input features (either (A or $\bar{A}$) and either (B or $\bar{B}$) and one output feature (either AB, $A\bar{B}$, $\bar{A}B$ or $\bar{A}\bar{B}$) are presented. $\bar{A}$ is presented at 10 ms, A at 11 ms, $\bar{B}$ at 12 ms and B at 14 ms. The output neurons are presented at 15 ms. The largest weights are on synapses that connect temporally adjacent neurons, like $\bar{B}$ and the first in ($A\bar{B}$), with smaller weights on more temporally distant connections.

An additional modification to the method from Sect. 3 is the use of multiplicative weight change instead of additive weight change in the STDP rule. Additive weight change can easily lead to the weight reaching its maximum or minimum so it is less stable.

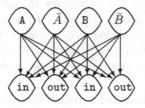

Fig. 1. The top row represents four input neurons, one for A and one for not A ($\bar{A}$), one for B and one for not B ($\bar{B}$). There are four output neurons, two for the in category and two for the out category. The network is well connected in a feedforward fashion.

After training, the synaptic weights are stored. When loaded in as static weights for testing, they perform perfectly, always categorising correctly.

Timing and multiple neurons for a category two of many options to support the integration of features. Another option is to build a separate subnetwork with neurons that only fire when a particular pair of feature values is present; indeed this could be extended to any number of feature values.

An example where this feature combination mechanism is needed can be seen in the Monks tasks [25]. This is an artificial data set designed to compare learning algorithms. It involves six features and three different binary categorisation tasks. The first task, Monk-1, is that either the fifth feature has a value of 1, or the first and second feature have the same values (or both).

Following the basic methodology from Sect. 3, a simple topology of 17 input neurons, and two output neurons was created. Presentation was modified so that, during training, the incorrect category neuron was presented before the input, then the correct category neuron. This strengthened long term depression. As expected, the fifth feature value 1 had roughly 0 synaptic weight to the out category. All other feature values had a positive value because each feature value co-occurred with both categories.

The system had insufficient synaptic weight to cause the output neurons to fire, which improved training. So, during testing, both category neurons were also primed when a test item was presented. The system correctly categorises 54 of the out category items and 29 of the in category items. When there is no firing on the output neuron or both fire only once and at the same time, it is a draw; three were draws, and there were 36 incorrect *in* categorisations, and two incorrect *out* categorisations. Of the inputs that had the fifth feature value 1, 29 were categorised correctly, and the other three were draws. Clearly this is evidence that the system needs to combine features to categorise correctly.

A second system with an extra layer of neurons to account for pairs is more effective. This system has weights from pairs of inputs to this extra layer of neurons. As there are 119 pairs, this layer has 119 neurons, and the synaptic weights are set from the neurons representing these input feature value pairs to these new neurons so that only the appropriate pairs fire. Training is repeated and leads to a test result of 51 *out* category items correct, 32 category *in* items correct, 11 draws, and 30 category *in* items incorrect. If all of the draws are categorised as category *out*, 56 are correct, with 36 category *in* items incorrect.

This data is also categorised using a covariance of feature value pairs with the output category. This gets the identical result (56 *out* correct, 32 *in* correct, and 36 *in* incorrect). So, the spiking system performs exactly the same as categorising by covariance.

Many categorisation tasks benefit from combining input feature values, and some require this combination to answer properly. This section has shown two tasks that require the combination of input feature value pairs, and how the basic spiking net STDP architecture can be used to properly categorise. Two feature combination mechanisms were shown; the first, for the xor task, was combination based on input and output time to allow STDP to resolve the problem; the second, for the monks task, used a neuron for each feature value pair with appropriate synaptic weights from input.

6   Discussion

This paper has shown an exploration of classification using a standard biological Hebbian STDP learning rule and a standard biological leaky integrate and fire neuron. With a simple feed forward topology, the system performs well on a novel task, and two benchmark tasks.

A modification, described in Sect. 5, of the presentation methodology and STDP rule leads the synaptic weights to accurately represent co-occurrence. Using multiplicative weight change instead of additive weight change in STDP eliminates the standard Hebbian problem of unlimited weight growth. Changing the presentation mechanism to present incorrect categories before the data, increases the power of long-term depression, and along with the presentation of the proper category after input, forces the synaptic weight to the co-occurrence value.

Two mechanisms for combining feature value pairs are presented. A modification to the training timing, which allows multiple outputs to be learned is used to solve the xor task. The addition of extra feature value pair neurons is another mechanism to allow value combinations; this is used to solve the first monks task.

The data presentation mechanism combined with the multiplicative STDP learning rule results in synaptic weights reflecting co-occurrence, either between feature values and categories, or pairs of feature values and categories. Section 4 has shown that, while this paper's training regime performs reasonably well, it does not perform as well as supervised learning mechanisms. While it is possible to integrate supervised learning with SNNs [6], unlike STDP, those mechanisms are not biologically plausible. An STDP based approach, which is different from the approach presented in this paper, is to use inhibition to force the categorising neurons to compete [7].

This approach, like the approach described in this paper, makes use of layers of neurons. This is not biologically plausible, as neurons are connected in reverberating circuits [4]. Another approach is to use reverberating cell assemblies (CAs) to form rules, and then learn to select the rules based on environmental feedback [1]. This reinforcement learning approach makes use of a compensatory Hebbian learning rule, which forces the total synaptic weight entering or leaving a neuron toward a constant. A third approach makes use of CAs and compensatory Hebbian learning to learn CAs that associate input features with categories [15]. Both the CA approach, and the reinforcement approach are more biologically plausible than the layered approach.

The promise of biological plausibility and the hope of systems that learn more like the brain contradict the evidence from the successes of deep nets, and supervised learning. It is likely that the power that can be gained from recurrent activity and the information that is passed by rapid (ms.) spike timing supports the brain's capacity to learn. Moreover, the long term nature of the brain allows it to bring a wealth of information to bear on a problem. The authors hope that further exploration of categorisation with biologically plausible nets will lead to improved machine learning systems.

7 Conclusion

This paper has shown that simple neural models with simple Hebbian learning rules can be used to learn effective categorisers. These models and rules are well founded in the sense that they are reasonably accurate descriptions of biological neurons, and the learning rules that they use to change synaptic weights.

This paper has shown that using a layered topology and an instance by instance presentation methodology, the network can learn synaptic weights that reflect the covariance of input and output features to an arbitrary degree of precision. These covariance weights are the basis of the effectiveness of the overall categoriser.

This layering is not a biological feature. However, commonly used machine learning systems, such as multi-layer perceptrons and deep networks, also make use of layering. They also make use of gradient descent training mechanisms, such as back propagation and unit models that are not biologically plausible. None the less, these systems are more effective categorisers than the SNNs described in this paper and elsewhere.

Future work may extend the SNN work described here and elsewhere. It could include lateral inhibition, recurrent topologies, reinforcement learning or a combination of these mechanisms. This may lead to the discovery of mechanisms that surpass existing machine learning algorithms.

References

1. Belavkin, R., Huyck, C.: Conflict resolution and learning probability matching in a neural cell-assembly architecture. Cogn. Syst. Res. **12**, 93–101 (2010)
2. Bi, G., Poo, M.: Synaptic modifications in cultured hippocampal neurons: dependence on spike timing, synaptic strength, and postsynaptic cell type. J. Neurosci. **18**(24), 10464–10472 (1998)
3. Brette, R., Gerstner, W.: Adaptive exponential integrate-and-fire model as an effective description of neuronal activity. J. Neurophysiol. **94**, 3637–3642 (2005)
4. Churchland, P., Sejnowski, T.: The Computational Brain. MIT Press, Cambridge (1999)
5. Davison, A., Yger, P., Kremkow, J., Perrinet, L., Muller, E.: PyNN: towards a universal neural simulator API in python. BMC Neurosci **8**(S2), P2 (2007)
6. Diehl, P., Cook, M.: Efficient implementation of STDP rules on spinnaker neuromorphic hardware. In: International Joint Conference on Neural Networks (IJCNN), pp. 4288–4295 (2014)
7. Diehl, P., Cook, M.: Unsupervised learning of digit recognition using spike-timing-dependent plasticity. Front. Comput. Neurosci **9**, 99 (2015)
8. Furber, S., Galluppi, F., Temple, S., Plana, L.A.: The spinnaker project. Proc. IEEE **102**(5), 652–665 (2014). https://doi.org/10.1109/JPROC.2014.2304638
9. Gewaltig, M., Diesmann, M.: NEST (NEural Simulation Tool). Scholarpedia **2**(4), 1430 (2007)
10. Goldberg, Y., Levy, O.: Word2vec explained: deriving mikolov et al'.s negative-sampling word-embedding method (2014). arXiv arXiv:1402.3722
11. Hao, Y., Huang, X., Dong, M., Xu, B.: A biologically plausible supervised learning method for spiking neural networks using the symmetric STDP rule. Neural Netw. **121**(8), 387 (2020)
12. Harnad, S.: The symbol grounding problem. Physica D **42**, 335–346 (1990)
13. Hebb, D.: The Organization of Behavior: A Neuropsychological Theory. Wiley, New York (1949)
14. Huyck, C.: Learning categories with spiking nets and spike timing dependent plasticity. In: International Conference on Innovative Techniques and Applications of Artificial Intelligence, pp. 139–144 (2020)
15. Huyck, C.R., Mitchell, I.G.: Post and pre-compensatory Hebbian learning for categorisation. Cogn. Neurodyn. **8**(4), 299–311 (2014). https://doi.org/10.1007/s11571-014-9282-4
16. Kaggle: New article classification using LSTMS (2020). https://www.kaggle.com/atechnohazard/news-article-classification-using-lstms
17. Kaggle: News article classifier with different models (2020). https://www.kaggle.com/amananandrai/ag-news-classification-dataset?select=train.csv
18. Kenter, T., Borisov, A., Rijke, M.D.: Siamese cbow: optimizing word embeddings for sentence representationst (2016). arXiv arXiv:1606.04640
19. Lisman, J.: The challenge of understanding the brain: where we stand in 2015. Neuron **86**(4), 864–882 (2015)

20. McCulloch, W., Pitts, W.: A logical calculus of ideas immanent in nervous activity. Bull. Math. Biophys. **5**, 115–133 (1943)
21. Oja, E.: A simplified neuron model as a principal component analyzer. J. Math. Biol. **15**, 267–273 (1982)
22. Rochester, N., Holland, J., Haibt, L., Dudag, W.: Tests on a cell assembly theory of the action of the brain using a large digital computer. Trans. Inf. Theory IT **2**, 80–93 (1956)
23. Silver, D., et al.: Mastering the game of go without human knowledge. Nature **550**, 354–59 (2017)
24. Song, S., Miller, K., Abbott, L.: Competitive hebbian learning through spike-timing-dependent synaptic plasticity. Nat. Neurosci. **3**(9), 919–926 (2000)
25. Thrun, S., et al.: The monk's problems: a performance comparison of different learning algorithms. Technical Report, CMU-CS-91-197, Carnegie Mellon University, Pittsburgh, PA (1991)
26. Vigneron, A., Martinet, J.: A critical survey of STDP in spiking neural networks for pattern recognition. In: 2020 International Joint Conference on on Neural Networks (IJCNN), pp. 1–9. IEEE (2020)

ORACLE: End-to-End Model Based Reinforcement Learning

Per-Arne Andersen$^{(\boxtimes)}$ ⓘ, Morten Goodwin ⓘ, and Ole-Christoffer Granmo ⓘ

Department of ICT, University of Agder, Grimstad, Norway
{per.andersen,morten.goodwin,ole.granmo}@uia.no

Abstract. Reinforcement Learning (RL) algorithms seek to maximize some notion of reward. There are two categories of RL agents, model-based or model-free agents. In the case of model-free learning, the algorithm learns through trial and error in the target environment in contrast to model-based where the agent train in a learned or known environment instead.

Model-free reinforcement learning shows promising results in simulated environments but falls short in the case of real-world environments. This is because trial and error do not fit with the reality where errors are related to an economic burden. On the other hand, Model-based reinforcement learning (MBRL) aims to exploit a known or learned dynamics model, which substantially increases sample efficiency. This paper focuses on learning a dynamics model and use the learned model to train several model-free algorithms by directly sampling the dynamics model. However, it is challenging to achieve good accuracy on dynamics models for highly complex domains due to stochasticity and compounding noise in the system. A majority of model-based RL focuses on dynamics models that derive policies from observation space. Deriving policies from observation space is problematic because it is often high dimensional with significant complexity.

This paper proposes an end-to-end model-based reinforcement learning algorithm for learning model-free algorithms to act in environments without trial and error in the real environment. This method is beneficial for existing installations that employ existing decision-making systems, such as an expert system. The proposed algorithm has the same fundamental learning principles as the Dreaming Variational Autoencoder but is substantially different architecturally. We show that the algorithm is more sample efficient and performs comparably with existing model-free approaches. We also demonstrate how the algorithm is actor agnostic, enabling existing model-free algorithms to operate in a model-based context.

Keywords: Reinforcement Learning · Markov decision processes · Neural networks · State space models · Model-based reinforcement learning

ⓒ Springer Nature Switzerland AG 2021
M. Bramer and R. Ellis (Eds.): SGAI-AI 2021, LNAI 13101, pp. 44–57, 2021.
https://doi.org/10.1007/978-3-030-91100-3_4

1   Introduction

Reinforcement Learning (RL) continues to be fruitful in many applications in recent literature. To mention a few, we have seen tremendous progress in learning computers to perform many tasks, such as complex strategies in games via self-play learning [25], autonomous driving [20], health care applications such as sequential decision making in tumor classification [30], and in industry decision making and efficiency optimization [8]. It is clear that RL has a significance in the present time, but also in going forward to understand and define artificial intelligence.

While reinforcement learning shows promise, it is still far from achieving super-intelligence and lacks sufficient generalization capabilities for mass adoption in disciplines such as industry. The various existing reinforcement learning algorithms suffers from catastrophic forgetting [29], Low sample efficiency [3], Few safety guarantees on decisions [11], and requires extensive hyper-parameter tuning [10] for optimal performance. On the bright side, RL algorithms often only have one of these negative traits making it possible to circumvent these issues altogether by choosing the correct algorithm for the correct task.

Reinforcement learning separates into two main categories, Model-based and Model-Free Reinforcement Learning. In Model-free RL, the goal is to derive a policy from samples, either in an on-policy or off-policy manner. Policy Gradients is an on-policy method and learns directly using samples collected from its policy. On-policy methods are regarded as less sample efficient and stable but can often reach higher convergence targets. On the other hand, off-policy algorithms use historic data sampled from previous policy snapshots or Monte-Carlo sampling. The benefit of reusing more distant experiences to prevent catastrophic forgetting and is widely accepted as more sample-efficient. On the other hand, Model-based reinforcement learning (MBRL) aims to exploit a known or learned dynamics model, which drastically increases sample efficiency and policy stability [21].

This paper focuses on learning a dynamics model and use the learned model to train several model-free algorithms by sampling directly from the dynamics model. However, it is challenging to achieve good accuracy on dynamics model trajectories for highly complex domains due to stochasticity and compounding noise in the system. A majority of model-based RL focuses on dynamics models to derive policies from observation space. Deriving policies from observation space is problematic because it is often high dimensional with significant complexity. One approach that we investigate in this work is to reduce the learning complexity by learning policies from latent space variables directly.

This paper attempts to address some fundamental issues with model-based RL by learning several agents concurrently using ensemble learning. The ensemble consists of on-policy and off-policy model-free algorithms that learn from samples of a learned world model. Each agent learns in parallel from interaction with its separate dream environment and, during inference, forms a majority voting system. The world model is trained separately by first observing expert systems or RL agents interact with the environment and finally learn its dynamics in a supervised manner. The world model learns markovian state transitions, rewards, state cost for measuring goal distance. ORACLE solve traditional reinforcement learning problems and shows promising progress on complex state-of-the-art test environments. The contributions of this work summarize as follows.

- A novel world-model approach based on stochastic recurrent neural networks (SRNN) from [9] for end-to-end model based RL.
- Ensemble Learning using multiple of model-free algorithms with majority voting for action selection

We organize the paper as follows.

Section 2 presents a in-depth background into reinforcement learning topics that ORACLE builds on and moves on to detail the algorithm architecture, design decisions and theoretical justifications. Section 3 presents empirical results in classical reinforcement learning problems, game environments, and in complex real-time strategy scenarios. We show that ORACLE outperforms both on and off-policy model-free alternatives in sample efficiency while maintaining comparable performance in most experiments. Section 4 presents recent related work in the field of model-based reinforcement learning. Finally, Sect. 5 discusses the good, the bad, and the ugly of ORACLE and concludes on the significance of our findings, We lay forth potential future paths of research for improving ORACLE performance and sample efficiency.

2   ORACLE: Observations Rewards Actions Costs Ensemble Learning

The Observations Rewards Actions Costs Learning Ensemble (ORACLE) is a novel end-to-end architecture for training model-free algorithms on a dynamics model of the ground truth environment. The ORACLE is a combination of several state-of-the-art deep learning techniques such as SRNN [9], variational autoencoders [18], and vector-quantization for latent space [24], and state-space models (SSM) [9]. This section aims to detail the algorithm and give the reader thorough insight into how ORACLE operates to learn a dynamics model for planning and executing decision-making.

Model-based reinforcement learning learns a dynamics model of a environment to derive a policy for decision making. The underlying mechanism is a Markov Decision Process (MDP), which mathematically defines the synergy between states, actions, rewards, and transitions. The problem is formalized as a tuple $M = (S, A, T, R)$, where $S = \{s_n, \ldots, s_{t+n}\}$ is a set of possible states and $A = \{a_n, \ldots, a_{t+n}\}$ is a set of possible actions. The state transition function $T : S \times A \times S \rightarrow [0, 1]$, which the dynamics model tries to learn is a probability function such that $T_{a_t}(s_t, s_{t+1})$ is the probability that current state s_t transitions to s_{t+1} given that the agent choses action a_t. The reward function $R : S \times A \rightarrow \mathbb{R}$ where $R_{a_t}(s_t, s_{t+1})$ returns the immediate reward received on when taking action a in state s_t with transition to s_{t+1}. The policy takes the form $\pi = \{s_1, a_1, s_2, a_2, \ldots, s_n, a_n\}$ where $\pi(a|s)$ denotes chosen action given a state. Model-based reinforcement learning divides primarily into three categories: 1) Dyna-based, 2) Policy Search-based, and 3) Shooting-based algorithms in which this work concerns Dyna-based approaches. The Dyna algorithm from [28] trains in two steps. First, the algorithm collects experience from interaction with the environment using a policy from a model-free algorithm (i.e., Q-learning). This experience is part of learning an estimated model of the environment, also referred to as a dynamics model. Second, the agent policy samples imagined data generated by the dynamics model and update its parameters towards optimal behavior.

Table 1. Set of tunable parameters in ORACLE. In addition to this incomplete list, the algorithm has options for controlling model complexity such as neuron counts and number of layers.

Hyperparameter	Values	Selected	Comment
Batch size	$\mathbb{Z}^+$	48	Number of sequence batches
Sequence size	$\mathbb{Z}^+$	48	Number of frames in a sequence
Buffer size	$\mathbb{Z}^+$	9 000	Replay buffer
Reward scaling	$\mathbb{R}$	1.0	Scaling of the reward objective
Cost scaling	$\mathbb{R}$	1.0	Scaling of the cost objective
VQ scaling	$\mathbb{R}$	0.1	Scaling of the VQ objective
KL scaling	$\mathbb{R}$	1.0	Scaling of the KL objective (KL-β)
KL minimum nats	$\mathbb{R}$	3.0	Minimal information loss
Optimizer		AdamW	AdamW improves generalization, see [19]
Gradient clipping	$\mathbb{R}$	100.0	Clip gradients to increase learning stability
Adaptive GC	$\mathbb{B}$	1	Based on the history of gradient norms [27]
Learning rate	$\mathbb{R}$	0.0001	Low Learning rate to improve stability
Latent leaps	$\mathbb{Z}^+$	30	Number of leaps into future states
Dynamics model RNN		LSTM	
Activation functions		ELU	
Enc/Dec neurons	$\mathbb{Z}^+$	1024	
Stochastic reward	$\mathbb{B}$	1	Sample rewards under Gaussian assumptions
Stochastic costs	$\mathbb{B}$	1	Sample costs under Gaussian assumptions

Dynamics Model: ORACLE's most crucial component is the dynamics model. The aim is to learn some parameters such that we can predict $s_{t+1} = F(s_t, a_t, \theta)$, the future state of a system or environment. Our approach is a combination of Variational Autoencoders (VAE) from [18] and Stochastic Recurrent State Space Models (SRSSM) from [9]. VAE and SRSSM's are highly expressive model classes for learning patterns in time series data and for system identification [7]. System identification, i.e. learning dynamics models from data is central in model-based reinforcement learning [6] and hence is a attractive concept for learning a functional dynamics model. We train the algorithm similarly to VAE's using amortized variational inference where we have two models, the generative model (prior) pr_θ and the inference model (posterior) po_θ.

$$\text{Prior Model} : pr(z_t, h_t | h_{t-1}, a_{t-1}) \tag{1}$$

$$\text{Posterior Model} : po(z_t | x_t, h_{t-1}, a_{t-1}) \tag{2}$$

Equation 1–2 define our models where a_t is the event that triggers the transition from observation o_t to o_{t+1} in the real dynamics system. The prior model has a recursive dependency on previous hidden state h_{t-1}, action a_{t-1}, and outputs the hidden state h_t including the latent state z_t as seen in Eq. 1. Internally, the prior performs the following operations:

1. Compute $u_t = concat(h_{t-1}, a_{t-1})$
2. forward concatenation to RNN such that $h_t = RNN(u_t)$
3. parameterize mean $\mu_t = NN_1(h_t)$ diagonal covariance matrix $\sigma = NN_2(h_t)$
4. sample from Gaussian distribution $p_\theta(z_t | h_t) \sim \mathcal{N}(z_t; \mu, \sigma)$

where all steps are performed for every sample and forms our prior beliefs of the latent variables. Note that we do input any information about the visual landscape (observation) into the prior, but the objective function, which we will describe later aims to learn these dynamics implicit via the posterior function.

We now move the attention to calculating the latent variable through a posterior model. As seen in Eq. 2, the posterior depends on the previous hidden state h_{t-1}, action a_{t-1} but has exclusive access to the encoded ground truth observation x_t. Similarly to the prior model, the input are concatenated and directly parameterize a Gaussian distribution. The posterior model can be summarized to the following procedure:

1. Compute $u_t = concat(h_{t-1}, a_{t-1}, x_{t-1})$
2. Parameterize mean $\mu_t = NN_3(u_t)$ diagonal covariance matrix $\sigma = NN_4(u_t)$
3. Sample from Gaussian distribution $p_\psi(z_t | h_t) \sim \mathcal{N}(z_t; \mu, \sigma)$

To optimize the dynamics model, we use variational bayes where the goal is to fit the posterior approximation such that $pr_\theta(z) = po_\theta(z|x)$, however, since $po(z|x) = \int_z \frac{po(x|z)po(z)}{po(x)} dz$, it becomes intractable as we are concerned with computing the integral over the entire latent space z. For this reason, we approximate the posterior using $po_\theta(z)$ and choose the *Kullback-Leibler* distance to approximate. Following the work in [18], we end up with **E**vidence **L**ower **BO**und [17] given by

$$(\underbrace{\mathbb{E}[logpr(X|z)]}_{transition-loss} + \underbrace{\mathbb{E}[logpr(R|z)]}_{reward-loss} + \underbrace{\mathbb{E}[logpr(C|z)]}_{cost-loss}) - \gamma \cdot \underbrace{D_{KL}[po_\theta(z|X) \| pr_\theta(z)]}_{KL-divergence}$$

$$\tag{3}$$

where log-likelihoods forms the reconstruction loss for observations, rewards, and costs, and KL-divergence act as a regularizer.

Rewards and Costs: ORACLE can predict rewards and costs using its dynamics model. During a transition in MDP's a feedback signal is emitted, which reinforcement learning agents utilize to fuel learning. We propose a novel, goal-directed approach where a cost-metric is added to the reward signal. This way, the reward signal is motivated by reaching the goal terminal state quickly.

Learning Ensemble: After ORACLE has trained in a supervised manner, an ensemble of model-free algorithms are trained on the dynamics model. Each actor learns separately in concurrent dynamics models. When the algorithm is sufficiently trained[1], the ensemble can perform decision making in the real environment. ORACLE can be configured to use the ensemble for decision making via majority voting or to use a single agent's decision.

Vector Quantization (VQ): We follow the VQ-VAE architecture from [24], and the motivation is to transform continuous latent-space variables into discrete latent variables, which has shown to be significantly better for reasoning planning, and predictive learning. Furthermore, VQ-VAE can model very long-term dependencies as it has a high compression rate compared to continuous space. [24].

Stochastic Weight Averaging (SWA) is a novel approach to ensemble learning where the objective is to widen the optima space such that it is easier to find and to give a better generalization of the model [16]. Compared to other ensemble learning techniques, SWA only requires a single model where snapshots are stored every n epochs. And are after m epochs averaged over. SWA has different learning rate strategies (i.e., cyclical learning rate), but we choose a fixed learning rate throughout training.

Hyperparameters: The ORACLE algorithm has a magnitude of different hyperparameters for tuning stability and performance. During the experiments, we found the algorithm to be rather robust to small changes in hyperparameters, and hence, we limit the scope to analyzing VQ, SWA, and Adaptive Gradient clipping (AGC) in Sect. 3. ORACLE supports numerous hyperparameters, and to limit the scope, we have focused on only a few in this work. The motivation for having such a substantial set of hyperparameters is that different environments have different requirements to learn a good generalized model. Specifically, we choose a long-short term memory (LSTM) layer in the Dynamics model for our deterministic prediction of a future state. Another notable choice is to enable adaptive gradient clipping, a novel approach to clip the gradient from historical norms[27]. Additionally, we clip the gradient if it exceeds 100.0 to limit training steps.

---

[1] The definition of 'sufficient' is to train up until a satisfactory performance in terms of average return.

Algorithm 1: ORACLE Training Routine

---

1 **Result 1:** Learned ensemble of policies $\pi = \{ \pi_1 \cdots \pi_n \}$
2 **Result 2:** Learned dynamics model $z_{t+1} = f(z_t, h_t, a_t)$
3 **Hyperparameters:** See Table 1.
4 **Assumptions:** Expert-system Ω
5 **while** *dynamics model is not trained* **do**
6 | Train dynamics model $po_\theta(\hat{o}_{t+1}, z_{t+1} | o_t, s_{t+1}, a_t)$ using equation 3
7 **end**
8 **while** *training model-free ensemble is not trained* **do**
9 | Choose action a from policy strategy
10 | Execute a at state s and get z_{t+1}, r, c via dynamics model
   | $po_\theta(z_{t+1}, r_{t+1}, c_{t+1} | z_t)$
11 | Perform policy update (depedening on algorihm)
12 **end**

Algorithm 1 shows pseudo-code for training ORACLE[2]. In essence, the algorithm has two training steps. First, the algorithm observes some policy-making decisions in the ground truth environment. The algorithm trains either directly as the samples are observed or store them in a buffer for delayed training. When the dynamics model is trained, which is indicated by learning objective graphs, the second training procedure for a model-free algorithm begins. The programmer is allowed to use any model-free algorithm but should note that the training procedure is different for off and on-policy algorithms. In off-policy algorithms, the algorithm should utilize a replay buffer and sample actions from an external policy for exploration, while on-policy algorithms should train directly without such storage. Each model-free algorithm is assigned a fixed number of batches, each representing a dream-world instance. When the model-free agent has reached a sufficient level of performance, the ensemble is ready for making decisions in the ground truth environment. In this implementation, we use majority voting, and when there is no consensus, random actions are selected.

3 Experiments

This section reveals that ORACLE can perform well across many different environments and outperforms existing RL approaches in the classical RL environment CartPole where the aim is to balance a pole on a moving cart. Furthermore, we show promising results in Deep RTS Deathmatch, a one versus one real-time strategy game [1]. Finally, we evaluate performance in the HalfCheetahPyBulletEnv-v0 from PyBullet, an open-source physics engine [5].[3] Our experimental evaluation aims to study the following questions:

---

[2] We refer the reader to https://github.com/perara/oracle for a detailed implementation in python.

[3] We take this opportunity to welcome the RL community to consider open-source benchmarks for easier comparison of scientific results.

– How well does ORACLE perform on reinforcement learning problems, compared to state-of-the-art model-based and model-free algorithms?
– What conclusions can we draw about ORACLE performance and are there any lessons for future study?

3.1 Hyperparameter and Sample Efficiency Evaluations

In the sample efficiency evaluations, we focus on how we can tune the ORACLE algorithm to improve sample efficiency while also maintaining acceptable performance. In this study, we only look at ORACLEbut significantly increase the number of hyperparameter variations in the experiments. We will investigate if SWA, VQ, latent leap (LL), and AGC have an advantageous effect on sample efficiency and if certain combinations show better performance. We intentionally leave out many hyperparameters that did not impact the performance in any meaningful capacity. However, we will detail our significant findings and discuss a guideline for choosing the correct hyperparameters for different environment types. We run the experiments five times for all environments and average the results. The round the convergence step to the nearest thousand and the algorithms fails the experiment if exceeding 1 million steps without reaching convergence. Finally, we use a ensemble of model-free algorithms for decision making, which we detail further in Sect. 3.2.

Table 2 illustrates the sample efficiency in terms of convergence rate for different hyperparameter settings with separate dynamics models per environment. The results clearly show that latent leap set to 30, AGC enabled, VQ disabled, and SWA enabled is the best choice for CartPole. For DeepRTS Deathmatch and HalfCheetahPyBulletEnv-v0, we observe the best results when VQ is enabled. We conclude that VQ performs worse in CartPole because it is a far simpler environment, and the algorithm cannot generalize well environments with few steps before termination state. This makes sense, as the VQ architectures double the number of trainable parameters in the model. The primary function of the VQ layer is to allow for encoding multiple environments in the same dynamics models, and hence it is natural to continue the experiments by using the same dynamics model for all environments.

Table 3 illustrates the sample efficiency of ORACLEwhen using the same model for all environments. This experiment aims to see if it is beneficial to feed the latent vector into a VQ to structure the latent space categorically. The results clearly show that ORACLE can generalize across several environments using the same parameters, using a VQ layer after the generative network.

We make the following conclusions on how to tune ORACLE. For simple environments with less than 1 000 timesteps before forced termination, we recommend disabling VQ and using LL = 30. If the environment exceeds 1 000 timesteps, enable VQ. When training the algorithm on all environments, we recommend having all hyperparameters enabled using LL = 30.

Table 2. The experiment setup for the limited hyperparameter search. The table clearly shows that a latent-leap of 30 is superior in reaching a convergence score for all tested environments.

CartPole-v1				
SWA	VQ	LL	AGC	Convergence step
On	On	10	On	N/A
On	On	30	On	755 000
On	On	60	On	N/A
On	**Off**	**30**	**On**	**390 000**
Off	On	30	Off	825 000
DeepRTS Deathmatch				
SWA	VQ	LL	AGC	Convergence step
On	On	10	On	N/A
On	**On**	**30**	**On**	**600 000**
On	On	60	On	N/A
On	Off	30	On	N/A
Off	On	30	Off	N/A
HalfCheetahPyBulletEnv-v0				
SWA	VQ	LL	AGC	Convergence step
On	On	10	On	N/A
On	**On**	**30**	**On**	**725 000**
On	On	60	On	N/A
On	Off	30	On	N/A
Off	On	30	Off	N/A

Table 3. The data depicts the average performance using a single dynamics model to learn all environments. The table clearly shows that enabling VQ has a positive effect on sample efficiency, and without, the environment can not converge before the step limit has passed.

SWA	VQ	LL	AGC	Average convergence step
On	On	10	On	895 000
Off	**On**	**30**	**On**	**565 000**
On	On	60	On	N/A
On	Off	10	On	N/A
On	Off	30	On	N/A
On	Off	60	On	N/A
On	On	10	Off	N/A
On	On	30	Off	695 000
On	On	60	Off	N/A
Off	On	10	On	N/A
Off	On	30	On	596 000
Off	On	60	On	N/A
Off	On	10	Off	N/A
Off	On	30	Off	650 000
Off	On	60	Off	N/A

3.2   Comparative Performance Evaluation

In our comparative performance evaluation, we aim to understand how the ORA-CLE algorithm performs in contrast to state-of-the-art model-based and model-free methods and how to tune the algorithm for different environments properly. We compare the ORACLE to RAINBOW [15] and PPO [26] for model-free and Dreamer [12] for model-based methods. We select PPO, DQN, RAINBOW, A3C, and VPG as the ensemble and perform majority voting for each evaluated action. In the case of a draw, we randomly select one of the actions. We run each experiment 5 times and measure steps for model-free algorithms parallel with training and model-based methods towards the real environment every 5 000 steps.[4] For the comparison, we use reference hyperparameters found in [15] for RAINBOW and [26] respectively.

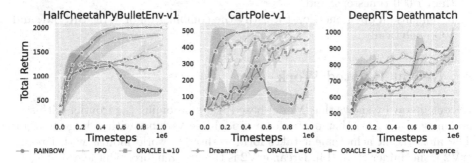

Fig. 1. The figure illustrates the accumulated return performance and sample efficiency of PPO, RAINBOW, Dreamer, and ORACLE. We observe that in all environments, ORACLE outperform the state-of-the-art algorithms with LL set to 30. The x-axis describes the environment step, while the y-axis describes the average return.

As seen in Fig. 1 ORACLE outperforms both model-free and model-based approaches for the selected environments. A dependent factor on how good ORA-CLE performs is the latent-leap parameter which represents how many steps the algorithm *leaps into the future* before resampling the real environment. Specifically, we see that a latent leap of 30 is a good compromise between sample efficiency and return performance.

3.3   Design Evaluation

We next discuss the findings in the hyperparameter tuning experiments and the comparative performance evaluation to understand better why ORACLE outperforms prior approaches.

---

[4] We make the reader aware that the experiments are compute-heavy, hence few experiment iterations. In total, the experiments take ~5 days of wall-clock time to train on consumer-level hardware.

Specifically, we think that ORACLE has strength in capturing large state-spaces and has a good ability to generalize well over sparse datasets. The dynamics model is primarily continuous with a combination of deterministic and stochastic variables, and it is well understood in the literature that variational inference is an excellent approach to model powerful generative models. Putting a VQ layer between the continuous probabilistic latent vector and transform it into a discrete latent vector before reconstructing the output. In parallel to our work [22] has the same conclusion and shows outstanding results on solving chess, outperforming previous methods. We conclude

- Using VQ in combination with VAE and SRSSM provides a powerful enhancement to model robustness, but it falls short when used for more simple problems,
- generally, we see that ORACLEis best suited for larger problems with more than 1 000 timesteps, and
- it remains an open question to justify the combination of VAE, SRSSM, and VQ analytically.

4   Recent Related Work

Recent literature shows that Model-based RL is becoming the frontier with several new algorithms that outperform model-free variants with a large margin. The most recent achievement takes form as discrete world models with DreamerV2 from Hafner et al. [14]. DreamerV2 is the first reinforcement learning agent that achieves human-level performance on the Atari benchmark by learning behaviors fully offline in a world-model. Prior work in [12] use similar architecture to [2] by deriving latent dynamics that form estimations of future observations given an action. Very Recently, Ozair et al. proposed Vector Quantized Models for planning in Reinforcement Learning [22]. The authors use a stochastic variant of the Monte Carlo tree search algorithm to plan the agent's actions and the discrete latent variables representing the system's dynamics model. This approach shows state-of-the-art results in chess and illustrates that the approach scales to DeepMind Lab, a first-person 3D environment with complex visual state observations with only partial observability.

Deep Planning Network (PlaNet) is a model-based agent that interpret the pixels of a state to learn the dynamics of an environment. The environment dynamics are stored into latent-space, where the agent sample actions based on the learned representation. The proposed algorithm showed significantly better sample efficiency compared to algorithms such as A3C [13].

[4] recently proposed Probabilistic Ensembles with Trajectory Sampling (PETS). The algorithm uses an ensemble of bootstrap neural networks to learn a dynamics model of the environment over future states. The algorithm then uses this model to predict the best action for future states. The authors show that the algorithm significantly lowers sampling requirements for environments such as half-cheetah compared to SAC and PPO.

5 Discussion and Future Work

We have investigated if the model-based reinforcement learning algorithm ORA-CLE performs well in classical and novel environments through a theoretical and empirical approach. We have shown that using state-space models combined with recurrent neural networks and variational inferences yields promising results towards advanced artificial intelligence that can perform well in tasks without directly interacting with the target environment. While it is difficult to explain the model analytically fully, we can show empirically that the model can generalize well in all tested environments. Furthermore, we show empirically that ORACLE substantially outperforms all tested model-free algorithms in performance and sample efficiency in tested environments, which is required for industry-near mission-critical environments. However, the algorithm still has several shortcomings, which we intend to approach in our continued work. First, we wish to increase the robustness to posterior collapse, a well-known problem in variational inference. Second, we wish to expand the scope of our experiments to include a substantially more comprehensive quantitive study with qualitative support to better understand the algorithm's strengths and weaknesses. Otherwise, we wish to

- Adopt the work in [23] to alleviate the posterior collapse phenomena and hopefully be able to provide better stability guarantees for the training procedure,
- Experiment with liquid time-constant networks (LTC)[27] for better learning the environment dynamics in the state-space model

References

1. Andersen, P., Goodwin, M., Granmo, O.: Deep RTS: a game environment for deep reinforcement learning in real-time strategy games. In: 2018 IEEE Conference on Computational Intelligence and Games (CIG), pp. 1–8 (2018). https://doi.org/10.1109/CIG.2018.8490409
2. Andersen, P.-A., Goodwin, M., Granmo, O.-C.: The dreaming variational autoencoder for reinforcement learning environments. In: Bramer, M., Petridis, M. (eds.) SGAI 2018. LNCS (LNAI), vol. 11311, pp. 143–155. Springer, Cham (2018). https://doi.org/10.1007/978-3-030-04191-5_11
3. Arulkumaran, K., Deisenroth, M.P., Brundage, M., Bharath, A.A.: Deep reinforcement learning: a brief survey. IEEE Signal Process. Mag. 34(6), 26–38 (2017). https://doi.org/10.1109/MSP.2017.2743240
4. Chua, K., Calandra, R., McAllister, R., Levine, S.: Deep reinforcement learning in a handful of trials using probabilistic dynamics models. In: Bengio, S., Wallach, H., Larochelle, H., Grauman, K., Cesa-Bianchi, N., Garnett, R. (eds.) Advances in Neural Information Processing Systems, vol. 31, pp. 4754–4765. Curran Associates, Inc. (2018)
5. Coumans, E., Bai, Y.: PyBullet, a Python module for physics simulation for games, robotics and machine learning. http://pybullet.org

6. Deisenroth, M., Rasmussen, C.E.: PILCO: A model-based and data-efficient approach to policy search. In: Proceedings of the 28th International Conference on Machine Learning ICML'11, pp. 465–472. Citeseer (2011)
7. Doerr, A., et al.: Probabilistic recurrent state-space models. In: Dy, J., Krause, A. (eds.) Proceedings of the 35th International Conference on Machine Learning. Proceedings of Machine Learning Research, vol. 80, pp. 1280–1289. PMLR (2018). http://proceedings.mlr.press/v80/doerr18a.html
8. Draganjac, I., Miklic, D., Kovacic, Z., Vasiljevic, G., Bogdan, S.: Decentralized control of multi-AGV systems in autonomous warehousing applications. IEEE Trans. Autom. Sci. Eng. **13**(4), 1433–1447 (2016). https://doi.org/10.1109/TASE.2016.2603781
9. Fraccaro, M.: Deep latent variable models for sequential data (2018). https://orbit.dtu.dk/en/publications/deep-latent-variable-models-for-sequential-data
10. Fuchs, A., Heider, Y., Wang, K., Sun, W.C., Kaliske, M.: DNN2: a hyper-parameter reinforcement learning game for self-design of neural network based elasto-plastic constitutive descriptions. Comput. Struct. **249**, 106505 (2021). https://doi.org/10.1016/j.compstruc.2021.106505
11. García, J., Fernández, F.: A comprehensive survey on safe reinforcement learning. J. Mach. Learn. Res. **16**, 1437–1480 (2015)
12. Hafner, D., Lillicrap, T., Ba, J., Norouzi, M.: Dream to control: learning behaviors by latent imagination. In: Proceedings 8th International Conference on Learning Representations, ICLR'20 (2020). https://openreview.net/forum?id=S1lOTC4tDS
13. Hafner, D., et al.: Learning latent dynamics for planning from pixels. In: Chaudhuri, K., Salakhutdinov, R. (eds.) Proceedings 36th International Conference on Machine Learning, ICML'18, vol. 97, pp. 2555–2565. PMLR, Long Beach (2019). http://proceedings.mlr.press/v97/hafner19a/hafner19a.pdf
14. Hafner, D., Lillicrap, T.P., Norouzi, M., Ba, J.: Mastering atari with discrete world models. In: Proceedings 9th International Conference on Learning Representations, ICLR'21 (2021). https://openreview.net/forum?id=0oabwyZbOu
15. Hessel, M., et al.: Rainbow: combining improvements in deep reinforcement learning. In: Proc. 32nd Conference on Artificial Intelligence, AAAI'18, pp. 3215–3222. AAAI Press, New Orleans (2018). https://www.aaai.org/ocs/index.php/AAAI/AAAI18/paper/download/17204/16680
16. Izmailov, P., Podoprikhin, D., Garipov, T., Vetrov, D., Wilson, A.G.: Averaging weights leads to wider optima and better generalization. In: R. Silva, A.G., Globerson, A. (eds.) 34th Conference on Uncertainty in Artificial Intelligence 2018, pp. 876–885. Association For Uncertainty in Artificial Intelligence (2018). http://arxiv.org/abs/1803.05407
17. Jordan, M.I., Ghahramani, Z., Jaakkola, T.S., Saul, L.K.: Introduction to variational methods for graphical models. Mach. Learn. **37**(2), 183–233 (1999). https://doi.org/10.1023/A:1007665907178
18. Kingma, D.P., Welling, M.: Auto-encoding variational bayes. In: Proceedings of the 2nd International Conference on Learning Representations (2013). https://doi.org/10.1051/0004-6361/201527329, http://arxiv.org/abs/1312.6114
19. Loshchilov, I., Hutter, F.: Decoupled weight decay regularization. In: Proceedings 7th International Conference on Learning Representations, ICLR'19 (2019). https://openreview.net/forum?id=Bkg6RiCqY7
20. Mallozzi, P., Pelliccione, P., Knauss, A., Berger, C., Mohammadiha, N.: Autonomous vehicles: state of the art, future trends, and challenges. In: Automotive Systems and Software Engineering, pp. 347–367. Springer, Cham (2019). https://doi.org/10.1007/978-3-030-12157-0_16

21. Moerland, T.M., Broekens, J., Jonker, C.M.: Model-based reinforcement learning: a survey (2020). arxiv preprint arXiv:2006.16712
22. Ozair, S., Li, Y., Razavi, A., Antonoglou, I., van den Oord, A., Vinyals, O.: Vector quantized models for planning. In: Proceedings 39th International Conference on Machine Learning, ICML'21 (2021). http://arxiv.org/abs/2106.04615
23. Razavi, A., van den Oord, A., Poole, B., Vinyals, O.: Preventing posterior collapse with delta-VAEs. In: Proceedings 7th International Conference on Learning Representations, ICLR'19 (2019). https://openreview.net/forum?id=BJe0Gn0cY7
24. Razavi, A., van den Oord, A., Vinyals, O.: Generating diverse high-fidelity images with VQ-VAE-2. In: Wallach, H., Larochelle, H., Beygelzimer, A., Alché-Buc, F., Fox, E., Garnett, R. (eds.) Advances in Neural Information Processing Systems, vol. 32. pp. 14837–14847. Curran Associates Inc., Vancouver (2019). http://papers.nips.cc/paper/9625-generating-diverse-high-fidelity-images-with-vq-vae-2
25. Schrittwieser, J., et al.: Mastering Atari, Go, chess and shogi by planning with a learned model. Nature 588(7839), 604–609 (2020). https://doi.org/10.1038/s41586-020-03051-4
26. Schulman, J., Wolski, F., Dhariwal, P., Radford, A., Klimov, O.: Proximal policy optimization algorithms (2017). arxiv preprint arXiv:1707.06347
27. Seetharaman, P., Wichern, G., Pardo, B., Roux, J.L.: Autoclip: adaptive gradient clipping for source separation networks. In: IEEE International Workshop on Machine Learning for Signal Processing, MLSP, vol. 2020-September. IEEE Computer Society (2020). https://doi.org/10.1109/MLSP49062.2020.9231926
28. Sutton, R.S.: Dyna, an integrated architecture for learning, planning, and reacting. ACM SIGART Bull. 2(4), 160–163 (1991). https://doi.org/10.1145/122344.122377
29. Varghese, N.V., Mahmoud, Q.H.: A survey of multi-task deep reinforcement learning. Electronics 9(9) (2020). https://doi.org/10.3390/electronics9091363
30. Yu, C., Liu, J., Nemati, S.: Reinforcement learning in healthcare: a survey (2019). arxiv preprint arXiv:1908.08796

Towards Explaining Metaheuristic Solution Quality by Data Mining Surrogate Fitness Models for Importance of Variables

Aidan Wallace, Alexander E. I. Brownlee$^{(\boxtimes)}$, and David Cairns

University of Stirling, Stirling, Scotland
{a.l.wallace,alexander.brownlee,david.cairns}@stir.ac.uk,
http://www.cs.stir.ac.uk/~alw
http://www.cs.stir.ac.uk/~sbr
http://www.cs.stir.ac.uk/~dec

Abstract. Metaheuristics are randomised search algorithms that are effective at finding "good enough" solutions to optimisation problems. However, they present no justification for generated solutions and these solutions are non-trivial to analyse in most cases. We propose that identifying the combinations of variables that strongly influence solution quality, and the nature of this relationship, represents a step towards explaining the choices made by a metaheuristic. Using three benchmark problems, we present an approach to mining this information by using a "surrogate fitness function" within a metaheuristic. For each problem, rankings of the importance of each variable with respect to fitness are determined through sampling of the surrogate model. We show that two of the three surrogate models tested were able to generate variable rankings that agree with our understanding of variable importance rankings within the three common binary benchmark problems trialled.

Keywords: Metaheuristics · Surrogates · Optimisation · Explainability

1 Introduction

With the uptake and utilisation of Artificial Intelligence (AI) driven systems across multiple sectors, we are seeing an increase in the presence of such systems within many businesses and organisations. As this continues these systems are being tasked to handle a larger number of decisions at greater levels of importance and with fewer checkpoints of human interference and guidance. It is thus vital that the decisions they are making can not only be trusted but more importantly understood by the end user as much as possible. It is hoped that, if individuals are able to build confidence in the suggestions of AI systems, they will be more likely to employ these systems and act on the solutions they provide. For this reason, enabling these processes to be understood and

© Springer Nature Switzerland AG 2021
M. Bramer and R. Ellis (Eds.): SGAI-AI 2021, LNAI 13101, pp. 58–72, 2021.
https://doi.org/10.1007/978-3-030-91100-3_5

explained is paramount to maximising the real world utility of many machine driven approaches [18].

One branch of AI, known as metaheuristics, comprises search-based methods that have been shown to efficiently find well performing solutions to difficult optimisation problems. Metaheuristics look for solutions that minimise or maximise a set of objectives that are often related to cost or performance. Optimisation problems are prevalent in many branches of industry and have an impact on numerous aspects of everyday life for many, from Computing Science and Engineering to the less traditional fields of Medicine and Retail [8,22,24], and can take many forms.

Whilst metaheuristics are able to produce well-performing solutions, the process by which they arrive at the suggested final solution remains largely unexplained to the end-user. This is problematic for a number of reasons. Firstly, a poorly understood solution will reduce the confidence an end user has in the highlighted solution that can have a knock-on effect in its uptake and implementation. Secondly, there can be additional criteria that were not included in the formal problem definition (e.g., aesthetics of a design, or having person X's working pattern accommodate their family life). Greater understanding of how the problem was solved could lead to a refinement of the problem that will, in turn, produce better performing solutions which can then lead to insight learned from this problem being applied to other similar problems. Thirdly, metaheuristics follow random processes that can lead to noise in the final outputs. It would be helpful to know what characteristics of a solution might simply be the result of this noise and can be eliminated with impacting solution quality. Finally, metaheuristics are very good at finding loopholes in the problem definition [19]. It would be helpful to know whether the solutions genuinely solve the problem or have just found a weakness in the specification.

These points together can reduce trust in an algorithm, meaning that suboptimal approaches may remain in practice that ultimately lead to wasted resources and inefficient practice. Whilst metaheuristics follow a relatively clear framework by which candidate solutions for a given problem are repeatedly generated, evaluated and modified, the search processes underpinning them are sufficiently complex as to be non-interpretable to humans and are regarded as a "blackbox". The problems metaheuristics solve are encompassed using a fitness function as a means to evaluate solutions, this is also difficult to interrogate directly for human understandable explanations and can take a variety of forms from truly blackbox examples driven by complex simulations to the more "grey box" optimisation examples where fitness is determined by a series of mathematical formulae.

In order for human users to adopt the recommendations of these automated decisions, it may be enough to provide explanation in the form of justifications for an individual outcome as opposed to interrogating and describing the inner processes by which an algorithm ultimately performs [1]. Research in explainability of deep learning can be seen to follow this type of approach, however there is little work of this type concerning metaheuristics, which address a different niche of problems than their deep learning siblings. When deciding whether to adopt a solution found by a metaheuristic, we suggest [7] that the decision maker is likely to want the focus to be on two main insights. Firstly: does the proposed solution actually solve the problem or have we stumbled upon a loophole in the problems definition; and, secondly: can we identify which characteristics of a solution are related to its performance and optimality for the problem, and which are simply an unrelated result of the random processes inherent to metaheuristics. The first of these points is more broadly applicable to any optimisation approach (including mathematical programming and brute-force optimisations), although here we focus purely on metaheuristics because of the ease with which the proposed solution approach (surrogate models) can be integrated with them.

Our focus within this paper is to offer some first steps towards making these insights. We propose a new approach to identify important characteristics of metaheuristic derived solutions to a series of binary benchmark problems, particularly which variables strongly influence solution quality and which are less important or can be ignored. The approach exploits *surrogate fitness functions* [9,16], a well-established technique for improving metaheuristic search efficiency. A computationally cheap model is trained in parallel with the optimization process, with the majority of the calls to a costly fitness function being replaced by a call to the surrogate model. Crucially, the surrogate is an explicit model of what the algorithm has learned about high-fitness solutions. Our approach takes a high-fitness solution returned by the metaheuristic and probes it with respect to the surrogate model to determine which variables are important, and their impact on fitness.

We begin in Sect. 2 by reviewing related work on trust and explanation in metaheuristics, before highlighting the role surrogates currently play in optimization problem solving and how we plan to utilise them for explainability in Sect. 3. The approach to mining the surrogate for problem information in the form of variable rankings is described in Sect. 4. We then demonstrate the approach with some easily understood simple benchmark problems being solved by a surrogate-assisted genetic algorithm in Sect. 5 and reflect on the results found in Sect. 6. Finally, we draw conclusions and set out our immediate plans for future work in this area in Sect. 7.

2 Related Work

Within the past decade, *Explainability* as a topic has seen a growing level of interest within the deep learning community as well as across other Machine Learning based approaches to problem solving. However there has been a noticeable gap in the research concerning metaheuristics and search algorithms with the closest examples being innovization proposed by Deb et al. in their 2014 paper [12] and illumination algorithms such as MAP-Elites discussed in a 2019 paper by Urquhart et al. [25].

Deb et al. [11,12] proposed "innovization" to generate additional problem based knowledge alongside the normally generated near-optimal solutions, by identifying common principles among Pareto-optimal solutions for multi-objective optimisation problems. This is based on the fact most optimization techniques adopted within industry are used to yield a single or small selection of optimal solutions and builds on it to allow these optimization techniques to yield additional problem-based knowledge alongside the generated optimal solution(s) via the innovization process. This process takes a generated set of high-performing trade-off solutions and looks for common principles concealed within them. The philosophy here is that principles common amongst this set of high performing solutions will represent properties that ensure Pareto-Optimality and are by extension valuable properties related to the problem as a whole.

More recently Urquhart's 2019 paper looked at using MAP-Elites [21] to increase trust in metaheuristics. This paper was based on the common complaint from end users when presented with a solution constructed via a metaheuristic approach that they themselves had no role in the solution construction. In order to address this the authors applied MAP-Elites, which creates a structured archive of high performing solutions that are mapped onto a set of solution characteristics defined by the user such as cost or time. These solutions are generated by mutation and recombination and each solution is then assigned a bin within the solution space; should a generated solution be assigned to an already occupied bin solution only the solution with the highest fitness is retained within this bin. MAP-Elites provides the end user with a structured archive of high performing yet diverse solutions: Urquhart et al. presented this archive via an interactive decision-making tool from which the user is ultimately responsible for choosing the preferred solution. It can be seen that MAP-Elites serves as filter of the solution space for an end user that takes a large and impractical search space and refines it to a diverse set of high-quality solutions that are more readily usable for the end user to interact with.

In 2017, Gaier et al. [13] described using surrogate modelling alongside MAP-elites, in order to speed up the MAP-Elites process by reducing the need for such a large number of evaluations normally required for MAP-Elites to produce worthwhile results, this was known as Surrogate-assisted illumination (SAIL). This is achieved by integrating approximate models in the form of surrogates as well as intelligent sampling of the objective function in question. Similarly to the original MAP-Elites approach the search space is partitioned into bins each holding a design with a different configuration of feature values. A surrogate is constructed on an initial population of candidate solutions and their fitness scores, MAP-elites then produces solutions seen to maximise the acquisition function in every region of the feature space producing our acquisition map. New solutions are then sampled from this map and sampled with the additional observations being used to improve the model. Repetition of the process results in increasingly accurate models of high fitness regions of the feature space. The performance predictions are then used by MAP-elites in place of the original objective function to produce a prediction map of estimated near-optimal designs.

The present work differs from the above approaches. In contrast to *Innovization*, we target single-objective optimisation problems. In contrast to the illumination methods using *MAP-elites*, we do not seek to present many solutions to the end user but, rather, seek to explain a single solution that was chosen by the algorithm.

3   Background: Surrogate Models

Metaheuristics, including evolutionary algorithms, follow a well-known general framework whereby a population of solutions are generated at random, then evaluated against a *fitness function*, and new solutions are generated, usually biased towards solutions known to be high in fitness. The fitness function measures solution quality and is used to guide the search but for many applied problems is costly, especially when a long running simulation or human-in-the-loop evaluation is used.

A common approach to speed up these metaheuristics is to build a surrogate model of this fitness function [4,15,16] and use this to suggest where near-optimal solutions fall within the decision space. The surrogate model uses machine learning techniques to approximate the true fitness function, ideally retaining some

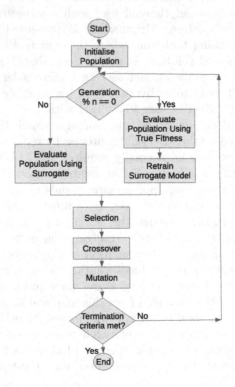

Fig. 1. The outline of the surrogate assisted genetic algorithm that we use on our experiments. In our study, n==5, i.e., the surrogate is retrained every 5 generations.

of its key properties such as regions of high fitness, but is capable of evaluating solutions at a faster rate than the fitness function. As well as offering a quicker way to evaluate potential solutions the surrogate represents an explicit model of the population and thus can be exploited to gain insight into the algorithm's understanding of the problem at hand. The outline framework for a surrogate-assisted genetic algorithm that forms the subject of our study is illustrated in the flow diagram in Fig. 1. In our work, the GA alternates between using the surrogate to evaluate solutions and using the true fitness function, with the surrogate being updated as new evaluations are carried out by the true fitness function. Many strategies for management and application of surrogate models exist and the interested reader is directed to [10,15,16] for more detail.

Surrogates are usually constructed through training a model in parallel with the optimization run, with the motivation for their use being an improvement in the speed of our search. For this reason any extra problem knowledge we are able to extract from them can largely be viewed as "free" in terms of additional resources and CPU time at least. The explicit model of the population in the form of our surrogate can then be mined, similarly to regression analysis in principle [14,17,20]. This mining of models has already been demonstrated when looking at Estimation of Distribution Algorithms (EDAs), which construct probabilistic models reflecting the distribution of high fitness solutions within the population, then sample this distribution to yield solutions likely to be high in fitness. With existing work highlighting how useful information can be extracted from these probabilistic models [3,6], it has been observed [7] within some real world problems the additional information gleamed from the EDA can prove just as advantageous as the optimisation results themselves.

It is important to note that the usefulness of this additional information is highly problem dependent and entirely reliant on the nature of the surrogate model used. More opaque black box modelling approaches involving neural nets are likely to be much harder to mine than any of the more transparent

Data: $x = (x_0 \ldots x_n), x_i = \{0,1\}$, near-optimal solution found by GA
Data: $S(X) \rightarrow f$, surrogate fitness function to estimate fitness f of a
    solution X
Result: $C = (c_0 \ldots c_n), c_i \in \mathbb{R}$, absolute change to surrogate fitness for
    each variable in x

```
C ← ∅;
f_org ← S(x)                    /* surrogate fitness of solution */
for i = 0 to n − 1 do           /* for each variable x_i */
    x_i ← (x_i + 1) mod 2       /* flip variable x_i */
    f̂_i              /* surrogate fitness of mutated solution */
    C ← |c_i|                   /* add to list */
end
```

Algorithm 1: Method for probing variables in a solution with respect to the surrogate fitness function

methods like functions derived using linear regression [23]. Our major hypothesis is that some semblance of explanation for the global optimum can be provided in the form of variable importance rankings, extracted by mining surrogate fitness models and visualisation of the results.

4   Methodology: Mining the Model

The proposed approach to determine and quantify the importance of individual variables takes the form of local sensitivity analysis [26], whereby the optimal solutions are perturbed and the resulting mutants tested against the surrogate model, following Algotithm 1. Once the metaheuristic run has completed and a surrogate fitness function built, the best-found solution over the metaheuristic run was retained. Due to the relative simplicity of binary benchmark problems this often lay on or near the true globally optimal solution s. Each binary variable within s was then flipped to form a neighbour $\hat{s}$. The fitness of $\hat{s}$ was calculated using the surrogate, allowing us to understand not only the importance a given variable may have on the overall fitness of a solution but, more importantly, whether our surrogate was able to accurately capture and utilize this information.

This method also brings insight into whether the problem contains variables which, when altered, would not impact negatively on performance. This is less relevant for benchmark problems but is significant should this approach be applied to more real life and noisy problems. This mutated fitness score was then compared to that of the original solution and the amount to which it has risen or fallen recorded. Once a value for each variable change was recorded the variables themselves were ranked in terms of absolute effect on fitness and these together constituted an experimental run. This entire process of GA and surrogate generation and subsequent surrogate model mining for variable importance was repeated 50 times to give us a set of repeat runs. From these 50 runs, the median absolute change in fitness and median ranking for each variable was calculated. An example of the outcome of these rankings can be seen in Fig. 3 and Fig. 4.

The idea here is that the importance of each variables is derived from the surrogate fitness function. This surrogate is biased towards high-quality solutions that have been visited by the metaheuristic, and so reflects something of the metaheuristic's understanding of the problem. Probing in this way also costs very little, because no additional calls to the fitness function are required.

5   Experiments

As a baseline, we focus on three well-known bit-string encoded benchmark functions (BinVal, AltOnes and Checkerboard) and use three problem sizes for each. In the case of BinVal and AltOnes these were 20, 50 and 100, whilst in the case of Checkerboard, a square structure was required so problems sizes of 25, 64 and 100 were used. These functions are well understood and, in each function, we have direct control over the interactions between variables and the importance of variables.

5.1 Benchmark Problems

Our experiments focus on three benchmark functions using a bit string representation. The three were chosen to give some basic variation in the importance attached to each variable and the presence or absence of interactions.

BinVal was chosen because the problem variables have a clear rank ordering of importance. In the standard version of this problem, fitness is simply the integer represented by the bit string in binary. In order to ensure that the importance of the least significant bits on fitness was not infinitesimal compared to the most significant bits, we flattened the growth in weight applied to each bit by changing the base c from 2 in the original benchmark to 1.1 in our experiments.

$$f(x) = \sum_{i=1}^{n-1} c^{ix_i} \tag{1}$$

AltOnes applies equal importance to all variables, and introduces interactions. Fitness is the count of directly neighbouring pairs of bits in the bit string that have differing values.

$$f(x) = \sum_{i=0}^{n-1} \delta(x_i, x_x + 1) \tag{2}$$

Checkerboard also introduces bivariate interactions, and though these are equally weighted in the fitness function, implicitly those in the centre of the grid have greater impact on fitness [5]. Solutions represent the rows of a s x s grid concatenated into one string, and the objective is to realise a grid with a checkerboard pattern of alternating 1s and 0s:

$$f(x) = 4(s-2)^2 - \sum_{i=2}^{s-1} \sum_{j=2}^{s-1} \left\{ \begin{array}{l} \delta(x_{ij}, x_{i-1j}) + \delta(x_{ij}, x_{i+1j}) \\ +\delta(x_{ij}, x_{ij-1}) + \delta(x_{ij}, x_{ij+1}) \end{array} \right\} \tag{3}$$

where δ is Kronecker's delta function,

$$\delta_{ij} = \left\{ \begin{array}{l} 1 \text{ if } i = j \\ 0 \text{ if } i \neq j \end{array} \right. \tag{4}$$

5.2 Experimental Procedure

When addressing each of the benchmark problems above, a similar experimental approach was undertaken. An initial random population of 100 candidate solutions was created and a Genetic Algorithm (GA) used with a view to determine a near-optimum solution. The GA has population size 100, tournament size 2, mutation gene rate of 0.1, and a crossover rate of 0.95 and ran for 100 generations. The GA also used elitism, with the single fittest solution being carried from one generation to the next without mutation.

The GA takes the initial population and iterates through a cycle of assessing the fitness of the population, selecting candidate solutions to take forward to the next newly formed population and breeding these solutions through a cycle of crossover and mutation, following the outline in Fig. 1. The best found solution over the entire metaheuristic run is returned to the end user once completed with no true explanation as to how it arrived at a given solution. In order to try and capture some of this explainability a surrogate model was constructed using the current GA population and calculated fitness scores at different periods throughout the GA run with retraining occurring at set intervals. Clearly for these simple benchmark functions the surrogate is unnecessary for the purpose of speeding up the process; but we aim to demonstrate its utility for mining the importance of problem variables.

For each problem, three different surrogate models were used in order to see how the problems performed over a variety of surrogate model types: linear regression; decision tree; and random forest. These were trained using the WEKA Java machine learning library[1], and used with the default hyperparameter configurations. In principle better modelling could be achieved by tuning of the hyperparameters, but as the purpose of this study is a proof of concept for mining the model, we have left this stage to future work for now.

6   Results and Discussion

Before we go onto to discuss the results, it is important to note that one of the surrogates failed to accurately grasp enough about any of the problems in question: this was the decision tree in the form of a WEKA RepTree. In the smaller sized instances of BinVal, RepTree was able to ascertain that greater importance lay in the lower numbered variables, nearer the beginning of the bit string but failed to pick up any further knowledge about variable importance. With both AltOnes and Checkerboard this surrogate did not pick up sufficient information to be of use to us. An example of the results that RepTree generated for BinVal can be seen in Fig. 2.

Looking firstly at the BinVal benchmark problem over the three problem sizes with linear regression and random forest as the surrogate models, we see similar results as shown in Fig. 3. The average bearing a variable has on fitness diminishes as the variable number increases. This is further reinforced by Fig. 4, which shows that, as the variable number increases, its rank and, by extension, its bearing on fitness, can be seen to reduce. This agrees with our understanding of the BinVal problem and paints a clear picture that surrogate mining has found information directly relevant to the quality of solutions in the optimisation problem at hand.

---

[1] Version 3.8.5—https://www.cs.waikato.ac.nz/ml/weka/.

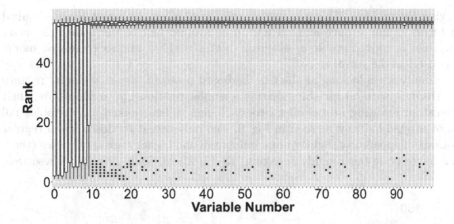

Fig. 2. This plot shows the distribution of importance ranks allocated to each variable over 50 runs (lower values indicate closer to 1st place; i.e., more important). In this case, showing the ability of the surrogate decision tree (RepTree) to capture problem knowledge. Even the most important variables (left-most) are often ranked far from first place, and after the tenth variable, rarely was any importance detected.

Similarly when looking at the AltOnes problem, where equal importance is seen across the suite of variables, it was observed both linear regression and random forest surrogates were able to detect that all variables shared the same level of change in absolute fitness. In each case, each variable had an impact of $1/n$ on overall fitness, indicating they shared a similar degree of importance in

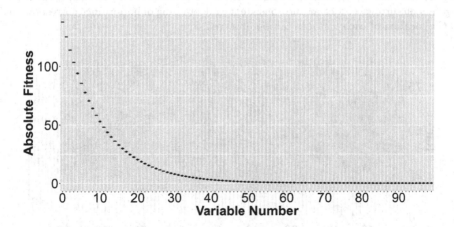

Fig. 3. The absolute fitness change resulting when individual variables are flipped with the BinVal problem of size 100, using a linear regression surrogate. Each box is the distribution of absolute fitness changes detected for each variable by mining the surrogate. A smooth drop off in importance can be observed.

solving the problem. This was further reinforced when the variables were ranked in terms of importance and all fell on or around half of the total number of variables in a given problem, as shown in Fig. 5, where a linear regression model was used as the surrogate.

Finally when looking at the Checkerboard problem, we see a similar pattern to AltOnes, with all variables sharing a similar relationship to fitness and their alteration resulting in a similar fitness change. When ranked, all variables fall on or around halfway, as seen in Fig. 6. The only caveat to this is small regular pockets of apparently slightly more influential and higher ranked variables (there is a lot of noise but roughly speaking, 13–17, 21–28, 55–61, 73–79). These were

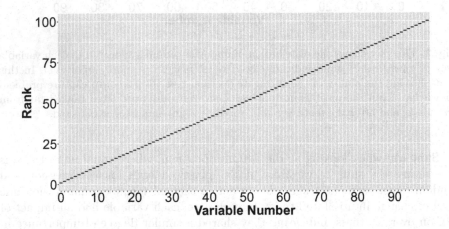

Fig. 4. The rankings of variables within the BinVal problem of size 100, using the linear regression surrogate. A clear and consistent rank ordering of importance corresponding to the location of each variable can be observed.

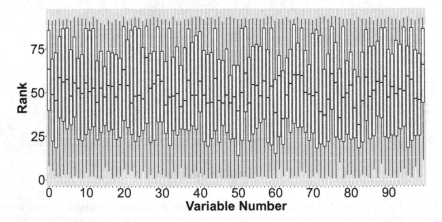

Fig. 5. Showing the variable ranking resulting when individual variables are flipped with the AltOnes problem of size 100

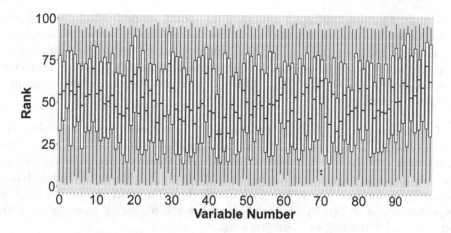

Fig. 6. Showing variable rankings within checkerboard problem

determined to be variables that lay nearer the central region of our hypothetical Checkerboard and thus had a higher number of neighbours surrounding them. At this stage, we are only concerned with the individual variable importance but, in future, more work could be done to investigate this neighbourhood element of the problem and how best to capture it.

7 Conclusion

This paper serves as an initial indicator for the potential to use a collection of machine learning algorithms to aid in the explainability of optimization processes utilizing metaheuristics. It focuses on the reporting of relationships between the location of variables within a given candidate solution and their bearing on this solutions ability to solve benchmark problems. It applies sensitivity analysis to a proposed solution with a surrogate model to achieve this. Some immediate benefits of this can be quickly seen:

- Outside of traditional benchmark problems, gaining knowledge about variable rankings and the sensitivity of individual variables can allow for solutions to be fine tuned for factors and constraints not initially considered during the optimization run, whilst retaining an idea of the effect a given change will have on the optimality of a given solution.
- More obviously, if the optimal solution/set of solutions returned by the meta-heuristic run agrees with the conclusions drawn from our surrogate model, it gives a decision maker more confidence in the optimality of solutions in question and increases the likelihood they will be utilized.
- Finally in the case of complicated or long running optimization algorithms, the surrogate is able to point towards the likely location of well performing solutions and by extension likely global optima. This has a possible two-fold

benefit. Firstly, allowing us to narrow the search space to filter out solutions we know to be of poorer quality and focus on only the higher quality solutions. Secondly, the potential to indicate where a stochastic technique such as those employed by many metaheuristic optimization techniques may have neglected or passed over a region of high fitness or perhaps even the globally optimal solution itself.

Comparing the results of the two successful surrogates (linear regression and random forest) we see very similar variable rankings generated for each of the benchmark problems. In the case of BinVal both showed a clear sliding level of variable importance as a variable is further from the beginning of the bit string. Similarly, in the case of AltOnes and Checkerboard a generally similar level of importance was shared by all variables within the bit string as expected with our own understanding of these problems.

We have looked at using surrogate fitness functions as a way to obtain additional information pertaining to variable importance rankings within a subset of common binary benchmark problems. Going forward from here additional focus needs to remain on introducing and disseminating the concept of applying surrogate model mining to a much wider range of problems particularly those traditionally solved using processes derived from metaheuristic approaches. This work has further strengthened the argument for using surrogates as a means of gaining additional problem knowledge and explaining metaheuristic optimisation results in the future.

Future work following this line could involve applying similar methods to real world and non-binary problems as well as multi-objective problems. We also wish to investigate whether taking surrogate models built at different stages of a GA run (after a set number of generations) will affect the surrogate's performance. Furthermore, we will seek to extend our current methods to work on problems involving interactions, such as the known neighbourhood structure in this benchmark problem, or following a structure learning procedure such as those set out in [2].

References

1. Adadi, A., Berrada, M.: Peeking inside the black-box: a survey on explainable artificial intelligence (XAI). IEEE Access **6**, 52138–52160 (2018). https://doi.org/10.1109/ACCESS.2018.2870052
2. Brownlee, A.E.I., McCall, J.A.W., Shakya, S.K., Zhang, Q.: Structure learning and optimisation in a markov-network based estimation of distribution algorithm. In: Proceedings of IEEE CEC, pp. 447–454. IEEE Press, Trondheim, Norway (2009)
3. Brownlee, A.E.I., Regnier-Coudert, O., McCall, J.A.W., Massie, S.: Using a Markov network as a surrogate fitness function in a genetic algorithm. In: Proceedings of IEEE CEC, pp. 4525–4532. Barcelona (2010)
4. Brownlee, A.E.I., Woodward, J., Swan, J.: Metaheuristic design pattern: surrogate fitness functions. In: MetaDeeP Workshop, Proceedings of GECCO Companion, pp. 1261–1264. ACM Press, Madrid, Spain (2015)

5. Brownlee, A., McCall, J., Zhang, Q.: Fitness modeling with Markov networks. IEEE Trans. Evolut. Comput. **17**(6), 862–879 (2013)
6. Brownlee, A.E.I., Regnier-Coudert, O., McCall, J.A.W., Massie, S., Stulajter, S.: An application of a GA with Markov network surrogate to feature selection. Int. J. Syst. Sci. **44**(11), 2039–2056 (2013)
7. Brownlee, A.E.I., Wallace, A., Cairns, D.: Mining Markov network surrogates to explain the results of metaheuristic optimisation. In: Proceedings of the SICSA XAI Workshop 2021, CEUR Workshop Proceedings, Robert Gordon University, Aberdeen, UK (2021)
8. Brownlee, A.E., Weiszer, M., Chen, J., Ravizza, S., Woodward, J.R., Burke, E.K.: A fuzzy approach to addressing uncertainty in Airport Ground Movement optimisation. Trans. Res. Part C Emerg. Technol. **92**, 150–175 (2018). https://doi.org/10.1016/j.trc.2018.04.020
9. Brownlee, A.E., Wright, J.A.: Constrained, mixed-integer and multi-objective optimisation of building designs by NSGA-II with fitness approximation. Appl. Soft Comput. **33**, 114–126 (2015)
10. Chugh, T., Rahat, A., Volz, V., Zaefferer, M.: Towards better integration of surrogate models and optimizers. In: Bartz-Beielstein, T., Filipič, B., Korošec, P., Talbi, E.-G. (eds.) High-Performance Simulation-Based Optimization. SCI, vol. 833, pp. 137–163. Springer, Cham (2020). https://doi.org/10.1007/978-3-030-18764-4_7
11. Deb, K., Srinivasan, A.: Innovization: Discovery of innovative design principles through multiobjective evolutionary optimization. In: Knowles, J., et al. (eds.) Multiobjective Problem Solving from Nature: From Concepts to Applications, pp. 243–262. Springer, Heidelberg (2008). https://doi.org/10.1007/978-3-540-72964-8_12
12. Deb, K., Bandaru, S., Greiner, D., Gaspar-Cunha, A., Tutum, C.C.: An integrated approach to automated innovization for discovering useful design principles: case studies from engineering. Appl. Soft Comput. **15**, 42–56 (2014). https://doi.org/10.1016/j.asoc.2013.10.011
13. Gaier, A., Asteroth, A., Mouret, J.B.: Data-efficient exploration, optimization, and modeling of diverse designs through surrogate-assisted illumination. In: Proceedings of the Genetic and Evolutionary Computation Conference, pp. 99–106 (2017)
14. Hauschild, M., Pelikan, M.: An introduction and survey of estimation of distribution algorithms. Swarm Evol. Comput. **1**(3), 111–128 (2011)
15. Jin, Y.: A comprehensive survey of fitness approximation in evolutionary computation. Soft Comput. **9**(1), 3–12 (2005)
16. Jin, Y.: Surrogate-assisted evolutionary computation: recent advances and future challenges. Swarm Evol. Comput. **1**(2), 61–70 (2011)
17. Larrañaga, P., Lozano, J.A.: Estimation of Distribution Algorithms: A New Tool for Evolutionary Computation. Kluwer, Boston (2002)
18. Le Bras, P., Robb, D.A., Methven, T.S., Padilla, S., Chantler, M.J.: Improving user confidence in concept maps: Exploring data driven explanations. In: Conference on Human Factors in Computing Systems - Proceedings 2018-April (2018). https://doi.org/10.1145/3173574.3173978
19. Lehman, J., Clune, J., Misevic, D.: The surprising creativity of digital evolution: A collection of anecdotes from the evolutionary computation and artificial life research communities. Artif. Life **26**(2), 274–306 (2020). https://doi.org/10.1162/artl_a_00319
20. Lozano, J.A., Larrañaga, P., Inza, I., Bengoetxea, E.: Towards a New Evolutionary Computation: Advances on Estimation of Distribution Algorithms (Studies in Fuzziness and Soft Computing). Springer, Heidelberg (2006)

21. Mouret, J.B., Clune, J.: Illuminating search spaces by mapping elites. arXiv preprint arXiv:1504.04909 (2015)
22. Ochoa, G., Christie, L.A., Brownlee, A.E., Hoyle, A.: Multi-objective evolutionary design of antibiotic treatments. Artif. Intell. Med. **102**, 101759 (2020). https://doi.org/10.1016/j.artmed.2019.101759
23. Rodriguez Rafael, G.D., Solano Salinas, C.J.: Empirical study of surrogate models for black box optimizations obtained using symbolic regression via genetic programming. In: Proceedings of GECCO Companion, pp. 185–186. ACM (2011)
24. Sajja, P.S.: Examples and applications on genetic algorithms. In: Illustrated Computational Intelligence. SCI, vol. 931, pp. 155–189. Springer, Singapore (2021). https://doi.org/10.1007/978-981-15-9589-9_5
25. Urquhart, N., Guckert, M., Powers, S.: Increasing trust in meta-heuristics using MAP-elites. In: Proceedings of GECCO Computation, pp. 1345–1348 (2019)
26. Wright, J.A., et al.: Multi-objective optimization of cellular fenestration by an evolutionary algorithm. J. Build. Perform. Sim. **7**(1), 33–51 (2014)

AI Techniques

Assessing the Impact of Agents in Weighted Bipolar Argumentation Frameworks

Areski Himeur[1], Bruno Yun[2(✉)], Pierre Bisquert[1,3], and Madalina Croitoru[1]

[1] LIRMM, Inria, Univ Montpellier, CNRS, Montpellier, France
`areski.himeur@etu.umontpellier.fr`, `pierre.bisquert@inra.fr`,
`croitoru@lirmm.fr`
[2] University of Aberdeen, Aberdeen, Scotland
`bruno.yun@abdn.ac.uk`
[3] IATE, Univ Montpellier, INRAE, Institut Agro, Montpellier, France

Abstract. Argumentation provides a formalism consisting of arguments and attacks/supports between these arguments and can be used to rank or deduce justified conclusions. In multi-agent settings, where several agents can advance arguments at the same time, understanding which agent has the most influence on a particular argument can improve an agent's decision about which argument to advance next. In this paper, we introduce an argumentation framework with authorship and define new semantics to account for the impact of the agents on the arguments. We propose a set of desirable principles that such a semantics should satisfy, instantiate such semantics from two popular graded based semantics, and study to which extent these principles are satisfied. These semantics will allow an observer to identify the most influential agents in a debate.

Keywords: Argumentation · Graded semantics · Authorship

1 Introduction

The Abstract Argumentation Framework (AAF), as introduced in Dung's seminal paper [8], is a powerful knowledge representation and reasoning paradigm which represents argumentation debates using directed graph where the nodes represent arguments and arcs represent attacks between the arguments. The weighted Bipolar Argumentation Framework (wBAF) [2] was later introduced as a generalization of AAF where arguments have an associated weight and another binary relation between arguments, called *supports*, is added alongside attacks. This particular framework has received much attention in the literature and most of the existing work have focused on defining semantics to reason with wBAFs [1,10,11]. One class of semantics, graded semantics, provides an acceptability degree for each argument of the graph, i.e. quantifying the "strength" of based on its initial weight and how much it is attacked and/or supported.

© Springer Nature Switzerland AG 2021
M. Bramer and R. Ellis (Eds.): SGAI-AI 2021, LNAI 13101, pp. 75–88, 2021.
https://doi.org/10.1007/978-3-030-91100-3_6

Let us consider the following situation where three systems of John's smart home, temperature sensor (p_1), general knowledge system (p_2) and user preference system (p_3), are communicating by exchanging arguments in real-time. The arguments are listed below:

p_1: The heater needs to be turned on (a_0).
p_2: Low temperature is acceptable during the night (a_1).
p_1: The inside temperature is 18 °C which is undesirable (a_2).
p_2: The residents are sleeping and low temperatures are beneficial (a_3).
p_3: John has specified that he is sensitive to cold (a_4).
p_3: In John's history, he has previously set the inside temperature to 18 °C (a_5).
p_2: It is unlikely that the inside temperature is 18 °C as the temperature of the area is 23 °C (a_6).

The relationship between these arguments and their initial strengths (representing the system confidence) is shown in Fig. 1.

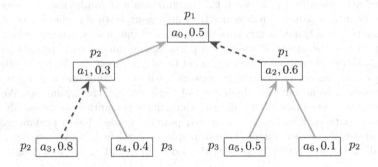

Fig. 1. Graph representation of the smart home example.

The question we are interested in here is: "Which system will be decisive in deciding whether the heater should be turned on?". More generally, in this paper, we turn our attention to the study of the impact of an agent on the final acceptability degree of an argument.

To illustrate the significance of our contribution, let us consider two motivating examples. For argument-based decision tool, it is useful to see the impact of an agent on the final result. On one hand, this study allows detecting agents that are the most influential. On the other hand, it may lead to a better identification of mischievous behavior that has a real impact on the final result. In addition, for educational purposes, formerly evaluate the impact of an agent on the final result makes it possible to advise a student who wants to learn how to argue. Moreover, it is particularly suited for automated remote training.

This paper is structured as follows. First, in Sect. 2, we recall the necessary definitions of weighted bipolar framework and graded semantics. Then, we present the contribution of this paper: (1) a novel bipolar argumentation framework with authorship (Sect. 3.1), (2) the definition of agent-based impact semantics and their desirable principles (Sect. 3.2), (3) concrete agent-based impact semantics instantiated using two popular graded semantics, namely Euler-based and DF-Quad based semantics, (Sect. 4.1) and (4) the analysis of the principles satisfied by the two aforementioned agent-based impact semantics (Sect. 4.2).

2   Background

We recall the standard weighted Bipolar Argumentation Framework (wBAF) introduced by Amgoud et al. [2,11]. We start by introducing a weighting on a set of elements as a function that associates to each element of this set, a number between 0 and 1 called its weight.

Definition 1 (Weighting). *Let X be a set of elements, a function $w : X \rightarrow [0, 1]$ is called a weighting on X.*

A weighted bipolar argumentation framework is triple composed of a set of arguments, two binary relations on arguments (attacks and supports) and a weighting on the set of arguments.

Definition 2 (wBAF). *A weighted bipolar argumentation framework (wBAF) is a tuple $F = \langle \mathcal{A}, \mathcal{R}, \mathcal{S}, w \rangle$ where $\mathcal{A}$ is a finite set of arguments, $\mathcal{R} \subseteq \mathcal{A} \times \mathcal{A}$ is a set of binary attacks, $\mathcal{S} \subseteq \mathcal{A} \times \mathcal{A}$ is a set of binary supports, and w is a weighting on $\mathcal{A}$.*

As it is common in the literature, we restrict ourselves to acyclic and non-maximal wBAFs, i.e. graphs without cycles nor arguments with a weight of 1. Note that this restriction allows for most of the usual graded semantics defined in the literature to converge.

Definition 3 (Acyclic and non-maximal). *A wBAF $F = \langle \mathcal{A}, \mathcal{R}, \mathcal{S}, w \rangle$ is acyclic iff for any non-empty finite sequence $\langle a_1, a_2, ..., a_n \rangle$ of arguments in $\mathcal{A}$, if for every $i \in \{1, 2, ..., n-1\}, (a_i, a_{i+1}) \in \mathcal{S} \cup \mathcal{R}$, then $(a_n, a_1) \notin \mathcal{S} \cup \mathcal{R}$. A wBAF F is non-maximal iff for every $a \in \mathcal{A}, w(a) < 1$.*

A graded semantics is a function assigning a value in $[0, 1]$ to each argument of a $wBAF$ such that arguments with higher values are considered more acceptable, i.e. less attacked.

Definition 4 (Graded semantics). *A semantics σ is a function mapping any wBAF $F = \langle \mathcal{A}, \mathcal{R}, \mathcal{S}, w \rangle$ into a weighting Deg_F^σ from $\mathcal{A}$ to $[0, 1]$. For any argument $a \in \mathcal{A}$, $Deg_F^\sigma(a)$ is called the acceptability degree of a.*

There are multiple graded semantics for wBAFs defined in the literature. In this paper, we restrict ourselves to two well-known graded semantics for (acyclic and non-maximal) $wBAFs$, namely the Euler-based [1] and DF-Quad semantics [15]. Of course, without loss of generality, our approach can be extended to other graded semantics.

Definition 5 (Euler-based semantics). *The Euler-based semantics σ_{EBS} is the function that maps any acyclic and non-maximal wBAF $\boldsymbol{F} = \langle \mathcal{A}, w, \mathcal{R}, \mathcal{S} \rangle$ to the weighting $Deg_{\mathcal{A}}^{\sigma_{EBS}} : \mathcal{A} \to [0,1]$, defined as follow:*

$$\forall a \in \mathcal{A}, Deg_{\boldsymbol{F}}^{\sigma_{EBS}}(a) = 1 - \frac{1 - w(a)^2}{1 + w(a)e^E}$$

$$\text{where } E = \sum_{s|(s,a)\in\mathcal{S}} Deg_{\boldsymbol{F}}^{\sigma_{EBS}}(s) - \sum_{r|(r,a)\in\mathcal{R}} Deg_{\boldsymbol{F}}^{\sigma_{EBS}}(r)$$

Please note that if a does not have any attackers nor supporters, $E = 0$.

Definition 6 (DF-Quad semantics). *The DF-Quad semantics σ_{DF} is the function that maps any acyclic and non-maximal wBAF $\boldsymbol{F} = \langle \mathcal{A}, \mathcal{R}, \mathcal{S}, w \rangle$ to the weighting $Deg_{\boldsymbol{F}}^{\sigma_{DF}} : \mathcal{A} \to [0,1]$ such that for every $a \in \mathcal{A}$, we have: if $v_s(a) = v_a(a)$, $Deg_{\boldsymbol{F}}^{\sigma_{DF}}(a) = w(a)$; else $Deg_{\boldsymbol{F}}^{\sigma_{DF}}(a) =$*

$$w(a) + (0.5 + \frac{v_s(a) - v_a(a)}{2 \cdot |v_s(a) - v_a(a)|} - w(a)) \cdot |v_s(a) - v_a(a)|$$

where:

$$- v_a(a) = 1 - \prod_{(b,a)\in\mathcal{R}} (1 - Deg_{\boldsymbol{F}}^{\sigma_{DF}}(b))$$
$$- v_s(a) = 1 - \prod_{(b,a)\in\mathcal{S}} (1 - Deg_{\boldsymbol{F}}^{\sigma_{DF}}(b)).$$

Please note that if a does not have any attackers $v_a(a) = 0$. Similarly, if a does not have any supporters $v_s(a) = 0$.

3   A Framework for Agent-Based Impact

In this section, we will introduce the framework allowing to study the impact of arguments and agents, i.e. authored wBAF (Sect. 3.1) and impact semantics (Sect. 3.2).

3.1   Authored wBAF

We extend the wBAF [2,13] framework by adding an additional label to each argument representing its author, i.e. the agent that owns it. The intuition of this label is that the agent that first states an argument in the debate is the one that "owns" it. For simplicity, our new framework only accommodates one author per argument but the approach of this paper can be easily extended to multiple authors per arguments by considering that each agent owns only one part of each argument.

Definition 7 (awBAF). *An authored wBAF (awBAF) is a tuple $\boldsymbol{A} = \langle \mathcal{A}, \mathcal{R}, \mathcal{S}, w, P, \mathcal{Y} \rangle$ where:*

- $\mathcal{A}$ is a finite set of arguments
- $\mathcal{R} \subseteq \mathcal{A} \times \mathcal{A}$ is a set of binary attacks
- $\mathcal{S} \subseteq \mathcal{A} \times \mathcal{A}$ is a set of binary supports
- w is a weighting on $\mathcal{A}$
- P is a finite set of agents such that $\mathcal{A} \cap P = \emptyset$
- $\mathcal{Y} : \mathcal{A} \to P$ is a function that associates to each argument, the agent that owns it.

Please note that $p \in P$ is the author of $a \in \mathcal{A}$ iff $\mathcal{Y}(a) = p$. Similarly, the set of arguments of an agent p is $\mathcal{A}_p = \{a \in \mathcal{A} \mid \mathcal{Y}(a) = p\}$. $P(\mathbf{A})$ is the set of agents owning arguments in $\mathbf{A}$, i.e. $P(\mathbf{A}) = \{p \in P \mid there\ exists\ a \in \mathcal{A}\ s.t.$ $\mathcal{Y}(a) = p\}$. Given $\mathbf{A} = \langle \mathcal{A}, \mathcal{R}, \mathcal{S}, w, P, \mathcal{Y} \rangle$ and $\mathbf{A'} = \langle \mathcal{A'}, \mathcal{R'}, \mathcal{S'}, w', P', \mathcal{Y'} \rangle$ such that $\mathcal{A} \cap \mathcal{A'} = \emptyset$, $\mathbf{A} \oplus \mathbf{A'}$ is $\langle \mathcal{A''}, \mathcal{R''}, \mathcal{S''}, w'', P'', \mathcal{Y''} \rangle$ such that $\mathcal{A''} = \mathcal{A'} \cup \mathcal{A}$, $\mathcal{R''} = \mathcal{R} \cup \mathcal{R'}$, $\mathcal{S''} = \mathcal{S} \cup \mathcal{S'}$, $P'' = P \cup P'$ and for all $a \in \mathcal{A'} \cup \mathcal{A}$, the following holds $w''(a) = w(a)$ if $a \in \mathcal{A}$ or $w''(a) = w'(a)$ if $a \in \mathcal{A'}$ and $\mathcal{Y''}(a) = \mathcal{Y}(a)$ if $a \in \mathcal{A}$ or $\mathcal{Y''}(a) = \mathcal{Y'}(a)$ if $a \in \mathcal{A'}$.

Quite naturally, disregarding the authors of an awBAF allows to obtain what we call the *induced wBAF*.

Definition 8 (Induced wBAF). *Given a awBAF* $\mathbf{A} = \langle \mathcal{A}, \mathcal{R}, \mathcal{S}, w, P, \mathcal{Y} \rangle$, *we call induced wBAF of* $\mathbf{A}$ *the wBAF* $\mathbf{F_A} = \langle \mathcal{A}, \mathcal{R}, \mathcal{S}, w \rangle$.

Example 1. The awBAF corresponding to the example in introduction, and represented in Fig. 1 $\mathbf{A} = \langle \mathcal{A}, \mathcal{R}, \mathcal{S}, w, P, \mathcal{Y} \rangle$ such that $\mathcal{A} = \{a_0, a_1, \ldots, a_6\}$, $\mathcal{R} = \{(a_1, a_0), (a_4, a_1), (a_6, a_2)\}$, $\mathcal{S} = \{(a_3, a_1), (a_2, a_0), (a_5, a_2)\}$, $P = \{p_1, p_2, p_3\}$.

Every square node represents an argument with its weight. Next to each square node, the corresponding author is represented, e.g. the author of a_0 is p_1. A dashed green arrow represents a support and a solid red arrow represents an attack. In this example, agent p_1 is trying to increase the acceptability of his own argument a_0 by adding the supporting argument a_2. On the contrary, p_2 is trying to decrease the acceptability of a_0 by using a_1, a_3 and a_6. Lastly, p_3 both decreases and increases the acceptability of a_0 with a_5 and a_4 respectively.

Definition 9 (Isomorphism). *Given two awBAFs* $\mathbf{A} = \langle \mathcal{A}, \mathcal{R}, \mathcal{S}, w, P, \mathcal{Y} \rangle$ *and* $\mathbf{A'} = \langle \mathcal{A'}, \mathcal{R'}, \mathcal{S'}, w', P', \mathcal{Y'} \rangle$, *we say that* f *is an isomorphism from* $\mathbf{A}$ *to* $\mathbf{A'}$ *iff there are two isomorphisms* f_1 *(from* $\mathcal{A}$ *to* $\mathcal{A'}$*) and* f_2 *(from* P *to* P'*) such that all the following items are satisfied:*

- *for every* $a, a' \in \mathcal{A}$, $(a, a') \in \mathcal{R}$ *iff* $(f_1(a), f_1(a')) \in \mathcal{R'}$
- *for every* $a, a' \in \mathcal{A}$, $(a, a') \in \mathcal{S}$ *iff* $(f_1(a), f_1(a')) \in \mathcal{S'}$
- *for every* $a \in \mathcal{A}$, $w(a) = w'(f_1(a))$
- *for every* $a \in \mathcal{A}$, $f_2(\mathcal{Y}(a)) = \mathcal{Y'}(f_1(a))$

In the next section, we will provide the general definition of an *agent-based impact semantics* and some desirable principles to assess the "quality" of such semantics, i.e. how accurate they are in depicting the attack and support relations of the awBAF.

3.2   Agent-Based Impact Semantics

As shown by Example 1 and Fig. 1, quantifying the impact that an agent has on the acceptability degree of an argument is not straightforward, especially for complex argumentation graphs. In this section, we define the notion of *agent-based impact semantics* and provide some desirable principles for it. Finally, we provide the first agent-based impact semantics.

Definition 10 (Agent-based impact semantics). *An (agent-based) impact semantics is a function δ that associates to each awBAF $A = \langle \mathcal{A}, \mathcal{R}, \mathcal{S}, w, P, \mathcal{Y} \rangle, a$ in $\mathcal{A}$, and $p \in P$, a positive real number $\delta(A, p, a)$. $\delta(A, p_2, a) \geq \delta(A, p_1, a)$ means that p_2 impacts at least as much as p_1 on the acceptability of a.*

In the rest of this subsection, we propose the first set of desirable principles for an (agent-based) impact semantics inspired by the principles for graded semantics in existing work on *wBAF* [2].

The *Anonymity* principle states that the agent-based impact semantics should not be defined based on the names of the arguments or the agents.

Principle 1 (Anonymity). *An impact semantics δ satisfies Anonymity iff for any two awBAFs $A = \langle \mathcal{A}, \mathcal{R}, \mathcal{S}, w, P, \mathcal{Y} \rangle$ and A' such that there exists an isomorphism from A to A' (and the corresponding isomorphisms f_1 and f_2 between the arguments and agents respectively), for any $a \in \mathcal{A}$, we have that for all $p_1, p_2 \in P, \delta(A, p_1, a) \leq \delta(A, p_2, a)$ iff $\delta(A', f_2(p_1), f_1(a)) \leq \delta(A', f_2(p_2), f_1(a))$.*

The following principle states that adding a dummy argument to an agent (an argument not involved in any attacks or supports) should keep the order of the agent impacts unchanged. Please note that a stricter variant of the dummy principle would imply that adding dummy arguments would keep the (agent-based) impact values unchanged.

Principle 2 (Dummy). *An impact semantics δ satisfies Dummy iff for any awBAF $A = \langle \mathcal{A}, \mathcal{R}, \mathcal{S}, w, P, \mathcal{Y} \rangle$, for any $p \in P$, for any $a \in \mathcal{A}$ and for any $r \notin \mathcal{A}$ such that $A' = \langle \mathcal{A} \cup \{r\}, \mathcal{R}, \mathcal{S}, w', P, \mathcal{Y}' \rangle$, where for all $b \in \mathcal{A}$, $w'(b) = w(b)$, $\mathcal{Y}'(b) = \mathcal{Y}(b)$ and $\mathcal{Y}'(r) = p$, for all $p_1, p_2 \in P$, if $\delta(A, p_1, a) \leq \delta(A, p_2, a)$ then $\delta(A', p_1, a) \leq \delta(A', p_2, a)$.*

The Silent Authorship principle states that an agent without arguments should have less impact than other agents. This is important as it highlights that only the agents that own arguments can affect the (agent-based) impact semantics.

Principle 3 (Silent Authorship). *An impact semantics δ satisfies Silent Authorship iff for any awBAF $A = \langle \mathcal{A}, \mathcal{R}, \mathcal{S}, w, P, \mathcal{Y} \rangle$, for any $a \in \mathcal{A}$, for any $p \notin P(A)$ and for any $p' \in P$, it holds that $\delta(A, p, a) \leq \delta(A, p', a)$*

Please note that silent authorship also implies that all the agents without arguments will always have the same amount of impact, and this amount will always be minimal.

Directionality states that the order of the agent impacts on a particular argument should only be based on its incoming attacks and supports.

Principle 4 (Directionality). *An impact semantics δ satisfies Directionality iff for any awBAFs $A = \langle \mathcal{A}, \mathcal{R}, \mathcal{S}, w, P, \mathcal{Y} \rangle$ and $A' = \langle \mathcal{A}, \mathcal{R}', \mathcal{S}', w, P, \mathcal{Y} \rangle$ with $a, b, x \in \mathcal{A}$, $p_1, p_2 \in P$ such that:*

- *$\delta(A, p_1, x) \leq \delta(A, p_2, x)$*
- *$\mathcal{R} \subseteq \mathcal{R}', \mathcal{S} \subseteq \mathcal{S}'$ and $\mathcal{R}' \cup \mathcal{S}' = \mathcal{R} \cup \mathcal{S} \cup \{(a, b)\}$,*
- *there is no path from b to x*

then $\delta(A', p_1, x) \leq \delta(A', p_2, x)$

The independence principle states that the impact of an agent on an argument a should be independent of any arguments (and thus agents) that are not connected to a.

Principle 5 (Independence). *An impact semantics δ satisfies Independence iff for any awBAFs $A = \langle \mathcal{A}, \mathcal{R}, \mathcal{S}, w, P, \mathcal{Y} \rangle$ and $A' = \langle \mathcal{A}', \mathcal{R}', \mathcal{S}', w', P', \mathcal{Y}' \rangle$ such that $\mathcal{A} \cap \mathcal{A}' = \emptyset$, it holds that for every $p_1, p_2 \in P$ such that $\delta(A, p_1, a) \leq \delta(A, p_2, a)$ then $\delta(A \oplus A', p_1, a) \leq \delta(A \oplus A', p_2, a)$.*

4   Instantiating Impact Semantics

4.1   Degree-Based Argument Impact

In this section, we provide the first instantiations of (agent-based) impact semantics for *awBAF* by using graded semantics. We start by defining the notion of *degree-based impact semantics* of an argument in a *wBAF*. Intuitively, the degree-based *impact* of an argument a on another argument r is the difference between acceptability degrees of r with or without a.

Definition 11 (Degree-based Argument Impact). *Let $F = \langle \mathcal{A}, w, \mathcal{R}, \mathcal{S} \rangle$ be a wBAF with $r, a \in \mathcal{A}$. Let σ be a graded semantics for wBAF. The impact of a on r (w.r.t. F) is $imp_F^{\sigma}(a, r) = |Deg_F^{\sigma}(r) - Deg_{F \setminus \{a\}}^{\sigma}(r)|$.*

Please note that for every $r \in \mathcal{A}$, the impact of r on itself is 0.

We can now define the way to aggregate multiple argument impacts to represent the impact of an agent's arguments.

Definition 12 (Aggregation function). *An aggregation function is a function $agg : [0, 1]^n \to \mathbb{R}$ for $n \in \mathbb{N}$.*

In this paper, we use the standard *average*, *median*, *sum* and *maximum* aggregation functions and introduce the *product* aggregation as follows. Let $X, X' \in [0,1]^n$ such that $X' = (x_1, x_2, \ldots, x_n)$ is the sequence resulting from sorting X in ascending order. We have $(average)$ $ave(X) = (\sum_{i=1}^n x_i)/n$, $(median)$ $med(X) = \frac{1}{2}(x_{\lfloor (n+1)/2 \rfloor} + x_{\lceil (n+1)/2 \rceil})$, (sum) $sum(X) = \sum_{i=1}^n x_i$, $(maximum)$ $max(X) = x_n$, and $(product)$ $prod(X) = (\prod_{i=1}^n 1 + x_i) - 1$.

An aggregation function satisfies *fairness aggregation* iff the order of the sequence has no effect on the output value, i.e. for all $X, Y, Z \in [0,1]^n$ such that Z is the sequence resulting from sorting X or Y in ascending order, then $agg(X) = agg(Y)$. All the aforementioned aggregation functions satisfy fairness aggregation.

We now define the notion of aggregated (agent-based) impact semantics as the aggregated impact of an agent's arguments.

Definition 13 (Aggregated agent-based impact semantics). *Let* $A = \langle \mathcal{A}, \mathcal{R}, \mathcal{S}, w, P, \mathcal{Y} \rangle$ *be a awBAF,* $F_A = \langle \mathcal{A}, \mathcal{R}, \mathcal{S}, w \rangle$ *the induced wBAF,* σ *a graded semantics, agg an aggregation function and* $r \in \mathcal{A}$ *an argument. The (aggregated agent-based) impact semantics w.r.t.* σ *and agg is* δ_{agg}^σ, *s.t. for any* $p \in P$, $\delta_{agg}^\sigma(A, p, r) = agg((imp_{F_A}^\sigma(a_1, r), \ldots, imp_{F_A}^\sigma(a_n, r)))$, *where* $\forall a_i, \mathcal{Y}(a_i) = p$.

4.2   Formal Analysis of the Principles

In this section, we study the similarities and differences of the Euler-based and DF-Quad-based aggregated impact semantics. First, we show, in Example 2, that these two semantics provide quite significant differences in terms of results.

Example 2. Let us consider the awBAF $A = \langle \mathcal{A}, \mathcal{R}, \mathcal{S}, w, P, \mathcal{Y} \rangle$, represented in Fig. 2, inspired from [3], where $\mathcal{A} = \{a, b, c, d, \ldots, j\}$, $\mathcal{R} = \{(d, a), (d, b), (e, b),$ $(e, c), (f, c), (g, e), (h, f)\}$, $\mathcal{S} = \{(j, i), (i, a), (i, b), (i, c)\}$, $w(a) = w(b) = w(c) = 0.6$, $w(d) = 0.22, w(e) = w(f) = 0.4, w(g) = 0, w(h) = w(j) = 0.99, w(i) = 0.1, P = \{p_0, p_1, p_2\}$, and $\mathcal{Y}$ is defined as $\mathcal{Y}(a) = \mathcal{Y}(b) = \mathcal{Y}(c) = \mathcal{Y}(i) = \mathcal{Y}(j) = p_0, \mathcal{Y}(e) = \mathcal{Y}(f) = p_2$, and $\mathcal{Y}(d) = \mathcal{Y}(g) = \mathcal{Y}(h) = p_1$.

In Table 1, we show the impact of the agents on the acceptability of b, e.g. the value 0.22 means that $\delta_{med}^{\sigma_{DF}}(A, p_0, b) = 0.22$. From the table, we can see that in the case of the Euler-based aggregated impact semantics, the agent p_2 has the most impact on argument b (for all aggregation functions), whereas in the case of the DF-Quad aggregated impact semantics, the agent p_0 is the one with the most impact. This is caused by the *big jump problem* [3] as the acceptability degree of i will be 0.991 with the DF-Quad semantics whereas with the Euler-based semantics it is only of 0.22. Given that i is connected to b, since it is a supporter, i has a huge impact in the case of $\delta^{\sigma_{DF}}$ compared to $\delta^{\sigma_{EBS}}$. The author of i, p_0, will hence have a much bigger impact on b in the former case.

In the second part of this section, we analyse the principles satisfied by the two aggregated agent-based impact semantics for each aggregation function. The results are summarised in Table 2. The remainder of this section provides the proofs and counter-examples.

Table 1. Impact of agents on b for the Euler-based and DF-Quad-based aggregated impact semantics w.r.t. different aggregation functions. The number 1.17 in column $\delta_x^{\sigma_{DF}}(\boldsymbol{A}, p_i, b)$, sub-column *Product* and row p_0 means that $\delta_{prod}^{\sigma_{DF}}(\boldsymbol{A}, p_0, b) = 1.17$.

	$\delta_x^{\sigma_{EBS}}(\boldsymbol{A}, p_i, b)$					$\delta_x^{\sigma_{DF}}(\boldsymbol{A}, p_i, b)$				
	Average	Median	Sum	Product	Max	Average	Median	Sum	Product	Max
p_0	0.01	0.01	0.04	0.04	0.03	0.24	0.22	0.95	1.17	0.5
p_1	0.01	0	0.03	0.03	0.03	0.02	0	0.05	0.05	0.05
p_2	0.03	0.03	0.06	0.06	0.06	0.06	0.06	0.12	0.12	0.12

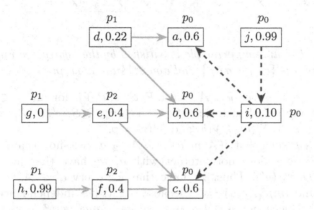

Fig. 2. An awBAF for which Euler-based and DF-Quad-based aggregated impact semantics give different results.

Theorem 1. *The anonymity principle is satisfied by the aggregated impact semantics δ_{agg}^{σ} where $\sigma \in \{\sigma_{EBS}, \sigma_{DF}\}$ and agg is an aggregation function that satisfies fairness aggregation.*

Proof. Let $\sigma \in \{\sigma_{EBS}, \sigma_{DF}\}$, $\boldsymbol{A} = \langle \mathcal{A}, \mathcal{R}, \mathcal{S}, w, P, \mathcal{Y} \rangle$ and $\boldsymbol{A}' = \langle \mathcal{A}', \mathcal{R}', \mathcal{S}', w', P', \mathcal{Y}' \rangle$ be two *awBAF* such that there exists an isomorphism from $\boldsymbol{A}$ to $\boldsymbol{A}'$ (and the corresponding isomorphisms f_1 and f_2 between the arguments and agents respectively).

We show the theorem by contradiction. We assume that there exists $a \in \mathcal{A}$ and $p_1, p_2 \in P(\boldsymbol{A})$ with $\delta(\boldsymbol{A}, p_1, a) \le \delta(\boldsymbol{A}, p_2, a)$ but $\delta(\boldsymbol{A}', f_2(p_2), f_1(a)) > \delta(\boldsymbol{A}', f_2(p_1), f_1(a))$.

As Euler-based and DF-Quad are only based on the structure of the graph, we have that for every $a' \in \mathcal{A}$, $Deg_A^{\delta}(a') = Deg_{A'}^{\delta}(f_1(a'))$. Thus, for all $a, r \in \mathcal{A}$ we have that $imp_A^{\sigma}(a, r) = imp_{A'}^{\sigma}(f_1(a), f_1(r))$. Consequently, for all $p \in P(\boldsymbol{A})$, we have $X_p = \{imp_A^{\sigma}(r, a) \mid \forall r \in \mathcal{A}, \mathcal{Y}(r) = p\}$, $X_p' = \{imp_{A'}^{\sigma}(r', f_1(a)) \mid \forall r' \in \mathcal{A}', \mathcal{Y}'(r') = f_2(p)\}$ such that $X_p = X_p'$. Thus, since *agg* satisfies fairness aggregation, for any sequences X_p^1 and X_p^2 obtained on X_p and X_p' respectively, we have $agg(X_p^1) = agg(X_p^2)$. By definition, we have that $\delta(\boldsymbol{A}', f_2(p_1), f_1(a)) \le \delta(\boldsymbol{A}', f_2(p_2), f_1(a))$, contradiction. $\square$

Table 2. Principles satisfied by the Euler-based and DF-Quad-based aggregated (agent-based) semantics; ✓ (resp. ✗) indicates that the principle is satisfied (resp. not satisfied).

	σ^{EBS}					σ^{DF}				
	Average	Median	Sum	Product	Max	Average	Median	Sum	Product	Max
Anonymity	✓	✓	✓	✓	✓	✓	✓	✓	✓	✓
Dummy	✗	✗	✓	✓	✓	✗	✗	✓	✓	✓
Silent Auth.	✓	✓	✓	✓	✓	✓	✓	✓	✓	✓
Directionality	✓	✓	✓	✓	✓	✓	✓	✓	✓	✓
Independence	✗	✗	✓	✓	✓	✗	✗	✓	✓	✓

Theorem 2. *The dummy principle is satisfied by the aggregated impact semantics δ_{agg}^{σ} where $\sigma \in \{\sigma_{EBS}, \sigma_{DF}\}$ and $agg \in \{sum, max, prod\}$.*

Proof. Let $\sigma \in \{\sigma_{EBS}, \sigma_{DF}\}$, $\boldsymbol{A} = \langle \mathcal{A}, \mathcal{R}, \mathcal{S}, w, P, \mathcal{Y} \rangle$, for any $p \in P$, for any $a \in \mathcal{A}$ and for any $r \notin \mathcal{A}$ such that $\boldsymbol{A}' = \langle \mathcal{A} \cup \{r\}, \mathcal{R}, \mathcal{S}, w', P, \mathcal{Y}' \rangle$, where for all $b \in \mathcal{A}$, $w'(b) = w(b)$, $\mathcal{Y}'(b) = \mathcal{Y}(b)$ and $\mathcal{Y}'(r) = p$.

Let $p_1, p_2 \in P$ such that $\delta(\boldsymbol{A}, p_1, a) \leq \delta(\boldsymbol{A}, p_2, a)$, we show that $\delta(\boldsymbol{A}', p_1, a) \leq \delta(\boldsymbol{A}', p_2, a)$. Since r does not interact with a, we have that for all $a' \in \mathcal{A}$, $Deg_{\boldsymbol{A}}^{\delta}(a') = Deg_{\boldsymbol{A}'}^{\delta}(a')$. Thus, we have that for every $a' \in \mathcal{A}$, $imp_{\boldsymbol{A}}^{\sigma}(a', a) = imp_{\boldsymbol{A}'}^{\sigma}(a', a)$ and $imp_{\boldsymbol{A}'}^{\sigma}(r, a) = 0$ (because σ satisfies independence for graded semantics) [6]. Hence, for $p \in \{p_1, p_2\}$, we have $agg(\langle imp_{\boldsymbol{A}}^{\sigma}(a, r) \mid \forall a, \mathcal{Y}(a) = p \rangle) = agg(\langle imp_{\boldsymbol{A}'}^{\sigma}(a, r) \mid \forall a, \mathcal{Y}(a) = p \rangle)$. Hence, $\delta(\boldsymbol{A}', p_1, a) \leq \delta(\boldsymbol{A}', p_2, a)$. ☐

Please note that the dummy principle is not satisfied by a aggregated impact semantics δ_{agg}^{σ} where $\sigma \in \{\sigma_{EBS}, \sigma_{DF}\}$ and $agg \in \{ave, med\}$. We show the counter-examples below.

Example 3. Let $\boldsymbol{A} = \langle \mathcal{A}, \mathcal{R}, \mathcal{S}, w, P, \mathcal{Y} \rangle$ be a awBAF such that $\mathcal{A} = \{a_1, r, a_2\}$, $\mathcal{R} = \{(a_1, r)\}$, $\mathcal{S} = \{(a_2, r)\}$, $w(a_1) = w(a_2) = w(r) = 0.5$, $P = \{p_0, p_1, p_2\}$, $\mathcal{Y}(a_1) = p_1, \mathcal{Y}(r) = p_0$ and $\mathcal{Y}(a_2) = p_2$. We define $\boldsymbol{A}' = \langle \mathcal{A} \cup \{a_3\}, \mathcal{R}, \mathcal{S}, w', P, \mathcal{Y}' \rangle$, where for all $b \in \mathcal{A}$, $w'(b) = w(b)$, $\mathcal{Y}'(b) = \mathcal{Y}(b)$ and $\mathcal{Y}'(a_3) = p_1$ (see Fig. 3).

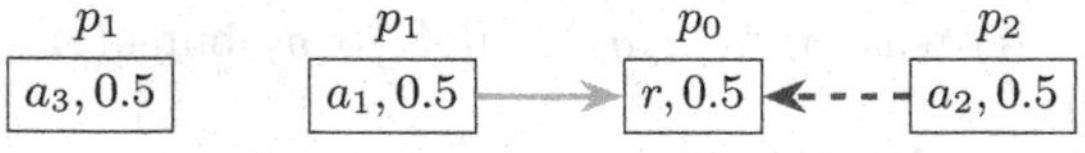

$$
\begin{array}{cccc}
p_1 & p_1 & p_0 & p_2 \\
\boxed{a_3, 0.5} & \boxed{a_1, 0.5} \longrightarrow & \boxed{r, 0.5} \xleftarrow{}- - - & \boxed{a_2, 0.5}
\end{array}
$$

Fig. 3. Counter-example for the satisfaction of the dummy principle when $agg \in \{sum, med\}$ (AF' is represented).

$Deg_{\boldsymbol{A}}^{\sigma_{EBS}}(r) = Deg_{\boldsymbol{A}'}^{\sigma_{EBS}}(r) = 0.5$, $Deg_{\boldsymbol{A} \setminus \{a_1\}}^{\sigma_{EBS}}(r) = Deg_{\boldsymbol{A}' \setminus \{a_1\}}^{\sigma_{EBS}}(r) \simeq 0.589$ and $Deg_{\boldsymbol{A} \setminus \{a_2\}}^{\sigma_{EBS}}(r) = Deg_{\boldsymbol{A}' \setminus \{a_2\}}^{\sigma_{EBS}}(r) \simeq 0.425$. Thus, $imp_{\boldsymbol{A}}^{\sigma_{EBS}}(a_1, r) = imp_{\boldsymbol{A}'}^{\sigma_{EBS}}(a_1, r) = 0.089$, $imp_{\boldsymbol{A}}^{\sigma_{EBS}}(a_2, r) = imp_{\boldsymbol{A}'}^{\sigma_{EBS}}(a_2, r) = 0.075$ and

$imp_{A'}^{\sigma_{EBS}}(a_3, r) = 0$. Consequently, $med(\langle 0, 0.089 \rangle) = ave(\langle 0, 0.089 \rangle) = 0.0445$ and $med(\langle 0.075 \rangle) = ave(\langle 0.075 \rangle) = 0.075$. As a result, we have that $\delta_{agg}^{\sigma_{EBS}}(A, p_2, r) \leq \delta_{agg}^{\sigma_{EBS}}(A, p_1, r)$ but $\delta_{agg}^{\sigma_{EBS}}(A', p_2, r) > \delta_{agg}^{\sigma_{EBS}}(A', p_1, r)$ for $agg \in \{med, ave\}$.

This counter-example also holds for σ_{DF}.

Theorem 3. *The silent authorship principle is satisfied by the aggregated impact semantics δ_{agg}^{σ} where $\sigma \in \{\sigma_{EBS}, \sigma_{DF}\}$ and $agg \in \{ave, med, sum, max, prod\}$*

Proof. This is trivially true, by definition, since an agent with no argument will have an impact of 0, formally for all $p \notin P(A)$ and for all $a \in A$, $\delta_x^{\sigma}(A, p, a) = 0$, where $x \in \{ave, med, sum, max, prod\}$ and $\sigma \in \{\sigma_{EBS}, \sigma_{DF}\}$.   □

Theorem 4. *The directionality principle is satisfied by the aggregated impact semantics δ_{agg}^{σ} where $\sigma \in \{\sigma_{EBS}, \sigma_{DF}\}$ and $agg \in \{ave, med, sum, max, prod\}$*

Proof. Let $A = \langle \mathcal{A}, \mathcal{R}, \mathcal{S}, w, P, \mathcal{Y} \rangle$ and $A' = \langle \mathcal{A}, \mathcal{R}', \mathcal{S}', w, P, \mathcal{Y} \rangle$ with $a, b, x \in \mathcal{A}$, $p_1, p_2 \in P$ such that $\delta_{agg}^{\sigma_{EBS}}(A, p_1, x) \leq \delta_{agg}^{\sigma_{EBS}}(A, p_2, x)$, $\mathcal{R} \subseteq \mathcal{R}', \mathcal{S} \subseteq \mathcal{S}'$ and $\mathcal{R}' \cup \mathcal{S}' = \mathcal{R} \cup \mathcal{S} \cup \{(a, b)\}$ and there is no path from b to x.

We know that σ_{EBS} satisfies directionality for graded semantics [2], thus the acceptability degree of x depends only on the arguments linked to it via a path. This means that for every $u \in \mathcal{A}$ such that u is not linked to x with a path, $imp_{A'}^{\sigma_{EBS}}(u, x) = 0$ and $imp_A^{\sigma_{EBS}}(u, x) = 0$. Similarly, for every $v \in \mathcal{A}$ such that v is linked to x with a path, $imp_{A'}^{\sigma_{EBS}}(v, x) = imp_A^{\sigma_{EBS}}(v, x)$. Hence, adding the interaction from a to b in A' does not change the impact of any argument on x. We conclude that $\delta_{agg}^{\sigma_{EBS}}(A', p_1, x) \leq \delta_{agg}^{\sigma_{EBS}}(A', p_2, x)$ for $agg \in \{ave, med, sum, max, prod\}$.

This reasoning is valid for any graded semantics that satisfies directionality, hence it covers σ_{DF} as well.   □

Theorem 5. *The independence principle is satisfied by the aggregated impact semantics δ_{agg}^{σ} where $\sigma \in \{\sigma_{EBS}, \sigma_{DF}\}$ and $agg \in \{sum, max, prod\}$*

Proof. We first show, by contradiction, that if a aggregated impact semantics δ satisfies dummy and directionality then it satisfies independence. Assume that δ satisfies dummy and directionality but not independence. This means that there exists two awBAFs $A = \langle \mathcal{A}, \mathcal{R}, \mathcal{S}, w, P, \mathcal{Y} \rangle$, $A' = \langle \mathcal{A}, \mathcal{R}', \mathcal{S}', w', P', \mathcal{Y}' \rangle$ such that $\mathcal{A} \cap \mathcal{A}' = \emptyset$ and there exists $p_1, p_2 \in P$ such that $\delta(A, p_1, a) \leq \delta(A, p_2, a)$ and $\delta(A \oplus A', p_1, a) > \delta(A \oplus A', p_2, a)$.

We know that by adding an argument from $\mathcal{A}'$ to A (without attacks nor supports), we have $\delta(A, p_1, a) \leq \delta(A, p_2, a)$ (by dummy). Thus, we can add all arguments from $\mathcal{A}'$ to A without any changes on the impact. Then, we know that by adding all attacks from $\mathcal{R}'$ and all supports from $\mathcal{S}'$ to A, we have $\delta(A, p_1, a) \leq \delta(A, p_2, a)$ (by directionality since there are no paths from arguments in $\mathcal{A}'$ to $a \in \mathcal{A}$). The resulting graph is $A \oplus A'$ and $\delta(A \oplus A', p_1, a) \leq \delta(A \leq A', p_2, a)$, contradiction.

Thus, from Theorems 2 and 4, δ_{agg}^{σ} satisfies independence, for $\sigma \in \{\sigma_{EBS}, \sigma_{DF}\}$ and $agg \in \{sum, max, prod\}$.

Please refer to Example 3 for a counter-example for δ_{agg}^{σ}, where $\sigma \in \{\sigma_{EBS},$ $\sigma_{DF}\}$ and $agg \in \{ave, med\}$, such that $\boldsymbol{A} = \langle \{r, a_1, a_2\}, \{(a_1, r)\}, \{a_2, r\}, w,$ $\{p_1, p_2\}, \mathcal{Y} \rangle$, with $\mathcal{Y}(r) = p_0$, $\mathcal{Y}(a_1) = p_1$ and $\mathcal{Y}(a_2) = p_2$, and $\boldsymbol{A}' = \langle \{a_3\}, \varnothing,$ $\varnothing, w, \{p_1\}, \mathcal{Y}' \rangle$ with $\mathcal{Y}'(a_3) = p_1$.   □

5 Discussion

In this paper, we have presented a novel way to rank agents with respect to their impact on the argumentation debate. Formally, we generalised the weighted bipolar framework, for the multi-agent context, by labelling each argument with an *author* and defined the notion of agent-based impact semantics. Those semantics allow to rank the agents from the most impactful to the least for a particular argument. We introduced a new framework, called *aggregated* agent-based impact semantics, to instantiate such impact semantics by using an aggregation function as well as a graded semantics (for bipolar argumentation frameworks). To illustrate, we used two classical graded semantics to instantiate this framework, the DF-Quad [15] and Euler-based semantics [1]. Finally, in order to assess the desirability of the instantiated impact semantics, we defined intuitive principles for such impact semantics, and assessed which principles were satisfied.

As far as we know, the only work that is similar to our approach is the work of Todd Robinson [16]. In this paper, the author introduces the notion of information value in Argumentation to identify the most "important" arguments. He uses two functions called *value of observed* and *value of observation* to represent respectively the value of arguments currently in the framework and the value of adding a new argument to the framework. His framework does not take into account the notion of Authorship which is essential in multi-agent contexts. Moreover, this framework is based on utility functions defined on extensions rather than graded semantics. This however could open up interesting avenues of research by combining the two approaches.

There are multiple possible future research avenues to extend our approach. First, we can study how the aggregated agent-based impact semantics behaves when it is instantiated with other graded semantics such as Potyka's *continuous modular semantics* [14] or quadratic energy model [12]. Second, we can broaden up this research by considering more general argumentation frameworks with additional features. For example, using a temporal argumentation framework [4,7], one can determine avant-gardist leaders that have an early influence on a specific argument, or using argumentation frameworks with sets of attacking arguments (SETAFs) to add expressivity to the attack/support relation [9,18]. Links can also be drawn from previous research in Argumentation Dynamics [5,17] to determine the effect of, say, a particular expansion (i.e. the addition of some arguments) on the impact of agents on particular arguments. This would allow to assess the interest, in terms of impact on the discussion, for an agent to enunciate some arguments.

References

1. Amgoud, L., Ben-Naim, J.: Evaluation of arguments in weighted bipolar graphs **99**, 39–55 (2018). https://doi.org/10.1016/j.ijar.2018.05.004, http://www.sciencedirect.com/science/article/pii/S0888613X1730590X
2. Amgoud, L., Ben-Naim, J.: Evaluation of arguments in weighted bipolar graphs. In: Proceedings of Symbolic and Quantitative Approaches to Reasoning with Uncertainty - 14th European Conference, ECSQARU 2017, Lugano, Switzerland, July 10–14, 2017, pp. 25–35 (2017)
3. Amgoud, L., Ben-Naim, J.: Weighted Bipolar Argumentation Graphs: Axioms and Semantics (2018)
4. Augusto, J.C., Simari, G.R.: Temporal defeasible reasoning. Knowl. Inf. Syst. **3**(3), 287–318 (2001). https://doi.org/10.1007/PL00011670
5. Baumann, R.: Normal and strong expansion equivalence for argumentation frameworks. Artif. Intell. **193**, 18–44 (2012). https://doi.org/10.1016/j.artint.2012.08.004
6. Bonzon, E., Delobelle, J., Konieczny, S., Maudet, N.: A comparative study of ranking-based semantics for abstract argumentation. In: Proceedings of the Thirtieth AAAI Conference on Artificial Intelligence, 12–17 February 2016, Phoenix, Arizona, USA, pp. 914–920 (2016). http://www.aaai.org/ocs/index.php/AAAI/AAAI16/paper/view/12465
7. Budán, M.C., Cobo, M.L., Martínez, D.C., Simari, G.R.: Bipolarity in temporal argumentation frameworks. Int. J. Approx. Reason. **84**, 1–22 (2017). https://doi.org/10.1016/j.ijar.2017.01.013
8. Dung, P.M.: On the acceptability of arguments and its fundamental role in non-monotonic reasoning, logic programming and n-person games. Artif. Intell. **77**(2), 321–358 (1995). https://doi.org/10.1016/0004-3702(94)00041-X
9. Nielsen, S.H., Parsons, S.: A generalization of dung's abstract framework for argumentation: arguing with sets of attacking arguments. In: Maudet, N., Parsons, S., Rahwan, I. (eds.) ArgMAS 2006. LNCS (LNAI), vol. 4766, pp. 54–73. Springer, Heidelberg (2007). https://doi.org/10.1007/978-3-540-75526-5_4
10. Pazienza, A., Ferilli, S., Esposito, F.: On the gradual acceptability of arguments in bipolar weighted argumentation frameworks with degrees of trust. In: Kryszkiewicz, M., Appice, A., Ślęzak, D., Rybinski, H., Skowron, A., Raś, Z.W. (eds.) ISMIS 2017. LNCS (LNAI), vol. 10352, pp. 195–204. Springer, Cham (2017). https://doi.org/10.1007/978-3-319-60438-1_20
11. Potyka, N.: Extending modular semantics for bipolar weighted argumentation (technical report) https://arxiv.org/abs/1809.07133v2
12. Potyka, N.: Continuous dynamical systems for weighted bipolar argumentation. In: Thielscher, M., Toni, F., Wolter, F. (eds.) Principles of Knowledge Representation and Reasoning: Proceedings of the Sixteenth International Conference, KR 2018, Tempe, Arizona, 30 October - 2 November 2018, pp. 148–157. AAAI Press (2018). https://aaai.org/ocs/index.php/KR/KR18/paper/view/17985
13. Potyka, N.: Extending modular semantics for bipolar weighted argumentation. In: Proceedings of the 18th International Conference on Autonomous Agents and MultiAgent Systems, AAMAS 2019, Montreal, QC, Canada, 13–17 May 2019. pp. 1722–1730 (2019). http://dl.acm.org/citation.cfm?id=3331903

14. Potyka, N.: Extending modular semantics for bipolar weighted argumentation. In: Elkind, E., Veloso, M., Agmon, N., Taylor, M.E. (eds.) Proceedings of the 18th International Conference on Autonomous Agents and MultiAgent Systems, AAMAS '19, Montreal, QC, Canada, 13–17 May 2019, pp. 1722–1730. International Foundation for Autonomous Agents and Multiagent Systems (2019). http://dl.acm.org/citation.cfm?id=3331903
15. Rago, A., Toni, F., Aurisicchio, M., Baroni, P.: Discontinuity-Free Decision Support with Quantitative Argumentation Debates. In: Principles of Knowledge Representation and Reasoning: Proceedings of the Fifteenth International Conference, KR 2016, Cape Town, South Africa, 25–29 April 2016, pp. 63–73 (2016). http://www.aaai.org/ocs/index.php/KR/KR16/paper/view/12874
16. Robinson, T.: Value of information for argumentation based intelligence analysis. CoRR abs/2102.08180 (2021). https://arxiv.org/abs/2102.08180
17. de Saint-Cyr, F.D., Bisquert, P., Cayrol, C., Lagasquie-Schiex, M.: Argumentation update in YALLA (yet another logic language for argumentation). Int. J. Approx. Reason. **75**, 57–92 (2016). https://doi.org/10.1016/j.ijar.2016.04.003
18. Yun, B., Vesic, S., Croitoru, M.: Ranking-based semantics for sets of attacking arguments. In: The Thirty-Fourth AAAI Conference on Artificial Intelligence, AAAI 2020, The Thirty-Second Innovative Applications of Artificial Intelligence Conference, IAAI 2020, The Tenth AAAI Symposium on Educational Advances in Artificial Intelligence, EAAI 2020, 7–12 February 2020, New York, pp. 3033–3040. AAAI Press (2020). https://aaai.org/ojs/index.php/AAAI/article/view/5697

Towards Explainable Metaheuristics: PCA for Trajectory Mining in Evolutionary Algorithms

Martin Fyvie[✉][ID], John A. W. McCall[ID], and Lee A. Christie[ID]

The Robert Gordon University, Garthdee Road, Aberdeen, UK
{m.fyvie,j.mccall,l.a.christie}@rgu.ac.uk

Abstract. The generation of explanations regarding decisions made by population-based meta-heuristics is often a difficult task due to the nature of the mechanisms employed by these approaches. With the increase in use of these methods for optimisation in industries that require end-user confirmation, the need for explanations has also grown. We present a novel approach to the extraction of features capable of supporting an explanation through the use of trajectory mining - extracting key features from the populations of NDAs. We apply Principal Components Analysis techniques to identify new methods of population diversity tracking post-runtime after projection into a lower dimensional space. These methods are applied to a set of benchmark problems solved by a Genetic Algorithm and a Univariate Estimation of Distribution Algorithm. We show that the new sub-space derived metrics can capture key learning steps in the algorithm run and how solution variable patterns that explain the fitness function may be captured in the principal component coefficients.

Keywords: Evolutionary algorithms · PCA · Explainability · Population diversity

1 Introduction

Non-Deterministic Algorithms such as population-based meta-heuristics have seen an increase in use in applications that involve end-user interactions such as transport route planning, delivery scheduling and medical applications. This increase has highlighted the need for the decision processes behind these system to be more understandable by end-users. This is turn may help build a level of trust in the solutions generated by these systems, as seen in conclusions and recommendations of the Public Health Genetics (PHG) foundation [1].

Two significant metaheuristic approaches are Genetic Algorithms (GA) and Estimation of Distribution (EDA) algorithms. Both are evolutionary algorithms and explore a solution space using a population-based search metaheuristic. As a GA explores the search space, solution populations generated represent the

© Springer Nature Switzerland AG 2021
M. Bramer and R. Ellis (Eds.): SGAI-AI 2021, LNAI 13101, pp. 89–102, 2021.
https://doi.org/10.1007/978-3-030-91100-3_7

implicitly learned structure of the problem it is solving. The EDA similarly represents this but also generates a sequence of explicit probabilistic models of the problem structure. Problem Structure refers to the graphical dependency relationship between solution variables and their joint influence on fitness value. This has been variously interpreted in the EDA literature through Bayesian, Markov or Gaussian probabilistic models [2]. For both GAs and EDAs, the collected populations generated over the course of a run can be considered the trajectory through the search spaces that the algorithm has taken as it converges on an ideal or near-ideal solution. These trajectories reflect the implicit knowledge gained.

We hypothesize that the trajectories generated in this process can be mined for valuable information regarding population changes that can aid in generating explanations for end-users. Our approach involves the projection of the high-dimension solutions space to a lower dimension space that can be used to generate more easily understood visualisations and provide a possible source of new metrics. This is accomplished through the application of Principal Components Analysis (PCA). The results can then be used to generate explanations with the aim of increasing an end-user understanding of the problem being solved and the process by which the algorithms have arrived at the provided set of solutions.

Previous work covering the visualisation of algorithm trajectories using PCA can be seen in [3] and more recent methods in which local optima networks are used to generate search trajectory networks for different algorithm runs in [4]. Other examples of work involving the exploration of algorithm paths via dimension reduction include [5] in which Sammon mapping is explored as a method of reduction for visualisation and [6] in which Euclidean Embedding is applied. These works focus on the visualisation of an algorithm through the search space however the approach taken in this paper using PCA has the potential to be used as a method extracting features from algorithm paths. These features can then be used to help support explanations by highlighting learning steps in the algorithm run and solution variable patterns that describe the fitness function.

The rest of the paper is structured as follows. Section 2 outlines the experimental setup that covers the algorithms used and the problems they were used to solve. Section 3 outlines the concept of Entropic Divergence and how this is used as measure of population diversity change. This is followed by the background method used to translate the algorithm trajectories into a lower dimension space as well as the new metrics derived from that space for comparison to the Entropic Divergence measurement. Section 4 highlights the results and performance between the newly created population metrics and the Entropic Divergence are shown and discussed. This section also highlights the findings regarding problem structure and post-PCA projection variable loading's. Section 5 sets out our conclusions based on the results of these tests.

2   Experimental Setup

2.1   Algorithm Runs

Two population-based solvers were selected to generate a series of population trajectories for use in this study. These were a Genetic Algorithm (GA) and a modified Population Based Incremental Learning (PBIL) Algorithm [7,8] in which a negative mutation rate and mutation shift value is introduced. These algorithms were selected for the purpose of comparing the results of a univariate solver and a more traditional genetic algorithm on problems with different structure. Each algorithm was run on the set of outlined problems in order to generate the trajectories used in the analysis phase of this trial.

The Genetic Algorithm used was an adaptation of the Canonical Genetic Algorithm (CGA) [9]. Figure 1 shows the main steps involved as the GA generates new populations during an optimisation run.

Table 1. GA run specifications

P	n	runs	maxGen	mutRate	Selection	Crossover
100	40	100	100	0.005	Tournament	Random 1-Point

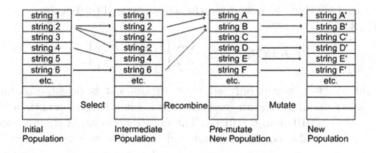

Fig. 1. CGA stages taken from [10]

Table 1 outlines the values used in the running of the GA during these experiments.

P shows the number of solutions in each population. **maxGen** is the maximum number of generations before termination. **mutRate** is the mutation rate within the GA. **Selection** is the selection method used within the GA for solution comparison and reproduction. **Crossover** is the crossover type used in this trial with a rate of 1 and so occurs each generation. **n** is the problem length. **runs** is the number of runs for each problem the GA ran for.

Population Based Incremental Learning (PBIL) is a form of Estimation of Distribution algorithm. The probability vector is updated and mutated each generation as seen in Eqs. 1 and 2:

Table 2. PBIL run specifications

P	n	runs	maxGen	mutRate	mutShift	learnRate	nlearnRate
100	40	100	100	0.005	0.05	0.1	0.075

$$p(X_1, \ldots, X_N) = \prod_{i=1}^{N} p(X_i) \quad (1) \qquad\qquad p(X_i) = \frac{1}{N} \sum_{j=1}^{N} x_{ij} \quad (2)$$

Here the vector of marginal probabilities $P_V = (p(X_1), \ldots, p(X_n))$ is created by calculating the arithmetic mean of each variable X in a population of size N. As the solutions are comprised of bit strings we will see that values will range from 0 to 1. Table 2 outlines the values used for the PBIL algorithm in this trial. Additional to these, the PBIL used a **mutShift** value that was applied to mutated probability vector values. **learnRate** is the learning rate of the algorithm as is the **nlearnRate** which shows the negative learning rate penalty if the best solution matches the worst in a solution when updating the probability vector.

2.2   Benchmark Problems

The 1D Checkerboard function scores the chromosome based on the sum of adjacent variables that do not share the same value [11]. The function is seen here in Eq. 3.

$$CHECK_{1D}^l(x) = \sum_{i=0}^{l-2} \begin{cases} 1, & x_i \neq x_{i+1} \\ 0, & x_i = x_{i+1} \end{cases} \quad (3)$$

Because the function scores only adjacent variables it is possible to have two possible global maxima. As an example, for a bit string of length 5 the two possible would be [01010] and [10101]. The implementation of the problem used in this experiment also checks the first and last allele to check if they match. This allows for a total fitness value equal to the bit-string length for an ideal solution

The Royal Road function scores chromosomes based on collections of variable values based on a specified set of schema that the solution must fulfil in order to score an optimal value [12]. below, Eq. 4 specifies the fitness function for the royal road problem with a schema block size of 5, as used in this experiment.

$$R_1(x) = \sum_{i=1}^{5} \delta_i(x) o(s_i), \text{ where } \delta_i(x) = \begin{cases} 1 & \text{if } x \in s_i \\ 0 & \text{if otherwise} \end{cases} \quad (4)$$

As noted in [12] the equation represents the fitness function, such that R_1 is a sum of terms relating to partially specified schema. The schemata are subsets of solutions that match the partial specification, s_i. As an example, one partially specified schema with a size of 5 could be represented as [11111*****...] where unspecified members are denoted by "*"

A given bit-string x is an instance of a specific schema s, $x \in s$ if x matches s in the defined positions within that schema. $o(s_i)$ defines the order of s_i which is the number of defined bits in s_i. The royal road function was designed to "capture one landscape feature of particular relevance to GAs: the presence of fit low-order building blocks that recombine to produce fitter, higher-order building blocks" [13].

The Trap-5 concatenated problem is designed to be intentionally deceptive [14,15], such that they "deceive evolutionary algorithms into converging on a local optimum. This is particularly a problem for algorithms which do not consider interactions between variables." [16]. As with the Royal Road problem, the bit-strings are partitioned into blocks and their fitness scored separately. Seen in Eq. 5a is the function of a trap of order k.

$$f(x) = \sum_{i=1}^{n/k} trap_k(x_{b_i,1} + ... + x_{b_i,k}) \tag{5a}$$

$$trap_k(u) = \left\{ f_{\text{high}} \text{ if } u = k, f_{\text{low}} - u\frac{f_{\text{low}}}{k-1} \text{ otherwise} \right\} \tag{5b}$$

Blocks within the bit-string are scored according to the fitness function in Eq. 5b. A Trap5 problem with a bit-string length of 10 would have the values $n = 10$, $k = 5$, $f_{\text{high}} = 5$ and $f_{\text{low}} = 4$.

The further from the goal of each Trap containing five 1's, the higher the fitness value, with only a maximum achieved when the whole Trap is comprised of 1s, leading the algorithm away from the optimal value.

2.3 Principal Components Analysis

The process of reducing the dimensionality of the algorithm trajectory population datasets is done through the use of Principal Components Analysis (PCA). This allows us to project the higher dimentional space of the solutions to a three-dimensional space as "PCA produces linear combinations of the original variables to generate the axes, also known as principal components, or PCs." [17]. This involves the calculation of a series of perpendicular, non correlated, linear combinations of the variables in the population such that each combination accounts for the maximum possible variation in the dataset through the use of singular value decomposition (SVD). A summary of the calculation of linear combination and weights from [17] can be seen below in the following series of Eqs. 6

$$\begin{aligned} PC_1 &= a_{11}X_1 + a_{12}X_2 + \ldots a_{1p}X_p \\ PC_2 &= a_{21}X_1 + a_{22}X_2 + \ldots a_{2p}X_p \\ PC_1 &= a_1^t X \\ PC &= XA \end{aligned} \tag{6}$$

In Eq. 6, matrix **A** denotes the matrix of eigenvectors. These are used to show the relationship between the original variables and the orientation of the principal components. The resulting datasets were then mined with the intent of finding features capable of explaining aspects of the optimisation problems that they were generated by.

3   Feature Extraction

3.1   Existing Population Diversity Measures

There exist several metrics used to measure the change in population diversity over the course of an optimisation run by genetic-based algorithms. In [18] a brief review of many of these metrics can be found. The metrics covered include the Hamming Distance, the sum of pair-wise comparison in the number of variable differences between two solutions although this method can be considered computationally expensive. An alternative to Hamming Distance is the Moment of Inertia [19] which provides a "..single method of computing population diversity that is computationally more efficient than normal pair-wise diversity measures for medium and large sized EA problems." When researching possible metrics for comparison, it was decided that the Kullback-Leibler Entropic Divergence distance measure [20] would be the best candidate as it was suitable for both population diversity monitoring and the detection of the "phase transition" point, in which it is said that a population based algorithm moves from the exploration of the search space to the exploitation of known problem structure to generate higher fitness solutions.

Entropic Divergence. The Kullback-Leibler Entropic Divergence (KL_d) is a population diversity distance measure based around the concept of information gain and Shannon's Entropy [22] in which "...the entropy of a random variable is defined in terms of its probability distribution." [20]. It can be defined in the following Equation:

$$KL_{\mathrm{d}}(P \parallel Q) = \sum_{x \in \mathcal{X}} P(x) \log \left(\frac{P^{(t)}(x)}{Q^{(t_0)}(x)} \right) \tag{7}$$

Where P and Q are vectors of marginal probabilities for two different populations in the trajectory [21].

Using the above Equation it is possible to track the information gain from the initial population generated by the algorithms as $Q(x)$ remains constant as the probability vector of the generation $t = 0$. This metric is called the "Global Learning" and it measures the total information gain from initial population to the population at any given t. The expected behaviour for this metric is to increase over time until a "steady state" is arrived at.

It is also shown in [20] that it is possible to use the above KL_d Equation to measure the information gain between two consecutive populations where $Q^{(i)}(x)$

and $P^{(i+1)}(x)$ are used. This is known as "Local Learning" with the expected behaviour of increasing until a "Phase Transition" point at which the algorithm moves from exploring the search space to exploiting knowledge learned. In the exploitation phase, higher fitness solutions are generated using this implicit knowledge. When this happens it is expected that the local learning rate will decrease as the diversity within the population decreases until convergence has been completed or a local basin of attraction is escaped [23]. This is of interest as it can be used to inform end-users when maximum population diversity is reached in a trajectory.

3.2   Sub-space Derived Features

Population Cluster Centers. The dimensionality of the dataset is reduced through the projection of the data into a lower dimension set based on the principal components calculated using 6. In this paper we project into a three-dimensional sub-space to help visualise the population as a cluster, illustrated in Fig. 2.a. The centroid of this cluster can be found by calculating the point that minimizes the sum of squared Euclidean distances between itself and each point in the set as seen in Eq. 8.

$$C = \frac{\mathbf{x}_1 + \mathbf{x}_2 + \cdots + \mathbf{x}_k}{k} \tag{8}$$

Figure 2.a is an example of a single trajectory visualisation post-PCA conversion. Each point in the trajectory represents the centroid of a population of solutions. For each generation in a given trajectory the centre point of the cluster is calculated. This process results in a set of points in 3D space that represents the algorithm trajectory, Fig. 2.b, from the initial population to the final population in terms of variation, as measured by the reduction in PCA coefficients over time from t = 0 to t = final.

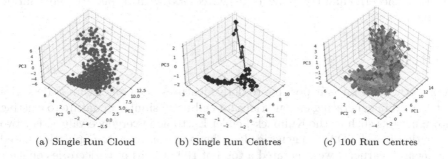

(a) Single Run Cloud   (b) Single Run Centres   (c) 100 Run Centres

Fig. 2. PBIL 1D checkerboard trajectory visualisation

It is important to note that this method does not chart the algorithm trajectory in objective space and does not explicitly reflect the fitness landscape but instead can be used to measure the direction and magnitude of changes in population diversity after being projected into this subspace. Seen in Fig. 2.c are all 100 trajectories created by the PBIL on the 1D Checkerboard problem, projected against the first three principle components.

Angle from Origin measures the angle between the centroid of the initial starting population in the trajectory and each subsequent population that was created. Each of the two points in the space are represented by the centroids coordinates as a vector of [PC1, PC2, PC3] coefficients in place of x, y and z coordinates. In order to calculate the acute angle α between two vectors we use the inverse cosine of vector products as seen in Eq. 9

$$\alpha = \arccos\left(\frac{C_0 \cdot C_i}{\|C_0\| \, \|C_i\|}\right)$$

$$C_0, C_i = \text{Cluster Centroids (x, y, z)}$$

(9)

Angle Between Clusters is calculated as in Eq. 9 using C_i and C_{i+1}, where ($i <= 0 <= maxGen$). This allows for the angle between consecutive populations to be calculated.

PCA Loading Values can be calculated using the resulting matrices from the principal component decomposition process outlined earlier in this paper. Loadings can be considered the weighting of each variable as they describe the magnitude of contribution each variable has to the calculation of each Principal component. Loading signs indicate the type of correlation between the PC and the variable in terms of negative and positive correlation and the strength of that relationship can be seen in the values – larger values indicate a stronger relationship. These loadings are shown in Eq. 6 as the matrix **A** and are the coefficients of the principal components (eigenvectors) with respect to the solution variables.

4   Results

We hypothesize that is it possible to derive features from algorithm trajectories that can aid in generating explanations for end-users similar in nature to existing known metrics such as the Kullback-Leibler Entropic Divergence values. For two population-based NDAs – a genetic algorithm and a univariate population based incremental learner – we generated a total of 100 algorithm trajectories on each of the three test functions used. These trajectories were transformed using PCA to allow the projection of the populations into a lower dimension space for the purpose of visualisation and feature extraction.

4.1   PCA Explained Variation

The values in Table 3 show the mean percentage of variation in the population data explained by the first three principal components, broken down by algorithm and problem.

Table 3. PCA variance explained by three components

Algorithm	Problem	PCA1 Exp %	PCA2 Exp %	PCA3 Exp %	Total %
PBIL	1D checker	25.6	5.2	3.6	34.4
GA	1D checker	32.5	10.8	7.6	50.9
PBIL	Royal road	25.1	5.9	3.8	34.8
GA	Royal road	28.8	10.0	7.4	46.2
PBIL	Trap5	27.0	4.6	3.3	34.9
GA	Trap5	37.9	11.0	7.6	56.6

These results show that for the PBIL, total variation explained by the first three principal components was 34.4% in the 1D Checkerboard problem, 34.8% in the Royal Road problem and 34.9% in the Trap5 Problem. The results also show that for the GA, explained variation was 50.9% in the 1D Checkerboard, 46.2 in the Royal Road and 56.6% in the Trap5 Problem.

4.2   Information Gain and Cluster Angle Results

Table 4 displays the Spearman Correlation Coefficients of Local and Global information gain to the Inter-Cluster and Angle from Origin features extracted. Global Information shows a strong positive correlation to the Angle from Origin feature with a range of 0.76 to 0.99 across all problems and algorithms. The PBIL coefficients were 0.99 for the 1D Checkerboard, 0.96 for the Royal Road and 0.88 for the Trap5. The GA coefficients were 0.98 for the 1d Checkerboard, 0.88 for the Royal Road and 0.76 for the Trap5 problem.

Table 4. Spearman Correlation Coefficient

Algorithm	Problem	Local to Inter-Cluster	Global to Origin
PBIL	1D checker	−0.69	0.99
GA	1D checker	0.83	0.98
PBIL	Royal road	0.36	0.96
GA	Royal road	0.94	0.88
PBIL	Trap5	0.39	0.88
GA	Trap5	0.79	0.76

Global Information Gain and Angle from Origin comparison results are shown in Fig. 3, split by algorithm and problem. It can be seen in the results and the correlation coefficients in Table 4 that for all three problems and both algorithms, the angle from origin metric closely matches the behaviour of the Global Information Gain behaviour. Both metrics detect the increase in information gained as the algorithms solve the supplied problem.

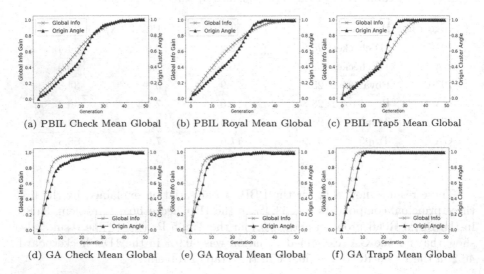

Fig. 3. Global information Vs PCA angles by problem and algorithm

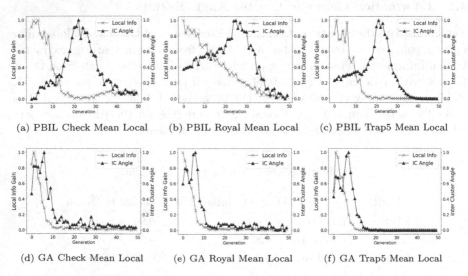

Fig. 4. Local information Vs PCA angles by problem and algorithm

Local information Gain and Inter-Cluster Angle comparison results are more varied and appear to be showing that learning behaviour differs between algorithms on the same problem, seen in Fig. 4. The inter-cluster angle calculated for the populations generated by the PBIL do not share the same pattern of behaviour as the Local Information gain. The results show a peak approximately 25 to 30 generations later than the local information gain and so these events do not co-occur at the same point in the trajectory in all problems tested. This difference in behaviour is reflected in the wider range of correlation coefficients calculated.

The results for the GA however do show a similar behaviour with a time lag of approximately 5 generations across all problems tested to the local information gain. Both sets of data peak early in the trajectory with the Inter-Cluster Angle peaking approximately 5 generations after the Local Information metric, displaying that the Inter-Cluster metric is detecting the occurrence of phase transition point only slightly later in the trajectory. The Inter-Cluster metric closely follows the profile of the Local Information as supported by the high positive correlation coefficients in Table 4.

The results show a clear difference between the two algorithms when Local Information Gain is compared to the Inter-Cluster-Angle results. This may be due to the fact that the PBIL increments the probabilistic model gradually over successive populations so local information gain accumulates before it is reflected in Inter-Cluster Angle change. As a GA can be considered a Markov process, the probability of each population is only dependant to the current state of the system. This can also be seen when Global information Gain is compared to Angle from Origin. The PBIL reaches maximum Global Information later in the trajectory than the GA with a shallower ascent. The PBIL reaches point at which Global Information Gain stops increasing between generations 25 and 40 whereas the GA has a steeper Global Information Gain rate, reaching the maximum value between generations 10 and 20. This may be due to the GA taking a more varied path across the search space than the PBIL which tends to have less varied performance. Together, these show that it is possible to detect differences in algorithm behaviour over the same optimisation problems through the differences in both sets of results.

4.3 Principal Component Loadings

The results of charting the mean loadings across all runs for each algorithm and problem can seen in Fig. 5.

The 1D Checkerboard results show that the loadings reflect the patterns of the coefficients. Adjacent variables in the solutions discovered have opposing values in both the PBIL Fig. 5.a and GA Fig. 5.b figures for the majority of cases. This matches closely the mathematical structure of the fitness functions. Both algorithms however show instances in which the loadings did not conform to the expected pattern, showing a flip in the alternating sequence at three or more points in the bit-string. The Royal Road results for the PBIL in Fig. 5.c do not show any clear pattern that would match the expected fitness function structure however the GA in Fig. 5.d does show some partial detection, with consecutive blocks of 5 bits having similar values that do not match the next block in 4 instances. The results for the Trap5 problem for the PBIL in Fig. 5.e do not show any strong relation to the expected fitness function structure however the GA in Fig. 5.f captures this correctly. It shows all 8 blocks of 5 consecutive bits possess similar values but are distinct from the next block. Since PBIL is univariate, it cannot detect multivariate interactions. 1D Checkerboard results show that some bivariate interaction was detected but this will be accidental. These results shows that the algorithm trajectories reflect the simpler features of the problem structure that the algorithms have learned but the higher order features are less likely to be recovered.

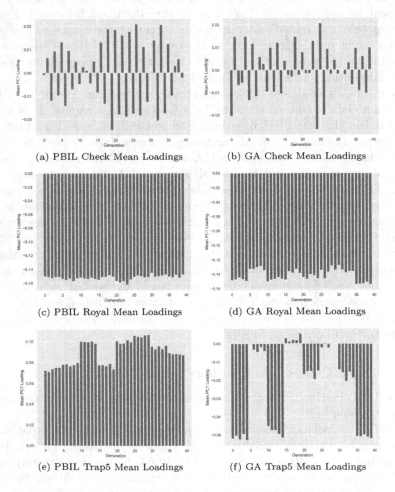

(a) PBIL Check Mean Loadings

(b) GA Check Mean Loadings

(c) PBIL Royal Mean Loadings

(d) GA Royal Mean Loadings

(e) PBIL Trap5 Mean Loadings

(f) GA Trap5 Mean Loadings

Fig. 5. PCA loading values by problem and algorithm

5   Conclusions

In this paper, we presented the results of the application of Principal Components Analysis (PCA) to the trajectories created by two population-based Non-Deterministic Algorithms (NDA). This was done to mine features that can enrich explanations regarding how these algorithms traverse the search space and present significant solution features detected by the algorithms. We generated a collection of algorithm trajectories by solving a set of benchmark problems with a Genetic Algorithm (GA) and modified Population Based Incremental Learning (PBIL) algorithm and projected the resulting trajectories into a lower dimensional space through the application of PCA. This process resulted in a dataset that was mined using a novel set of angular based metrics. Our evaluation of these metrics when compared to the Kullback-Leibler Entropic Divergence measure of both Local Information and Global Information gain shows that there is potential to capture a similar level of detail regarding the Global information learned. These metrics were used to detect differing algorithm behaviour on the same problems as seen between that of the PBIL and GA in the Inter-Cluster Angle values. Finally, it was shown that principal component loadings were used to represent what the algorithms have learned in terms of variable contributions to overall fitness. This is a move towards the generation of explanation of solutions returned by the algorithm. This can be seen in the Eigenvector values for the GA that implied the fitness function structure of the optimisation problem for the 1D Checker and Trap 5 Problem. This feature in the PBIL results show partial structure detection only in the 1D Checker problem and shows that some structure has not been captured using the features used in these tests. Being univariate, PBIL is incapable of creating probability features that capture higher level features with interactions as found in the remaining problems. The results of this paper have shown that the PC derived features are associated with the algorithm learnings regarding problem structure. These techniques can be considered a stepping stone towards supporting explanations by relating changes in information gain to the discovery of specific interaction features.

References

1. Ordish, J., Brigden, T., Hall, A.: Black Box Medicine and Transparency. PHG Foundation, Cambridge, p. 34 (2020)
2. Shakya, S., McCall, J., Brownlee, A., Owusu, G.: DEUM - distribution estimation using markov networks. In: Shakya S., Santana R. (eds) Markov Networks in Evolutionary Computation. Adaptation, Learning, and Optimization, vol. 14, pp 55–71. Springer, Heidelberg (2012). https://doi.org/10.1007/978-3-642-28900-2_4
3. Collins, T.D.: Applying software visualization technology to support the use of evolutionary algorithms. J. Vis. Lang. Comput. 14(2), 123–150 (2003). ISSN 1045–926X. https://doi.org/10.1016/S1045-926X(02)00060-5
4. Ochoa, G., Malan, K.M., Blum, C.: Search trajectory networks: a tool for analysing and visualising the behaviour of metaheuristics. Appl. Soft Comput. 109, 107492 (2021). ISSN 1568-4946. https://doi.org/10.1016/j.asoc.2021.107492

5. Pohlheim, H.: Multidimensional scaling for evolutionary algorithms-visualization of the path through search space and solution space using Sammon mapping. Artif. Life **12**(2), 203–209 (2006). PMID: 16539764. https://doi.org/10.1162/106454606776073305

6. Michalak, K.: Low-dimensional Euclidean embedding for visualization of search spaces in combinatorial optimization. IEEE Trans. Evol. Comput. **23**(2), 232–246 (2019). https://doi.org/10.1109/TEVC.2018.2846636

7. Baluja, S., Caruana, R.: Removing the genetics from the standard genetic algorithm. In: ICML, pp. 38–46 (1995)

8. Baluja, S.: An empirical comparison of seven iterative and evolutionary function optimization heuristics, Carnegie Mellon University, Pittsburgh, PA, Technical report CMU-CS-95-193 (1995)

9. Holland, J.H.: Adaptation in Natural and Artificial Systems: An Introductory Analysis with Applications to Biology, Control, and Artificial Intelligence. Oxford. U Michigan Press, England (1975)

10. Goldsmiths University of London Computational Creativity Research Group. http://ccg.doc.gold.ac.uk/ccg_old/teaching/artificial_intelligence/lecture16.html. Accessed 12 Nov 2020

11. Baluja, S., Davies, S.: Using optimal dependency-trees for combinatorial optimization: Learning the structure of the search space. Technical report, DTIC Document (1997)

12. Forrest, S., Mitchell, M.: Relative building-block fitness and the building block hypothesis. In: Foundations of Genetic Algorithms 2 (San Mateo), Morgan Kaufmann, pp. 109–126 (1993)

13. B.2.7.5: Fitness Landscapes: Royal Road Functions. Handbook of Evolutionary Computation M MitchellS Forrest

14. Goldberg, D.E.: Genetic algorithms and Walsh functions: part i, a gentle introduction. Complex Syst. **3**(2), 129–152 (1989)

15. Goldberg, D.E.: Genetic algorithms and Walsh functions: part ii, deception and its analysis. Complex Syst. **3**(2), 153–171 (1989)

16. Brownlee, A.E.I.: Multivariate Markov networks for fitness modelling in an estimation of distribution algorithm. Robert Gordon University, PhD thesis (2009)

17. Holland, S.M.: Principal Components Analysis (PCA) (2019). Strata.uga.edu. https://strata.uga.edu/software/pdf/pcaTutorial.pdf. Accessed 19 Jun 2021

18. Hien, N.T., Hoai, N.X.: A Brief Overview of Population Diversity Measures in Genetic Programming (2006). http://gpbib.cs.ucl.ac.uk/aspgp06/diversityMeasures.pdf. Accessed 20 Jun 2021

19. Morrison, R.W., De Jong, K.A.: Measurement of population diversity. In: Collet, P., Fonlupt, C., Hao, J.-K., Lutton, E., Schoenauer, M. (eds.) EA 2001. LNCS, vol. 2310, pp. 31–41. Springer, Heidelberg (2002). https://doi.org/10.1007/3-540-46033-0_3

20. Cutello, V., Nicosia, G., Pavone, M., Stracquadanio, G.: Entropic divergence for population based optimization algorithms. In: IEEE Congress on Evolutionary Computation, pp. 1–8 (2010). https://doi.org/10.1109/CEC.2010.5586044

21. MacKay, D.J.C.: Information Theory, Inference, and Learning Algorithms (First ed.). Cambridge University Press, p. 34 (2003). ISBN 9780521642989

22. Shannon, C.E.: A mathematical theory of communication. SIGMO BILE Mob. Comput. Commun. Rev. **5**(1), 3–55 (2001)

23. Protter, M.H., Morrey, Jr., Charles, B.: College Calculus with Analytic Geometry (2nd ed.) (1970)

AI Methods of Autonomous Geological Target Selection in the Hunt for Signs of Extraterrestrial Life

Alexander Tettenborn[✉] and Alex Ellery

Carleton University, 1125 Colonel By Dr, Ottawa, ON K1S 5B6, Canada
alex.tettenborn@cmail.carleton.ca, alexellery@cunet.carleton.ca

Abstract. This report presents a comparison of the accuracy of algorithm developed to allow autonomous visual identification of rock types by extracting texture data from rock images. Approaches differed by their methods of transforming texture data to achieve rotational invariance in the texture feature vector. These vectors were then used for training and testing a Gaussian naïve Bayes classifier. This algorithm will in future allow planetary rovers to select objects of scientific interest to take advantage of the downtime between sending data to Earth and receiving instructions.

The various methods were trained and tested on a set of images of rocks of different types. It was determined from the results of these testing that the accuracy of the algorithms, as well as the length of the feature vectors needed to achieve high accuracy correlates with the degree of information lost in converting the extracted texture information to a rotationally invariant form. The highest accuracy in positive rock type identification was 85% which was achieved by using a weighted binarization of the texture features to perform a circular shift on the feature vector.

Keywords: Texture extraction · Robotic vision · Gabor filter

1 Introduction

The possibility of past life on Mars has long been a subject of scientific interest. One of the primary requirements for life as we know it, liquid water, is not stable anywhere on Mars under present environmental conditions [1]. However, there is evidence that this was not always the case: when exposed to liquid water, rocks like basalt, the primary rock type of the surface of Mars, become chemically weathered into new secondary minerals which incorporate water into their crystalline structures. Such minerals have been detected on the Martian surface [2]. Additionally, geomorphic evidence, including river valleys, lake basins, and evidence of precipitation, points to a time in the past when liquid water existed in abundance on the Martian surface [3]. There is certainly enough water present on Mars to produce such features under the requisite climate; the amount of ice on the surface has been estimated at 5×10^6 cubic kilometers, which corresponds

© Springer Nature Switzerland AG 2021
M. Bramer and R. Ellis (Eds.): SGAI-AI 2021, LNAI 13101, pp. 103–116, 2021.
https://doi.org/10.1007/978-3-030-91100-3_8

to a layer 35 m deep over the surface of the planet [4]. This evidence of abundant surface water suggests that Mars at one point could have supported microbial life.

The motivation for the study of aqueously-deposited sedimentary rocks when searching for indications of past microbial life, or conditions favourable to such, is driven by the known importance of liquid water to life. Aeolian (wind deposited) sedimentary rocks and igneous rocks are not created in environments conducive to microbes and surface dust is exposed to ultraviolet light and oxidants in the environment which degrade organic molecules [5].

While humankind is unable to send geologists and astrobiologists to Mars to examine the Martian environment directly, we must rely on robotics to do the work for us. A prevalent issue in the use of planetary rovers in scientific research is the delay caused by line-of-sight communication windows between other planets or moons and Earth. Rovers do not contain communication equipment with sufficient power to transmit data directly to earth and so must rely on orbiting communication satellites [6]. This necessity produces a delay as a rover must wait for its satellite to pass overhead, then the satellite must orbit until it has line-of-sight to Earth. Once the data has been examined by Earth-side scientists the reverse process must occur to send instructions to the rover producing an unavoidable delay during which the rover is mostly inactive. For the Mars Exploration Rovers Spirit and Opportunity, this operational cycle was approximately 4 days in length [7]. This delay has spurred action to develop autonomous capabilities in rovers to capitalize on this unused time. A major part of this effort, which has seen limited success, is the goal of allowing rovers to autonomously select objects of scientific interest from their environment. Of particular interest is the ability to identify aqueously deposited sedimentary rocks. These are highly relevant to astrobiology and geological history as they provide insight into the history of water on Mars and are most likely to contain indications of past microbial life or conditions favourable to such life [5].

Past attempts at detecting rocks on extraterrestrial landscapes include the use of 3-d surface modeling [8], intensity-based image segmentation [9], and boundary and edge detection [10]. In McGuire et al. (2014) [11] a 'cyborg astrobiologist' system was developed which used compression and juxtaposition of geological images to detect novelty textures and alert to similarities of a new image to previously observed textures. They reported accuracy of 64% in novelty detection and 91% in similarity detection. In an attempt developed for the purposes of fossil fuel extraction, Gancalves and Leta (2010) [12] used binary space partitioning to classify rocks by texture using Haralick parameters and Hurst coefficients, achieving 73% accuracy. In Sharif, Ralchenko, Samson and Ellery (2015) [13] used Haralick parameters and a Bayesian network to classify rock images based on texture information and achieved a success rate of 80%.

In previous work we presented an algorithm which used Gabor filtering applied at multiple angles and wavelengths to extract texture information from rock images [14]. These features were then used by a Gaussian naïve Bayes classifier to determine probabilities of rock types. We subsequently compared those attempts with the use of Cauchy and Mexican Hat wavelets [15]. It was determined that Gabor filtering resulted in the highest accuracy. The loss of information that resulted from transforming the extracted feature vectors to be rotationally invariant seemed to put an upper limit on the accuracy of the algorithm.

In this work an algorithm is present for the extraction of texture data from rock images. The identification accuracies of using four methods of transforming texture data to produce rotational invariance in the extracted texture vector are compared. The two methods which were not in the previous work were selected because they involve less information loss.

2 Feature Extraction

2.1 Gabor Filter

The Gabor filter is an orientation sensitive linear filter used in a range of applications including edge detection and texture analysis. Meng, Yilong, Yang and Xiaoming (2013) [16] used Gabor to build a robust retinal identification algorithm capable of identifying retinas with an error rate of only 0.65%. Chaki and Parkj (2012) [17] built a system for plant classification by leaf characteristics capable of 83% accuracy for classifying among 10 leaf types and 90% accuracy for classifying among 4 leaf types. Wei et al. (2008) [18] used Gabor filters for identification of Chinese characters with an error rate ranging from 92.5% to 99.4% depending on image quality.

Image analysis using Gabor has been shown to bear significant similarity to the way images are processed by mammalian vision [19]. The filter itself is made up of a complex sinusoidal waveform modulated by a Gaussian curve. When extended to two dimensions, the filter is similarly a sinusoidal plane wave which is modulated by a Gaussian kernel, as shown in Eq. 1–3. When applied to an image as a convolution mask the response produced varies in magnitude based on the presence of spatial textures in the image and the scale (wavelength of the sinusoid) and orientation (direction perpendicular to the sinusoid parallel lines).

$$g(x, y) = exp\left(i\left(2\pi\frac{x'}{\lambda} + \varphi\right)\right)exp\left(-\frac{x'^2 + \gamma^2 y'^2}{2\sigma^2}\right) \tag{1}$$

$$x' = xcos(\theta) + ysin(\theta) \tag{2}$$

$$y' = -xsin(\theta) + ycos(\theta) \tag{3}$$

Where λ and φ are respectively the wavelength and phase shift of the complex sinusoid s, and σ and γ are the standard deviation and spatial aspect ratio of the Gaussian envelope w. θ is the normal to the parallel lines of the sinusoid. This gives the angle at which the filter applies and determines what orientation of texture features responds. A filter with a θ of 0° responds only to horizontal texture features while a value of 90° would respond only to vertical texture features. This can be seen in Fig. 1 where the filters applied at $\theta = 0°$ and $\theta = 45°$ and $\theta = 90°$ show response in different parts of the image of sedimentary sandstone depending on the direction of the striations.

2.2 Gabor Banks and Gabor Filter Parameter Optimization

To apply the Gabor filter to texture extraction a single filter is not sufficient. Instead, a bank of filters must be applied to an image to extract texture information at different angles and scales. Table 1 lists the different applicable values associated with generating a bank of Gabor filters.

Table 1. List of important parameters for texture extraction with a Gabor filter bank

Parameter	Description
FM	Highest frequency used in filter bank
F_R	Frequency or spatial resolution. The ratio between a frequency and the one directly after it
ϑ_D	Angular resolution. The difference between two successive angles
n	Number of frequencies ($F = 1/\lambda$) used
m	Number of orientations (ϑ) used
σ	Standard deviation of Gaussian envelope in direction of sinusoidal wave
γ	Aspect ratio of Gaussian envelope
φ	Phase shift of the sinusoid

Given a bank of Gabor filters $G_{ij}(x,y)$ the Gabor transform of an input image I is

$$T_{ij}(x, y) = \sum_{a=1}^{X} \sum_{b=1}^{Y} I(a, b)\overline{G}_{ij}(x - a, y - b) \tag{4}$$

The maximum frequency, FM (the reciprocal of the smallest wavelength), used in the filter bank is often selected in order to maintain filter response within the Nyquist frequency. In the case of image analysis frequencies are denoted in pixels-1 and the sampling rate is taken to be 1. The Nyquist frequency, defined as half the sampling rate, is therefore 0.5. Proposed values range from 0.18 to 0.5 with $\sqrt{2}/4$ and 0.4 being common [20].

The ratio between successive wavelengths, FR, is selected in order to control the amount of overlap in the frequency plane by the filters used. Common values are 1/2 and $\sqrt{2}/2$ which correspond to an octave interval and a half octave interval. Some publications also calculate FR specifically to produce a filter bank whose half-peak magnitude iso-curves touch, but do not overlap in the frequency domain [20].

The difference between successive angles, θ_D, is usually chosen simply as π/m radians, so that the Gabor filters cover a range from 0 radians to ($\pi - \theta_D$) radians, the angle π radians being redundant with the angle 0 radians [20].

The number of frequencies (n) and number of orientations (m) are widely accepted as the two parameters with the most influence over texture classification accuracy [21]. The proper n and m depend highly on the specific problem being attempted they will be the primary independent variables used when examining the accuracy of the proposed algorithm in this work. The effect of the standard deviation, σ, and aspect ratio, γ of the

Gaussian envelope, referred to as the 'smoothing parameters', are not widely explored in literature. It has been suggested, based on physiological evidence that an aspect ratio of 0.6 might improve texture discrimination [22]. It can be assumed that, since the scale of the sinusoid increases exponentially when a filter bank is generated from a given FM and FR, that the standard deviation should also scale with the wavelength so that the Gaussian envelope does not reduce the sinusoid so quickly that it becomes irrelevant to the filter.

The phase shift φ of the sinusoid does not seem to be an important factor in texture discrimination, to the point that in much of the literature it is neglected from the equations entirely (equivalent to setting it to zero) [20, 21].

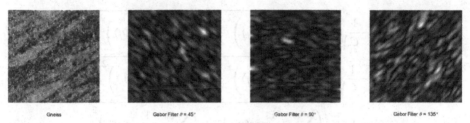

Gneiss   Gabor Filter θ = 45°   Gabor Filter θ = 90°   Gabor Filter θ = 135°

Fig. 1. Image of gneiss processed by Gabor filter at 45°, 90° and 135° showing the difference in response.

2.3 Rotation Invariance in Texture Features

A set of digital images of prepared rock samples was used for the training and testing of the algorithms described in the previous sections. The set is comprised of 360 images of 21 different rock types, with between 12 and 36 images of each type. The image dataset used here was provided by Sharif, Ralchenko, Samson and Ellery (2015) [13]. Of these, half were used as a training set for the naïve Bayesian classifier while half were used as a test set to determine accuracy. One significant difficulty involved in using such test images is the rotational invariance of the Gabor and Cauchy techniques. As we can see from Fig. 1, anisometric techniques such as these the orientation of the texture feature makes a major difference to the response received. This can be highly useful as it allows the algorithm to extract more information from a single texture. However, it is a drawback when similar textures in different images are shown at different orientations. This is the case with the test images, as striations were not aligned between different images. It would also be the case in real world applications as rocks on extraterrestrial landscapes will not be conveniently oriented to always show texture features travelling in the same direction, especially when they are photographed at oblique angles. Four methods were used to remedy this.

2.3.1 Response Weighted Semi-circular Distribution Method

For the first method of achieving rotational invariance the assumption is made that for the same texture photographed at different orientations, the peak response will occur at different values of θ but the distribution of response for different values of θ will be similar if λ is held constant.

To train the Bayes network an n-by-m array of filters was applied to each image. In the case of the Gabor filter this corresponded to n different spatial scales (values of λ) such that the values ranged from 3 to 128 pixels, and m orientations (values of θ) such that the values were distributed evenly between 0 and 180°. The Gabor filter was applied with $\sigma = 3/2\lambda$, $\varphi = 0$ and $\gamma = 0.5$. The mean and standard deviation of the magnitude of the response is then taken with μ_{ij} and σ_{ij} denoting the mean and standard deviation of the ith spatial scale and jth orientation. These are then used to calculate the features $S_{\mu i}$ and $S_{\sigma i}$, as shown in Eq. 5–7 for each spatial scale, which represent the amount of variation in μ_{ij} and σ_{ij} respectively.

$$S_{\mu i} = -\frac{1}{C}\sqrt{\left(\sum_{j=1}^{m}\mu_{ij}cos(\theta_j)\right)^2 + \left(\sum_{j=1}^{m}\mu_{ij}sin(\theta_j)\right)^2} + \frac{1}{C} \tag{5}$$

$$S_{\sigma i} = -\frac{1}{C}\sqrt{\left(\sum_{j=1}^{m}\sigma_{ij}cos(\theta_j)\right)^2 + \left(\sum_{j=1}^{m}\sigma_{ij}sin(\theta_j)\right)^2} + \frac{1}{C} \tag{6}$$

$$C = 1 - \sqrt{\left(\sum_{j=1}^{m}\frac{1}{m}cos(\theta_j)\right)^2 + \left(\sum_{j=1}^{m}\frac{1}{m}sin(\theta_j)\right)^2} \tag{7}$$

These equations are formulated such that they produce values ranging from 0 in the case that all orientations have the same magnitude or standard deviation, to 1 if a single magnitude or standard deviation is so large that all others are negligible. It is visualized as the magnitude of the averaged position of points around a semicircle, weighted by the corresponding values of mean and standard deviation. These equations are used to achieve rotational invariance. The values of $S_{\mu i}$ and $S_{\sigma i}$ become elements of the feature vector for the image. In addition, the maximum value of μ_{ij} and σ_{ij} for the i'th value of λ are stored respectively as $M_{\mu i}$ and $M_{\sigma i}$ respectively. This finally produces a number of features equal to 4 times the number of spatial scales used.

2.3.2 Fourier Coefficient Magnitude Method

In the second method the feature vector of the anisotropic extraction methods is expressed as a set of N one-dimensional signals whose length M is the number of orientations used, where N is the number of spatial resolutions. These can be treated as if they are N periodic signals where $f^m{}_n(m)$ is the signal for the nth spatial resolution and the mth orientation. Rotation invariant features can then be obtained by taking the discrete Fourier coefficients $C_{k,n}$ of $f^m{}_n(m)$ as shown in Eq. 8 [23].

$$C_{k,n} = \left|c_k(f)_n\right| = \left|\frac{1}{M}\sum_{m=0}^{M}f_n^m(m)exp(-2i\pi km/M)\right| \tag{8}$$

Doing so produces a vector of extracted texture features of length $m * n$. This is significantly longer than the previous method which increases computation time both for training and identification, however it may contain more vector information. One indication that it likely contains more information than the previous method is that this method can be inverted to retrieve the original signal.

2.3.3   Fourier Based Rotation Invariant Features with Imbedded Phase Data

One disadvantage of the method using Fourier coefficients is that in taking the magnitude of the Fourier components, the phase data of the Fourier transform is lost. The overall shape of the original signal depends on the phase data, so this represents a loss of information from the original signal. In Mavandadi, Aarabi and Plataniotis (2009) [24] a novel method is developed which combines both the phase and magnitude information of the signal to achieve invariance. First the discrete Fourier transform of the signal is taken. Then the coefficients are transformed as shown in Eq. 9.

$$M_f[n] = \frac{1}{N}F_0 + \frac{1}{N}\sum_{k-1}^{N-1}|F_k|e^{j\angle F_k \lambda_k}e^{j2\pi k^n/N} \tag{9}$$

This is similar to the inverse discrete Fourier transform with the exception of that the phase angle is multiplied by the coefficient $\lambda_k = k - 1$. They show that when compared to a circularly shifted function g such that g[n] = f[n − m] this transformation gives

$$M_f[n] = \frac{1}{N}G_0 + \frac{1}{N}e^{-j2\pi k^m/N}\sum_{k-1}^{N-1}|F_k|e^{j\angle F_k \lambda_k}e^{j2\pi k^n/N} \tag{10}$$

Because the factors within the summation are the same between both functions, this leads to the equality

$$\left|M_f[n] - \frac{1}{N}F_0\right| = \left|M_G[n] - \frac{1}{N}G_0\right| \tag{11}$$

Thus the rotation invariant signal transform can be given as

$$D[r, n] = \left|M_P[r, n] - \frac{1}{N}P[r, 0]\right| \tag{12}$$

Where r corresponds to the rows for each angle and n corresponds to the features along the row. This gives a feature vector which is rotationally invariant, and which has imbedded within the phase information from the original extracted texture feature. No information is lost prior to taking the magnitude of the final feature.

2.3.4   Rotation Invariant Feature Vectors Through Weighted Binarization Shifting

The ideal feature vector for rotational invariance would be one which, for a circularly shifted vector, keeps all information except for the degree of circular shift. In other words, the method for turning the initial feature vector into a rotationally invariant one would keep all information about the initial shape, but simply not know which feature was the first in the initial vector. To achieve this, a method was developed that shifts the initial feature vector by an amount determined by its shape. The initial step is to take the initial feature vector (corresponding to all orientations at a single frequency) and binarize it.

$$b[m] = \begin{cases} 1 \ if \ f(m) \geq E[f(m)] \\ 0 \ if \ f(m) < E[f(m)] \end{cases} \tag{13}$$

Then each element of this feature vector is scaled by a binomial factor 2 m and summed to achieve a number which spatially characterizes the images local texture information.

$$B = \sum_{m=0}^{M} b_m 2^m \tag{14}$$

Then, this same method is applied to the same binarized feature vector after circular shifts from 0 to M − 1. This results in M binarized texture descriptors Bm. Next the rotation is noted which produces the maximum B_m.

$$J_{rotation} = j | B_j = \max\left(\sum_{m=0}^{M} rotate(b_m | j = 0 \ldots M - 1) 2^m\right) \tag{15}$$

Then this rotation is applied to the original feature vector. This method is rotationally invariant such that the resulting feature vector is constant given a circular shift of features in the orientation direction, and it results in no loss of information of the original shape. The only information lost is which element of the initial feature vector was f(0).

For all methods of rotational invariance, the Gaussian naïve Bayes classifier is trained by applying these methods to each of the training images to produce feature vectors and taking the mean and standard deviation of each feature separated by rock type. These are denoted as μ_{kl} and σ_{kl}, where k denotes the class of rock, and l is the total number of features in each vector.

3   Classification

The methods of feature extraction discussed in Sect. 2 all produce a feature vector that can be used to classify them by their visual textures. These methods were applied to a set of rock images.

3.1   Gaussian Naïve Bayes Classifiers

For a given set of n features, $x_1, \ldots, x_n$ a naïve Bayes classifier can be used to assign a probability that the feature belongs to each of k possible classes Ck. The probability is assigned using Bayes' Theorem.

$$p(C_k | x_1, \ldots, x_n) = \frac{p(C_k)p(x_1, \ldots, x_n | C_k)}{p(x_1, \ldots, x_n)} \tag{16}$$

If the assumption is made that these features are conditionally independent of each other, then the conditional probability of the feature vector given the class can be expressed as a product of the posterior probability of each element given the class.

$$p(C_k | x_1, \ldots, x_n) = \frac{p(C_k)\prod_{i=1}^{n} p(x_i | C_k)}{p(x_1, \ldots, x_n)} \tag{17}$$

The prior probability for each class p(Ck) is found by dividing the number of images of each class in the sample set by the total number of images. This leaves only the conditional probability of each element given the class. In this case the assumption was made that the features in each class followed a roughly Gaussian distribution which allows us to use Eq. 3.3 to find the condition probabilities.

$$p(x_i = v | C_k) = \frac{1}{\sqrt{2\pi\sigma_{k,i}^2}} e^{\frac{(v - \mu_{k,i})^2}{2\sigma_{k,i}^2}} \tag{18}$$

3.2 Rock Type Identification

With the Bayes classifier trained, the same methods described in Sect. 2.3 are then applied to the test images, producing feature vectors. For each image the feature vector is used to compute the probability the image belongs to each of the image classes, in this case rock types, using Eq. 17. The μ_{kl} and σ_{kl} for each rock type and feature allow for the calculation of the likelihood of the observed value for that feature given each rock type.

The denominator of Eq. 17 is selected to cause the sum of probabilities for all rock types to sum to 1. The final array of probabilities is then plotted. Each test is a success if the maximum of the returned vector of $p(x_i = x_1 | C_k)$ corresponds to the rock type the image is labelled with.

4 Results

The algorithm described in Sect. 3 was implemented in the MATLAB numerical computing environment. For each set of parameters in each texture extraction and rotational invariance method the Bayes classifier was trained using the training images. The rock type identification in Sect. 3.2 was then applied to the remaining test images. The rate of success in selecting the correct rock type was recorded.

4.1 Accuracy of Gabor Filter Parameters

For simplicity the methods of achieving rotational invariance the response weighted semi-circular distribution method will be referred to as the 'weighted point method' and the Fourier transform coefficient method with be referred to as the "Fourier method", the method using Fourier Based Rotation Invariant Features with Imbedded Phase Data will be referred to as "phase Fourier method" and the Rotation Invariant Feature Vectors Through Weighted Binarization Shifting method will be referred to as the "binarized shifting method".

Figure 2 shows how the accuracy of the identification methods vary as the number of spatial resolutions is changed. The accuracy of the Gabor filter with all methods reach their maximum with respect to the number of scales by $n = 6$. As the spatial resolutions used varied by octave, starting at 2 pixels, this corresponds to a maximum spatial wavelength of 64 pixels. It makes sense that scales higher than this would not provide much more information from images that are only 256×256 pixels. Of the

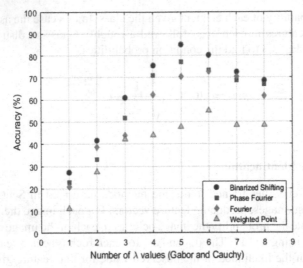

Fig. 2. Results of trials with varying number of spatial resolutions used in identification with 8 orientations.

four methods, the binarized shifting method seems to achieve the highest accuracy, followed by the phase Fourier method, the Fourier method and lastly, the weighted point method. In addition, the binarized shifting method and phase Fourier method improve more quickly starting at low number of scales used. This allows for a robust accurate algorithm with a smaller feature vector, which greatly reduces computation time. This is especially true with regards to spatial orientation, as the convolution window of the Gabor filter is scaled based on the value of λ, so larger scales require significantly more computation time to apply the filter.

Figure 3 shows how the accuracy of the algorithm varies with the number of orientations used over the four methods of rotation invariance. Again, we can see that the weighted point method requires more orientations to achieve its maximum accuracy and achieves a lower accuracy than the other methods. The best performing method is again the binarized shifting, followed by the phase Fourier and Fourier methods.

Overall, the weighted point method reached a maximum of 67.7% accuracy using an array of 6 scales and 14 orientations. The Fourier method achieved 78.8% accuracy at 6 scales and 12 orientations, the phase Fourier method achieved 81.1% accuracy at 5 scales and 10 orientations and the binarized shifting method achieved 85% accuracy at 5 scales and 8 orientations. The maximum accuracies for the weighted point and Fourier methods are slightly lower than those found in Tettenborn and Ellery 2018 [15]. This is because the previous work used a half octave between scales. This resulted in higher accuracy for the methods evaluated, but significantly longer computation time and a larger feature vector. In the case of binarized shifting and phase Fourier methods using full octave between scales showed a slightly better result with reduced computation time, so it was applied to all methods for comparison.

It can be observed that the accuracy achieved, and the size of the feature vector needed to achieve it are correlated with the amount of information preserved by the

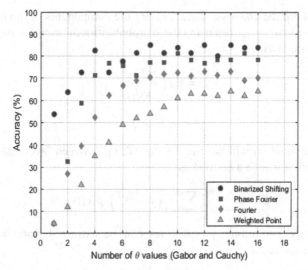

Fig. 3. Results of trials with varying number of orientations used in identification with 5 spatial resolutions.

method of achieving rotational invariance. The weighted point method loses much of the shape information, the Fourier method loses all the phase information from the Fourier Coefficients, the phase Fourier method embeds the phase information in the feature vector, but still loses information when the magnitude is taken, and the binarized shifting method maintains the entire shape of the feature vector while losing only the knowledge of how much it was shifted.

5   Conclusions and Future Work

In this report texture feature extraction using Gabor filter arrays at varying numbers of scales and orientations was examined using four methods of transforming texture data to achieving rotational invariance. This was done to assess their potential use in allowing planetary rovers to autonomously identify types of rocks. The methods examined were weighted Binarization shifting which saw the most success, with a peak identification rate of 85%, followed by the method of Fourier based features with embedded phase information achieving 81.1%, the method using Fourier coefficients directly achieving 78.8% and finally the semi-circular weighted point methods achieving 67.7%. It was observed that methods achieve higher accuracy the less information is lost in the shift to rotationally invariant features.

The next step in this work will be to use a novel method of combining the pre-trained probabilities of a Bayesian network with the powerful capabilities of artificial neural networks. The goal is to successfully use the conditional probabilities of the Bayesian network to preconfigure the weights and biases of a 3-layer multi-layer perceptron.

The probabilities associated with the Bayesian net are given by the formula

$$p(C_k|x_1, ..., x_n) = \frac{p(C_k)p(x_1, ..., x_n|C_k)}{p(x_1, ..., x_n)} \tag{19}$$

Where C_k is are the classes and $x_i,...,x_n$ are the components of the texture feature array. If we take $x_i = x_i,...,x_n$ then using these probabilities the weights and biases of the MLP can be encoded as

$$w_{ij} = log\left(\frac{p(C_i|x_j)}{p(C_i)}\right) \tag{20}$$

$$w_{i0} = log p(y_i)$$

The sigmoid function will be used for squashing between layers and the squared error cost function for such a network is

$$E =< \sum_{j=1}^{n} \sum_{i=1}^{m} \left(y_i - y_i^d\right)^2 p(c_i|x_i) > \tag{21}$$

Conversely the conditional probabilities can be extracted from the connection weights using the formula

$$p(y_i|x_j) = 1 - exp\left(-\sum_{j<i} w_{ij}x_j\right) \tag{22}$$

Once the initial ANN has been built from the Bayesian probabilities, further training of the network will be achieved using the Levenburg-Marquardt algorithm, which is a particular case of the extended Kalman filter [25]. The change in weights is given as

$$\Delta w = -(H + \lambda I)^{-1} \nabla J(w) \tag{23}$$

Where J and H are the sum of square cost function with weight decay and the Hessian respectively, given by

$$J(w) = \frac{1}{2}\sum_{k=1}^{n} e_k^2 + kw^2 = \frac{1}{2}\sum_{k=1}^{n} \left(y_k^d - f(x_k, w)\right)^2 + kw^2 \tag{24}$$

$$H_{ij} = \sum_{k=1}^{n} \frac{\partial e_k}{\partial w_i} \frac{\partial e_k}{\partial w_j} \tag{25}$$

And λ is a training parameter.

The motivation behind this fusing of Bayesian and artificial neural nets is to produce a neural net that is already capable of classification with only its initial weights. This produces several advantages over deep convolutional neural networks (CNNs). Firstly, it reduces the initial dataset requirement as CNNs require a large amount of data for training while Bayesian networks are robust with relatively small initial datasets. Secondly it allows for a lower computational time cost as Bayesian nets and MLPs require significantly less processing overhead than CNNs which are often implemented using graphic processing units (GPUs). Lastly it allows for transparency in the algorithm. The logic used by the hidden layers in CNNs and most other ANNs is opaque. The many weights and biases connecting each node to each other node makes it an intractable task to follow a chain of logic from the input to the output. This is not true of the algorithm proposed here as the Bayesian conditional probabilities can be extracted from the network and examined. This would allow scientists on Earth to understand how an autonomous rover was making its decisions, even as it continued to learn from new data. In addition to these advantages, the proposed algorithm will provide more novelty to the final thesis than would a CNN approach.

This will culminate in a robust algorithm for use aboard planetary rovers. Without the need for human intervention in the selection of objects of scientific interest the productivity of future missions should be greatly improved.

References

1. McSween, H.Y.: Water on Mars. Elements 2(3), 135–137 (2006)
2. Ming, D., Morris, R., Clark, R.: Aqueous Alerations on Mars. The Martian Surface: Composition, Mineralogy, and Physical Properties, pp. 519–540 (2008)
3. Baker, V., Strom, R., Gulick, V., Kargel, J., Komatsu, G., Kale, V.: Ancient oceans, ice sheets and the hydrological cycle on Mars. Nature 352, 589–594 (1991)
4. Christensen, P.: Water at the poles and in permafrost regions of Mars. Geosci. World 2(3), 151–155 (2006)
5. Westall, F., Foucher, F., Bost, N., Bertrand, M., Loizeau, D., Vago, J.: Biosignatures of Mars: What, Where and How? Implications for the search for Martian life. Astrobiology 15(11) (2015)
6. Horne, W., Hastrup, R., Cesarone, R.: Telecommunications for Mars rovers and robotic missions. Space Technol. 17, 205–213 (1997)
7. Erickson, J., Adler, M., Crisp, J., Mishkin, A., Welch, R.: Mars exploration rover: surface operations. In: Proceedings of 53rd International Astronautical Congress. Houston, TX (2002)
8. Li, R., Di, K., Howard, A., Matthies, L., Wang, J.: Rock modelling and matching for autonomous long-range Mars rover localizations. J. Field Robot. 24(3), 187–203 (2007)
9. Castano, A., Anderson, C., Castano, R., Estlin, T., Judd, M.: Intensity-based rock detection for acquiring onboard rover science. In: 35th Lunar and Planetary Science Conference Proceedings (2004)
10. Gui, C., Li, Z.: An autonomous rock identification method for planetary exploration. In: Wong, W.E., Ma, T. (eds.) Emerging Technologies for Information Systems, Computing, and Management. LNEE, vol. 236, pp. 545–552. Springer, New York (2013). https://doi.org/10.1007/978-1-4614-7010-6_61
11. McGuire, P., et al.: The Cyborg Astrobiologist: matching of prior textures by image compression for geological mapping and novelty detection. Int. J. Astrobiol. 13(3), 191–202 (2014)
12. Goncalves, L., Leta, F.: Macroscopic Rock Texture Image Classification Using a Hierarchical Neuro-Fuzzy Class Method. Mathematical Problems in Engineering (2010)
13. Sharif, H., Ralchenko, M., Samson, C., Ellery, A.: Autonomous rock classification using Bayesian image analysis for rover-based planetary exploration. Comput. Geosci. 83, 153–167 (2015)
14. Tettenborn, A., Ellery, A.: Geological identification of rocks for planetary rovers. In: Proceedings of the 2017 Advanced Space Technologies for Robotics and Automation Conference. Leiden (2017)
15. Tettenborn, A., Ellery, A.: Comparison of Gabor filters and Wavelet transform methods for extraction of lithological features. In: Proceedings of the 2018 International Symposium on Artificial Intelligence, Robotics and Automation in Space. Madrid (2018)
16. Meng, X., Yilong, Y., Yang, G., Xiaoming, X.: Retinal identification based on an improved circular Gabor filter and scale invariant feature transform. Sensors 13(7), 9248–9266 (2013)

17. Chaki, J., Parekj, R.: Plant leaf recognition using Gabor filter. J. Comput. Appl. **56**(10), 26–29 (2012)
18. Wei, L., Wang, F., Decian, Z., Zhixiao, Y., Zhiyan, Z., Fei, S.: The application of Gabor filter in Chinese writer identification. In: Proceedings of 2008 IEEE International Symposium on IT in Medicine and Education, pp. 360–362. Xiamen (2008)
19. Marcelja, S.: Mathematical description of the responses of simple cortical cells. J. Opt. Soc. Am. **70**, 1297–1300 (1980)
20. Bianconi, F., Fernandez, A.: Evaluation of the effect of Gabor filter parameters of texture classification. J. Pattern Recogn. **40**, 3325–3335 (2007)
21. Moreno, P., Bernardino, A., Santos-Victor, J.: Gabor parameter selection for local feature detection. In: Marques, J.S., Pérez de la Blanca, N., Pina, P. (eds.) IbPRIA 2005. LNCS, vol. 3522, pp. 11–19. Springer, Heidelberg (2005). https://doi.org/10.1007/11492429_2
22. Turner, M.: Texture discrimination by Gabor functions. Biol. Cybern. **55**, 71–82 (1986)
23. Van de Wouwer, G., Vautrot, P., Scheunders, P., Liven, S., Van Dyck, D., Bonnet, N.: Rotation-invariant texture segmentation using continuous Wavelets. In: Proceedings of the IEEE UK Conference on Applications of Time Frequency and Time Scale Methods, (pp. 129–132). Warwick, United Kingdom (1997)
24. Mavandadi, S., Aarabi, P., Plataniotis, N.: Fourier-based rotation invariant image features. In: 16th IEEE International Conference on Image Processing (ICIP), pp. 2041–2044 (2009)
25. Horvath, S., Neuner, H.: Comparison of Levenberg-Marquardt and extended Kalman filter based parameter estimation of artificial neural networks in modelling deformation processes. In: The 3rd Joint International Symposium on Deformation Monitoring, Vienna (2016)

Probabilistic Rule Induction
for Transparent CBR Under Uncertainty

Martin Jedwabny[1]([✉]), Pierre Bisquert[1,2], and Madalina Croitoru[1]

[1] LIRMM, Inria, Univ Montpellier, CNRS, Montpellier, France
{martin.jedwabny,madalina.croitoru}@lirmm.fr, pierre.bisquert@inrae.fr
[2] IATE, Univ Montpellier, INRAE, Institut Agro, Montpellier, France

Abstract. CBR systems leverage past experiences to make decisions. Recently, the AI community has taken an interest in making CBR systems explainable. Logic-based frameworks make answers straightforward to explain. However, they struggle in the face of conflicting information, unlike probabilistic techniques. We show how probabilistic inductive logic programming (PILP) can be applied in CBR systems to make transparent decisions combining logic and probabilities. Then, we demonstrate how our approach can be applied in scenarios presenting uncertainty.

Keywords: Case-based reasoning · Probabilistic logic programming · Inductive logic programming · Explanability

1 Introduction

Case-based reasoning (CBR) [1] is a problem-solving technique that uses previously encountered experiences to solve a problem. When novel problems are encountered, similar past cases are retrieved and their solutions are adapted to the situation at hand. Furthermore, soft case-based reasoning [15] allows for uncertainty in the form of missing information or when a single description has been solved using multiple solutions. Here, we focus on this second type of uncertainty, in which a single problem might have been solved using different solutions in the past. Indeed, this scenario can easily present itself as a consequence of multiple domain experts providing conflicting solutions, or when a single one has different confidence levels over the space of possible solutions.

Lately, there has been a major interest from the Artificial Intelligence community to make systems that provide explanations to their answers, giving birth to what is known as explainable AI (XAI). Due to several concerns stemming from the lack of transparency and interpretability [3], several approaches have been proposed to make up for these issues for various AI subfields, including CBR systems [21]. Indeed, some literature [13,20] even includes computing explanations as part of the fundamental workflow of CBR systems.

Past literature in XAI has developed two main ways of achieving explainability [3]: transparent systems and post-hoc models to explain black-box systems

© Springer Nature Switzerland AG 2021
M. Bramer and R. Ellis (Eds.): SGAI-AI 2021, LNAI 13101, pp. 117–130, 2021.
https://doi.org/10.1007/978-3-030-91100-3_9

[17]. Some authors consider the second type of explanations as limited due to the fact that they provide reconstructions which might not be really linked to the actual reasoning process of the black-box system. On the other hand, transparent systems often sacrifice the quality of the answers or computational performance, in order to fully offer interpretable results.

Recently, there has been a growing interest in the XAI community in frameworks that combine symbolic and probabilistic approaches, which allows to both handle uncertainty in the form of conflicting information, and deliver transparent results. A state-of-the-art probabilistic rule induction system, called ProbFOIL+ [8] allows to infer probability annotated rules from noisy data. However, this approach will often suffer from time complexity issues when the available information is too large.

In this paper, we argue that case-based reasoning in conjunction with ProbFOIL+ is a feasible and interesting approach to both tackling the time complexity issues of probabilistic rule induction, and providing transparent answers in soft case-based reasoning problems featuring problems with conflicting solutions.

The following sections are structured as follows. Section 2 introduces the basic notions required to present our framework. Then, Sect. 3 covers the general architecture of our framework, the CBR case representation, and the reasoning mechanism from a theoretical perspective. Section 4 goes into the implementation details of our system. In Sect. 5, the reader will find a the results obtained by the implementation of our framework. Finally, Sect. 6 summarizes our results, discusses different perspectives upon which our work contributes to, and compares our work to previous research.

2   Preliminaries

In this section, we describe the logical language we will use to represent the cases of our CBR system and some basic concepts of probabilistic inductive logic programming [8] which our system uses to perform the case adaptation phase described in the upcoming sections.

2.1   Logic Language

We build upon a first-order logic language $\mathcal{L}$ composed of *constants* $\{a, b, \ldots\}$, *variables* $\{X, Y, \ldots\}$, *function* symbols $\{f, g, \ldots\}$, and *predicate* symbols $\{P, Q, \ldots\}$. A *term* t is a constant, a variable or a functor. An *atom* $P(t_1, \ldots, t_n)$ is a predicate P of arity $n \in \mathbb{N}_0$ applied to terms $t_1, \ldots, t_n$. A *rule* $H \leftarrow B_1, \ldots, B_n$ is a construct composed of a *head* atom H and a finite conjunction of *body* atoms $B_1, \ldots, B_n$. A *fact* is a rule with an empty body. A *substitution* $\theta = \{X_1/t_1, \ldots X_k/t_k\}$ is a mapping from variables to terms. Applying a substitution θ to an atom a is denoted as $a\theta$ and it replaces the variables in the domain of θ with their corresponding terms. In the case $a\theta$ contains no variables, we say that the operation is a grounding of a and we call $a\theta$ a ground atom.

2.2 Probabilistic Logic Language

We can extend logic rules with probabilistic annotations in order to deal with uncertain information. ProbLog [9] is a probabilistic first-order logic language that extends the notions presented above with *probabilistic rules* (and facts) $p_i :: r_i$ where $p_i \in [0, 1]$ denotes a probability and r_i is a rule. Its semantics is based on what is known as a distribution semantics [19] (a well-known semantics for probabilistic logics).

A ProbLog *program* $T = \{p_1 :: r_1, \ldots, p_n :: r_n\}$ consists of a finite set of probabilistic rules. Given a finite set of possible grounding substitutions $\{\theta_{i,1}, \ldots, \theta_{i,m_i}\}$ for each probabilistic rule $p_i :: r_i \in T$, a ProbLog program T defines a probability distribution over the subsets $L \subseteq L_T$ of possible groundings $L_T = \{r_1\theta_{1,1}, \ldots, r_1\theta_{1,n_1}, \ldots, r_n\theta_{n,1}, \ldots, r_n\theta_{n,m_n}\}$ of (strict) rules in T as:

$$P(L \mid T) = \prod_{r_i\theta_j \in L} p_i \prod_{r_i\theta_j \in L_T \setminus L} (1 - p_i)$$

Moreover, ProbLog defines the *success probability* of a query q (i.e. finite conjunction of atoms) as the overall probability that a random subset $L \subseteq L_T$ entails q:

$$P_s(T \models q) = \sum_{\substack{L \subseteq L_T \\ L \cup D \models q}} P(L \mid T)$$

2.3 Probabilistic Inductive Logic Programming

PILP [8] is a subfield of statistical relation learning (SRL) [11] that addresses the task of inferring a set of logic rules that justify a target predicate from examples and background knowledge, when the examples and learnt rules may be annotated with probabilities.

As mentioned before, the PILP setting is the task of finding an hypothesis in the form of a set of probabilistic rules from which a set of examples of a target predicate can be derived with minimal loss. More precisely (based on [8]):

Definition 1 (PILP problem). *Given the following:*

1. *A set of examples E, composed of pairs (x_i, p_i) where x_i is a grounding for the target predicate t and p_i its probability,*
2. *A background theory B containing information related to the examples in the form of a ProbLog program,*
3. *A loss function $loss(H, B, E)$, measuring the error of a hypothesis (set of rules) H w.r.t B and E (in [8]: $loss(H, B, E) = \sum_{(x_i,p_i)\in E} |P_s(B \cup H \models x_i) - p_i|$), and*
4. *A space of possible clauses L_h specified as in [14].*

Find a hypothesis $H \subseteq L_h$ such that $H = \underset{H' \subseteq L_h}{\operatorname{argmin}}\ loss(H', B, E)$.

Notice that the definition above accounts for probabilistic rules in the background theory B and hypothesis H unlike [8], which only accounts for probabilistic facts. However, as mentioned in [9] this definition is equivalently general, as probabilistic rules can be replaced in this setting by strict rules by adding a fresh probabilistic fact (with the same probability annotation) to its body. We modified this definition for ease of use in later sections.

3   Our Framework

In this section, we will present our framework from a theoretical perspective, while the implementation details will be described in the following one. It utilizes the mechanisms of probabilistic inductive logic programming to adapt previously encountered cases so that it allows them to have conflicting solutions.

As mentioned before, CBR is a methodology which consists of finding and reusing past problems to solve novel ones, which present similar features. We will denote the *case base* (i.e. the past cases) of a CBR system as a collection of (possibly non-unique) pairs $\mathcal{CB} = \{(x_i, y_i)\}_i$ where $x_i \in \mathcal{P}$ is called the problem and $y_i \in \mathcal{S}$ its solution.

Both $\mathcal{P}$ the *problem space* and $\mathcal{S}$ the *solution space*, are typically assigned a fixed structure by the CBR implementation. More precisely, their structure should be contained in its prespecified *background knowledge* $\mathcal{BK}$ consisting of (i) the case base structure, (ii) integrity constraints, (iii) the case base itself, and (iv) additional knowledge for the many stages of the decision process.

Given a case base and a novel problem x^{new}, a CBR system should assign an appropriate solution y^{new}. More precisely, case-based reasoners suppose that $\mathcal{CB}$ follows an unknown relation $Sols \subseteq \mathcal{P} \times \mathcal{S}$ and its objective is to replicate its behaviour such that $(x^{new}, y^{new}) \in Sols$.

When confronted with a novel case x^{new}, CBR systems normally follow an architecture consisting of four distinct steps [1]:

1. *Retrieve* previously seen cases that are similar to the current one. This step is often performed by extracting the k cases from $\mathcal{CB}$ that maximize a similarity function (reflexive and symmetric) $sim : \mathcal{P} \times \mathcal{P} \mapsto [0, 1]$ between the case in question and x^{new}.
2. *Reuse* the retrieved cases from the previous step by selecting or integrating their solutions to produce a set of candidate solutions.
3. *Revise* the candidate solution(s) and adapt it(them) into a solution for x^{new}.
4. *Retain* the new solution after validation into the case base if necessary.

3.1   Representation

We will model our cases using a first-order logical language $\mathcal{L}$ as the one presented in Sect. 2.3. The solution space will be characterized by a set of (reserved) constants $\mathcal{S} = \{s_1, s_2, \ldots\}$. Then, we say that:

Definition 2 (Case). *A case base* $\mathcal{CB} = \{(x_i, y_i)\}_i$ *is a collection of (possibly non-unique) cases where* $y_i \in \mathcal{S}$, *and* x_i *is a set of ground atoms of the form* $P(a_1, \ldots, a_n)$ *or* $P(s, a_1, \ldots, a_n)$ *where* $s \in \mathcal{S}$, P *is a predicate and* $a_1, \ldots, a_n$ *are (non-solution) constants* $(\forall i, j, a_j \neq s_i)$ *of* $\mathcal{L}$.

The intuition behind this model is that the atoms of the form $P(a_1, \ldots, a_n)$ describe the scenario of the case, whereas $P(s, a_1, \ldots, a_n)$ are used to represent the properties of each possible solution, denoted by $s \in \mathcal{S}$. This representation will later allow us to encode the adaptation phase of the CBR cycle as a PILP problem as defined in the previous section.

In order to exemplify our framework, let us consider this example from [2]:

Example 1 (Assisted driver). We set ourselves in the context of an AI-equipped vehicle which can spontaneously take control from the human driver under dangerous circumstances. As such, each case revolves around either taking control of the vehicle, or doing nothing. These two options are always mutually exclusive. The characterization of the problem is given by a set of duties at stake. These are (i) prevention of collision, (ii) respect for driver autonomy, (iii) keeping within speed limit, and (iv) prevention of imminent harm to people.

More precisely, each case x_i is represented by a set of predicates of the form $Duty(Option, Value)$ where $Duty \in \{preventCollision, respectAutonomy, withinLimit, preventHarm\}$, $Option \in \{takeControl, doNothing\}$, $Value \in \{yes, no\}$, and each solution $y_i \in \{takeControl, doNothing\}$. For example, if a case contains the predicate $preventCollision(takeControl, yes)$, it would imply that taking control of the car in the current scenario guarantees preventing a collision. If a duty is not present in a case, it's deemed as irrelevant.

– Case 1: There is an object ahead in the driver's lane and the driver moves into another lane that is clear.

$$x_1 = \{preventCollision(takeControl, yes), respectAutonomy(takeControl, no),$$
$$preventCollision(doNothing, yes), respectAutonomy(doNothing, yes)\}$$

– Case 2: The driver has been going in and out of his/her lane with no objects discernible ahead.

$$x_2 = \{preventCollision(takeControl, yes), respectAutonomy(takeControl, no),$$
$$preventCollision(doNothing, yes), respectAutonomy(doNothing, yes)\}$$

– Case 3: The driver is speeding to take a passenger to a hospital. The GPS destination is set for a hospital.

$$x_3 = \{respectAutonomy(takeControl, no), withinLimit(takeControl, yes),$$
$$preventHarm(takeControl, no), respectAutonomy(doNothing, yes),$$
$$withinLimit(doNothing, no), preventHarm(doNothing, yes)\}$$

– Case 4: Driving alone, there is a bale of hay ahead in the driver's lane. There is a vehicle close behind that will run the driver's vehicle upon sudden braking and he/she can't change lanes, all of which can be determined by the system. The driver starts to brake.

$$x_4 = \{preventCollision(takeControl, no), respectAutonomy(takeControl, no),$$
$$preventHarm(takeControl, yes), preventCollision(doNothing, no),$$
$$respectAutonomy(doNothing, yes), preventHarm(doNothing, no)\}$$

3.2 Reasoning

Having defined our structure for cases, we can now describe our framework using the classical CBR cycle. As explained before, it's composed of four distinct phases, (i) *retrieval* of similar past cases, (ii) *reuse* of their solutions by integration, (iii) *revision* of candidate solutions, and (iv) *retention* of the new solution after validation.

Retrieval. Given a novel case (x, y) defined using our representation above, the reasoner searches for similar encountered cases in its base. Typically, CBR systems have a fixed limit $K \in \mathbb{N}$ of cases to retrieve. The system starts by determining the K past cases that maximize a similarity function $sim : \mathcal{P} \times \mathcal{P} \mapsto [0, 1]$. There are numerous ways of defining such a function in the literature [6]. For our purposes, we'll use a generic yet general weighted function:

$$sim(x_1, x_2) = \frac{\sum_{p \in A(\mathcal{CB})} w_p \times sim_p(x_1, x_2)}{\sum_{p \in A(\mathcal{CB})} w_p} \tag{1}$$

where $x_1, x_2 \in \mathcal{P}$ are two problems, $A(\mathcal{CB})$ is the set of all ground atoms of $\mathcal{L}$ in $\mathcal{CB}$, $sim_p(x_1, x_2)$ is a local similarity function, and $w_p \in \mathbb{R}_{>0}$ is an optional weight describing the relative importance of p.

For a given case base $\mathcal{CB}$, we denote the K most similar cases to problem $x \in \mathcal{P}$ as $sim_{\mathcal{CB}}^K(x) \subseteq \mathcal{P}$, containing exactly K elements if $|\mathcal{CB}| \geq K$, or all the problems in the base otherwise.

Adaptation. Then, the *reuse* and *revision* steps are implemented by (i) generalizing the solutions from $sim_{\mathcal{CB}}(x^{new})$ through PILP, and (ii) computing the probability that an answer is correct for x^{new} using the ProbLog semantics.

Step (i) reduces generalization to the PILP setting as in Procedure 1. Given a case base $\mathcal{CB}$, an input problem x^{new}, and its K most similar cases $sim_{\mathcal{CB}}^K(x^{new})$, the procedure reduces the adaptation of the these cases to a PILP problem.

The intuition behind this transformation is that it allows conflicting solutions for the same problem by defining p_i as the proportion of times the answer was chosen. In doing so, a PILP solver obtains as output a set of ProbLog rules of the form:

Procedure 1: Generalize results from the retrieval step using PILP

Input: Case base $\mathcal{CB}$, problem x^{new}, cases $C = sim^K_{\mathcal{CB}}(x^{new})$

Output: Hypothesis H

1 $E \leftarrow \{(answer(id_x, y), p_y)\}$ such that $(x, y) \in C$ are retrieved cases, 'id_x' maps a problem (set of ground atoms) to a (fresh) constant, '$answer$' is the target predicate of arity 2, and $p_y = \frac{|\{(x,y)\in C\}|}{|\{(x,y')\in C: y\neq y'\}|}$.

2 $B \leftarrow P(id_x, a_1, ..., a_n)$ (or, $P(id_x, s, a_1, ..., a_n)$) for each predicate $P(a_1, ..., a_n)$ (or, $P(s, a_1, ..., a_n)$) in x, for all $(x, y) \in C$.

3 Define $loss(H, B, E) = \sum_{(x_i,p_i)\in E} |P_s(B \cup H \models x_i) - p_i|)$ as in [8].

4 Define the space of possible clauses L_h such that:
   - Only allows the variabilized atom $answer(X, Y)$ in a rule's head.
   - Only allows atoms of the form $P(X, a_1, ..., a_n)$ or $P(X, Y, a_1, ..., a_n)$ where $P(a_1, ..., a_n)$ or $P(s, a_1, ..., a_n)$ are atoms appearing in C, respectively, X, Y are the variables appearing in the rule's head, and $a_1, ..., a_n$ remain as constants (are not replaced by variables).

5 Find a hypothesis $H \subseteq L_h$ such that $H = \underset{H'\subseteq L_h}{argmin} \ loss(H', B, E)$.

$$p_i :: answer(X, Y) \leftarrow P_{i_1}(X, a_{i_{1,1}}, ..., a_{i_{1,n_1}}), ..., P_{i_m}(X, a_{i_{m,1}}, ..., a_{i_{m,n_m}})$$
$$Q_{i_1}(X, Y, a_{i_{1,1}}, ..., a_{i_{1,n_1}}), ..., Q_{i_t}(X, Y, a_{i_{t,1}}, ..., a_{i_{t,n_t}})$$

where p_i is the probability annotation of the ProbLog rule, $answer(X, Y)$ the target predicate, P, Q body predicates, X, Y variables, and $a_{i_{j,k}}$ constants.

Example 2 (Assisted driver continued). Suppose $\mathcal{CB}$ is composed of 1 instance of each pair $(x_1, doNothing)$, $(x_2, takeControl)$, $(x_3, doNothing)$, $(x_4, takeControl)$ and 4 instances of $(x_2, doNothing)$, $(x_3, takeControl)$, $(x_4, doNothing)$. For this case base, a hypothesis that minimizes the loss function is the following:

$0.8 :: answer(A, B) \leftarrow preventHarm(A, B, yes), preventCollision(A, B, no)$

$0.8 :: answer(A, B) \leftarrow respectAutonomy(A, B, yes), preventHarm(A, B, yes)$

$0.2 :: answer(A, B) \leftarrow withinSpeedLimit(A, B, yes)$

$0.2 :: answer(A, B) \leftarrow preventCollision(A, B, yes)$

Notice that for ProbLog semantics, the last rule obtained by the solver, i.e.: $0.2 :: answer(A, B) \leftarrow preventCollision(A, B, yes)$, doesn't imply there is 0.2 probability of a solution being correct given that it prevents a collision, but rather, that there is a 0.2 chance that the rule itself is valid.

It's also worth mentioning that the space and time complexity of finding H depends on the PILP implementation. However, our transformation produces a knowledge base of size linear with respect to the amount of ground clauses in C

(retrieved cases). This in turn is extremely useful as various sizes K of similarity bounds can be tested at decision-making time. For a experimental analysis of an existing PILP solver please refer to [8]. A more in depth theoretical analysis of the time and space complexity of our framework as a whole is left for future work.

Step (ii) of the adaptation phase consists of executing a ProbLog solver [8] using the hypothesis H obtained from phase (i), (optional) background knowledge B that can be used to enforce certain behaviour at decision-making time, and the ground atoms in the current problem x^{new}. In summary this ProbLog program consists of:

1. H the hypothesis obtained from step (i), i.e.: a set of ProbLog rules with head $answer(X, Y)$,
2. B the (optional) background knowledge,
3. All facts of the form $P(id_{x^{new}}, a_1, \ldots, a_n)$ or $P(id_{x^{new}}, s, a_1, \ldots, a_n)$ contained in x^{new}, where $id_{x^{new}}$ is a (fresh) constant, and
4. A query $q = answer(id_{x^{new}}, Y)$ where Y is the variable to be grounded.

Example 3 (Assisted driver continued). Consider the novel case 5, characterized by:

$$x_5 = \{respectAutonomy(takeControl, no), preventHarm(takeControl, no),$$
$$preventCollision(takeControl, yes), respectAutonomy(doNothing, yes),$$
$$preventHarm(doNothing, yes), preventCollision(doNothing, yes)\}$$

Computing the query $q = answer(x_5, Y)$ for the hypothesis H obtained in the previous part of the example, and adding the ground facts of x_5, gives us:

$$answer(x_5, doNothing) : 0.84$$
$$answer(x_5, takeControl) : 0.2$$

With the result of step (ii), the response of our CBR framework is determined by the solution with the highest probability of being correct according to the ProbLog solver. Notice that the sum of the probabilities don't have to add up to 1, because we want to allow multiple solutions to be valid at the same time, which can be useful depending on the application domain.

Retention. Finally, the last step of the CBR cycle is implemented by adding the case with the infered solution after validation from a human user, if retention is necessary in the application domain's context. Because our main focus was on the adaptation phase, we leave other retention strategies [7] for future work.

4 Implementation

Having defined the overall idea of our framework in the previous section, here we'll describe our current implementation and the technologies involved in it. Figure 1 depicts the high-level architecture of our CBR system.

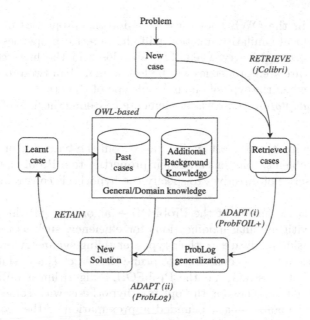

Fig. 1. Overview of the architecture of our CBR system

For the representation of our framework, we used a simplified version of CBROnto [10], an OWL-based domain-agnostic ontology for representing CBR systems. CBROnto allows to define cases, complex properties, similarity measures, and many other useful elements for a CBR system. At the same time, it can combat the main problem of knowledge-intensive CBR systems, the 'knowledge acquisition bottleneck' by reusing knowledge from other ontology libraries to create complex knowledge structures. This choice of design was useful twofold: (i) it facilitated case and general knowledge elicitation by organizing the information in a generic yet extensible manner, and (ii) it allowed the system to reuse previous research work based on CBROnto.

Our system was mainly developed using the Java language, and is comprised of several subsystems that implement the different phases of the CBR cycle.

The *retrieval* step is performed by using jColibri [16] as a Java library. jColibri is an adaptable CBR framework and full-fledged system that offers an overarching architecture for the phases of case-based reasoning. In our case, we mainly used the library version for the *retrieval* and *retention* steps. It allowed us to easily parse and query the OWL knowledge base in order to retrieve the K most similar cases while being flexible enough to implement our own similarity measures.

As for the similarity-based retrieval function, we used a modified version of the one described in Eq. 1. In our version, the local similarity measure used was the *fdeep* function mentioned in [16]. This method utilizes the hierarchical description-logics based similarity of the ontology to determine which properties of two problems are similar. In other words, given a complex hierarchy of types and subtypes in the OWL knowledge base for the properties of a case base problem, this local similarity function will characterize properties as having a higher measure of similarity when they are closer in the hierarchy tree. For example, two unrelated properties will be less similar than two properties of the same type, or when the type of one in a subtype of the other.

Next, the *adaptation* phase was implemented as along the lines of the previous section:

1. After retrieving the K most similar cases from the base, our program translates the problems, solutions and their properties to a ProbLog program and appends a series of directives to specify the hypothesis constraints as in Procedure 1.
2. Then, it runs a version of the ProbFOIL+ algorithm [8] which is publicly available[1] with minimal modifications for efficiency, such as restricting the constants inside predicates to their types, enabling symmetry breaking and a set of generic integrity constraints to prune the search space while preserving generality. Let us stress that the ProbFOIL+ algorithm is an approximate algorithm that searches for the optimal hypothesis with some greedy subroutines and maintaining a bounded approximation of the score of partial answers. As such, we found that these integrity constraints had a considerable impact in the efficiency of the algorithm. For more information, please refer to the implementation link below.
3. Subsequently, our system parses the result of the ProbFOIL+ algorithm and it appends them with the description of the novel case. This in turn generates a ProbLog program that is run with its standard implementation[2]. The mechanism for transforming this information to a ProbLog program is straightforward, and we only add the queries before execution time.
4. Finally, the result of the ProbLog program is parsed and our system choses the solution for which the success probability as described previously is the highest.

The implementation of our system is publicly available[3].

5   Experimentation

For our experiments, we constructed a dataset from an online game-like survey based on the TV series 'Breaking bad', in which users were presented with various ethically nuanced situations and given a set of possible alternatives to choose from. Users chose a character from TV series and where tasked to give a series of 5–7 answers for the series of questions that guided the overall story leading into one of many possible paths. In total, we acquired over 150 user histories with an average of 6 answers for each user.

---

[1] https://bitbucket.org/problog/prob2foil/.

[2] https://github.com/ML-KULeuven/problog.

[3] https://github.com/martinjedwabny/cbr-edm.

Similar to the running example, we represented the problem x in each case (x, y) by the duties each solution fulfills. I.e. as a set of values $Duty(Option, Value)$ where $Duty \in \{fidelity, reparation, gratitude, non-maleficence, beneficence, self-improvement, justice\}$, $Option$ a possible solution for the problem, and $Value \in \{extremely\text{-}bad, really\text{-}bad, bad, neutral, good, really\text{-}good, extremely\text{-}good\}$.

These duties were inspired by Ross's [18] theory of *prima facie* duties:

- Fidelity: strive to keep promises and be honest.
- Reparation: make amends when we have wronged someone.
- Gratitude: repay others when they perform actions that benefit us.
- Non-maleficence: refrain from harming others in any way.
- Beneficence: improve other peoples health and well-being.
- Self-improvement: improve our own health and well-being.
- Justice: be fair and try to distribute benefits and burdens evenly.

Each answer provided by the users was stored using our OWL case base architecture as a pair (x, y) with x as described before and y the solution chosen from a predefined set of choices which was described in natural language.

We evaluated our system by in two ways, a quantitative and a qualitative manner. These tests were performed at least 10 times each and the numbers depicted in the figures represent averages over these runs. They were performed in a 1,6 GHz Intel Core i5 computer with 8 GB 2133 MHz LPDDR3 RAM.

The first experiment was designed to test the computational cost of the proposed mechanisms. In particular, we tested for different choices of K, the added cost of the retrieval and adaptation phases, of which, unsurprisingly the generalization step inside of the adaptation was the most costly. We can see the results in Fig. 2. For reference, when $K = 50$ the total amount of facts produced by our translation of this form was around 250, and over 550 in total counting past solution examples and data-type predicates. Using our current system, we can see the adaptation time growing steadily. In practice, the system could handle cases up until $K = 50$ in at most around 2 min. However, finer grained experimentation would be required in future work to determine the acceptable bounds of the execution time.

Then second, we tested the quality of the generalizations made by testing over a reserved dataset containing 16 situations, and inserting the rest in the case base. An example of an answer obtained during these tests is the one shown in Fig. 3.

We analysed the quality of the answer using the loss equation defined before: $loss(H, B, E) = \sum_{(x_i, p_i) \in E} |P_s(B \cup H \models x_i) - p_i|)$. Table 1 shows the results obtained. As we can see, the loss is relatively similar for $K = 10$ and $K = 20$ and then degrades heavily. For reference, the predicted probabilities were tested against the 16 situations with 2 possible solutions each, making up for a total of 32 ground atoms to predict, and a maximum loss of 32 (the sum of the absolute values of their differences). The results, while showing room for improvement, seem reasonable enough especially considering the complexity of ethical decision making. With a simple model of ethics as the one presented here, the system

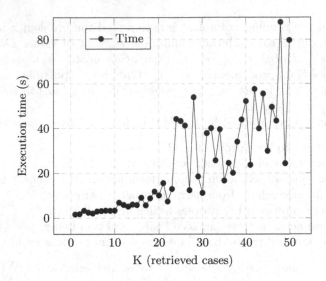

Fig. 2. Running time assessment

$0.43877551 :: answer(A, B) \leftarrow hasDuty(A, B,' justice',' really\_good')$.

$0.55555556 :: answer(A, B) \leftarrow hasDuty(A, B,' beneficence',' really\_good')$.

$0.5 :: answer(A, B) \leftarrow hasDuty(A, B,' honesty',' good')$.

$0.2 :: answer(A, B) \leftarrow hasDuty(A, B,' non\_maleficence',' really\_good')$.

Fig. 3. Example result of the adaptation step

could consistently predict reasonable answers in this domain. However, a greater K didn't improve the results, potentially showing that only including the most related cases in our domain can improve the performance of our system, and large K values degraded it by including less related ones. Moreover, it would be interesting to see what results our system would get with a finer characterization of the domain.

Table 1. Testing loss as the sum of absolute errors

K	10	20	30	50
Loss	9.581	9.874	12.464	10.224

6   Conclusion

We have developed a framework for case-based reasoning which can handle noisy datasets and provide explainable solutions to novel cases by profiting from the adaptability of the probabilistic inductive logic programming setting. Then, we described the implementation of our system, which is publicly available, making it easier to specify cases and elicit knowledge by utilizing various state-of-the-art technologies from the representation to the retrieval and adaptation stages of our system. We have depicted how our system fares against a real-world inspired scenario in the context of a ethical dilemmas and shown results from the computational complexity and qualitative viewpoints.

Discussion. As mentioned in [1], CBR differs from machine learning approaches in that it favours learning from experience as a natural by-product of problem solving, as opposed to generalizing from it. Our work adds to this research venue by proposing a further technique with which uncertainty can be handled in CBR systems. Concretely, we combine the ideas of CBR and probabilistic inductive logic programming by generalizing/learning only after the similarity-based retrieval step from CBR systems.

By leveraging the noise-handling capabilities of ProbFOIL+, our system can also be seen as a contribution to soft case-based reasoning [15]. This in turn, shows the adaptability and generality of the probabilistic logic setting, which has also been previously used to develop explainable AI systems in other subfields, such as decision-making [4] and recommender systems [5].

The manner in which our framework handles uncertainty is also related to multi-criteria fuzzy decision making systems [12] in that it allows multiple decision makers to provide different answers for the same problem, which our system uses to compute a consensus. However, our CBR adds two layers to the reasoning process, namely the similarity-based case selection which filters decisions to the most relevant cases, and secondly the abstraction layer in the form of background knowledge which can be used to extend the properties of cases and potentially use different past cases to compute the answer of a novel one.

From a XAI perspective, our framework is a contribution to *transparent* systems [3], by making it easy for the user to understand the reasoning process, and increasing the confidence in the solution of the system by making the reasoning steps of the CBR cycle depend on well-defined rules.

Future Work. We wish to expand our work in the scale of experimentation and compare the quality of our results to other similar CBR systems. It would also be interesting to compare the performance of our reduction of the adaptation step in the CBR cycle to other different encodings. In addition, other datasets coming from both knowledge-intensive and knowledge-light CBR domains could be used to test our implementation.

References

1. Aamodt, A., Plaza, E.: Case-based reasoning: foundational issues, methodological variations, and system approaches. AI Commun. **7**(1), 39–59 (1994)

2. Anderson, M., Anderson, S.L.: Geneth: a general ethical dilemma analyzer. Paladyn J. Behav. Robot. **9**(1), 337–357 (2018)
3. Arrieta, A.B., et al.: Explainable artificial intelligence (XAI): concepts, taxonomies, opportunities and challenges toward responsible AI. Inf. Fusion **58**, 82–115 (2020)
4. Van den Broeck, G., Thon, I., Van Otterlo, M., De Raedt, L.: Dtproblog: A decision-theoretic probabilistic prolog. In: Proceedings of the AAAI Conference on Artificial Intelligence, vol. 24 (2010)
5. Catherine, R., Cohen, W.: Personalized recommendations using knowledge graphs: a probabilistic logic programming approach. In: Proceedings of the 10th ACM Conference on Recommender Systems, pp. 325–332 (2016)
6. Cunningham, P.: A taxonomy of similarity mechanisms for case-based reasoning. IEEE Trans. Knowl. Data Eng. **21**(11), 1532–1543 (2008)
7. De Mantaras, R.L., et al.: Retrieval, reuse, revision and retention in case-based reasoning. Knowl. Eng. Rev. **20**(3), 215–240 (2005)
8. De Raedt, L., Dries, A., Thon, I., Van den Broeck, G., Verbeke, M.: Inducing probabilistic relational rules from probabilistic examples. In: Proceedings of 24th International Joint Conference on Artificial Intelligence (IJCAI), vol. 2015, pp. 1835–1842. IJCAI-INT JOINT CONF ARTIF INTELL (2015)
9. De Raedt, L., Kimmig, A.: Probabilistic (logic) programming concepts. Mach. Learn. **100**(1), 5–47 (2015). https://doi.org/10.1007/s10994-015-5494-z
10. Díaz-Agudo, B., González-Calero, P.A.: Cbronto: a task/method ontology for CBR. In: Proceedings of the 15th International FLAIRS, vol. 2, pp. 101–106 (2002)
11. Getoor, L., Taskar, B.: Statistical relational learning (2007)
12. Hong, D.H., Choi, C.H.: Multicriteria fuzzy decision-making problems based on vague set theory. Fuzzy Sets Syst. **114**(1), 103–113 (2000)
13. Kolodner, J.L.: An introduction to case-based reasoning. Artif. Intell. Rev. **6**(1), 3–34 (1992)
14. Muggleton, S.: Inverse entailment and progol. New Gener. Comput. **13**(3–4), 245–286 (1995)
15. Pal, S.K., Shiu, S.C.: Foundations of Soft Case-Based Reasoning, vol. 8, Wiley, Hoboken (2004)
16. Recio-Garía, J.A., Díaz-Agudo, B.: Ontology based CBR with jCOLIBRI. In: Ellis R., Allen T., Tuson A. (eds.) Applications and Innovations in Intelligent Systems XIV. SGAI 2006, pp. 149–162. Springer, London (2006). https://doi.org/10.1007/978-1-84628-666-7_12
17. Ribeiro, M.T., Singh, S., Guestrin, C.: Why should i trust you? explaining the predictions of any classifier. In: Proceedings of the 22nd ACM SIGKDD International Conference on Knowledge Discovery and Data Mining, pp. 1135–1144 (2016)
18. Ross, D., Ross, W.D.: The Right and the Good. Oxford University Press, Oxford (2002)
19. Sato, T.: A statistical learning method for logic programs with distribution semantics. In: ICLP (1995)
20. Slade, S.: Case-based reasoning: a research paradigm. AI Mag. **12**(1), 42–42 (1991)
21. Sørmo, F., Cassens, J., Aamodt, A.: Explanation in case-based reasoning-perspectives and goals. Artif. Intell. Rev. **24**(2), 109–143 (2005)

Short Technical Stream Papers

Detection of Brain Tumour Using Deep Learning

Waqar Ahmed and Savas Konur[(⊠)]

Department of Computer Science, University of Bradford, Bradford, UK
{wahmed22,s.konur}@bradford.ac.uk

Abstract. Brain tumour is an uncontrollable growth of abnormal cells in the brain that may lead to cancer. Tumours are detected and diagnosed by manually analyzing Magnetic Resonance Imaging (MRI) scans. It is a time and resource consuming process which leads to prolonged waiting times for brain tumour patients and adversely affect their life expectancy. Deep learning has been widely researched to automate this process. Previous studies conducted in this area have not systematically analyzed how different factors affect the accuracy rate of a Convolutional Neural Network (CNN). These factors include the size of the dataset, data augmentation and the number epochs used in a model. This paper addresses these issues by proposing a workflow that systematically analyses the contributing factors to a CNN's accuracy. The results from the proposed methodology show that the size of the dataset and data augmentation are some of the important factors which affect the accuracy rates of a CNN model.

Keywords: Machine learning · Deep learning · Classification · CNN · Brain tumour

1 Introduction

Manual analysis of MRI to detect brain tumours is a time and resource consuming process which is prone to perceptual and cognitive errors and may affect the timely treatment of the disease [9]. Recently, deep learning algorithms and CNN's in particular have achieved an accuracy of up to 98% in the detection of brain tumours and are believed to be a potential solution to automate the process of tumour detection [7, 8].

Hossain et al. [1] used small sized dataset and achieved a high accuracy, however, the factors leading to the results were not systematically analyzed. Similarly, the system proposed by P Gokila Brinda et al. [2] was applied to a larger dataset but no data augmentation was applied. Although the results were compelling but the paper does not mention the factors leading to the accuracy rate. The model proposed by Siar et al. [3] used a larger and achieved a high accuracy but factors leading to the results were not specified.

In this paper, we aim to address the factors mentioned above which may limit the performance of a CNN, which includes data size, data augmentation and number of epochs in a model. Here, we present a CNN which uses a combination of a larger dataset and data augmentation with a high number of epochs and systematically analyses the factors that may contribute to a CNN's accuracy.

© Springer Nature Switzerland AG 2021
M. Bramer and R. Ellis (Eds.): SGAI-AI 2021, LNAI 13101, pp. 133–138, 2021.
https://doi.org/10.1007/978-3-030-91100-3_10

A dataset of 3000 MRI images is initially used in a CNN model with 250 epochs. In the next step, data augmentation is employed and the model is retrained with the same parameters. The results from both models suggest that dataset size, number of epochs and data augmentation play an important role in the performance of a CNN model. The paper is organized as follows. Sect. 2 summarizes the related work. Sect. 3 presents the methodology applied in this paper. Sect. 4 presents the experimental results. Sect. 5 concludes the paper and discusses our future work.

2   Related Work

A CNN is a class of deep learning networks which commonly deals with image classification and computer vision [4]. It is composed of multiple layers which are connected to each other through artificial neurons. A neuron receives an input signal, processes the signal and produces an output. The final layer compiles all the inputs and produces an output which is based on all of the outputs from the previous layers.

A 5-Layer CNN was trained and tested on a dataset of 217 images [1]. Image size was set to $64 \times 64 \times 3$ pixels. A convolution kernel with 32 filters of size 3×3 was applied. Rectified Linear Unit (ReLU) was used as the activation function. The dataset was divided for training and testing with the ratio of 70:30 and 80:20 at two stages. Data augmentation was applied and the model achieved an accuracy of 97.87% after 9 epochs. In Siar et al. [3] a 5-Layer CNN used a dataset of 1892 images and achieved an accuracy of 98.67%. In the next stage, a clustering algorithm was combined with a CNN and a softmax classifier which increased the accuracy to 99.12%. No data augmentation technique was mentioned in the methodology. P Gokila Brinda et al. [2] Presented a CNN based on five convolution and five Max Pooling layers. The model was trained and tested on a dataset of 2065 MRI images using 200 epochs and achieved an accuracy of 94%. Data augmentation was not mentioned in the methodology. In this paper it is studied, how the data size, data augmentation and number of epochs effect the accuracy of a CNN model.

3   Methodology

The dataset was obtained from (https://www.kaggle.com/ahmedhamada0/brain-tumor-detection). The dataset contained 3000 MRI images.

3.1   Workflow

The dataset is given as input to the program. The details of the dataset: folder name, categories and number of images are displayed to the user. The category named "yes" contains tumorous images whereas the category named "no" contains non-tumorous images. A batch size of 32 is defined, prediction is compared to output variable after the completion of each batch [5]. The dataset is split into training and validation data with the ratio of 80% and 20%, respectively. The pixel values in the images are scaled down by a factor of 255. After rescaling the dataset is given as input to the CNN model. Initially the model is trained and tested on the original dataset using 250 epochs. In the next step, data augmentation with random rotation, flip and zoom is applied to the dataset and the model is retrained with same parameters.

3.2 CNN Model Architecture

The proposed CNN includes an input layer, a rescaling layer followed by 3 convolution and 3 Max Pooling layers followed by flatten, dense and an output layer. The input layer receives the image in the original shape (180 × 180 pixels). The image is rescaled into values between 0–255 in the rescaling layer. The first convolution layer consist of 16 feature maps with the kernel size of (3 × 3). The second and third convolution layers consist of 32 and 64 feature maps respectively. The kernel from the convolution layer extracts useful features from the image. Rectified Linear Unit (ReLU) is the activation function used in the proposed CNN and mathematically represented as follows.

$$Y = \text{Activation}\left(\sum (\text{weight} * \text{input}) + \text{bias}\right) \tag{1}$$

The convolution layer passes the data onto the Max Pooling layers where the dimensionality of the data is reduced. The flatten layer converts the incoming data into a 1D array (vector). The data from the flatten layer is received by the dense layer which is composed of 128 neurons. The data is then passed onto the output layer which consists of 2 neurons which is equal to the number of categories. The dimensionality reduction and feature extraction can be observed in Fig. 1.

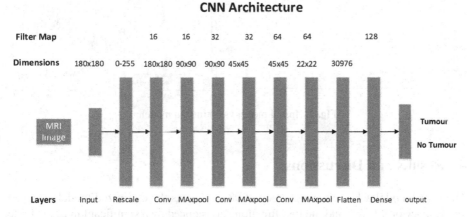

Fig. 1. Image dimensionality reduction and feature extraction in the CNN.

3.3 Compile CNN Model

To compile the model we defined the loss function, optimizer and metrics. The loss function used in the proposed model is "sparse_categorical_crossentropy". It is commonly used for multiclass classification. Formally it is designed to quantify the difference between probability distributions. Adam is an adaptive learning rate method which is used as optimizer in the proposed model [6]. The third parameter in the compilation of the model is accuracy. It is defined as the number of correct predictions made by the model over all the predictions made.

3.4 Model Evaluation and Optimization

The initial model achieved an accuracy of 98%, however, the accuracy values were fluctuating and a high loss function was being produced. To address this issue, data augmentation with random rotation of (0.1), random flip and a random zoom of (0.1) and a dropout of (0.2) was applied to the dataset. The model was then retrained using the same parameters. The optimized model provided better results and achieved an accuracy of 99.95%. The results from both models are shown in Fig. 2.

Normal Data   Data Augmentation

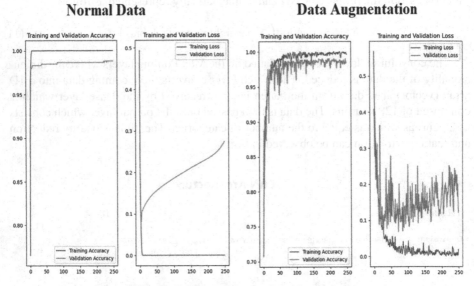

Fig. 2. Initial model vs optimized model.

4   Results and Discussions

The initial model achieved an accuracy of 98% whereas the optimized model achieved an accuracy of 99.95% and the loss function was reduced by a significant margin. Table 1 represent the results from both models and it can be observed that the optimized model achieve a higher accuracy rate with no fluctuation in the accuracy.

The results from this experiment signify that the factors which contributed to a higher accuracy are: larger dataset, higher number of epochs and data augmentation. Although, these techniques have been mentioned in previous studies but a combination of all these factors in a single experiment is not mentioned. Table 2 compares the methodology of the proposed system to previous studies.

The results obtained from the initial CNN model and the optimized CNN model clearly signify that the size of the dataset, number of epochs and data augmentation are some of the important factors which contribute to a higher accuracy rate. The proposed model achieve an accuracy of 99.95% which is higher than those of previous studies. Table 3 compares the results of this study with previous studies.

Table 1. Results comparison, normal data and data augmentation.

MRI and actual class		No data augmentation		Data augmentation	
Image	Actual class	Predicted class	Accuracy	Predicted class	Accuracy
No1	No	No	51%	NO	99.99%
No2	No	No	76%	NO	99.74%
No3	No	No	92%	NO	98.90%
Yes2	Yes	Yes	84%	YES	99.95%
Yes3	Yes	Yes	96%	YES	99.99%

Table 2. Methodology comparison of the proposed system with previous studies.

CNN by	Dataset size	Epochs	Data augmentation
Hossain et al. [1]	217	9	Yes
P Gokila Brinda et al. [2]	2065	200	No
Siar et al. [3]	1892	Not specified	No
Proposed CNN	3000	250	Yes

Table 3. Accuracy comparison to previous studies.

Methodology	Classification success
P Gokila Brinda et al. [2]	94%
Hossain et al. [1]	97.87%
Siar et al. [3]	99.12%
Proposed CNN model	99.95%

5   Conclusion and Future Work

The proposed CNN model achieved an accuracy of 99.95% with a split of 80:20 of 3000 images. The results suggest that large sized dataset with a high number of epochs and data augmentation lead to a higher accuracy rate. The previous studies do not mention the combination of all these factors combine in a single experiment. Although the proposed model achieved a higher accuracy rate, further study needs to be conducted on datasets from different sources, since machine learning has a high error-susceptibility which means that a biased dataset may lead to biased results.

In the future, we plan to work on larger datasets from different sources with different settings to analyze this model for further improvement. The results obtained in this experiments suggest that deep learning may potentially automate the process of brain tumour detection and assist clinical decisions in future. This study may lay foundation for further research in this area.

Acknowledgements. The work presented in this paper is supported by EPSRC research grant EP/R043787/1.

References

1. Hossain, T., Shishir, F.S., Ashraf, M., Al Nasim, A., Shah, F.M.: Brain tumor detection using convolutional neural network. In: 1st International Conference on Advances in Science, Engineering and Robotics Technology, pp. 1–6. ICASERT (2019)
2. Brindha, P.G., Kavinraj, M., Manivasakam, P., Prasanth, P.: Brain tumor detection from MRI images using deep learning techniques. In: IOP Conference Series: Materials Science and Engineering (2021). https://doi.org/10.1088/1757-899x/1055/1/012115
3. Siar, M., Teshnehlab, M.: Brain tumor detection using deep neural network and machine learning algorithm. In: 9th International Conference on Computer and Knowledge Engineering, pp. 363–368. ICCKE (2019)
4. Yamashita, R., Nishio, M., Do, R.K.G., Togashi, K.: Convolutional neural networks: an overview and application in radiology. Insights Imaging **9**(4), 611–629 (2018). https://doi.org/10.1007/s13244-018-0639-9
5. Brownlee, J.: Difference Between a Batch and an Epoch in a Neural Network. shorturl.at/desH0
6. Bushaev, V.: Adam—Latest Trends in Deep Learning Optimization. shorturl.at/wGOT8.
7. Ari, A., Hanbay, D.: Deep learning based brain tumor classification and detection system. Turk. J. Electr. Eng. Comput. Sci. **26**, 2275–2286 (2018)
8. Cruz, J.A., Wishart, D.S.: Applications of machine learning in cancer prediction. Cancer Inf. **2**, 59–77 (2006)
9. Nazir, M., Shakil, S., Khurshid, K.: Role of deep learning in brain tumour detection and classification. Comput. Med. Imaging Graph. **91**, 101940 (2021)

GaussianProductAttributes: Density-Based Distributed Representations for Products

Hossein Ghodrati Noushahr[(✉)], Jeremy Levesley, Samad Ahmadi,
and Evgeny Mirkes

University of Leicester, Leicester, UK
{hgn2,jl1,s.ahmadi,em322}@leicester.ac.uk

Abstract. Multivariate Gaussian probability distributions have been used as distributed representations for text. In comparison with traditional vector representations, these density-based representations are able to model uncertainty, inclusion and entailment. We present a model to learn such representations for products based on a public e-commerce dataset. We qualitatively analyse the properties of the proposed model and how the learned representations capture semantic relatedness, similarity and entailment between products and text.

Keywords: Representation learning · Distributional semantics · Machine learning · E-commerce

1 Introduction

Distributed representations in form of lower dimensional vectors for words have seen a dramatic increase in research and real-world applications in recent years. Inspired by this, the same idea was pursued for entire sentences, paragraphs or documents. In the domain of e-commerce, product embeddings have become popular, but mostly applied in the context of recommender systems.

Vilnis and McCallum [9] presented a new form of word embeddings where each word is represented by a probability distribution. These density-based representations caught the attention of the research community and triggered a sequence of new research directions including theoretical foundations and specific applications. The representation of words by multivariate Gaussian probability distributions makes it possible to model uncertainty, inclusion and entailment [9].

We propose *GaussianProductAttributes*, a model to learn density-based distributed embeddings for products based on multivariate Gaussian distributions in this paper. While the product embeddings are the primary output of the model, representations for words (text), e-commerce companies and product categories (attributes) are also learned. This model allows us to estimate inclusion and entailment between words that describe a product and the product itself.

© Springer Nature Switzerland AG 2021
M. Bramer and R. Ellis (Eds.): SGAI-AI 2021, LNAI 13101, pp. 139–145, 2021.
https://doi.org/10.1007/978-3-030-91100-3_11

The main contributions of this paper are 1) a novel technique to learn dense representations for products, 2) an extensive qualitative evaluation of the learned representations, and 3) an analysis that sheds light on the general patterns and specific exceptions how entailment is modeled with the learned representations.

2   Related Work

Traditional distributed representations for words are *vectors* [6,7]. Vilnis and McCallum [9] propose a model to learn distributed representations that are *densities*. These *probabilistic embeddings* are implemented via multivariate Gaussian probability distributions. The aim is to better capture uncertainty about a representation and its relationships and to measure asymmetries [9]. The similarity between two words is measured by the *expected likelihood* or *probability product kernel* [4] in the symmetric case, and the *Kullback-Leibler (KL) divergence* [5] in the asymmetric case. Athiwaratkun and Wilson [1] built an extension of the probabilistic embedding idea that can be *multimodal*.

Grbovic et al. [3] introduced *prod2vec*, a model to find low-dimensional representations for products. The model is based on Word2Vec and shopper's purchase sequences are treated as sentences where each individual purchased product resembles a word [3]. Products with similar contexts will have similar vector representations, that is, products that are bought frequently together by shoppers will be embedded in the same vector space [3].

Meta-Prod2Vec, first introduced by Vasile et al. [8], is another extension of the prod2vec model that leverages categorical product attributes to learn representations. These attributes are included in the training algorithm in that they are treated as additional "words" in the artificial "sentences" [8]. Meta-Prod2Vec can be considered a collaborative filtering method that overcomes the *cold-start problem*.

3   GaussianProductAttributes

In this section, we present *GaussianProductAttributes*, a model to learn density-based distributed embeddings for words, products, companies, and product categories, purely based on product attributes. Each word, product, company and product category is represented by a multivariate Gaussian distribution $\mathcal{N}$ with mean vector μ and covariance matrix Σ. μ and Σ are initialised by sampling from a random variable for all words.

GaussianProductAttributes builds on top of Skip-gram's initial procedure [7] to find word representations that have high predictive power to identify surrounding words in a sentence. We extend this approach and perform a multi-objective optimisation to find 1) product representations that have high predictive power identifying words that appear in the product title, 2) company representations that have high predictive power to identify products they list on their website, and 3) product category representations that have high predictive power to identify products assigned to the category.

The model parameters $\theta = \{\mu_i, \Sigma_i\}, i \in N$ are learned via energy-based optimisation, minimising the *Bhattacharyya distance* D_B [2] between two multivariate Gaussian probability distributions $\mathcal{N}_1$ and $\mathcal{N}_2$:

$$D_B(\mathcal{N}_1, \mathcal{N}_2) = \frac{1}{8}(\mu_1 - \mu_2)^T \Sigma^{-1} (\mu_1 - \mu_2) + \frac{1}{2} \ln \left(\frac{\det \Sigma}{\sqrt{\det \Sigma_1 \det \Sigma_2}} \right) \quad (1)$$

where $\Sigma = (\Sigma_1 + \Sigma_2)/2$ and N is the number of words, products, companies and product categories. More formally, given a sequence of words $w_1, w_2, w_3, \cdots, w_T$ describing a product p, sold by company o and belonging to a category l, the objective of ProductAttributes is to minimise the maximum-margin *Hinge* loss L with regard to the model parameters θ in Eq. 2:

$$
\begin{aligned}
L(\theta) = \frac{1}{T} \sum_{t=1}^{T} &\left[\sum_{-c \le j \le c, j \ne 0} \sum_{k_w=1}^{K_w} max \left(0, m + D_B(\mathcal{N}_{w_t}, \mathcal{N}_{w_j}) - D_B(\mathcal{N}_{w_t}, \mathcal{N}_{w_{k_w}}) \right) \right. \\
&\left. + \sum_{k_p=1}^{K_p} max \left(0, m + D_B(\mathcal{N}_{w_t}, \mathcal{N}_p) - D_B(\mathcal{N}_{w_t}, \mathcal{N}_{p_{k_p}}) \right) \right] \\
&+ \sum_{k_m=1}^{K_m} max \left(0, m + D_B(\mathcal{N}_p, \mathcal{N}_o) - D_B(\mathcal{N}_p, \mathcal{N}_{o_{k_o}}) \right) \\
&+ \sum_{k_l=1}^{K_l} max \left(0, m + D_B(\mathcal{N}_p, \mathcal{N}_l) - D_B(\mathcal{N}_p, \mathcal{N}_{l_{k_l}}) \right) \quad (2)
\end{aligned}
$$

where D_B is the Bhattacharyya distance and c the size of the context. K_w, K_p, K_o and K_l are the number of negative samples for words, products, companies and categories drawn from the respective noise distributions $P_n(w)$, $P_n(p)$, $P_n(o)$ and $P_n(l)$.

4   Evaluation

We use the *MWPD2020 - Task 2* dataset [10] to train the GaussianProductAttributes model and perform two qualitative evaluation tasks on the learned embeddings: similarities and entailment. For the former, we inspect the results of similarity-based retrieval of words and products for a given query. For the latter, we inspect whether the embeddings learned are able to capture the concept of entailment measured by the KL divergence. Standard datasets and evaluation tasks for product embeddings do exist mostly in the domain of recommender system research and more traditional classification problems. To the best of our knowledge, there are no dedicated evaluation datasets to capture the quality of distributed representations for products similar to the word analogy task [6,7]. For this reason, no quantitative evaluation is performed.

4.1   Similarities

We inspect the most similar words that were retrieved for a given query word. The similarity is measured by the previously presented Bhattacharyya distance D_B. Table 1 lists the results for 10 representative words. The retrieved words are semantically related, e.g. 'shirt' and 'sweatshirt,' 'hoodie' and 'pullover,' 'bag' and 'tote,' 'adidas' and 'polo' or 'printer' and 'laserjet.' But also some results that look not relevant at first sight turn out to be related upon further inspection. Saris, Vilano and Thule are companies that produce products related to bicycles. The more obvious example holds also true for watches: Rolex, Tissot or Seiko.

Table 1. Most similar words for a given query word in descending order measured by the Bhattacharyya distance D_B.

Query	Similar words in descending order
Shirt	Sweatshirt zip pullover flannel polo sleeve hoodie secondary cufflinks 47
Hoodie	Pullover sweatshirt shorts denim polo zip cufflinks shirt sweatpants skirt
Bag	Tote denim duffel duffle name messenger reusable marissa mcarthur franchise
Adidas	Polo jacket shorts men sweatshirt zip scarf cufflinks maternity tcu
Printer	Laserjet mfp multifunction officejet copier scanner 9050 ultra3 multifunctional tlz10
Scanner	Kodak dura printer equestrian mfp copier raglan jessica tlz10 woven
Watch	Swiss rolex tissot dial chronograph colosseum superdry seiko aquatimer gucci
Toddler	Name sweatshirt polo splatter ponytail scarf pullover girls crossbody skirt
Oil	Essential lemon cuticle peppermint seed neem fenugreek castor ml organic
Bike	Bicycle saris recumbent vilano hitch road shimano thule rockymounts suspension

4.2   Entailment

We use the KL divergence between two multivariate Gaussian distributions that represent two concepts such as words, products, companies or product categories to measure the entailment of one concept by the other. We denote this by $c_2 \models c_1$ where all instances of c_2 are (part of) $c1$. More formally, c_1 encompasses c_2 if $KL(c_2||c_1) < KL(c_1||c_2)$.

Our first qualitative entailment evaluation focuses on the GPC product categories. For the Level 1 clothing category '67000000_Clothing' we retrieve the most similar Level 3 classes as measured by the Bhattacharyya distance D_B (Table 2). We can see that nine out of the ten most similar Level 3 classes belong to the clothing category. We now check for each of these nine Level 3 clothing categories if the top-level category (c_1) entails the more granular Level 3 category (c_3) or vice versa and each of the nine cases $KL(c_3||c_1) < KL(c_1||c_3)$ holds true.

Table 2. Most similar Level 3 classes for Level 1 class '67000000_Clothing' (c_1) in descending order measured by the Bhattacharyya distance D_B and pairwise KL divergence between c_1 and other Level 3 classes (c_3).

Level 3 class	D_B	$KL(c_3||c_1)$	$KL(c_1||c_3)$
67010100_Clothing Accessories	0.12767	0.48231	0.55097
67010800_Upper Body Wear/Tops	0.13813	0.50417	0.61831
67010300_Lower Body Wear/Bottoms	0.14669	0.56757	0.62251
67010200_Full Body Wear	0.15267	0.55476	0.69020
67010700_Underwear	0.17933	0.70366	0.75286
67010900_Protective Wear	0.20814	0.77453	0.91736
67010500_Sleepwear	0.23007	0.85619	1.02656
67010600_Sportswear	0.24125	0.89856	1.07775
67011100_Clothing Variety Packs	0.24401	0.90010	1.10123
10111600_Pet Food	0.41256	–	–

This is an interesting result for two reasons: first, the model does not calculate any loss between the different GPC category levels directly, but between products and GPC category levels 1, 2 and 3 separately. The noise contrastive loss in form of the hinge loss from Eq. 2 is calculated with the Bhattacharyya distance D_B between the multivariate Gaussian probability distribution $\mathcal{N}_p$ for product p and the multivariate Gaussian probability distribution $\mathcal{N}_{l_i}$ for GPC category level l_i: $D_B(\mathcal{N}_p, \mathcal{N}_{l_i})$ with $i \in \{1, 2, 3\}$. It is not calculated for different GPC category levels with each other: $D_B(\mathcal{N}_{l_i}, \mathcal{N}_{l_j})$ with $i, j \in \{1, 2, 3\}, i \neq j$. And second, the learned representations correctly reflect the hierarchy between the different GPC category levels.

We now inspect the learned embeddings for words and products as our second qualitative evaluation tasks with regards to entailment. For each word (token), all products in which it appears are retrieved. For each such product-token combination, the KL divergence is calculated to determine whether the token entails the product. These are rolled up by token and the ratio (percentage) of products each token entails calculated. Table 3 provides detailed statistics for the most and least frequent tokens. We observe that the density-based embeddings for the most frequent tokens entail to a high degree the embeddings of the products in which they appear. The contrary is observed for lower frequency tokens. Figure 1 plots the same statistic across the whole vocabulary smoothed with a window aggregation for better graphical illustration.

The first intuition behind this observation suggests that words that occur very frequently, appear in a larger number of documents. Given the loss function of the model, the Bhattacharyya distance D_B between high-frequency words and all documents in which they appear must be low. As such, the variance of the embeddings for the high-frequency words must be wider. For low-frequency tokens that appear only in a few products, this does not hold true. We validate this hypothesis by inspecting the variance of the Gaussian distributions for all tokens and observe the variance of the token embeddings decreasing with the frequency of the words while it remains approx. constant across all products.

Table 3. Token-product entailment statistics of most frequent and least frequent tokens. Rank: rank of token in vocabulary. Products: number of distinct products in which token appears. Entailments: number of products entailed by token. Pct. Entailments: ratio of products entailed by token over all products in which token appears.

Rank	Token	Products	Entailments	Pct. Entailments
1	Shirt	2,079	2,076	99.86%
2	t	2,038	2,000	98.14%
3	Black	1,224	884	72.22%
4	Blue	1,095	989	90.32%
5	Sleeve	961	943	98.13%
...	...	...	...	...
6618	Wiggle	2	0	0.00%
6619	Will	2	0	0.00%
6620	Winco	2	0	0.00%
6621	Windshirt	2	2	100.00%
6622	Wingtip	2	0	0.00%

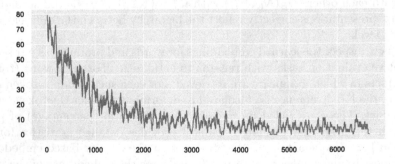

Fig. 1. Global product-token entailments: percentage of products each token entails across entire vocabulary. Smoothing applied with window size 32.

5   Conclusion and Future Work

We presented a novel technique to learn density-based distributed representations for products that make it possible to model inclusion and entailment. While the primary aim of our model is to learn product representations, it produces in parallel representations for text, the associated e-commerce companies and product categories in the same space. The learned representations not only capture semantic relatedness between products, but also between products and the words that describes a product. Furthermore, the hierarchy of the product category taxonomy is correctly reflected by their learned representations. Our initial objective to model inclusion and entailment between products and words was met and the subsequent analysis shed light on the general patterns and specific exceptions of how entailment is modeled with the learned representations. In the future, multimodal density-based product embeddings can capture more nuanced attributes of products in the form of Gaussian mixture models.

References

1. Athiwaratkun, B., Wilson, A.G.: Multimodal word distributions. In: Proceedings of the Conference on 55th Annual Meeting of the Association for Computational Linguistics (Long Papers), ACL 2017, vol. 1, pp 1645–1656 (2017)
2. Bhattacharyya, A.: On a measure of divergence between two multinomial populations. Sankhya Indian J. Stat. **7**, 401–406 (1946)
3. Grbovic, M., et al.: E-commerce in your inbox: product recommendations at scale. In: Proceedings of the ACM SIGKDD International Conference on Knowledge Discovery and Data Mining, vol. 2015, pp. 1809–1818 (2015)
4. Jebara, T., Kondor, R., Howard, A.: Probability product kernels. J. Mach. Learn. Res. **5**, 819–844 (2004)
5. Kullback, S., Leibler, R.A.: On information and sufficiency. Ann. Math. Stat. **22**(1), 79–86 (1951)
6. Mikolov, T., Chen, K., Corrado, G., Dean, J.: Efficient estimation of word representations in vector space. In: Proceedings of the International Conference on Learning Representations, ICLR 2013, pp. 1–12 (2013)
7. Mikolov, T., Sutskever, I., Chen, K., Corrado, G., Dean, J.: Distributed representations of words and phrases and their compositionality. In: Advances in Neural Information Processing Systems, pp. 3111–3119 (2013)
8. Vasile, F., Smirnova, E., Conneau, A.: Meta-Prod2Vec - product embeddings using side-information for recommendation. In: Proceedings of the 10th ACM Conference on Recommender Systems, RecSys 2016, pp. 225–232 (2016)
9. Vilnis, L., McCallum, A.: Word representations via Gaussian embedding. In: 3rd International Conference on Learning Representations, ICLR 2015 - Conference Track Proceedings, pp. 1–12 (2015)
10. Zhang, Z., Bizer, C., Peeters, R., Primpeli, A.: MWPD2020: semantic web challenge on mining the web of HTML-embedded product data. In: CEUR Workshop Proceedings, vol. 2720 (2020)

Modelling Emotion Dynamics in Chatbots with Neural Hawkes Processes

Ahmed Abouzeid$^{(\boxtimes)}$ ⓘ, Ole-Christoffer Granmo ⓘ, and Morten Goodwin ⓘ

University of Agder, Kristiansand, Norway
{ahmed.abouzeid,ole.granmo,morten.goodwin}@uia.no

Abstract. Conversation partners tend to stick to a particular emotional state unless some external motivation excited them to change that state. Usually, the excitation comes from the other conversation partner. This preliminary study investigates how an Artificial Intelligence model can provide excitation for the other partner during a dyadic text-based conversation. As a first step, we propose a Neural Emotion Hawkes Process architecture (NEHP) for predicting future emotion dynamics of the other conversation partner. Moreover, we hypothesize that NEHP can facilitate learning of distinguishable consequences of different excitation strategies, and thus it allows for goal-directed excitation behavior by integrating with chatbot agents. We evaluate our preliminary model on two public datasets, each with different emotion taxonomies. Our preliminary results show promising emotion prediction accuracy over future conversation turns. Furthermore, our model captures meaningful excitation without being trained on explicit excitation ground-truths as practiced in earlier studies.

Keywords: Knowledge representation · Non-parametric Hawkes process · Chat-bots · Neural networks · Emotion dynamics

1 Introduction

Nowadays, sequential events are in our every day life, we can observe that in the huge amount of online data being generated at every second. Data generated on social media platforms such as Facebook and Twitter is an example. In such mediums, each user shares a sequence of events though self-opinions and interactions with others [1]. Besides social media, sequential events also exist in domains like regular conversations [2]. In general, sequences are characterized by the particular order of their elements and either their occurrences were temporal, spatial, or both. However, what actually distinguishes the characteristic of a sequence from another is the pattern of its behaviour. For instance, some sequences are synchronous where the temporal or spatial arrivals of events are synced together. On the other hand, some sequences are asynchronous [3] which means the time intervals between event arrivals is as important as their order. In the latter scenario, both self and mutual excitation between events exist [4], and

© Springer Nature Switzerland AG 2021
M. Bramer and R. Ellis (Eds.): SGAI-AI 2021, LNAI 13101, pp. 146–151, 2021.
https://doi.org/10.1007/978-3-030-91100-3_12

that constructs the dynamics of their behaviour. To this end, point processes [5] were utilized to capture the hidden influence caused by event excitation through the different time intervals.

Traditionally, Poisson point process [4] is used as an example for point processes. However, the complicated dynamics usually found in asynchronous events are beyond the capacity of Poisson processes, due to their event history stateless nature. Hence, Hawkes processes (HPs) [4] were utilized to capture the historical dependencies between events, which led to more accurate prediction and inference of the hidden excitation. However, some generated events could still be unrelated to each other which is not assumed by the classic HP. That is due to the static computation of its parameters where the latter is estimated from the data before prediction. Therefore, alternative approaches were proposed for a non-parametric HP. First, recurrent neural networks (RNNs) and their variants (e.g., LSTM) were utilized [6,7] to model the HP dynamics through the network hidden state vector, where historical dependencies were implicitly captured. The advantage of this method is how the process parameters were mutable over different time intervals which is more likely in real-world scenarios. However, due to the limitations [8] of the RNN and LSTM, the neural network struggles in longer sequences with some unrelated dependencies. Hence, a self-attentive HP was proposed [9] to overcome the challenge of long-term dependencies. In the latter approach and unlike RNNs, the self-attention mechanism improved the prediction accuracy by eliminating unrelated dependencies.

According to the definition of *emotional inertia* [10], conversation partners tend to stick to a particular emotional state, unless some external motivation excited them to change that state. Usually, the excitation comes from the other conversation partner. Therefore, by considering one partner as a chatbot agent [11], this preliminary study investigates how to learn hidden excitation patterns in emotional conversations, so the agent can control the outcome from other partner's emotions by re-planning its own (chatbot) expressed emotions.

As a first step, we propose a Neural Emotion Hawkes Process (NEHP) for the conversation emotion dynamics prediction. Moreover, we investigate how the NEHP input conversation emotions should be represented to allow for high prediction accuracy, and successful excitation from further developed controller models on top of the NEHP. For instance, a reinforcement learning chatbot agent that interacts with NEHP as its emotional dynamics environment. To evaluate a potential successful integration with chatbot agents in further studies, we manually re-plan the expressed emotions of one partner in the NEHP emotion sequence input. We define the re-planning of one partner's emotions as the replacement of a certain emotion in its associated conversation utterances sequence. Then, we evaluate if such plan will succeed to excite the other partner for a more positive emotional outcome. We conduct a T-test and accept only significant emotion change outcomes where $P\text{-}value \leq 0.05$. Two public text-based conversational datasets are studied for the preliminary experiments, one is from imagined conversations in movies [12], and the other is sentiment-annotated human-to-human conversations [13].

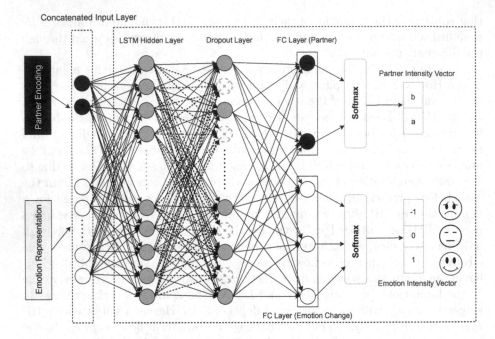

Fig. 1. LSTM-based MHP for dyadic conversation emotion change prediction.

2   Proposed Prediction Model

Figure 1 shows our proposed End-to-End architecture of the Neural Emotion Hawkes Process (NEHP). The model utilizes a long short-term memory network (LSTM). We believe the utilization of an LSTM would be sufficient as a preliminary study, where the input sequence length is relatively short and the conversation expressed emotions are completely related, due to the complementary nature of emotions [14] in dialogues. However, self-attention mechanisms are recommended for the analysis of long and multi-context conversations.

NEHP is fed by two categories of inputs: (1) the two partners one-hot-encoding vector R^2 over n steps, where n is the emotion change sequence length, and (2) the emotion change feature representation vector R^n. The core idea behind the proposed sequence prediction model is a multivariate Hawkes process (MHP). In an MHP, the excitation between different categories of sequential events can be modelled via a parametric intensity function λ. In our case, we are interested in modelling the asynchronous sequential emotion changes from conversation turns. The term asynchronous is adopted to best describe the importance of the time interval for when an emotion change occurs, e.g., excitation planning. Time intervals in a dyadic conversation setting can be viewed as the turns indices, with the clarification that if one partner interacted with consequent adjacent utterances, all these turns will be considered one single interval. That is, the intervals even indices will be associated with one partner while the odd ones will be representing the other partner. The formal description of a parametric classic MHP is given below in Eq. 1 with its conditional intensity function. The conditional intensity λ predicts the intensity of an emotion change event to occur in a particular interval, given some history of a relevant observation. The prediction captures the mutual excitation between two conversation partners by considering hidden patterns in the given history [4].

$$\lambda(e_i, t_i | H_{t_s}) := \mu(e_i, t_i) + \sum g(e_i - e_s, t_i - t_s) : s < i \qquad (1)$$

Where g is some kernel function over the history with a decay factor over time, and H_{t_s} is the history of emotion change prior to the interval t_i. Equivalently, the index i indicates the current conversation turn index. Typically, g is calculated over an influence matrix A where its entries estimate self and mutual excitation between events, e.g., emotion changes. In a short conversation setting, we can consider no decay of influence since the latter is usually adopted for long temporal sequence analysis and prediction. Moreover, in a neural network setting such as our proposed NEHP, the non-parametric conditional intensities are calculated as per Eq. 2, Where h_t is the hidden state vector from the LSTM network.

$$\lambda(e_{i+1}, t_{i+1} | H_{t_{i+1}}) = \tanh(h_{t_i}) \qquad (2)$$

3   Preliminary Results

Table 1 shows the preliminary results for our proposed NEHP where four emotion representation techniques were evaluated. Our preliminary results show promising prediction accuracy and potential successful excitation over two future turns of the other conversation partner. The reported excitation results do not involve any reinforcement learning methods for the control task, but the latter was simplified as a manual modification of the emotion sequence input.

The emotion representation methods vary from each others in terms of how emotion taxonomies scalar values sequence is being prepared as an input to the NEHP. For example, partner difference means that we only focus on the sequence turns associated each partner alone and calculate the differences for each. So, we obtain a transformed sequence that represents an emotion change pattern for each partner independently. On the other hand, partners difference means that we calculate the differences from each two adjacent turns emotion scalar values. Since each two adjacent turns in our setting are associated with two different partners, then, the latter technique allows for creating dependencies between partners in the representation. Eventually, the incremental technique allows for accumulated differences, so that it could capture dependencies over time. It is important to highlight that raw emotion scalar values sequence is not a good choice for representing the NEHP input. Since the latter gave a very low prediction accuracy. To reproduce the results, source code and data made available at (https://github.com/Ahmed-Abouzeid/rnn_mhp_emotion).

Table 1. Prediction accuracy of other conversation partner over two turns in future.

Dataset	Emotion representation	Acc (1)	Acc (2)	Avg Acc	Excitation
Topical	Partner difference	0.82	0.51	0.67	**0.16**
Movies	Partner difference	0.80	0.35	0.57	0.40
Topical	Incremental partner difference	0.89	**0.62**	**0.76**	0.05
Movies	Incremental partner difference	0.82	0.20	0.51	**0.45**
Topical	Partners difference	0.85	0.54	0.64	0.06
Movies	Partners difference	0.81	0.37	0.59	0.24
Topical	Incremental partners difference	**0.94**	0.57	**0.76**	0.06
Movies	Incremental partners difference	**0.92**	**0.76**	**0.84**	0.16

4   Conclusion and Future Work

Conversational emotional dynamics has two main properties: (1) self and (2) inter-personal dependencies. We consider such setting is applicable with Hawkes Processes, where the latter is a point process for modeling mutual and self-excitation in asynchronous events. This preliminary study presented how we could predict emotion changes for n text-based conversation turns in the future. Our Neural Emotion Hawkes Process (NEHP) captured hidden excitation of an emotion change point process, and hence could simulate partners' emotion changes as well. Although the NEHP performs a supervised learning for the prediction task, the inferred excitation was not boosted by any supervised learning as practiced in [15]. Therefore, the only given ground-truths were partner ids and their associated emotion change values. The latter capability of the NEHP highlights how the utilization of Hawkes Processes is beneficial in this domain. Furthermore, the prediction of both partners' emotions means that the NEHP can be either an observer or an actor during a conversation. Observing conversations and predicting their dynamics could be useful in social media analysis to predict the popularity of a post, or the occurrence of critical events in the future. On the other hand, as an actor in a conversation, the NEHP excitation simulation could be considered an environment for a reinforcement learning-based chatbot, where the latter learns to develop emotional intelligence.

The domain of emotion recognition is evolving rapidly, opening the venue for many research questions. Future work can be applying a self attentive-NEHP model on video recordings-based conversations, where facial and audio features can be extracted. We believe the NEHP could be utilized for other semantic events as well, such as context change in conversations. Moreover, this preliminary study could be a first step towards understanding the behavior patterns of individuals, by studying some semantic shifts in their conversations.

Acknowledgments. This work is part of the Chatbot Interaction Design project, funded by the Norwegian Research Council. The project is a collaboration between

SINTEF and the Center for Artificial Intelligence Research (CAIR) in Norway, University of Agder. We would like to thank all colleagues and the project manager Asbjørn Følstad for all the insights and discussions.

References

1. Yang, S.-H., Long, B., Smola, A., Sadagopan, N., Zheng, Z., Zha, H.: Like like alike: joint friendship and interest propagation in social networks. In: Proceedings of the 20th International Conference on World Wide Web, pp. 537–546 (2011)
2. Cappers, B.C.M., van Wijk, J.J.: Exploring multivariate event sequences using rules, aggregations, and selections. IEEE Trans. Vis. Comput. Graph. **24**(1), 532–541 (2017)
3. Ross, S.M.: Stochastic Processes, vol. 2. Wiley, New York (1996)
4. Hawkes, A.G.: Spectra of some self-exciting and mutually exciting point processes. Biometrika **58**(1), 83–90 (1971)
5. Cox, D.R., Isham, V.: Point Processes, vol. 12. CRC Press (1980)
6. Xiao, S., Yan, J., Yang, X., Zha, H., Chu, S.: Modeling the intensity function of point process via recurrent neural networks. In: Proceedings of the AAAI Conference on Artificial Intelligence, vol. 31 (2017)
7. Du, N., Dai, H., Trivedi, R., Upadhyay, U., Gomez-Rodriguez, M., Song, L.: Recurrent marked temporal point processes: embedding event history to vector. In Proceedings of the 22nd ACM SIGKDD International Conference on Knowledge Discovery and Data Mining, pp. 1555–1564 (2016)
8. Zhao, J., et al.: Do RNN and LSTM have long memory? In: International Conference on Machine Learning, pp. 11365–11375. PMLR (2020)
9. Zhang, Q., Lipani, A., Kirnap, O., Yilmaz, E.: Self-attentive Hawkes process. In: International Conference on Machine Learning, pp. 11183–11193. PMLR (2020)
10. Kuppens, P., Allen, N.B., Sheeber, L.B.: Emotional inertia and psychological maladjustment. Psychol. Sci. **21**(7), 984–991 (2010)
11. Li, R., Wu, Z., Jia, J., Li, J., Chen, W., Meng, H.: Inferring user emotive state changes in realistic human-computer conversational dialogs. In: Proceedings of the 26th ACM International Conference on Multimedia, pp. 136–144 (2018)
12. Danescu-Niculescu-Mizil, C., Lee, L.: Chameleons in imagined conversations: a new approach to understanding coordination of linguistic style in dialogs. arXiv preprint arXiv:1106.3077 (2011)
13. Gopalakrishnan, K., et al.: Topical-chat: towards knowledge-grounded open-domain conversations. In: INTERSPEECH, pp. 1891–1895 (2019)
14. Turner, J.H., Stets, J.E.: Sociological theories of human emotions. Ann. Rev. Sociol. **32**, 25–52 (2006)
15. Poria, S., et al.: Recognizing emotion cause in conversations. Cogn. Comput. **13**(5), 1317–1332 (2021). https://doi.org/10.1007/s12559-021-09925-7

Knowledge-Based Composable Inductive Programming

Edward McDaid$^{(\boxtimes)}$ (iD) and Sarah McDaid (iD)

Zoea Ltd, 20-22 Wenlock Road, London N1 7GU, UK
edward.mcdaid@zoea.co.uk

Abstract. Zoea is a knowledge-based inductive programming system that generates code directly from a set of test cases. It also allows developers to combine generated software in a variety of ways to form programs of arbitrary size. The Zoea compiler is built using a modern variant of the blackboard architecture. Zoea integrates a large number of knowledge sources that encode different elements of programming language and software development expertise, using test cases as a ubiquitous basis for knowledge representation. Hypotheses are managed through the creation of synthetic test cases and blackboard recursion. We briefly outline the text-based and visual specification languages, and the associated composable inductive programming development paradigm. The benefits of the approach and some plans for future development are also identified.

Keywords: Inductive programming · Knowledge-based system · Blackboard

1 Introduction

The use of AI to support developers in the creation of code is currently receiving increased attention. Yet this is the latest chapter in a series of research efforts that have spanned much of the last five decades [1–3]. In that time inductive programming and related disciplines have made many advances however the overarching goal of generating non-trivial software automatically from some form of specification has remained elusive.

One important question that has rarely been considered regards the nature of the user experience for inductive programming, if and when it finally becomes available. The prevalence of test-driven development and associated practices make test cases a compelling candidate as the basis for a simple and intuitive software specification language. Many people who cannot code already define software requirements as test cases.

Zoea was conceived as an AI system that would support the incremental production of software from a specification and which would be simple enough to be used by anyone with very little training. It was built using a knowledge-based approach and Zoea uses a blackboard architecture as a simple and effective means of integrating many diverse knowledge sources. Conventional compilers use a parser and an abstract syntax tree to translate source code into machine instructions. Zoea on the other hand, identifies or hypothesises, data and code elements, based on features in test cases and integrates these in a manner that is similar to the operation of a chart parser.

© Springer Nature Switzerland AG 2021
M. Bramer and R. Ellis (Eds.): SGAI-AI 2021, LNAI 13101, pp. 152–157, 2021.
https://doi.org/10.1007/978-3-030-91100-3_13

2 Related Work

Inductive programming (IP) encompasses a number of related research areas that have been active during the last five decades [1]. Automatic programming is a broader and somewhat more nebulous term that has at different times been applied to a variety of code generation techniques including compilers, domain specific languages and templating systems. Program synthesis is a related discipline that is concerned with generating and verifying programs from a mathematical description.

Broadly inductive programming involves the generation of programs based on a combination of example data and background knowledge. IP approaches can be characterised according to a number of dimensions [2]. In terms of programming paradigm inductive functional programming and inductive logic programming account for most current work in the field. The combinatorial explosion of the hypothesis space is a significant problem for all IP systems. As a result even the most advanced IP systems are currently able to produce relatively small programs [3].

3 Zoea Approach

Zoea uses a knowledge-based approach that encodes expertise about various programming language elements and how they can be combined in different ways. Pattern recognition is also used to extract as much information about the required program as possible from the test cases. In operation Zoea focuses initially on the production of values rather than code. This effectively conflates the consideration of often numerous equivalent solutions or solution fragments.

When a human developer is presented with a set of test cases they can often identify characteristics of the corresponding program. This is because the test case input and output values can provide important clues about the code that they describe. For a start the data types can indicate directly in some cases that specific type conversions may be required. The actual values of inputs and outputs can also be useful. Simply by inspection people are often able to determine if an input and output pair of lists has been sorted, reversed, mapped, filtered or selected in any combination. Zoea is designed to take advantage of the fact that a user is actively trying to communicate their requirements through the test cases that they create.

Each time a knowledge source detects a pattern in a test case input it is effectively creating a hypothesis. Zoea captures and manages such hypotheses by creating synthetic test cases (STCs). A synthetic test case is no different to a real test case except in its provenance. The knowledge source also creates an associated code fragment that converts the data in the original test case into the STC. STCs are then processed in exactly the same way as real test cases which may include the creation of additional STCs and so on. STCs allow Zoea to explore different interpretations of the test cases it has been provided with. They also serve to partition different lines of reasoning.

The combination of pattern matching against test case data and relatively coarse grained programming knowledge (where application of that pattern is at least plausible in the current context) help to guide Zoea towards producing partial and complete solutions that reflect the users intention as articulated through the test cases.

4 Composable Inductive Programming

Composable inductive programming (CIP) is a simple, iterative software development paradigm in which all software is automatically generated through inductive programming from a specification in the form of a set of test cases. In CIP smaller programs can also be combined through various forms of composition to form software of arbitrary size. Zoea supports CIP using either a text-based or a visual notation.

Each test case normally includes both an input and an output value. It is also possible to describe one or more derived values, which represent an intermediate state of the data during processing at some point between the input and the output. Using derived values the user can articulate any number of potentially complex data transformations deep within the code path that corresponds to a test case. During compilation Zoea treats derived values as representing multiple back-to-back test cases. Zoea also allows any number of existing programs to be composed to form larger programs of any size. Included programs temporarily extend the target language instruction set.

5 Zoea Specification Language

Zoea Specification Language (ZSL) is a text-based notation used to describe a program as a set of test cases. A ZSL program consists of one or more terms where each term has the form <Tag> : <Value>. Terms must be separated by white space but layout is not significant. ZSL supports the following set of tags: program, use, data, case, step, input, derive, and output. The mandatory program tag defines the program name. The optional use tag can identify one or more existing programs to include. An optional data tag allows static reference data to be embedded within a program.

One or more test cases are introduced by the case tag, which is optional for a single case. Each case can have any number of optionally identified steps where a step contains a single input, derive or output tag. Data, input, derive and output values are basically JSON data although quotes are optional for strings that contain no special characters. Listing 1 provides a simple example of a ZSL program.

```
program: is_day_of_week
data:   [monday,tuesday,wednesday,thursday,friday,
           saturday,sunday]
case: 1 input: thursday output: day_of_week
case: 2 input: 'MONDAY' output: day_of_week
case: 3 input: banana   output: not_day_of_week
```

Listing 1. Example ZSL Program

6 Zoea Visual

Zoea Visual is a visual programming language for describing Zoea test cases that is built on top of ZSL (see Fig. 1). In Zoea Visual all data is represented visually as input fields, tables, etc. Elements are placed in named columns that correspond to ZSL tag names. Zoea Visual supports any number of input and output values.

Zoea Visual introduces the concept of dependencies, which are data flow links between pairs of elements in different columns. These are used to indicate that one or more source elements are involved in some way in the production of a target element. This allows the user to construct a data flow diagram for each test case that provides more detail about the user intention to the compiler.

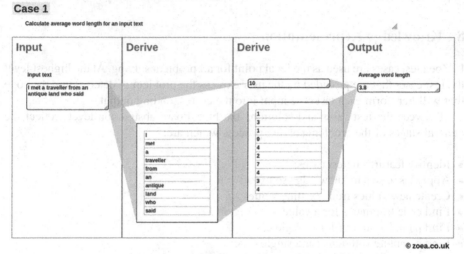

Fig. 1. Example Zoea Visual program

Zoea Visual also introduces a further form of composition called subsidiary test cases. A subsidiary test case allows the code for a given element to be elaborated as a completely separate Zoea Visual program. This facility allows complex logic and multiple code paths to be expressed using a linear rather than exponential number of test cases.

7   Zoea Architecture

Zoea uses a version of the blackboard architecture in which many knowledge sources update and react to changes in a central data store. There are a number of differences between the Zoea blackboard and the classical model:

- Knowledge sources are distributed across any number of physical computers;
- Knowledge sources work on local copies of relevant subsets of the blackboard data that are synchronised in both directions through deltas;
- The central copy of the blackboard data is mainly used for data integration and redistribution;

- Global scheduling involves the allocation of time and resource budgets;
- Activated knowledge sources act concurrently within their allocated budgets;
- Control knowledge that relates to a specific knowledge source is part of the knowledge source rather than an external scheduler.

The knowledge sources are built on top of a distributed computing framework that allows arbitrary compute jobs to be unicast or multicast to a pool of workers located on any number of physical nodes. A central controller monitors the activity of all workers, and distributes jobs including knowledge source activations and blackboard updates as required. Modern engineering provides high performance and scalability.

8   Knowledge Representation

In Zoea test cases are used as the focal point for all problem solving. At the highest level the test cases that are provided by the user express the problem of determining the code that will transform each test case input into the corresponding output.

Between the test cases and solutions the blackboard abstraction levels reflect the general stages of the problem solving process which are:

- Identify features in test cases;
- Apply test cases to knowledge sources;
- Create new values from existing values;
- Find code fragments for a value;
- Find partial solutions for a single case;
- Find complete solutions for a single case;
- Find a set of case solutions that work for all cases;
- Generate the raw code for a solution set;
- Generalise the raw solution set code.

The entries on the Zoea blackboard do not form a simple linear hierarchy. Rather, the creation of synthetic test cases and the knowledge source activations form a large and multiply recursive tree in which the code elements of any solution are both sparsely distributed and also mutated as a result of synthetic test case transformations.

9   Discussion and Future Work

ZSL and Zoea Visual are novel, highly declarative and simple programming languages. CIP also represents a completely new software development paradigm.

A set of ZSL and Zoea Visual code examples has been released [4], and the complete ZSL language specification is also available in the public domain [5]. ZSL code is similar in terms of size but approximately half the complexity of equivalent code in a conventional language. In addition ZSL has only 25–30% of the language complexity of the simplest conventional languages such as Go or Python.

Both ZSL and Zoea Visual have been used internally to create programs that are the equivalent to hundreds of lines of code in conventional languages. Automated testing with randomised programs has produced hundreds of thousands of programs – many of which are equivalent to over a thousand lines of conventional code.

The construction of Zoea involved no element of training nor the use of any third party source code. It therefore avoids any imputations of intellectual property misuse.

While the compiler is functional work continues to improve performance and to provide more end user tooling. In particular we want to make hypotheses visible to the user, allowing them to be optionally accepted or rejected.

The synthetic test case transformations carried out by the knowledge sources could be defined in more abstract terms. This might be useful for reasoning about interaction between knowledge sources, for example to identify any redundant activations.

Currently Zoea is run on a dedicated cluster of physical servers. While this is suitable for development and testing it limits access for other purposes. At some stage we would like to make Zoea more publicly available and this will require migration to some form of cloud-based infrastructure.

10   Conclusions

Zoea is the first inductive programming system that was designed to support the creation of code of arbitrary size. It is a knowledge-based system that integrates many diverse knowledge sources using a blackboard architecture. Knowledge source activations are driven by pattern recognition and test cases are used as a ubiquitous basis for all reasoning. In giving rise to simple, novel programming languages and processes, Zoea also demonstrates the potential for AI to revolutionise software development.

Acknowledgements. This work was funded and carried out by Zoea Ltd (https://zoea.co.uk). Zoea is a trademark of Zoea Ltd. Other trademarks are the property of their respective owners.

References

1. Flener, P., Schmid, U.: An introduction to inductive programming. Artif. Intell. Rev. **29**(1), 45–62 (2008)
2. Kitzelmann, E.: Analytical inductive functional programming. In: Hanus, Michael (ed.) LOP-STR 2008. LNCS, vol. 5438, pp. 87–102. Springer, Heidelberg (2009). https://doi.org/10.1007/978-3-642-00515-2_7
3. Galwani, S., Hernandez-Orallo, J., Kitzelmann, E., Muggleton, S.H., Schmid, U., Zorn, B.: Inductive programming meets the real world. Commun. ACM **58**(11), 90–99 (2015)
4. Zoea Code Examples. http://rosettacode.org/wiki/Category:Zoea. Accessed 2 Sept 2021
5. McDaid, E., McDaid, S.: Zoea – Composable Inductive Programming Without Limits (2019). arXiv:1911.08286

Named Entity Recognition and Relation Extraction for COVID-19: Explainable Active Learning with Word2vec Embeddings and Transformer-Based BERT Models

M. Arguello-Casteleiro[1]([✉]), N. Maroto[2], C. Wroe[3], C. Sevillano Torrado[4],
C. Henson[5], J. Des-Diz[4], M. J. Fernandez-Prieto[6], T. Furmston[1],
D. Maseda Fernandez[5], M. Kulshrestha[5], R. Stevens[1], J. Keane[1], and S. Peters[1]

[1] University of Manchester, Manchester, UK
m.arguello@manchester.ac.uk
[2] Universidad Politécnica de Madrid, Madrid, Spain
[3] BMJ, London, UK
[4] Hospital do Salnés, Pontevedra, Spain
[5] Midcheshire Hospital Foundation Trust, Crewe, UK
[6] University of Salford, Salford, UK

Abstract. Deep learning for natural language processing acquires dense vector representations for n-grams from large-scale unstructured corpora. Converting static embeddings of n-grams into a dataset of interlinked concepts with explicit contextual semantic dependencies provides the foundation to acquire reusable knowledge. However, the validation of this knowledge requires cross-checking with ground-truths that may be unavailable in an actionable or computable form. This paper presents a novel approach from the new field of explainable active learning that combines methods for learning static embeddings (word2vec models) with methods for learning dynamic contextual embeddings (transformer-based BERT models). We created a dataset for named entity recognition (NER) and relation extraction (REX) for the Coronavirus Disease 2019 (COVID-19). The COVID-19 dataset has 2,212 associations captured by 11 word2vec models with additional examples of use from the biomedical literature. We propose interpreting the NER and REX tasks for COVID-19 as Question Answering (QA) incorporating general medical knowledge within the question, e.g. "does 'cough' (n-gram) belong to 'clinical presentation/symptoms' for COVID-19?". We evaluated biomedical-specific pre-trained language models (BioBERT, SciBERT, ClinicalBERT, BlueBERT, and PubMedBERT) versus general-domain pre-trained language models (BERT, and RoBERTa) for transfer learning with COVID-19 dataset, i.e. task-specific fine-tuning considering NER as a sequence-level task. Using 2,060 QA for training (associations from 10 word2vec models) and 152 QA for validation (associations from 1 word2vec model), BERT obtained an F-measure of 87.38%, with precision = 93.75% and recall = 81.82%. SciBERT achieved the highest F-measure of 94.34%, with precision = 98.04% and recall = 90.91%.

Keywords: Deep learning for natural language processing · Transfer learning · Embeddings · Transformer-based models · Explainable active learning

© Springer Nature Switzerland AG 2021
M. Bramer and R. Ellis (Eds.): SGAI-AI 2021, LNAI 13101, pp. 158–163, 2021.
https://doi.org/10.1007/978-3-030-91100-3_14

1   Introduction

Artificial Intelligence (AI), and more specifically Deep Learning, may contribute to deliver better healthcare [1, 2], e.g. by helping clinicians to diagnose and treat disease, while avoiding serious diagnostic errors and mistakes in managing the disease. Deep Learning algorithms are considered *black box algorithms* that create an uncomfortable situation for physicians and patients [1, 2]: a close examination by humans does not reveal the features used to generate the prediction.

This paper belongs to explainable AI [3]: seeking to provide predictions (outcome) with accompanying justifications (outcome explanation). The approach presented belongs to the new field of explainable active learning (XAL) [4], combining active learning (AL) [5] and local explanations [6].

Deep learning is a subfield of Machine Learning (ML) [7] and "the most common form of machine learning, deep or not, is supervised learning" [7]. Transformer-based models such as BERT (Bidirectional Encoder Representations from Transformers) [8] are the state-of-the-art in deep learning for natural language processing (NLP). BERT models are pre-trained on large-scale corpus of unlabeled text, and then they are trained on supervised downstream tasks such as Named Entity Recognition (NER) and Relationship Extraction (REX). NER and REX are information extraction tasks considered to be high-level NLP tasks [9]. Sentiment analysis, topic classification, and filtering (e.g. "relevant" and "non-relevant") are text classification tasks [5]. Both information extraction and text classification are sophisticated learning tasks [5], where labeled instances are difficult, time-consuming, or expensive to obtain [5]. Question answering (QA) is another sophisticated learning task, where a training corpus of questions is needed [10]. Devlin et al. [8] fine-tuned BERT models for downstream tasks considering QA and NER as token-level, while text classification was considered a sequence-level task.

Labeling the biomedical literature is a large-scale annotation that requires domain expertise. Our goal is to extract clinical terms related to a disease like COVID-19 from raw text. We combine methods for learning static embeddings with methods for learning dynamic contextual embeddings to provide the prediction (i.e. clinical term relatable to the disease under stud) together with an explanation. Methods such as word2vec [11] and GloVe [12] learn static embeddings, i.e. one fixed vector for each term in the vocabulary [10]. Transformer models like BERT learn dynamic contextual embeddings, where the vector for each term is different according to context [10].

AL needs less labeled training instances for greater accuracy by choosing the data from which the ML algorithm learns [5]. Examples of recent studies that applied AL to label text in the biomedical/clinical domain and employed embeddings: [11] used word2vec and GloVe embeddings; and [12] used BERT embeddings.

The novelty of our approach is 3-fold: 1) fine-tuning BERT models adhering to XAL, differing from AL; 2) shaping the data for fine-tuning BERT models in NER and REX as QA; and 3) systematically injecting domain knowledge into the fine-tuning of BERT models by incorporating general medical knowledge into the queries.

2   Experimental Setup for XAL: NER and REX for COVID-19

We interpreted NER and REX tasks as acquiring the clinical presentation/symptoms, the diagnostic test/findings, the treatments, and the co-existing medical conditions for the COVID-19. We focused on a fixed set of relations between entities.

Figure 1 has the XAL setup overview. Vector arithmetic formulas act as the active learning sampling strategy, i.e. the scoring functions to select the data for the queries to fine-tune pre-trained BERT models.

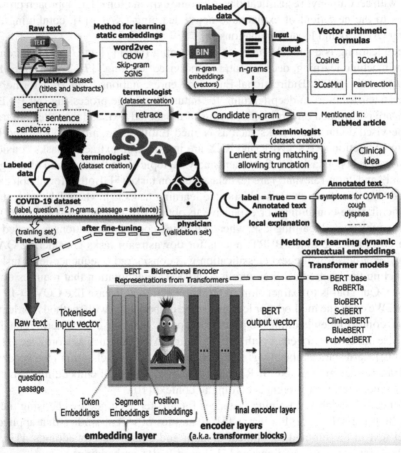

Fig. 1. Overview of the explainable active learning (XAL) setup: NER and REX for COVID-19

Wor2vec Models. Using titles and available abstracts of PubMed articles [13], we obtained different datasets. We used word2phrase [11] to obtain n-grams (i.e. sequence of tokens) for each dataset; and word2vec [11] to learn the vectors for the n-grams. Table 1 has the number of n-grams and the method for learning embeddings, i.e. skip-gram and skip-gram with negative sampling (SGNS). The word2vec models were created around

Table 1. Information about the word2vec models created.

Date	Word2vec model	Word2vec algorithm	Number of n-grams
10-August-2020	M1	skip-gram	6,883
10-July-2020	M2, M3, M4	skip-gram	6,509
10-June-2020	M5	skip-gram	5,689
11-May-2020	M6	skip-gram	4,471
10-August-2020	M7	skip-gram	94,155
10-July-2020	M8	skip-gram	76,434
10-June-2020	M9	skip-gram	57,659
11-May-2020	M10	skip-gram	34,765
10-June-2021	M11	SGNS	12,569

the date displayed (1st column). The number of unique n-grams from models M1 to M10 is 98,901.

AL Process. We considered 10 iterations. For each iteration, the model Mi from Table 1 with i = [1, 10] can provide the instances for training the BERT models.

AL Sampling Strategy. A physician chose few n-grams as "prior knowledge" (*what is known*), e.g. fever n-gram is a symptom for the COVID-19 [14]. Vector arithmetic formulas are applied in an unsupervised way, using the "prior knowledge" as input, to recover relational similarities that are encoded in each model Mi.

AL Query Strategy. The COVID-19 dataset has 3-tuples (label, question, passage). The fine-tuning can be seen as reading comprehension [10], passing the question and passage to BERT models. The label is the prediction True/False also interpretable as yes/no answer for QA task. The question consists of an n-gram representing a general medical term together with an input/output n-gram from vector arithmetic formulas.

Local Explanations. The passage is a sentence automatically selected by retracing the input/output n-gram into the dataset, which was re-organised by date and source. The sentence selected is validated by a biomedical terminologist (human annotator) and may be changed if deemed inappropriate. The sentence acts as a local explanation that justifies only the reason for the prediction on a specific input instance [6].

BERT Models. Transformer models such as BERT base are trained on a supervised downstream task by fine-tuning all pre-trained parameters [8]. Transformers models map sequences of input vectors {x1,…, xn} to sequences of output vectors {y1,…, yn} of the same length [10]. Both BERT and RoBERTa [15] are general-domain pre-trained language models. RoBERTa was obtained by modifying the BERT pre-training procedure expecting it to lead to better downstream task performance [15]. There are several biomedical-specific pre-trained language models, such as BioBERT [16], SciBERT [17], ClinicalBERT [18], BlueBERT [19], and PubMedBERT [20].

Performance Metrics. Vector arithmetic formulas may bring "relevant" and "non relevant" information according to a broad category, such as symptoms. We fine-tune BERT models adhering to XAL to filter the information retrieved, to better provide "explanations" for the "predictions", such as terms retrieved that seem "relevant" symptoms for a disease. We report precision, recall, F-measure, and accuracy [10] of BERT models for the downstream task after the fine-tuning. We report the observed agreement [21], i.e. the percentage of agreed instances with 2 domain experts.

3   Results for XAL: NER and REX for COVID-19

The COVID-19 dataset created contains 2212 instances, each instance has a value for the prediction: True = 1 or False = 0. All n-grams that are the input/outputs of the vector arithmetic formulas for the SGNS model M11 act as the foundation to build the validation set. There is no overlap between the training and validation set:

- Training set has 2060 instances: 1575 are False and 485 are True.
- Validation set has 152 instances: 97 are False and 55 are True.

Table 2 shows the performance for the validation set of the transformer-based models after the fine-tuning. SciBERT achieved the highest F-measure of 94.34%. The biomedical-specific pre-trained language models yielded a superior performance for the downstream task than BERT base - the only exception being BlueBERT.

Table 2. Measuring the performance for NER and REX as QA for COVID-19.

Fine-Tuned model	Accuracy	F-measure	Precision	Recall
BERT base	91.45%	87.38%	93.75%	81.82%
RoBERTa	84.21%	77.78%	79.25%	76.36%
BioBERT	94.74%	92.73%	92.73%	92.73%
SciBERT	96.05%	94.34%	98.04%	90.91%
ClinicalBERT	92.76%	89.72%	92.31%	87.27%
BlueBERT	89.47%	84.91%	88.24%	81.82%
PubMedBERT	94.74%	92.45%	96.08%	89.09%

A second biomedical terminologist (human annotator) had an observed agreement of 98.10% on the whole COVID-19 dataset. A medical consultant audited the 152 instances of the validation set and had an observed agreement of 98.68%, providing feedback when disagreeing with the local explanation.

4   Concluding Remarks

Our COVID-19 dataset has a relatively modest number of 2K instances for training, although the initial pool of unique n-grams from models M1 to M10 was 99K.

XAL with word2vec and BERT models give balance to: a) the number of training instances that needed peer-review and labeling by a biomedical terminologist; b) the performance achieved by the transformer-based models after fine-tuning; and c) making it feasible to obtain feedback/perceptions from physicians for local explanation.

The low level of disagreement between the 2 biomedical terminologists and the high level of observed agreement with the medical consultant encourages a systematic application of the semi-automatic XAL approach presented to other diseases.

References

1. Fogel, A.L., Kvedar, J.C.: Artificial intelligence powers digital medicine. NPJ Digit. Med. **1**, 5 (2018). https://doi.org/10.1038/s41746-017-0012-2
2. Durán, J.M., Jongsma, K.R.: Who is afraid of black box algorithms? on the epistemological and ethical basis of trust in medical AI. J. Med. Ethics **47**(5), 329–335 (2021)
3. Gunning, D., Stefik, M., Choi, J., Miller, T., Stumpf, S., Yang, G.Z.: XAI—Explainable artificial intelligence. Sci. Robot. **4**, 37 (2019)
4. Ghai, B., Liao, Q.V., Zhang, Y., Bellamy, R., Mueller, K.: Explainable active learning (XAL) toward AI explanations as interfaces for machine teachers. In: ACM, pp. 1–28 (2021)
5. Settles, B.: Active learning literature survey. Computer Sciences Technical Report (2009)
6. Guidotti, R., Monreale, A., Ruggieri, S., Turini, F., Giannotti, F., Pedreschi, D.: A survey of methods for explaining black box models. In: ACM, pp.1–42 (2018)
7. LeCun, Y., Bengio, Y., Hinton, G.: Deep learning. Nature **521**, 436–444 (2015)
8. Devlin, J., Chang, M.W., Lee, K., Toutanova, K.: Bert: pre-training of deep bidirec-tional transformers for language understanding. In: 2019 NAACL, pp. 4171–4186 (2019)
9. Nadkarni, P.M., Ohno-Machado, L., Chapman, W.W.: Natural language processing: an introduction. J. Am. Med. Inform. Assoc. **18**(5), 544–551 (2011)
10. Jurafsky, D., Martin, J.H.: Speech and Language Processing, 3rd ed. draft. (2020)
11. Word2vec. http://code.google.com/p/word2vec/. Accessed 16 June 2021
12. GloVe. https://nlp.stanford.edu/projects/glove/. Accessed 16 June 2021
13. PubMed. https://pubmed.ncbi.nlm.nih.gov/
14. COVID-19. https://bestpractice.bmj.com/topics/engb/3000168. Accessed 16 June 2021
15. Liu, Y., et al.: Roberta: A Robustly Optimized BERT Pretraining Approach (2019)
16. Lee, J., et al.: BioBERT: a pre-trained biomedical language representation model for biomedical text mining. Bioinformatics **36**(4), 1234–1240 (2020)
17. Beltagy, I., Lo, K., Cohan, A.: Scibert: a pretrained language model for scientific text. In: 2019 EMNLP-IJCNLP, pp. 3615–3620 (2019)
18. Alsentzer, E., Murphy, J.R., Boag, W., Weng, W.H., Jin, D., Naumann, T., McDer-mott, M.: Publicly available clinical BERT embeddings. In: NAACL, pp. 72–78 (2019)
19. Peng, Y., Yan, S., Lu, Z.: Transfer learning in biomedical natural language processing: an evaluation of BERT and ELMo on ten benchmarking datasets. In: 18th BioNLP Work-shop and Shared Task, pp. 58–65 (2019)
20. Gu, Y., et al.: Domain-Specific Language Model Pretraining for Biomedical Natural Language Processing (2021). https://doi.org/10.1145/3458754
21. Artstein, R., Poesio, M.: Inter-coder agreement for computational linguistics. Comput. Linguist. **34**(4), 555–596 (2008)

Application Papers

Patients Forecasting in Emergency Services by Using Machine Learning and Exogenous Variables

Hugo Álvarez-Chaves$^{(\boxtimes)}$(iD), David F. Barrero(iD), Mario Cobos(iD),
and Maria D. R-Moreno(iD)

Universidad de Alcalá, Departamento de Automática, Madrid, Spain
{hugo.alvarezc,david.fernandezb,mario.cobos,malola.rmoreno}@uah.es

Abstract. Emergency Departments (ED) in hospitals around the world are a critical service in medical care of patients. Being able to predict the number of patients every day, week or month could be of great help to the healthcare system, and especially in the current situation.

In this paper we present some results in forecasting the admissions, the inpatients and the discharges series in EDs by using Machine Learning algorithms. We have considered different time aggregations (specifically: eight hours, twelve hours, one day and the official shifts of the workers) and exogenous variables (in particular, the Spanish public holiday calendar, the academic calendar, the phase of the lunar cycle and national football matches).

Results show that the best performance is obtained for the admissions series using eight hours aggregations and the biggest improvement is with the daily aggregation in the admission series. The academic calendar and public holidays were the most selected variables.

Keywords: e-Health · ED forecasting · Machine learning

1 Introduction

The Emergency Department (ED) is a critical hospital service and plays a key role in the patients healthcare. In contrast to other hospital services, the patients' arrivals are not pre-planned due to the nature of the department. This apparent randomness poses a challenge in the service resources planning task.

Preventing service overcrowding without wasting resources is one of the most important challenges in ED management. This challenge is revolved around two main terms: service quality and service efficiency. Perhaps the most relevant quality metrics are patient waiting time and ED overcrowding. Both are associated,

First author is supported by Consejería de Ciencia, Universidades e Innovación of Comunidad de Madrid (PEJ-2020-AI/TIC-19375). This study was funded by Junta de Comunidades de Castilla-La Mancha (SBPLY/19/180501/000024) and Ministerio de Ciencia e Innovación (PID2019-109891RB-I00).

M. Bramer and R. Ellis (Eds.): SGAI-AI 2021, LNAI 13101, pp. 167–180, 2021.
https://doi.org/10.1007/978-3-030-91100-3_15

the former being a consequence of the latter. In addition to the obvious nuisance to patients, waiting time has more serious consecuences such as increased mortality rates of the patients [1]. On the other hand, the efficiency of the ED refers to the service cost. Resources are limited, and they must not be wasted.

There are various ways to handle this problem in the literature. Most approaches can be classified by the data format they use: a time series or a features matrix [2]. Time-series studies apply algorithms focused on the temporal association of the data, where the values are time-related. Time-series algorithms take advantage of time association using past values from the series to forecast the number of patients for the following hours, days, weeks or months. Sometimes, depending on the type of algorithm used, exogenous variables are also added to complement the time-series information. By contrast, features matrix-based approaches follow a classical Machine Learning (ML) strategy, where each data instance is independent of others. The time relation in a matrix of features is explicit usually adding at least one time-related feature [3]. Exogeneous variables can be integrated in the data matrix to enhance its predictive power.

The literature has dedicated significant effort to identifying exogeneous variables able to increase the performance of forecast models. Some exogenous variables used in previous studies are calendar [4], weather conditions [5], pollution [6] or hospital demographic data [7]. Each variable can impact results differently depending on the location where the study is performed; therefore, it is essential to select significant variables for improving the performance of the forecast models.

The aim of this work is to analyse the impact of some exogenous variables selected and determine if they can improve results from univariate modelling. The variables used in this study have been selected due to regional sociodemographic concerns and the support of experienced clinical professionals. The end goal is to improve performance when forecasting three variables of interest: admissions, inpatients and discharges. We selected these variables after interviewing several ED managers, who agreed on identifying them as the most relevants for ED management.

To specify the impact of the variables, we proceed to analyse them over three different time series and four time aggregations. The time series are related to patient admissions, inpatients and discharges. The time aggregations correspond to eight-hours, twelve-hours and one-day periods, and official shifts of the service workers.

The paper has been organised in the following way: Sect. 2 provides an overview of the related literature to our topic, Sect. 3 shows the univariable results as a baseline for this work, Sect. 4 details the dataset process collection, Sect. 5 explains the methodology used for feature selection and Sect. 6 presents the experimental results which are discussed in Sect. 7. Finally, Sect. 8 presents conclusions and future works.

2   Literature Review

ED service forecast modelling is a widely treated topic in literature [2]. Many studies in the literature use only the time series values for forecasting modelling. Nevertheless, other authors try to introduce external variables to improve forecasting accuracy and the understanding of the factors that affects ED demand.

Usually, time series forecasting and time series grouping tend to be on the scale of days, weeks or months [2]. The amount of studies that focus on more fine-grained scales, such as the hourly scale, is much lower. Among these studies, Rocha and Rodrigues [8] use ten years of ED service data. They apply different time series algorithms such as ARIMA or Recurrent Neural Networks (RNN) and a feature matrix approach, such as XGBoost. Regarding the feature matrix approach, the following dependent variables are used: year, month, day of the week, time of day, holiday, preceding one-year admissions and preceding admission values at 1, 2, 3, 4, 50, 51, 52, 53, 54 weeks.

Boyle et al. wrote one of the most relevant studies with hourly scales [7]. The study starts from five years of data and different hospitals and tries to develop an application to help ED service management. In addition to the time-series, variables extracted from the calendar are introduced into the ARIMA modelling using labels to describe the calendar specifications (1 = Sunday, 7 = Saturday, 8 = Public holiday, 9 = day before/after holiday, 2–6 = Monday–Friday). Other studies use calendar variables to analyse the impact on predictions when the variables are added to ARIMA and the linear regressions [4]. Kam et al. [9] and Sun et al. [6] use calendar variables only in the ARIMA model. Furthermore, the latter not only feed the model with calendar variables but also use climatic variables. McCarthy et al. [5] also included these weather variables, although they do not seem to influence the arrival of patients to the service. Some authors have studied the influence of exogenous variables concluding that it seems to be closely associated with the hospital location where the service is analysed [7].

In order to know the goodness of the algorithms used, it is necessary to quantify the success of the forecasts of the applied models. An analysis of the most commonly used metrics for the ED service forecasting problem is presented in Gul and Celik [2]. Said work identifies the Mean Absolute Percentage Error (MAPE) and R^2 as the most common metrics. In addition, the symmetric variant of MAPE, called SMAPE, is used when the time-series has values equal to zero to avoid problems in its calculation, as in our study.

Other studies from a more classical data mining perspective are Poole et al. [10] and Graham et al. [11]. These studies use prior information about a patient when accessing the service, such as previous admissions within a specific previous time. Unfortunately, such approaches require sensitive information such as patient identification, so it is difficult to obtain due to privacy restrictions from hospitals in many cases.

The best data representation for ED forecast and the determination of the exogeneous variables with the best predictive power is still an open issue. In the following section, we present a simple univariable time-series approach to serve as baseline of the study.

3 Univariable Time-Series Forecasting

In this section we briefly establish a basic univariate baseline to discern whether any external variable improves the model performance. We use time series representations with classical algorithms: AutoRegressive Integrated Moving Average (ARIMA), Autoregressive models (AR) and Holt-Winters seasonal exponential smoothing (H-W). The prediction horizon is four months to satisfy the hospital requirements.

Our study uses a private dataset from the Hospital Universitario de Guadalajara (HUGU), Castilla-La Mancha, Spain. HUGU is in Guadalajara, a town located 65.4 km north-east of Madrid and it has near 85000 citizens. The region around HUGU has low population density and its main economical activity is agriculture.

The dataset contains records from each patient who accessed the ED service from January 1, 2018 until December 31, 2019. The dataset features are date and time of the patient's access to the service, date and time of discharge, and the reason for service discharge. The reason for discharge allows us to differentiate whether the patient was hospitalised in another hospital service or whether the patient left the service successfully. Note that our dataset consists of records previous to the COVID-19 pandemic.

Starting from the original dataset, we aggregated the patients to create four study time series for each series. The aggregations made are eight hours, twelve hours, one day and by the official shifts of the service workers. The official shifts at HUGU are from 8:00 a.m. to 3:00 p.m., called morning shift or first shift, from 3:00 p.m. to 10:00 p.m., called afternoon shift or second shift, and from 10:00 p.m. to 08:00 a.m., called evening shift or third shift.

Table 1 shows a summary of all the series and time-aggregations (Freq. column) considered for modelling. For all series, the best model is H-W. By contrast, each series obtains the best result for a different time grouping. For instance, looking at the R^2 metric for comparing different aggregations (due to the nature of each metric), the best aggregation for the admissions series is eight hours, while twelve hours is the best grouping for the inpatient series.

Results from Table 1 follows a time series approach. Exogenous data cannot be added to H-W and AR algorithms by default, whereas ARIMA accepts them apart from time-series values. In the initial phase of our study, the use of ARIMA with external variables was tested, but in no case did it alter the results of using univariable ARIMA. These initial results did not allow us to analyse the impact of exogenous variables. Therefore, we decided to change our approach from a time-series approach to a feature matrix approach.

Table 1. Forecast performance using univariate timeseries. Shift refers to the official shifts of ED service workers. Due to zero values in inpatients series, some infinite MAPE values appear.

Series	Freq	Model	MAPE (%)	SMAPE (%)	R^2
Admissions	8H	H-W	13.19	12.15	0.93
	Shift	H-W	11.76	11.05	0.87
	12H	H-W	8.22	7.92	0.90
	1D	H-W	5.89	5.77	0.40
Inpatients	8H	H-W	∞	28.44	0.53
	Shift	H-W	∞	31.07	0.66
	12H	H-W	31.99	25.20	0.75
	1D	H-W	14.48	14.17	0.11
Discharges	8H	H-W	15.41	14.12	0.84
	Shift	H-W	12.65	12.26	0.60
	12H	H-W	12.59	12.04	0.90
	1D	H-W	6.89	6.80	0.15

4   Data Preprocess

Due to the application of regressive algorithms in this study, it is necessary to adapt the time series detailed in the previous section. The transformation applied will allow us to convert each of the time series into feature matrices that maintain some relationship with previous values of the series.

To carry out the time series conversion, the first point to consider is that the time series value at an instant in time is the dependent variable in the algorithms subsequently applied. Thus, the first features are obtained from the same dependent variable. To this end, the time series are shifted by days so that one value of the time series is an independent variable of the next value. In this way, we get a matrix with a time series value for a specific time instant and its immediate previous values in the same record. The number of movements applied was 56 days due to the tests that performed better results. Figure 1 summarize the process described.

The second part of creating the feature-based dataset consists of adding the exogenous variables to analyse their impact. The first exogenous variables chosen are related to calendars. Among these variables, we select five variables to indicate public holidays in binary format: a first variable indicating whether the date is a bank holiday in Spain, the second one indicating whether the holiday is a regional holiday, the third one indicating whether it is a local holiday in Guadalajara, a fourth indicating all public holidays regardless of their category, and the last indicating whether the previous day was a public holiday. Continuing with the variables extracted from the calendar, we also introduce the academic calendar of the schools in binary format, which will indicate whether the day is a school day or not. Finishing with the calendar variables and enhancing the

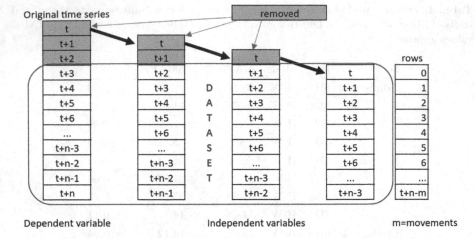

Fig. 1. Time series to feature matrix process. Our study selects 56 days for movements, so the first 56 days of feature matrix are removed due to null values.

seasonality contained in the initial time series, we also introduce the lunar phase cycle for each day. The influence of the lunar phase was suggested by the ED managers, who hipotetized a relationship between tides and childbirths.

The last selected exogenous variables are relevant events for the local culture. They have been selected due to the indications of human experts. These events are related to the football matches of the Real Madrid, F.C. Barcelona, Atlético de Madrid and the Spanish National Team. The way to add them to the dataset is using a binary format. The binary format indicates whether a team played a match on a specific day or not. The match's result is not added because we aim to generate predictive models, and the result is unknown a priori.

Table 2 shows a summary of all the variables in our dataset.

Table 2. All features of our final dataset. Our dependent variable is the current value from time series.

Variable name	Description	Type
prev$i$	Time series value at previous lag i	Integer value
all_fest	Current day is a public holiday (national, regional and local)	Binary $\{0,1\}$
prev_fest	Previous day was a holiday	Binary $\{0,1\}$
national_fest	Current day is a bank holiday (Spain)	Binary $\{0,1\}$
regional_fest	Current day is a regional holiday (Castilla-La Mancha)	Binary $\{0,1\}$
local_fest	Current day is a local holiday (Guadalajara)	Binary $\{0,1\}$
academic_class	Current day is a school day (Guadalajara)	Binary $\{0,1\}$
moon_pos	Lunar phase cycle	Binary $\{0,1\}$
atm_match	Current day Atlético de Madrid plays a football match	Binary $\{0,1\}$
bcn_match	Current day F.C. Barcelona plays a football match	Binary $\{0,1\}$
mad_match	Current day Real Madrid plays a football match	Binary $\{0,1\}$
spain_match	Current day Spanish National Team plays a football match	Binary $\{0,1\}$

5   Methodology Based on Feature Selection

In order to understand the influence of the exogenous attributes, we have trained several predictive models and compared the attributes selected by the models. We included two classical regression models, linear regression and ElasticNet regression, and also included a much more recent tree-based regressor, XGBoost. For each one of these algorithms we followed the same procedure to assess the impact of exogenous variables.

The procedure starts by tuning an algorithm to forecast the independent variable, i.e. the value of the time-series, using only the feature of the value of the same time-series at the last instant. Then, for each model fitted, we use 10-folds cross-validation on the training set and extract the R^2 metric by averaging results obtained by all folds. This provides a naïve baseline for the following steps.

The second step consists of analysing, also using 10-fold cross-validation, the impact of each of the other variables and sorting them by the R^2 metric. From all the variables considered, we add the one with the best results to the selected variables set, whether it represents a considerable improvement for the baseline. We understand a considerable improvement as one that exceeds the baseline results by a threshold greater than 0.001. The result obtained by this new selected variables set will be fixed as the new baseline for the next iteration.

Our procedure ends at the point where none of the unselected variables improves the results of their baseline by the defined threshold. Once we have the final variables selected, we will fit the treated model again but this time with the entire training set to obtain the final metrics. Algorithm 1 shows the pseudocode of the implemented process for feature selection.

After defining the general process, the procedure to be followed by each algorithm is set out in concrete terms, as previous steps may be required in some cases.

5.1   Linear Model

As the simplest model, the linear model only follows the steps detailed above. Therefore, no extra steps are required.

5.2   ElasticNet

The ElasticNet model has three hyperparameters to fit: alpha, l1 ratio, and maximum iterations. Before fitting, we proceed to find the hyperparameters that optimize the model for our data. Using a *GridSearchCV*, we perform a hyperparameters optimization search. The value params used for the search are alpha values of 0.0001, 0.001, 0.01, 0.1, 1, 10 and 100; l1 ratio values of 0.1–1.0 with steps of 0.1; and maximum iterations values between 1 and 10.

ElasticNet is capable of detecting which variables are helpful for regression, so it is not necessary to apply the base algorithm described above. The variables selected in this case will be those whose regression coefficients are non-zero.

Algorithm 1: Feature selection algorithm pseudocode.

Data: Dataset divided on train (to August 7, 2019) and test (from August 8, 2019)

$selected\_features = list()$;
$threshold = 0.001$;
$selected\_features.append(previous\_time\_series\_value)$;
$baseline = 10fold\_cross\_validation(selected\_features, train)$;
while *exists unselected features* **do**
    $impact\_list = list()$;
    for *each unselected feature* **do**
        $value = $
            $10fold\_cross\_validation(list(selected\_features, new\_feature), train)$;
        $impact\_list.append(value)$;
    end
    $best\_feature = best\_value(impact\_list)$;
    if $best\_feature > (baseline + threshold)$ **then**
        $selected\_features.append(best\_feature)$;
        $baseline = 10fold\_cross\_validation(selected\_features, train)$;
    else
        $break$;
    end
end
$fit\_model(selected\_features, train)$;

5.3   XGBoost

The XGBoost model, like ElasticNet, has some hyperparameters that require optimization. To this end, the hyperparameters adjustment is made after selecting the attributes but before making the final adjustment in the general process. The hyperparameters to be tuned are the number of estimators (we test with values of 100, 500 and 1000), the depth of the estimators (we introduce values from 5 to 10), the number of variables we introduce for each estimator (we test with 40%, 60% and 80% of dataset variables) and the learning rate (we introduce values of 0.001, 0.01 and 0.1). The rest of the parameters are the default ones from the Python XGBoost library. The hyperparameter search is performed with *GridSearchCV*. The rest of the procedure follows the described methodology.

6   Experimental Results

Table 3 shows the performance metrics for the algorithms applied to all the time aggregations along with the univariate performance to ease comparison. Considering admissions, multivariate regression techniques improve the baseline for the eight-hour, official shift and twelve-hour aggregations. However, the difference is minimal. On the other hand, we obtain significantly better results for the one-day time aggregation, going from 0.40 in R^2 to 0.51 for the linear regression with exogenous variables. Thus, the results for this series hints at there being no single model providing the best fit for all possible aggregations. As a result, depending on the chosen aggregation, linear regression or XGBoost will provide the best results.

Regarding the inpatients series, only aggregating by shifts improves the univariate modelling results on the R^2 metric, but not for the SMAPE metric. For the rest of the frequencies, modelling with exogenous variables does not improve the univariate results. Exogenous variables used may not be associated with the time-series. It is noted that models based on a feature matrix may not be selecting exogenous variables when selecting variables because they are not providing relevant information.

Finally, looking at the discharges series' results, we find that the features appear to be adding value to the time series only for the twelve-hour frequency. However, the improvement is minor, from an R^2 of 0.90 to 0.91, and a SMAPE from 12.04 to 12.59.

Considering the applied models, linear regressions and XGBoost alternate as the best model among the ones studied. ElasticNet achieves the best fit only for the inpatients series in eight-hour aggregations. At the same time, ElasticNet is also the model that least often improves the univariate modelling.

The number of variables that have been selected the most during the process might provide relevant knowledge. Figure 2 examines the frecuency of the selected variables for each output variable. In the admissions, the regional and local holidays, Real Madrid matches and Spanish National Team matches are not chosen in any case. Therefore, these variables have not improved the predictions in our experiments. This lack of improvement may be caused because their information is contained in other variables, the time series itself, or it may be irrelevant. On the other hand, the academic calendar, Real Madrid and Atletico Madrid matches are the most frequently selected for inpatient modelling. Finally, the most frecuently chosen atributes for discharges were whether the previous day was a public holiday and the academic calendar.

Analysing exogenous variables by time aggregation, the academic calendar is the most prominent variable among all the groupings and variables, except admissions. It is also remarkable that daily frequency has the highest number of selected variables. This result coincides with the greatest improvement over univariate modelling. In this situation, it seems that exogenous variables provide new information not contained in the time series. Figure 3 shows the distribution of the selected variables according to the time grouping.

7   Discussion

Based on the previously described results, some relevant observations can be made. Firstly, our time series seems to provide enough relevant information on its own to hamper improvement via the addition of exogenous variables. As observed during our experimentation, the progressive inclusion of additional features offers minimal improvement over our baseline H-W model. Furthermore,

Table 3. Regression performance with different algorithms and time aggregations. Due to zero values in inpatients series, some infinite MAPE values appear.

Serie	Freq	Model	MAPE	SMAPE	R^2
Admissions	8H	Linear regression	13.53	12.75	0.94
		XGBoost	12.15	11.58	0.94
		H-W	13.19	12.15	0.93
		Elastic net	14.98	13.96	0.92
	Shift	XGBoost	10.83	10.54	0.88
		Linear regression	12.08	11.63	0.87
		H-W	11.76	8.22	0.87
		Elastic net	13.11	12.46	0.85
	12H	XGBoost	8.09	8.02	0.90
		H-W	8.22	7.92	0.90
		Linear regression	8.48	8.38	0.89
		Elastic net	9.50	9.39	0.87
	1D	Linear regression	5.41	5.35	0.51
		XGBoost	5.58	5.53	0.46
		Elastic net	5.87	5.81	0.41
		H-W	5.89	5.77	0.40
Inpatients	8H	H-W	∞	28.44	0.53
		Elastic net	∞	29.00	0.50
		XGBoost	∞	29.88	0.49
		Linear regression	∞	30.28	0.48
	Shift	XGBoost	∞	31.85	0.67
		H-W	∞	31.07	0.66
		Linear regression	∞	32.74	0.65
		Elastic net	∞	31.82	0.64
	12H	H-W	31.99	25.20	0.75
		Linear regression	30.63	25.85	0.75
		XGBoost	33.11	26.22	0.73
		Elastic net	32.85	25.83	0.72
	1D	H-W	14.48	14.17	0.11
		Linear regression	14.95	14.58	0.05
		Elastic net	15.18	14.70	0.03
		XGBoost	15.49	15.02	0.01
Discharges	8H	H-W	15.41	14.12	0.84
		XGBoost	13.95	13.40	0.84
		Linear regression	13.96	13.39	0.84
		Elastic net	14.68	13.95	0.81
	Shift	H-W	12.65	12.26	0.60
		Linear regression	12.95	12.60	0.58
		XGBoost	13.37	12.99	0.56
		Elastic net	13.39	12.93	0.56
	12H	XGBoost	11.19	11.04	0.91
		Linear regression	11.67	11.35	0.91
		H-W	12.59	12.04	0.90
		Elastic net	13.24	12.86	0.89
	1D	XGBoost	6.84	6.80	0.18
		Linear regression	7.00	6.98	0.17
		Elastic net	7.05	7.01	0.17
		H-W	6.89	6.80	0.15

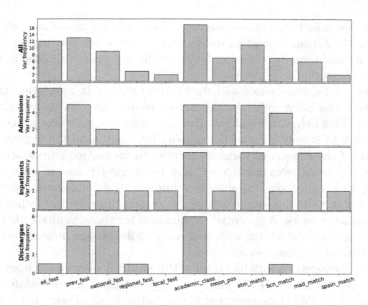

Fig. 2. Number of exogenous variables selections for each variable. At the top, the accumulation of all selections for all series and all time aggregations. Subsequently, the division by each series for all time aggregations.

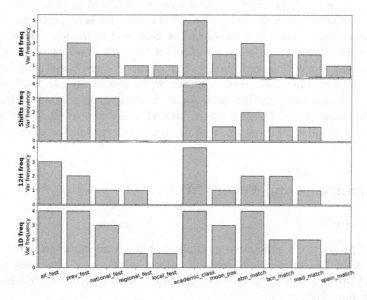

Fig. 3. Number of exogenous variables selections for each time aggregation. Exogenous variables are selected more times when the time aggregation eliminates the daily series seasonality. This is consistent with improvements in the predictions for each of the series in this aggregation.

due to its comparatively simpler approach, this baseline model minimizes time needed for the fitting process to complete, offering a sensible balance between performance and required resources for model fitting when compared to the rest of the models studied.

Regarding the time series and its aggregations, it is interesting that the admissions series offers substantially better results once its daily stationality is removed. This behavior highlights the importance of said seasonality, as well as the ability to supply some of the missing information in the aggregation by using some of the exogenous variables mentioned for our experimentation.

Another relevant conclusion that may be derived from our study is that modelling with exogenous variables can improve the admissions series, albeit only slightly, but the same approach offers no clear improvements when applied to the inpatients series. A potential explanation for these results is that people who come to the ED service with serious pathologies are independent of the calendar date or the matches analysed.

As for the exogenous variables used in this study, it seems quite relevant that the academic calendar and the public holiday calendar may be related to ED attendance. A variable being selected in our methodology means that it helps to model the noise of the time series. In our case, it seems these types of variables provide the most information. In addition, it seems that Atlético de Madrid and Real Madrid matches are helping to forecast the inpatients series, but as they do not improve on the univariate results, we cannot conclude that they provide more information than the time series itself.

Finally, experimental results suggest that no single algorithm is better than the others for all series and aggregations. Therefore, for each problem, a specific study needs to be carried out to select the best suited model. This same idea extends to exogenous variables: depending on the series and aggregations, their utility may vary, as well as with the location of the selected hospital, as indicated in the literature. Therefore, results obtained by our study are limited to the specific timeframe and location used for it, without any guarantees that they may be extended to a different context. Nevertheless, the results align with the literature on calendar information seeming to be a relevant factor when modelling ED service data.

8   Conclusions and Future Work

8.1   Conclusions

This work presents the predictive modelling of three relevant variables from the perspective of ED service management, along with some exogenous variables that could provide an insight to its behaviour. These variables were admissions, inpatients and discharges.

We made different time aggregations, of eight hours, twelve hours, one day, and the service workers' official shifts for each series. The exogenous variables chosen for our study were, on the one hand, variables extracted from the calendar: public holidays, national holidays, regional holidays, local holidays, academic calendar and the phase of the lunar cycle; on the other hand, events related to football matches of Real Madrid, F.C. Barcelona, Atlético de Madrid and the Spanish National team.

Results obtained with our process significantly improve the prediction for the admissions when the frequency is daily from an R^2 score of 0.40 in the univariate modelling to 0.51 with linear regression. For admissions, there is a slight improvement over the univariate modelling at all other frequencies. Regarding inpatients, the results obtained do not improve the univariate H-W modelling with the selected variables. Concerning the discharges series, the greatest improvement also occurs in the daily frequency, with the R^2 going from 0.15 to 0.18.

During the variable selection process, the academic calendar and public holidays (including a variable indicating that the previous day was a public holiday) were the most selected variables.

8.2 Future Works

The results presented in this paper may suggest future works to better understand the ED service's affluence. The first would be the inclusion of more exogenous variables of different kinds. One of them could be to test the influence of climate or the level of pollution. The main reason for not including them in our study was the smaller time window available to obtain them, compared with our prediction window. In the case of climate, it would limit our predictive range. However, it could be an interesting indicator to measure its impact for predictions within a smaller time frame.

Another work that could be interesting would be to try to quantify more concretely the impact that each of the variables has over the value of the time series. Thus, peaks in the series could be associated with specific, meaningful events.

Due to data limitations, it would be interesting to apply the procedure followed in our paper to a larger amount of data gathered from different locations, to understand the ED service better in a more general way.

Acknowledgements. The authors would like to acknowledge the clinical support of Mr. Francisco López Martínez, Mrs. María Isabel Pascual Benito and Mrs. Helena Hernández Martínez. Also, the authors want to thank the support of the Hospital Universitario de Guadalajara (HUGU), Spain.

References

1. Guttmann, A., Schull, M.J., Vermeulen, M.J., Stukel, T.A.: Association between waiting times and short term mortality and hospital admission after departure from emergency department: population based cohort study from Ontario, Canada. BMJ 342(7809), 6 June 2011. https://doi.org/10.1136/bmj.d2983

2. Gul, M., Celik, E.: An exhaustive review and analysis on applications of statistical forecasting in hospital emergency departments. Health Syst. **9**(4), 263–284 (2020). https://doi.org/10.1080/20476965.2018.1547348
3. Collado-Villaverde, A., R-Moreno, M.D., Barrero, D.F., Rodriguez, D.: Machine learning approach to detect falls on elderly people using sound, pp. 149–159. Springer, Arras, France, June 2017. https://doi.org/10.1007/978-3-319-60042-0_18
4. Hertzum, M.: Forecasting hourly patient visits in the emergency department to counteract crowding. Ergon. Open J. **10**(1), 1–13 (2017). https://doi.org/10.2174/1875934301710010001
5. McCarthy, M.L., Zeger, S.L., Ding, R., Aronsky, D., Hoot, N.R., Kelen, G.D.: The challenge of predicting demand for emergency department services. Acad. Emergency Med. **15**(4), 337–346 (2008). https://doi.org/10.1111/j.1553-2712.2008.00083.x
6. Sun, Y., Heng, B.H., Seow, Y.T., Seow, E.: Forecasting daily attendances at an emergency department to aid resource planning (2009). https://doi.org/10.1186/1471-227X-9-1
7. Boyle, J., et al.: Predicting emergency department admissions. Emergency Med. J. **29**(5), 358–365 (2012). https://doi.org/10.1136/emj.2010.103531
8. Rocha, C.N., Rodrigues, F.: Forecasting emergency department admissions. J. Intell. Inf. Syst. **56**(3), 509–528 (2021). https://doi.org/10.1007/s10844-021-00638-9
9. Kam, H.J., Sung, J.O., Park, R.W.: Prediction of daily patient numbers for a regional emergency medical center using time series analysis. Healthc. Inform. Res. **16**(3), 158–165 (2010). https://doi.org/10.4258/hir.2010.16.3.158
10. Poole, S., Grannis, S., Shah, N.H.: Predicting emergency department visits. AMIA Joint Summits on Translational Science proceedings. AMIA Joint Summits on Translational Science 2016, pp. 438–445 (2016)
11. Graham, B., Bond, R., Quinn, M., Mulvenna, M.: Using data mining to predict hospital admissions from the emergency department. IEEE Access **6**, 10458–10469 (2018). https://doi.org/10.1109/ACCESS.2018.2808843

Applications of Machine Learning

Automatic Information Extraction from Electronic Documents Using Machine Learning

Nishanthan Kamaleson[✉], Dominique Chu, and Fernando E. B. Otero

School of Computing, University of Kent, Canterbury, UK
{N.Kamaleson,D.F.Chu,F.E.B.Otero}@kent.ac.uk

Abstract. The digital processing of electronic documents is widely exploited across many domains to improve the efficiency of information extraction. However, paper documents are still largely being used in practice. In order to process such documents, a manual procedure is used to inspect them and extract the values of interest. As this task is monotonous and time consuming, it is prone to introduce human errors during the process. In this paper, we present an efficient and robust system that automates the aforementioned task by using a combination of machine learning techniques: optical character recognition, object detection and image processing techniques. This not only speeds up the process but also improves the accuracy of extracted information compared to a manual procedure.

Keywords: OCR · Layout analysis · Image detection · Information extraction

1 Introduction

In the last few years, the applications of machine learning (ML) have displayed a strong positive impact in various industrial sectors. With the help of ML, most of the complex and tedious tasks have been transformed into smartly automated tasks. For example, ML-enabled chatbots have started assisting the customers with product related questions, henceforth, the sales cycle became more efficient. Since the interventions of ML, a paradigm shift has started towards digitalisation. As a result, many sectors decided to move beyond paper documents and adopt digital document management systems. Nevertheless, use of paper documents is still widespread within some sectors such as financial and legal. The key information (KI) from such documents need to be extracted and stored electronically to adhere to the paradigm of digitalisation. This process has been done manually by humans until the introduction of optical character recognition (OCR), which makes it possible to convert text within an image into machine readable text.

© Springer Nature Switzerland AG 2021
M. Bramer and R. Ellis (Eds.): SGAI-AI 2021, LNAI 13101, pp. 183–194, 2021.
https://doi.org/10.1007/978-3-030-91100-3_16

As OCR systems have evolved in recent years, the recognition of hand-written and printed text from scanned images has significantly improved. However, extracting the values of interest from varying complex structures still is a challenging problem. Previously, there have been many methods introduced to tackle this problem in various contexts [3,4,6–8]. However, they are either very generic or too specific and complex to solve the problem of extracting values from more than 2000 different types of electronic documents, where the number of types could possibly increase over time.

In this paper, we present a novel system for KI extraction, named as *Doctract*, which is effective and robust in handling complex documents of various structures. *Doctract* is composed of multiple sophisticated tools and techniques including state-of-the-art open-source OCR engine *Tesseract*[1] and object detection model *YOLOv4*.[2] It utilises the features of documents, such as text, layout, position and visual cues, to obtain a semantic representation that enables the efficient and precise extraction of KI. For a certain document type, these features should be defined for every KI of interest using a document template file. Later, when processing a document, Doctract system will refer to the document template file and extract KI accordingly.

The rest of the paper is organised as follows. Section 2 describes the problem of extracting key information. Section 3 describes prior works related to key information extraction from electronic documents. Section 4 details the proposed system and how it uses machine learning techniques to solve the problem. The evaluation of our approach is discussed in Sect. 5, followed by conclusion in Sect. 6.

2   Problem: Extracting Key Information

The problem of extracting key information that we are addressing in this paper can be exemplified as follows. An anonymous company collects different documents that enclose KI of their clients from external sources with their consent. In their current work flow, such KI are manually extracted and uploaded into their systems for record keeping. This process consumes on average between 5 to 10 min per document with up to 15% likelihood of human error (85% accuracy). Each of these external sources could have more than one type (structure) of document and there are about 2000 different external sources, therefore a KI can be located at different sections of the document and equivalent KI can be identified by different labels (e.g., member number, account number, member ID).

---

[1] https://opensource.google/projects/tesseract.
[2] https://github.com/AlexeyAB/darknet.

Our goal is to automate their KI extraction process to improve the processing time and eliminate the need for human resources while making sure the likelihood of error is below 15%. As the processing of documents can be parallelised, our focus is only on extracting the precise KI as more computational resources could be allocated to speed up the overall process. In this paper, the document corpus was created from 6 different external sources where 1 of them has 3 different document types whilst the rest has only two. Overall, we obtained 50 document instances with at least 3 samples for each of the document type. Although we are working with scanned documents, the proposed system is capable of handling any electronic documents.

3   Related Work

The extraction of KI from scanned images of complex structured documents has been explored and studied extensively by many researchers [4,5,7].

Ishitani [5] proposed a document analysis method which enables automated extraction of KI and their logical relationship from scanned documents using a set of pre-stored models, which defines the type of each document. The KI extraction pipeline of this particular work is very similar to our proposed solution, where their models are referred in our context as document templates. However, their models assume that the documents have fixed structure for a given type. In our documents, KI is not only spanned across multiple pages but also their geometric positions are likely to change within a same type of document.

Peanho et al. [7] proposed another similar solution where their document model is a set of relations between text segments which describes positional and geometric relations. Although their document model considers significant positional displacement of KI within a same type of document, it assumes the document model is always known a priori. When the document model is unknown, their system applies all the models to the corresponding document and selects the appropriate model. This approach is not efficient in our case as we are dealing with more than 2000 types of document layouts.

Commercial products such as Google's Cloud Vision[3] and Amazon's Textract[4] have good performance in carrying out OCR tasks. However, the flexibility of their layout analysis is limited. For example, Textract can identify text, forms and tables but there is not an option to selectively extract only the values of a particular section of the text or table from documents. Additionally, they do not provide a facility to extract the same information from documents with different layout or structure. In this work, we overcome these limitations by introducing document templates, which allows a user to define the relative location of a KI, together with an automatic document detection to select the specific template to extract the information.

---

[3] https://cloud.google.com/vision.
[4] https://aws.amazon.com/textract/.

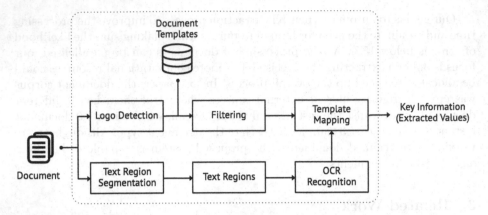

Fig. 1. Pipeline of key information extraction process

4 Proposed System

This section describes the architecture of the proposed Doctract system and the underlying tools and techniques used to achieve our goal, including the state-of-the-art object detection architecture, image processing techniques used in computer vision and an optical character recognition (OCR) tool.

4.1 Overview

The Doctract system performs the KI extraction process over three phases. During the first phase, it detects logos within the given electronic document, henceforth, identifies the respective external source. In the second phase, it initially performs text segmentation and then constructs a dictionary using the OCR outputs and bounding box coordinates of those respective text segments. Finally, it selects all document templates matching the identified logo and maps each of them against the constructed dictionary. Thereafter, it picks the appropriate template based on confidence scores, which measures the relevance of a document template to the document. Finally, returns the KI that was extracted using the best template. Figure 1 shows the pipeline of the Doctract System including all of these phases.

4.2 Object Detection

Image classification [2] is the process of categorising and labeling groups of pixels within an image based on a set of rules. Image localisation [9] is a regression problem where the output is x and y coordinates around the object of interest to draw bounding boxes. Object detection is a complex problem that combines the concepts of both image localisation and classification to return bounding boxes around all objects of interest and assign a class to them.

When classifying an electronic document into a certain type, we would normally consider using image classification techniques. However, we have access to only a small number of documents and their structures vary significantly even within the same document type. Therefore, we decided to focus on image objects that uniquely identifies the type of a given document. Based on our investigation, we learned that the logos in these documents are a good candidate to identify the external source as they do not change often.

However, these logo objects are too small comparing to the size a document page. Unlike image classification, the likelihood of preserving the classification signal is very high in object detection as it generates features from images at more fine-grained level. In our particular scenario, therefore, we could achieve better performance with object detection over the image classification even when we are not interested in the exact location or counts of the object.

As we have small number training image samples, it is necessary for us to augment our existing training dataset so that our machine learning model will be able to learn from a wider array of situations. The authors of the YOLOv4 [1], a widely used object detector, built in a set of techniques called Bag-of-Freebies, which includes some popular techniques, such as data augmentation, random cropping and shadowing, to improve the accuracy and robustness of the model during training and post-processing. Therefore, we decided to use YOLOv4 as our object detector, which in our case eliminated the necessity to augment the training data further.

4.3   Optical Character Recognition

Optical Character Recognition (OCR) can be quite sensitive to the quality (resolution) of the document. The rudimentary document quality standards which we recommend to pay attention to when scanning the documents are the dot per inch (dpi), brightness and contrast level. The widely used rule of thumb for dpi and brightness levels are between 300 to 600 dpi and 50% brightness level, respectively. Keeping the dpi below 300 may produce unclear and incomprehensible results whilst keeping the dpi above 600 will lead to only larger output files and no further improvements in the quality of the results. The brightness levels that are too high or low could negatively impact the OCR quality. However, when it comes to contrast level, only the lower settings would result in poor OCR accuracy. Therefore, keeping the contrast level above 50% is recommended. We can improve the accuracy of an OCR process either by maintaining the list of document quality standards we mentioned before at the acquisition stage and by applying a combination of image processing techniques as appropriate at the preprocessing stage. We will discuss the commonly used image processing techniques and how we leveraged them to achieve our goals in the next section.

There are currently plenty of commercial and open-source OCR tools available in the market. Cloud services from Google (Google Vision API), Microsoft (Azure Computer Vision API)[5], Amazon (Textract API) are providing their

---

[5] https://azure.microsoft.com/en-gb/services/cognitive-services/computer-vision/.

own OCR models as subscription services. Tesseract[6], GOCR[7] and CuneiForm[8] are widely used open-source OCR Tools. Among the open-source OCR Tools, the performance of the Tesseract OCR engine is comparable to the commercial tools. Therefore, we decided to select Tesseract as the OCR tool of our choice to perform KI extraction in the Doctract system.

4.4   Image Processing

The main objective of the preprocessing stage in the OCR process is to improve the readability of the document for the OCR system to recognise a character/-word from the background. Most commonly used image preprocessing techniques are binarization, skew correction, noise reduction. However, in this specific phase, we apply the following techniques in the given order:

1. Binarisation
2. Noise removal
3. Horizontal and vertical line detection
4. Add vertical spaces before and after horizontal lines
5. Remove horizontal and vertical lines.

First, we converted the RGB image into a grayscale image and then we applied adaptive thresholding to binarize the image. Any noises introduced during the scanning process were reduced using the morphological operations such as opening and closing. Most of our document instances included tables where the paddings between cells were too small to perform precise segmentation. Thus, we added spaces before and after the detected horizontal lines which allowed us to easily separate the cells from each other during the text segmentation phase. Moreover, we decided to remove all the lines as we are only interested in the textual content.

Later, we inverted the image and applied the morphological transformation operation called dilation using a rectangle kernel. As a result of this process, we will obtain white rectangle blocks which could possibly represent the location of a sentence, a phrase or a word. We finally extract the bounds of these white rectangle blocks. The knowledge of these bounds are not only used to distinguish the text segments but also used during the application of document templates to compare the relative positions of key text segments against each other.

---

[6] https://github.com/tesseract-ocr/tesseract.

[7] http://jocr.sourceforge.net/.

[8] https://en.wikipedia.org/wiki/CuneiForm_(software).

```
1   <Templates>
2     <Company name="ABC Ltd.">
3       <Document id="1" name="Form">
4         <Term name="Start Date">
5           <DataType>Date</DataType>
6           <Content type="key-value">
7             <Key>Commencement Date</Key>
8             <Context>
9               <Neighbour>
10                <Detail>
11                  <Text>Job Title</Text>
12                  <Location>Above</Location>
13                </Detail>
14              </Neighbour>
15            </Context>
16          </Content>
17        </Term>
18      </Document>
19    </Company>
20  </Templates>
```

Listing 1.1. Sample Document Template

4.5 Document Templates

The templates for documents were introduced with the intention of locating KI within a given document. We realised that during an extraction process, we have to deal with different types of values such as currency, dates, names and IDs. In addition to this, our values could be found either as a key-value pair (e.g. "Start Date: 01/02/2019") or located within a cell of a table. Finally, we decided to include the contextual information of neighbours as constraints to increase the confidence. Document templates are specified in XML – the XML code snippet shown in Listing 1.1 is an example for an application form of fictitious "ABC Ltd." company.

In this application form, we are aiming to extract the corresponding value for the term "start date". It is also given that the value's data type is "Date". As this value is expected to appear as a key-value pair in the document, we should look for that particular key in the dictionary which we constructed during the image processing phase. Later, the algorithm verifies whether the "Job Title" is above this particular key. If the value satisfies the neighbour constraint, Doctract looks for the values immediately on the right or bottom of the given key and verifies whether it is a type of "Date" or not; if so, returns the value.

We have defined a metric which allows us to evaluate the performance of our Doctract system in extracting these values. Let T be the number of times a value is repeated, the confidence score C for the ith term (where $i < n$ and n is the total number of terms) is defined as below:

$$C_i = \frac{T_i^2}{\sum\limits_{j=0}^{n} T_j^2} \tag{1}$$

For example, assume we are trying to extract a value for the term "name" from an application form. The Doctract system extracted the values "David" and "Tom" from the given document three times and one time, respectively. As "David" repeated more times, we are more confident that "David" is likely to be the right value. If we substitute these values into Eq. 1, we get a 90% confidence score that "David" is the correct value.

4.6 Algorithm

The Doctract algorithm illustrated in Algorithm 1, begins with identifying the logo located within the document. If the logo detection is successful, every page in the document will be preprocessed and the relevant document template will be pulled from the templates XML file. Thereafter, the algorithm loops through each of these preprocessed pages and detects the elements such as words/phrases/sentences. Using the coordinates of the bounding boxes of these elements, the original page is cropped and passed to the Tesseract OCR tool for extracting the text within those bounding boxes.

Once the text is extracted, a dictionary will be constructed where the bounding boxes and the extracted texts are keys and values, respectively. Finally, the template is applied on the constructed dictionary to extract the values of interest based on the relative locations defined in the templates. The results from all the pages are aggregated and returned. If multiple values that satisfies the specification of a given term have appeared within the document then the most frequent one is selected.

5 Evaluation

In this section, we present the evaluation results of the proposed system. The performance was measured comparing the values extracted by the system against the actual values in the documents. As these documents hold sensitive information, we keep the context as well as the values from these documents anonymous. We also discuss details of the runtime environment of the proposed system and the steps carried out to perform the experiment. Our dataset contained 50 documents from 6 different providers and each provider had 2 document types except provider "D" which had 3 different document types. In total, we created 13 different document templates.

All experiments were carried out on a system of Intel(R) Core(TM) i9-9980HK CPU @ 2.40 GHz (16 CPUs) with 32 GB RAM and NVIDIA GeForce GTX 1650 4 GB Graphics card.

Algorithm 1. Doctract algorithm

Require: Scanned document d
```
1:  l := DetectLogo(d)
2:  if l in supportedDocs then
3:      globalResults := {}
4:      prepDoc := preprocess(doc)
5:      t := findTemplate(l)
6:      for page in prepDoc do
7:          bounds := extractBound(page)
8:          d := {}
9:          for b in bounds do
10:             roi := prepDoc.crop(b)
11:             text := tesseract.read(roi)
12:             dictionary.add(roi, text)
13:         end for
14:         pageResults := applyTemplate(d, t)
15:         globalResults.agg(pageResults)
16:     end for
17:     return globalResults
18: else
19:     return {}
20: end if
```

5.1 Logo Detection Model Accuracy

In Sect. 4, we discussed in detail why the object detection approach is a better fit than image classification in our context. In order to train any supervised machine learning models, we need labelled data. For object detection task, images with corresponding bounding box coordinates and classes are the labelled data. As we have obtained only a few scanned documents, we created our own training dataset using these documents as well as images of logos retrieved from the internet.

All of these documents were converted into images and then the logos were annotated with the help of an open-source image annotation tool, known as LabelImg[9]. In our training dataset we labelled six different logos, are for each different external source, and created around 100 samples for each of these logos. *YOLOv4* achieved the mean average precision of 90% in 3000 iterations on our logo dataset.

5.2 Performance of Doctract System

We evaluated the performance of the Doctract system by comparing the results against the manually extracted values. In this context, these values can be a type of currency, ID or date. Table 1 shows the results of evaluation against 6 different logos (each logo represents an external source) and 11 different types

---

[9] https://github.com/tzutalin/labelImg

Table 1. Accuracy of extracted key information from the scanned documents. In this experiment, Doctract confidence score is calculated using Eq. 1 for each extracted value and then averaged across all the documents. Accuracy refers to whether the value extracted by Doctract is same as the value present in the document. Highlighted value refers to the case when Doctract extracted an incorrect value from one of the "D01" documents due to poor scanned quality of the document.

Logo	Doc type	Docs count	No. of extracted values per doc	Logo detection accuracy	Average confidence	Average accuracy
A	A01	3	5	100%	100%	100%
	A02	3	5	100%	100%	100%
B	B01	7	5	100%	100%	100%
	B02	3	5	100%	100%	100%
C	C01	3	5	100%	100%	100%
	C02	10	5	100%	100%	100%
D	D01	3	5	100%	**100%**	**93.3%**
	D02	3	3	100%	100%	100%
	D03	3	5	100%	100%	100%
E	E01	3	5	100%	100%	100%
	E02	3	5	100%	100%	100%
F	F01	3	5	100%	100%	100%
	F02	3	5	100%	100%	100%

of documents. Our results show that for all the documents the Doctract system accurately extracted the expected values, apart from *D01*. In the case of document type *D01*, the Doctract system is 100% confident that the values it extracted were the right ones. However, during the manual inspection, it was revealed that one of the extracted values was incorrect due to an erroneous reading by the OCR tool.

Table 2 shows the time taken to process a page within the three phases of the extraction process. From the table, we can see that the presence of lines in a page does not impact the time taken to detect the logo or the application of a template as they do not deal with the lines. On the other hand, the time of the second phase is increased by a few seconds as it is the place where the lines in a page are identified and removed so that an OCR system can read the values with more clarity.

Our corpus mostly includes documents of pages 6 to 40. The proposed Doctract system was able to extract the key information from the smallest one within 2 min whilst it took 10 min to process the largest one. In general, it takes about 5 to 10 min for an experienced person to complete this task. As we can parallelise

Table 2. Performance of Doctract system across different phases

Document structure	Logo detection (s/page)	Preprocessing and OCR (s/page)	Application of template (s/page)
With lines	2.13	17.27	0.006
Without lines	2.09	12.10	0.006

the processing at document level, the Doctract system can certainly improve the efficiency of the existing workflow.

6 Conclusion

Our main objective in this work was to improve the existing work flow of manually extracting key information from electronic documents. Henceforth, we have proposed a system, called Doctract, as a solution to aid the existing work flow. Our system was able to recognise different types of documents from various external sources and extracted KI with the support of document templates. Our evaluation shows that Doctract can extract information with high accuracy (99.4%) across 50 real-world documents.

Our future work concentrates on developing a graphical user interface to assist users with generating document templates with ease. In addition to this, we are also exploring in the direction of leveraging the power ML to automate the generation of templates. Currently, adding a new provider requires the collection of logo samples and re-training the logo detection model, which can be a time consuming task. Therefore, we are exploring a more efficient way to detect the type of document to make the system more scalable and perform experiments with a larger set of documents.

References

1. Bochkovskiy, A., Wang, C.Y., Liao, H.Y.M.: YOLOv4: optimal speed and accuracy of object detection. arXiv preprint arXiv:2004.10934 (2020)
2. Druzhkov, P.N., Kustikova, V.D.: A survey of deep learning methods and software tools for image classification and object detection. Pattern Recogn. Image Anal. **26**(1), 9–15 (2016). https://doi.org/10.1134/S1054661816010065
3. Hirano, T., Okano, Y., Okada, Y., Yoda, F.: Text and layout information extraction from document files of various formats based on the analysis of page description language. In: 9th International Conference on Document Analysis and Recognition, ICDAR 2007, vol. 1, pp. 262–266. IEEE (2007)
4. Huang, Z., et al.: ICDAR 2019 competition on scanned receipt OCR and information extraction. In: 2019 International Conference on Document Analysis and Recognition (ICDAR), pp. 1516–1520. IEEE (2019)
5. Ishitani, Y.: Model based information extraction and its application to document images. In: Proceedings of the Workshop on Document Layout Interpretation and its Applications (2001)

6. Meier, R., Urbschat, H., Wanschura, T., Hausmann, J.: Methods for automatic structured extraction of data in OCR documents having tabular data. US Patent 9,251,413, 2 February 2016
7. Peanho, C.A., Stagni, H., da Silva, F.S.C.: Semantic information extraction from images of complex documents. Appl. Intell. **37**(4), 543–557 (2012)
8. Takasu, A., Aihara, K.: Quality enhancement in information extraction from scanned documents. In: Proceedings of the 2006 ACM Symposium on Document Engineering, pp. 122–124 (2006)
9. Vaillant, R., Monrocq, C., Le Cun, Y.: Original approach for the localisation of objects in images. IEE Proc. Visi. Image Sig. Process. **141**(4), 245–250 (1994)

Modelling Satellite Data for Automobile Insurance Risk

Sam Richardson[✉], Yixie Shao, Dana Khartabil, and Simon Thompson

GFT Financial Ltd, 9th Floor, 107 Cheapside, London EC2V 6DN, UK
{sam.richardson,yixie.shao,dana.khartabil,
simon.thompson}@gft.com

Abstract. High-resolution satellite data opens new applications for personalised hyper-local insurance risk scores. In this paper, open-source satellite imagery and accident incident data are aggregated to model road network risk for the generation of a risk map to be used in insurance quotation. Two machine learning approaches are outlined – an unsupervised clustering of the images based on extracted features and a supervised labelled data approach. These are tried against the data; results illustrating the potential utility of this approach for estimating insurance risk are given. For the unsupervised approach, distinct risk levels were produced which reflected historic levels of accident for visually similar road sections. With supervised methods, we performed a binary classification to identify accident sites with a recall of 82% and precision of 80%.

Keywords: Insurance · Risk · Satellite images · Transfer learning · Deep learning model · Unsupervised learning

1 Introduction

The availability and exploitation of high-resolution satellite imagery presents a range of new opportunities for the insurance industry with applications such as claim review and fraud detection. In this paper, we describe two potential approaches for generating a map of automobile accident risk by modelling satellite images and accident data which could be used to inform policy quotations. High-resolution satellite data is now widely available from several commercial suppliers such as Maxar and Airbus with modern satellites reaching resolutions of up to 30 cm [1]. Many of the initial applications of satellite imagery for insurance were in the agricultural space where the features of interest cover a large area [2]. With improved resolution, the ability to resolve a wider variety of objects such as roads, houses, and trees opens new opportunities for insurance application development. In the past, processing large unstructured datasets such as satellite data for this kind of application was unrealistic, presenting a challenge that was difficult to address whilst working with in-house data centres. Modern cloud platforms provide scalable storage and compute capable of addressing these issues, and a range of managed services that can be exploited to rapidly build reliable and maintainable solutions. Additionally, the development of open API's and configurable engines such

© Springer Nature Switzerland AG 2021
M. Bramer and R. Ellis (Eds.): SGAI-AI 2021, LNAI 13101, pp. 195–208, 2021.
https://doi.org/10.1007/978-3-030-91100-3_17

as Guidewire [3], Insuresoft [4] and Insurity [5] for managing business processes such as quote generation in retail insurance provides a straightforward route to deploying this kind of technology.

There are a variety of factors that can lead to an increased risk of automobile accidents such as, time of day, weather conditions and the type of road. In conventional risk estimation, several factors relating to the demographic and location of the policyholder are combined with historical claims and accident counts to generate a risk score, often based upon the predicted frequency and severity of claims within the upcoming policy period. The established approach of considering a home location in relation to historical accidents is only able to accommodate risks due to the local road network when the infrastructure has been in place for a prolonged period allowing accident records to be measured. An alternative approach is to use the complexity or type of road networks in an area to infer a risk score for those wanting to insure a vehicle there. The hypothesis is that more complex or anomalous sections of road are likely to lead to a higher risk of accidents occurring. Studies have indicated that most accidents occur when driving near the home [6] demonstrating the importance of understanding local risk. In addition, complex junctions are reported to lead to a greater level of accidents with much consideration of road network planning to reduce the potential risk [7].

To implement a local risk assessment method, it is necessary to generate a geographical risk map that provides a score for the risk of driving a vehicle in a particular location. Such a score could then be referred to when generating policy quotations. Previous studies from the literature have demonstrated an association between historical accident records and visual features found in satellite images of roads [8]. Alternative labels associated with high-risk areas such as social media warnings [9] and telematics readings [10] have also shown a link to features extracted from road images.

In this paper, we describe two methods for generating a road network risk map based on unsupervised and supervised learning methods. First, we demonstrate an unsupervised approach to clustering satellite data to generate distinct risk levels. By clustering images into visually similar road sections, we can generate risk levels considering accident statistics across the entire group which aims to avoid potential issues around the sparsity of accident data. This approach follows the hypothesis that road network risk is related to the structure of the network with visually similar road sections clustered together within in the image embedding space. For this model, clusters are fit for varying values of k with a manual search to find the optimal number of risk levels where distinct separation of images is achieved. Previous studies have looked to address the issue of sparse accident data with alternative datasets [9, 10], here we address the sparsity by averaging accident counts over visually similar road sections. Second, in our supervised modelling study, we utilise transfer learning with a pre-trained ResNet50 model. Supervised modelling was chosen as an alternative approach which is potentially simpler to implement as a binary classification does not require a search for an appropriate number of risk levels. Along with the supervised method we propose pre-processing method to improve model focus upon the road complexity by masking non-road areas on satellite images using open mapping data to remove often irrelevant features such as buildings. For this study, mapping data was available for the geographical region which we modelled were this not the case alternative approaches have been reported for extracting road networks directly from satellite images [11]. Following the road masking, we used a transfer learning approach to classify areas as high or low risk with a measured performance of 82% recall and 80% precision. For both modelling approaches, we detail potential future directions for expanding upon this work.

2 Data

For the modelling experiments, we sourced public high-resolution satellite datasets from the SpaceNet project [12] and Google Earth Engine [13] covering cities in the US along with records of American automobile accidents from the United States Department of Transportation [14].

SpaceNet is a collection of satellite datasets designed for machine learning training, with datasets built around different community challenges. For the unsupervised modelling work, we utilized images from the SpaceNet3 dataset taken of Las Vegas at a single time point in 2015 by the WorldView-3 satellite with images pre-sliced to a size of 400 × 400 m [15]. Google Earth Engine contains several public geographical datasets along with tools for analysis. For supervised modelling, we used the Planet SkySat Public Ortho imagery collection from Google Earth with images collected from Planet Labs SkySat satellites. This collection contained images taken over the period 2014-07-03 to 2016-12-24 with a resolution of 0.8 m [16]. To create the labelled dataset, we extracted satellite images from Google Earth Engine at known sites where accidents had and had not occurred. For accident sites, 600 × 600 m images were extracted centred on the accident location. For non-accident sites, images of the same size were extracted centred on random points all 1 km away from any known accident. This resulted in a dataset of 1750 images with 250 images where accidents were recorded and 1500 where no accidents were found. Examples of extracted images are shown in Fig. 1. This method led to some areas where multiple accidents were recorded being featured in multiple images allowing for a greater emphasis on high-risk areas when modelling.

Fig. 1. Examples of an image labelled as a risky area (left) and another labelled as safe (right). RGB bands were used for modelling, presented here in greyscale.

To increase the model's focus upon the road networks rather than the surrounding areas we also created a dataset with the background non-road areas masked in black as shown in Fig. 2. Here, we utilise road vector files from United States Census Bureau

[17] to provide a boundary for clipping the satellite images. The general steps of pre-processing for obtaining road-only images were as follows: 1. overlay the road vector map on top of satellite image 2. select the road vectors within the boundary of 600 × 600 m square with accident location or safe point as the centre, 3. create a buffer along the roads, 4. clip the satellite image with the buffered road to generate the road-only image, 5. Extract the 600 × 600 m processed image. Generation of clipped images was automated using the Google Earth Engine API.

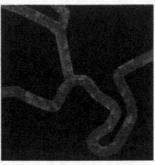

Fig. 2. Examples of road-only images for images shown in Fig. 1.

3   Modelling Overview

Two modelling approaches were trialled for generating risk maps based upon unsupervised and supervised methods. For the unsupervised modelling, we generated clusters of road network images from 1000 pre-sliced satellite images. To generate clusters, we produced encodings for each image using a pre-trained neural network, ResNet50 [18] and then generated clusters using a K-means algorithm. For the supervised approach, we utilised a labelled dataset, described in the previous section with image tiles labelled whether there had been an automobile accident in the image region from 2017–2019.

3.1   Unsupervised Models for Satellite Data

For the unsupervised modelling, embeddings were generated for each image using a pre-trained ResNet model. These image encodings represent the content of each image tile as a vector allowing traditional clustering methods such as k-means to be used. The satellite images were prepared for input to the ResNet model by extracting the 3 visual bands (RGB) and downsampling to the size of the model's input layer (224 × 224 × 3). The pre-trained model was imported using Keras without the classification head originally used to train the model on ImageNet. To generate the satellite image embeddings, inference was performed on each image and the flattened vector from the final max pooling layer was extracted. With a feature vector for each image, we generated clusters using a k-means algorithm; groupings were generated across a sequence of initial cluster counts (k) with the process performed multiple times to assess the stability of solutions. Once the clusters were defined, a mean accident count (MAC) was assigned for each group. To calculate this, we initially assigned each image tile an accident count by checking the accident records 2017–2019 within the geographical boundaries of each image. MAC was then defined as the count of accidents across all images in the group, divided by the total number of images in the group. A MAC score was assigned to each group as the mean number of accidents per image.

$$MAC = \#accidents \ in \ group/\#images \ in \ group \tag{1}$$

We repeated the clustering process across 10 repeat fits and measured the mean accident count for each cluster. The full results of this experiment are shown in Fig. 3. Here a low-risk group with a mean accident count ~0.02 accidents/image can be observed where k = 2,3,4,5. A single low-risk group is found in all repeat fits indicating that there is a visual feature within this group of images that corresponds to low levels of accidents. On inspection, this group was found to primarily contain regions without roads or large masked areas due to being at the edge of the satellite measurement swath.

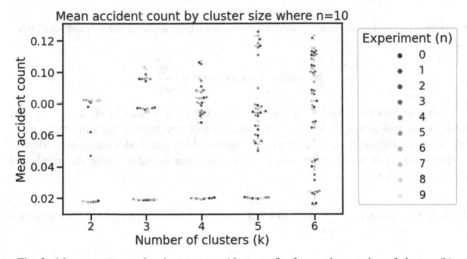

Fig. 3. Mean event count by cluster across 10 repeat fits for varying number of clusters (k).

From the results in Fig. 3 the k = 3 and k = 5 model fits were identified as good candidates for further investigation due to the observed separation of mean accident count across repeat fits. For k = 3, each fit resulted in 3 clusters with distinct accident counts which could be ranked by mean accident count as low (MAC ~ 0.02), medium (MAC ~ 0.08) and high-risk groups (MAC ~ 0.10). The results for the k = 3 fit are shown in Fig. 4, where the clusters are ranked from low (risk level 1) to high (risk level 3).

It is important to understand that the images contained at the clusters at each rank are consistent across each iteration of fitting. To assess this, we measured the Jaccard index for the ranked clusters across multiple repeat experiments [19]. The Jaccard index

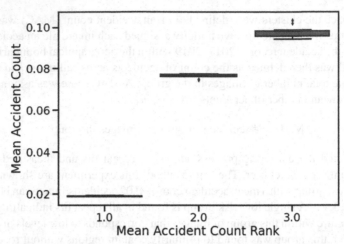

Fig. 4. Mean accident count across ranked clusters where k-means was fit with k = 3 across 10 repeat experiments.

measures the normalised intersection between sets which for multiple sets can be defined as,

$$\text{Normalised intersection} = \frac{\cap s_i}{\cup s_i} \tag{2}$$

Table 1 shows the results for this measurement of similarity in the k = 3 fit. The table shows that across all levels of risk the clusters generated in each fit are found to often contain the same images. This result indicated that the model was able to identify a visual feature of the road network images which was correlated with the number of historical accidents.

Table 1. Normalised intersection across k = 3 fit across 10 repeat fits. A high level of intersection is seen across each level of risk.

Risk level	Union total	Intersection total	Normalised intersection
1	106	103	97%
2	679	667	98%
3	216	207	96%

We repeated this analysis for the k = 5 fit with results for the average of the clusters ranked by mean event count as shown in Fig. 5. For the k = 5 fit the clusters are again ranked from low to high now with 1 lowest and 5 as highest risk. Here, a large amount of overlap is observed between the rank 3 and 4 clusters.

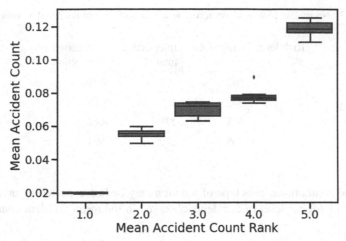

Fig. 5. Mean event count across ranked clusters for the k = 5 fit across 10 repeat fits.

Table 2. Normalised intersection across 10 repeats of k = 5 fit. A high level of intersection is observed in all but risk level 3 and 4 clusters.

Risk level	Union total	Intersection total	Normalised intersection
1	102	97	95%
2	343	289	84%
3	324	0	0%
4	314	0	0%
5	308	229	74%

This result indicates there is a large amount of mixing between images for clusters rank 3 and 4 which is consistent with the normalised intersection results shown in Table 2. Here, the clusters for risk ranks 3 and 4 show that 0% of images appear in every iteration demonstrating a high level of mixing between these two clusters.

As the clusters representing risk ranks 3 and 4 appeared to often mix these levels were combined into a single level rank 3/4. This resulted in more distinct risk levels with a low level of intermixing as shown in Table 3.

Finally, we plotted a sample of images from the clusters taken from a single model run for the k = 3 and k = 5 fits as shown in Figs. 6 and 7 respectively. For the risk groups defined in the k = 3 fit the low-risk (level 1) images contain edges and mostly desert regions where there are no roads. The two higher risk regions both contain populated areas with roads. Images from the medium risk group (level 2) appear to show image tiles where roads mostly run parallel to the boundary of the image (where north is up) with right angles seen at cross and T junctions. The higher risk group (level 3) includes images that feature some roads running non-parallel to the image boundary with a variation of

Table 3. Normalised intersection across k = 5 fit with risk ranks 3 and 4 combined.

Risk level	Union total	Intersection total	Normalised intersection
1	102	97	95%
2	343	289	84%
3/4	333	278	83%
5	308	229	74%

angles found at junctions. This type of junction may be less expected by drivers which could lead to a higher level of accidents observed in the mean accident counts for the groups.

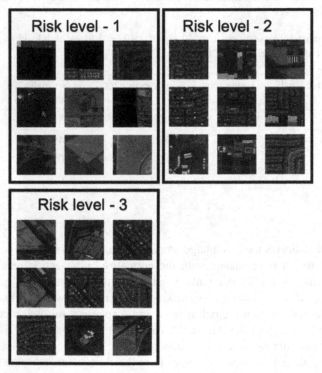

Fig. 6. Sample of image clusters for k = 3 fit where image clusters are listed according to risk level, low to high (1–3).

For the k = 5 fit, a similar pattern was observed with the two lowest risk groups showing desert/edge images (level 1) as very low risk and dense grid-based residential streets (level 2) and the second lowest risk. Above this, the combined 3/4 risk groups showed roads running non-parallel to the image boundary as well as some larger non-residential

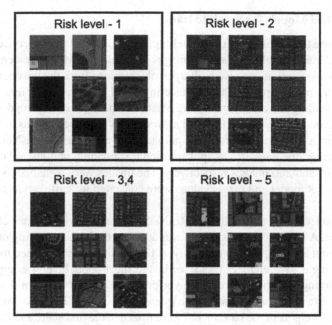

Fig. 7. Sample of image clusters for k = 5 fit with risk levels 1–5 (low to high).

buildings. The images in the highest risk level (5) mostly seemed to feature large non-residential buildings. It seems from these results that the background surrounding the road made an impact on the groupings which indicates that the road complexity had less impact on these groupings. For the k = 5 fit the 3/4 risk levels were chosen to be merged due to their observed intermixing across repeat experiments. This decision was due to a robust separation not being found with the current approach but had the downside of reducing the granularity of the risk assessment. If a set number of risk levels was a requirement a different approach would be required. One approach would be to set k to the required number of risk levels and then assign areas to a group based on where they most commonly were found in repeat fittings. Another approach could be to search higher k values until the target number of risk levels was found as distinct non-mixing groups. Automating the search strategy to define risk levels with the required granularity should be considered moving forwards. From these results, this unsupervised approach appears to be a promising method to generate a geographical risk map for road networks. The two values of k we investigated both provide distinct levels of risk which could be used by an insurer to inform policy quotations with localised risk scores. The use of cluster-wide accident statistics to classify visually similar groups allows us to utilise sparse accident data to evaluate road network design with respect to risk. By considering the average risk across a large group, we can reduce the impact of the intrinsic randomness found in accident records.

3.2 Supervised Models for Satellite Data

As an alternative to the unsupervised modelling, we also looked at a supervised approach where we extracted a labelled dataset of images covering sites where accidents did or did not occur. For this section, we also built upon observations from the unsupervised modelling where the model appeared to be clustering based upon the entire image including the area surrounding the roads by creating a dataset where the background was masked as black. The images tiles were classified as to whether we expected this to be a high or low risk region using a transfer learning approach with a pre-trained ResNet50 network. Before modelling, the dataset was split into train, validation, and test sets which contained 656, 165 and 206 images respectively. The images were reshaped to fit the input layer of a ResNet model and pixels values were converted to 'caffe' style where values were centred.

For our model, we used a pre-trained ResNet50 as the base with the final classification layer removed. A new classification head was added to the base consisting of an average pooling, dropout and single node dense layer. The pooling layer was used to convert the features to a single 2048-element vector per image, the dropout layer was applied to help prevent overfitting and the final dense layer provided a score between 0 and 1 which corresponded to a prediction of a safe or risky area respectively. The model was trained in two stages, the weights of the base model were frozen in the first stage and then unfrozen in the second to allow for fine-tuning. For the second stage, we used a lower learning rate of 10% of the base rate (0.0001) to prevent overfitting. The initial restricted training took place over 10 epochs with the fine-tuning run for 20. The number of epochs for the 1st and 2nd stages was chosen from the heuristic observation of a levelling-off of the loss curve; further training would be expected to have seen reduced benefit for the additional computation cost. Figure 8 shows the learning curves of the whole training process; the dotted vertical line indicates the starting point of the fine-tuning. We observed that in both the initial training and the fine turning that the training and validation accuracy increased while the loss decreased.

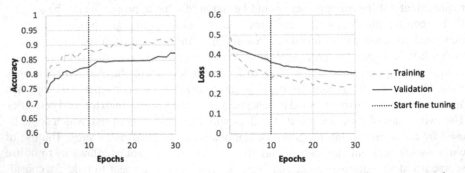

Fig. 8. Learning curves for the entire training process. The dotted vertical line indicates where the fine-tuning stage began.

Supervised Modelling Results. Table 4 shows the evaluation metrics in two steps: initial training and fine-tuning. The overall performance of the model post fine-tuning is better than after the initial training section with the precision, recall and F1 score all improved following the fine-tuning step.

Table 4. Evaluation metrics for supervised modelling.

	Initial training	Fine-tuning
Loss	0.286	0.242
Accuracy	0.888	0.908
Precision	0.783	0.8
Recall	0.735	0.816
F1 score	0.758	0.808

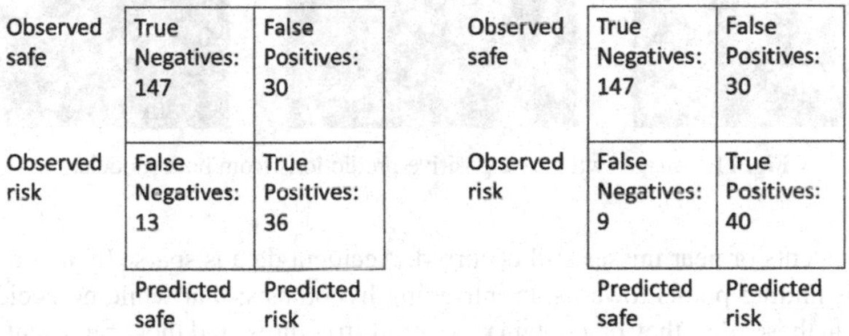

Observed safe	True Negatives: 147	False Positives: 30
Observed risk	False Negatives: 13	True Positives: 36
	Predicted safe	Predicted risk

Observed safe	True Negatives: 147	False Positives: 30
Observed risk	False Negatives: 9	True Positives: 40
	Predicted safe	Predicted risk

Fig. 9. Confusion matrix for test prediction following initial restricted training (left) and fine-tuning (right).

Figure 9 shows the confusion matrix of the model in the initial training step (left), and fine-tuning step (right). True positives are increased from 36 to 40, with false negatives decreased following the second training stage. Meanwhile, the true negatives and false positives remain fixed. Hence, the recall is increased from 0.74 to 0.82, an 11% improvement after fine-tuning. When assessing the model performance, we focused on the false negative performance of the classifier – in this application overall accuracy in terms of label prediction is a poor indicator of model quality because we have a skewed class distribution so a default model would achieve 75% accuracy. However, a classifier with a higher recall that rarely misses a risk indicator is desirable.

The current results show a marginal improvement from fine-tuning with more risky images picked up by the tuned classifier. Figure 10 shows two of the four images, which are identified as safe ones in the initial training step but corrected by the tuned classifier. Among all these images, we can find large complex road junctions.

The images shown in Fig. 11 were observed as safe areas but predicted as being high risk in both the initial training and fine-tuning stages. Based on the image labelling we know that no major accidents occurred in these regions over the time period studied. Our accident covers major incidents only, so it is possible that an increased level of

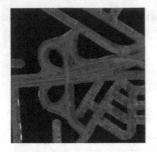

Fig. 10. Two of the 'corrected' images in the fine-tuning step.

Fig. 11. Images with false positive predictions from both models.

minor accidents or near misses still occurred. Accident data is sparse by nature, potentially, this finding points towards an intriguing hypothesis: that while no accident has occurred in these tiles, they do contain risky road structures, and these represent a safety liability. In this study we utilised a basic MLP classification head in combination with the embeddings generated by the pre-trained ResNet50 model, further work in this area could expand upon this by testing a range of different classification approaches such as tree-based models or support vector machines.

4 Future Directions

Currently, we are planning an extension of this work in terms of further validation and testing of the modelling in addition to productionisation of the risk map concept for use in policy quotations. For this work to be utilised effectively in insurance quote processes it will have to be integrated into a quote production workflow such as Guidewire or other similar systems.

To build upon the modelling from these promising initial findings, we plan to expand this study to a larger geographical area for additional validation. In terms of generalisation, we would expect some re-training would potentially be required if implementing into a distinct new region such as a new country due to the variation of road infrastructure observed globally, for example, the density of roundabouts vs. crossroads found in the UK compared to the USA. We would anticipate that in real-world use, a risk mapping model would be trained for a particular geographical area which matches the locations an insurer provided policies for.

A pressing question about both modelling processes was around what visual features are being identified by the models. We plan to build upon the pre-processing work in this study where non-road areas were masked by performing further manipulations to control the complexity of image content and better understand which features are most important. In the future, given the discussion about confirming latent safety detection capabilities, we also anticipate being able to use this approach to both assess the impact of newly proposed road schemes on intrinsic risk and to identify the optimal mitigations available in a road network to create the largest possible reduction in risk. Modelling potential risk could also be of value for route planning (avoiding risk) and urban planning and simulation decisions. For this work, we used a relatively large grid size (400/600 m^2) which was chosen as an appropriate resolution for mapping risk. With a reasonably coarse grid size, visual similarity of road networks sections will potentially be defined by long-range network features rather than short-range features from individual junctions which could result in underestimating the risk of problem junctions which sit within an otherwise low risk area. A sensitivity study with manually selected or synthetic data could be performed to understand how grid size effects the model. Ultimately a method which captures short-range information for individual junctions in combination with long-range information about where they sit within a network is likely to be most effective.

To identify potentially risky areas, we utilised historical accident data which is expected to be sparse and potentially unrepresentative of the potential for future accidents. Historical risk could be assessed more accurately by combining multiple risk indicators such as telematics and social media data [9, 10].

5   Conclusion

In this paper, we have evaluated two approaches for modelling satellite data to generate a risk map for insurance policy quotation. For the unsupervised study, we detailed a new method for assessing the risk across visually similar groups of roads sections which aims to avoid issues around the sparsity of public accident records, in the supervised study we utilised a masking technique to improve model focus upon the road network itself rather than the surrounding area. Both approaches provided promising results as a means of generating a risk map and we have discussed plans to expand upon this work with additional exploration and validation in addition to developing a production-ready infrastructure for serving localized-risk scores during the quotation process.

References

1. WorldView-4 information page. https://eoportal.org/web/eoportal/satellite-missions/v-w-x-y-z/worldview-4. Accessed 7 Sept 2021
2. Sinha, S., Tripathi, N.K.: Assessing the challenges in successful implementation and adoption of crop insurance in Thailand. Sustainability **8**, 1306 (2016). https://doi.org/10.3390/su8121306
3. Guidewire homepage. https://www.guidewire.com. Accessed 7 Sept 2021
4. Insuresoft homepage. https://www.insuresoft.com. Accessed 7 Sept 2021
5. Insurity homepage. https://www.insurity.com. Accessed 7 Sept 2021

6. Burdett, B., Starkey, N., Charlton, S.: The close to home effect in road crashes. Saf. Sci. **98**, 1–8 (2017)
7. European Commission: Road safety planning 2014/10. https://ec.europa.eu/transport/road_s afety/sites/default/files/pdf/national-road-safety-strategies_en.pdf. Accessed 7 Sept 2021
8. Najjar, A., Kaneko, S., Miyanaga, Y.: Combining satellite imagery and open data to map road safety. In: Proceedings of the AAAI Conference on Artificial Intelligence (2017)
9. Zhang, Y., Lu, Y., Zhang, D., Shang, L., Wang, D.: Risksens: a multi-view learning approach to identifying risky traffic locations in intelligent transportation systems using social and remote sensing. In: 2018 IEEE International Conference on Big Data (Big Data) (2018)
10. Wijnands, J.S., et al.: Identifying safe intersection design through unsupervised feature extraction from satellite imagery. Comput. Aided Civ. Infrastruct. Eng. **36**(3), 346–361 (2020)
11. He, S., et al.: Encoding, Sat2Graph: Road Graph Extraction through Graph-Tensor. arxiv.org, 19 July 2020. arXiv:2007.09547v1
12. SpaceNet homepage. https://spacenet.ai. Accessed 7 Sept 2021
13. Google Earth Engine. https://earthengine.google.com/. Accessed 7 Sept 2021
14. United States Department of Transportation: Fatality Analysis Reporting System Data (2019). https://www.nhtsa.gov/file-downloads?p=nhtsa/downloads/FARS. Accessed 7 Sept 2021
15. SpaceNet3: Las Vegas dataset overview. https://spacenet.ai/las-vegas. Accessed 7 Sept 2021
16. Planet SkySat Public Ortho Imagery. https://developers.google.com/earth-engine/datasets/cat alog/SKYSAT_GEN-A_PUBLIC_ORTHO_RGB. Accessed 7 Sept 2021
17. U. S. Census: 2021 Road Vector Files. https://www2.census.gov/geo/tiger/TIGER2020/ ROADS. Accessed 7 Sept 2021
18. He, K., Zhang, X., Ren, S., Sun, J.: Deep residual learning for image recognition. In: Computer Vision and Pattern Recognition (2016)
19. Leskovec, J., Rajaraman, A., Ullman, J.D.: Mining of Massive Datasets. Cambridge University Press, New York (2012)

Ranking Pathology Data in the Absence of a Ground Truth

Jing Qi[1]([⊠]), Girvan Burnside[2], and Frans Coenen[1]

[1] Department of Computer Science, The University of Liverpool,
Liverpool L69 3BX, UK
`J.QI7@Liverpool.ac.uk`
[2] Department of Biostatistics, Institute of Translational Medicine,
The University of Liverpool, Liverpool L69 3BX, UK

Abstract. Pathology results play a critical role in medical decision making. A particular challenge is the large number of pathology results that doctors are presented with on a daily basis. Some form of pathology result prioritisation is therefore a necessity. However, there is no readily available training data that would support a traditional supervised learning approach. Thus some alternative solutions are needed. There are two approaches presented in this paper, anomaly-based unsupervised pathology prioritisation and proxy ground truth-based supervised pathology prioritisation. Two variations of each were considered. With respect to the first, point and time series based unsupervised anomaly prioritisation; and with respect to the second kNN and RNN proxy ground truth-based supervised prioritisation. To act as a focus, Urea and Electrolytes pathology testing was used. The reported evaluation indicated that the RNN proxy ground truth-based supervised pathology prioritisation method produced the best results.

Keywords: Data ranking · Time series · Deep learning · Pathology data

1 Introduction

It has been well documented that, facilitated by advances in IT technology, large quantities of data are produced on a continuous basis. An exemplar application, and the focus for the work presented in this paper, is in the medical domain where large amounts pathology data are produced continually. Some clinicians may have hundreds of pathology results to review on a single shift; a classic *information overload* situation. A potential solution is to adopt the tools and techniques of machine learning to prioritise pathology results. However, a challenge is the absence of ground truth data. Clinicians observe that they "know a priority result when they see one", and can explain why, however typically there is no resource available to generate appropriate prioritised training data (especially given the current COVID-19 pandemic). This means that traditional,

© Springer Nature Switzerland AG 2021
M. Bramer and R. Ellis (Eds.): SGAI-AI 2021, LNAI 13101, pp. 209–223, 2021.
https://doi.org/10.1007/978-3-030-91100-3_18

well established, supervised learning techniques are unavailable. This is a very much unexplored domain of application for machine learning.

This paper presents an exploration of two approaches whereby such data can be ranked, or at least categorised. The first approach is founded on the idea of anomaly detection, the second one using supervised learning but with a proxy for the ground truth data. Anomaly, or outlier, detection has a long history within the context of machine learning [27]. One established technique, and that adopted in this paper, is cluster analysis-based outlier detection [6,12]. Two variations are considered: point-based and time series based. The first assumes all pathology results are independent, and is used as a bench-mark technique with respect to the work presented. The second variation acknowledges that pathology results are typically part of a sequence and/or part of a set of parallel results, and therefore individual pathology results should not be considered in isolation.

The second approach is founded on the observation that although ground truth data is typically not available, information about what happened to patients is available. For example the final destination of patients: Emergency Patient (EP), In-Patient (IP) or Out-Patient (OP). This information can thus be used to construct a proxy ground truth training set from which classification models can be generated. Two variations are considered, a kNN classification model as traditionally used in time series analysis [10,17] and a Recursive Neural Network (RNN) deep learning model as popularised in more recent work on time series analysis [9].

To act as a focus for the work the domain of Urea and Electrolytes (U&E) pathology testing is considered. The proposed approaches are compared using U&E data provided by Arrowe Park Hospital in Merseyside in the UK.

The remainder of this paper is organised as follows. A review of relevant previous work is presented in Sect. 2. This is followed by a review of the Urea and Electrolytes pathology testing application domain, used as a focus for the work, in Sect. 3. The two proposed approaches are considered in Sects. 4 and 5. The comparative evaluation of the two approaches is then discussed in Sect. 6. The paper is concluded in Sect. 7 with a summary of the main findings and some suggested avenues for future work.

2   Previous Work

Prioritisation is significant with respect to many application domains and fields of study. The most common application domain, and that most frequently referenced in the literature, is the information retrieval domain [20]. For example the ranking of documents as the result of a web search or a document repository search. However, the prioritisation models considered in this paper are not ranking models but classification models. The proposed mechanism are designed to build models to label data according to a set of class labels C indicating priority, namely $C = \{high, medium, low\}$. The challenge, as noted above, is the absence of training data. This makes the application domain considered in this paper unique. To address this challenge two approaches are considered and compared:

1. Anomaly-based unsupervised prioritisation.
2. Proxy ground truth-based supervised prioritisation.

Anomaly detection is concerned with the detection of points, observations or events within a data collection which do not satisfy the dataset's normal distribution [8]. A common technology, and that adopted with respect to the work presented in this paper, is unsupervised learning. A typical application domain for unsupervised anomaly detection is cyber security, where anomalous network behaviour is considered to be an indicator of an attack. Examples can be found in [1], [11] and [15]. In [1] a k-medoid customized clustering technique was presented for anomaly detection in wireless sensor network to detect misdirection attacks and blackhole attacks. In [11] a network anomaly detection method based on fuzzy clustering was presented. In [15] a mechanism was presented for anomaly detection with respect to traffic patterns in computer networks. In [16] a survey was presented of unsupervised approaches to identify anomalies in system log files for anomalous events detection relevant to cyber security. There are many other applications where unsupervised learning has been applied for anomaly detection. In [18] the use of unsupervised anomaly detection was used to detect the abnormal operation of aircraft and in [2] to detect abnormal behaviour in the financial domain. A range of techniques are available for unsupervised anomaly detection, there has been some interesting recent work using autoencoders [31]. Unsupervised learning has, of course, been more generally applied to pathology data for analysis purposes, see for example [23]. Whatever the case, the broad concepts that feature in the above referenced work underpin the work presented here with respect to anomaly-based unsupervised pathology data prioritisation.

The challenge of creating training data to support supervised learning is well established and has led to the growing research area of *self-supervised learning*. Broadly, self-supervised learning is a means for training computers to do tasks without humans providing labeled data [13]. An alternative, which was adopted with respect to the work presented here, is to identify a proxy for the training data. There has been some work on using proxy data for classification purposes. Examples can be found in [7], [3] and [30]. In [7], in the context of market segmentation, it was observed that ground truth data is often scarce or unavailable; a proxy labeling scheme was proposed for labeling a population according to a postulated set of shopping behaviors. In [3] a proxy data set was created, using a clustering approach, for anomaly detection in enterprise and cloud networks. In [30] machine learning was applied to internet search behaviour as a proxy for human behaviour. In [5], in the context of the domain of Psychophysiology, the authors argue that training data is frequently flawed and that proxy data is more able to produce a quality classification model. They go on to present a review of techniques whereby a proxy ground truth can be created, and conclude that there is no single technique that is sufficient for the accurate generation of ground truth data for classification and suggest a hybrid approach. The above provides support for the second approach presented in this paper, the proxy ground truth-based supervised prioritisation approach.

3   U&E Testing Application Domain

The work presented in this paper is focused on Urea and Electrolytes pathology test data (U&E testing). U&E testing is usually performed to confirm normal kidney function or to exclude a serious imbalance of biochemical salts in the bloodstream. The U&E test data considered in this paper comprised, for each test, measurement of levels of: (i) Sodium (ii) Potassium (iii) Urea (vi) Creatinine and (v) Bicarbonate. The measurement of each is referred to as a "task", thus we have five tasks per test. Thus each U&E test results in five pathology values. Abnormal levels in any of these tasks may indicate that the kidneys are not working properly. However, a one time abnormal result does not necessarily indicate priority. A new task result that is out of range for a patient who has a previous recent history of out of range task results, but the latest result indicates a trend back into the normal range, may not be a priority result either. Conversely, a new task result that is within the normal range for a patient who has a history of normal range task results, but the latest result indicates a trend heading out of the normal range, may be a priority result. Given a new set of pathology values for a U&E test we wish to determine the priority to be associated with this set of values.

The U&E data comprised a set of clinical patient records, $\mathbf{D} = \{P_1, P_2, \dots\}$. Each record $P_j \in \mathbf{D}$ was of the form:

$$P_j = \langle PatientID, TestDate, Gender, T_{So}, T_{Po}, T_{Ur}, T_{Cr}, T_{Bi}, c \rangle \qquad (1)$$

Where: (i) $PatientID$ is the ID for the patient in question; (ii) T_{so} to T_{Bi} are five three dimensional time series, one per task, representing, in sequence, pathology results for: Sodium (So), Potassium (Po), Urea (Ur), Creatinine (Cr) and Bicarbonate (Bi) and (iii) c is the class label taken from a set of classes C. Each time series T_i has three dimensions: (i) pathology result value, (ii) normal low and (iii) normal high. The normal low and high dimensions indicate a "band" in which pathology results are expected to fall. These values are less volatile than the pathology result values, but can change over time.

For the purpose of building prioritisation models training data was required. The data set $\mathbf{D}$ was used to create individual training data sets, one per task, D_{So}, D_{Po}, D_{Ur}, D_{Cr} and D_{Bi}. Two data formats were used, one for the point-based outlier detection method and one for the three time series methods considered. For the first each data set comprised a set of pathology result values $D_i = \{p_1, p_2, \dots\}$ where each point p_i comprised a tuple of the form $\langle v, n_l, n_h \rangle$ (pathology result value, normal low and normal high respectively). For the other methods each data set comprised a set of time series $D_i = \{T_1, T_2, \dots\}$ where each time series T_i comprises a sequence of tuples, of the form $\langle v, n_l, n_h \rangle$.

4   Anomaly-Based Unsupervised Pathology Prioritisation

The fundamental idea under-pinning the anomaly-based pathology data prioritisation approach is that an anomalous result should be prioritised. More specifically the first approach presented in this paper proposes that this can be achieved by clustering existing records and attempting to assign new records to this cluster configuration. If a new record cannot be easily allocated to a cluster it is considered to be an *outlier* and hence a priority record. This is an approach that has been frequently adopted with respect to cyber security applications [1,11,15,16].

The outlier/anomaly detection approach to pathology data prioritisation produces a binary classification, a new pathology record is either an outlier (a priority record) or not. This is in itself useful, but we would like a finer grained outcome. Thus, for the outliers the distance to the centroid of the nearest cluster is determined to produce a ranking which can be used to produce a more fine grained prioritisation. In the evaluation presented later in this paper outlier records are labelled either as "high priority" or "medium pririty" according to a predefined threshold λ which needs to be established; non-outlier records are labelled a "low priority". Thus we have a three class prioritisation, $C = \{high, medium, low\}$.

In the context of the U&E test application focus for this paper, as discussed above, we have five tasks. Hence, we have five cluster configurations and consequently five predictions that need to be reconciled, and so five thresholds to be identified λ_{So}, λ_{Po}, λ_{Ur}, λ_{Cr} and λ_{Bi}.

The high level process is as follows, given:

1. For each data set $D_i \in \mathbf{D}$, $D_i = \{p_1, p_2, \dots\}$, where each point p_i is a tuple of the form, $\langle v, n_l, n_h \rangle$, create a cluster configuration, one per task, hence five configurations.
2. For each configuration, given the set of outliers A, for each $a \in A$ calculate the distances to the nearest centroid. To give a set of distances.
3. For each set of distances calculate the average, these are then the thresholds, λ_{So}, λ_{Po}, λ_{Ur}, λ_{Cr} and λ_{Bi}, that will be used to determine whether an outlier record is high or medium priority.

Given a new pathology record, it will be compared to the cluster configuration, generated as described above, which will produce five class labels, one for each task. The following rule is then applied.

Rule 1 If one of the class labels is "high" the overall class label is high, otherwise use voting to derive the overall class label.

Any one of a number of clustering algorithms could have been adopted. However, for the evaluation presented later in this paper the DBSCAN clustering algorithm [14] was adopted with respect to the work presented in this paper, because it readily supports outlier detection, and because it is a well established and understood clustering algorithm.

Two variations of the anomaly-based pathology data prioritisation approach were considered.

Point Based: Assumes that any new record is independent of any previous records for the same patient and hence can be considered in isolation.

Time Series Based: Assumes that any new record is not independent of previous records for the same patient and hence should be considered in context; in other words as a time series.

Each is discussed in further detail in the following two sub-sections.

4.1 Point Based Outlier Detection Unsupervised Pathology Prioritisation

The point-based approach considers each pathology result, pertaining to the same patient, to be independent. In this case the data set used, to create a desired cluster configuration, simply comprised a set of pathology results obtained from historical patient data.

DBSCAN uses two parameters: (i) $minPts$, the minimum number of data points that can be held in a cluster, and (ii) ε, the maximum distance between two data points whereby they are considered to be neighbours and thus should appear in the same cluster. If $minPts = 1$ is used this will result in every record forming its own cluster; if $minPts = 2$ is used, this will result in a hierarchical clustering as clusters will be repeatedly split into two. Therefore $minPts$ needs to be greater than 2. In [26] it was suggested that the value of $minPts$ should be at least $|A|+1$ (where A is the attribute set). The reasoning was that each attribute represents a dimension in a $|A|$-dimensional space. To determine a value for ε the approach proposed in [21] was adopted. For each record the distance to the kth nearest neighbouring record was determined and plotted using an "elbow plot". A range of values for k was considered starting with $k = minPts - 1$. For each value of k, the input data records were listed in ascending order according to distance. The elbow plot has k plotted along the x-axis and distance along the y-axis. The plot will feature an "elbow" marking a significant change in the gradient of the slope. The most appropriate value for ε is then the distance associated with the point where the elbow first starts to appear.

4.2 Time Series Based Outlier Detection Unsupervised Pathology Prioritisation

The main difference between the time series approach and the point approach is that the time series approach considers patient history. In other words the "trajectory" for the patient in question. The intuition was that this would provide a better prioritisation. As in the case of the point based approach, the idea was to cluster existing trajectories to produce a cluster configuration. Given a new record this will be added to the time series for the corresponding patient (if the record does not belong to an existing patient, the point approach will need to be used) and the resulting time series compared to the cluster configuration. Again, if the time series associated with the new record is found to be an outlier the record is considered to be a prioritiy record.

The DBSCAN clustering algorithm was again adopted. However, whereas the point based approach used Euclidean distance as the distance measure with which to generate a cluster configuration, for the time series based approach Dynamic Time Warping (DTW) was used [25] which gives a distance measure (the *warping distance*) between two time series. For applying DTW the Sakoe-Chiba band, as also proposed in [25], was used as a global constraint to accelerate the algorithm. The same mechanisms for determining the most appropriate values for $minPts$ and ε as used with respect to the point based approach described above were adopted, those given in [26] and [21] respectively.

5   Proxy Ground Truth-Based Supervised Pathology Prioritisation

The fundamental idea underpinning the proposed proxy ground truth-based supervised pathology prioritisation approach was that although no ground truth training data was available, the final destinations of patients where known, and hence these could act as a proxy for a ground truth. Consequently, supervised time series learning could be used to generate a pathology data prioritisation model. For the evaluation presented later in this paper, three outcome events were considered: (i) Emergency Patient (EP), (ii) In-Patient (IP) and (ii) Out Patient (OP), which were correlated with the priority descriptors "high", "medium" and "low" respectively.

Two variations of the proxy ground truth-based pathology data prioritisation approach were considered.

KNN Based: Uses k Nearest Neighbour (kNN) classification, the most frequently adopted form of time series classification.

RNN Based: Uses Recurrent Neural Network (RNN) classification, a time series classification model that is gaining increasing popularity.

Each is discussed in further detail in the following two sub-sections.

5.1   KNN Proxy Ground Truth-Based Supervised Pathology Prioritisation

The kNN classification model uses a parameter k, the number of best matches we are looking for. For the evaluation presented later in this paper, $k = 1$ was used, because $k = 1$ often provides better accuracy when comparing time series using DTW [4]. Note that DTW was used for similarity measurement because of its ability to operates with time series of different length and because it has been shown to be more effective than alternatives such as Euclidean distance measurement [29]. The disadvantage of DTW, compared to the Euclidean distance measurement, is its high computational time complexity of $O(x \times y)$ where x and y are the lengths of the two time series under consideration. The complexity for Euclidean distance time series comparison is $O(x)$ (x is required to be equal to y).

There are many techniques available for reducing the time complexity of DTW coupled with kNN classification. Two that were adopted with respect to the work presented here were: (i) early-abandonment and (ii) lower bounding. The first is a strategy whereby the accumulative distance between two time series is repeatedly checked as the calculation progresses and if the distance exceeds the best distance so far the calculation will be "abandoned" [22]. The second involves pre-processing the time series to be considered by comparing the time series using an alternative "cheaper" technique and pruning those that are unlikely to be close matches and applying DTW to the remainder. One example of this, and that adopted with respect to the work presented in this paper, is the lower bounding technique proposed in [28], the so called the *LB-Keogh technique*. This operates by superimposing a band, defined by a predefined offset value referred to as the lower bound, over each time series in the bank, and calculating the complement of the overlap with the new time series. Where the calculated value exceeds a given threshold ϵ the associated time series is pruned.

The traditional manner in which kNN is applied, in the context of time series analysis, is to compare a query time series with the time series in the kNN bank. In the case of the U&E pathology prioritisation scenario considered here, as noted in Sect. 3, individual pathology results comprised five values, one per task making up the overall A&E test. The kNN process thus involved five comparisons, once for each task time series in the query record, $T_{q_{so}}$, $T_{q_{po}}$, $T_{q_{ur}}$, $T_{q_{cr}}$ and $T_{q_{bi}}$. In addition, traditional kNN is applied to univariate time series, in the U&E pathology case each task time series was a three-dimensional multi-variate time series: (i) pathology value, (ii) normal low and (iii) normal high. Thus, from the foregoing, for each comparison five distance measures were obtained. These five distance measures therefore need to be combined to give a final prioritisation.

The overall process was as follows, given a new pathology result for a patient p_q, that has been appended to the patient's history of pathology results to give five three-dimensional component time series $T_{q_{so}}$, $T_{q_{po}}$, $T_{q_{ur}}$, $T_{q_{cr}}$ and $T_{q_{bi}}$.

1. Calculate the average LB-keogh overlap for the five component time series and prune all records in D where the overlap for any one time series was greater than ϵ, to leave D'.
2. Apply DTW, with early-abandonment to compare each T_{q_j} with each $T_{i_j} \in D'$, where j indicates the U&E task, and use the class label c associated with the most similar record to assign to each time series T_{q_j}.
3. Use the class label c to define a priority for p_q and then apply Rule 1 from Sect. 4 to determine the final prioritisation, "high", "medium" or "low".

With respect to the above the choice of the value for ϵ is of great importance as it affects the efficiency and the accuracy of the similarity search. According to [19], there is a threshold value for ϵ whereby the time complexity for the lower bounding is greater than simply using DTW distance without lower bounding. The experiments presented in [19] demonstrated that this threshold occurs when the value for ϵ prunes 90% of the time series in D. For the parameter setting in the work presented in this paper, $\epsilon = 0.159$ was used because, on average, this resulted in 10% of the time series in D being retained.

5.2 RNN Proxy Ground Truth-Based Supervised Pathology Prioritisation

For the RNN-based approach a Long Short Term Memory (LSTM) architecture was adopted. Given the U&E pathology prioritisation scenario used as a focus in this paper the proposed approach commenced with the training of five LSTM models, one per task: $LSTM_{so}$, $LSTM_{po}$, $LSTM_{ur}$, $LSTM_{cr}$ and $LSTM_{bi}$. Figure 1 illustrates the construction and structure of the proposed LSTM approach to prioritise pathology data.

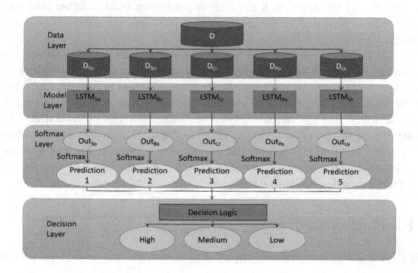

Fig. 1. LSTM architecture for proxy ground truth pathology prioritisation

With reference to Fig. 1 the process and structure is expressed in terms of four layers: (i) Data, (ii) Model, (iii) Softmax, (iv) Decision. The input is the data set D divided into of its component parts D_{So}, D_{Po}, D_{Ur}, D_{Cr} and D_{Bi}. Each data set comprised a set of multi-variate time series $T_i = \{V_1, V_2, \ldots, V_m\}$, where V_j is a tuple of the form $\langle v, n_l, n_h \rangle$ where v is the pathology value, n_l is the normal low and n_h is the normal high. Where necessary each time series T_i was padded to the length of the longest time series in D_i, using the mean value of the v, n_l and n_h values, because the LSTM model requires all time series to be of the same length.

Next, for each of the five tasks, once a time series data set had been constructed, each was passed to the model layer and the LSTM constructed. Note that each LSTM comprised two hidden layers. The output produce, Out_i, was used to define the softmax layer where predictions will be made. The Softmax Layer, and the Softmax function for normalising the output of each single task LSTM model was as follows:

$$y_i = \frac{e^{a_i}}{\Sigma_{k=1}^{|C|} e^{a_k}} \quad \forall i \in 1\ldots C \qquad (2)$$

Where: (i) $|C|$ is the number of classes (three in this case), (ii) a_i is the output of the LSTM layer.

The last layer is the decision layer where the final label is derived. After obtaining all of the five outputs and the predicted labels from the five LSTM models, a decision logic module was added to decide the final prioritisation level of the patient. This included the rule: *"If there exists a prediction that equates to 'High' for one of the tasks then the overall prediction is high, otherwise average the five outputs produced by the Softmax function and choose the class with the maximum probability"*.

For the LSTM, there are five parameters thaqt need to be tuned during the training process. The parameters belong to two categories: (i) optimization parameters and (ii) model parameters. The optimization parameters are: Learning rate, batch size and number of epochs. The model parameters are the number of hidden layers and the number of hidden units. For the optimization, Adam optimization was chosen due to its efficiency and the nature of the adaptive learning rate. For finding the optimal parameters, cross-entropy was used as the loss function, and the parameters tuned by observing the loss and accuracy plots of the training and validation data.

6   Evaluation

From the for going we have two approaches each with two associated variation:

1. Anomaly-Based Supervised Pathology Prioritisation.
   (a) Point-based
   (b) Time series-based
2. Proxy Ground Truth-Based Supervised Pathology Prioritisation.
   (a) kNN
   (b) RNN-based

A significant challenge of ranking pathology data without a ground truth is how to evaluate any proposed approach. There is also no previous work in this area, to the best knowledge of the authors, whereby any direct comparison between the proposed approaches and any existing approaches can be conducted. In the case of the anomaly-based approach we can of course measure the quality of the cluster configuration produced using cohesion and separation measures, such as the well-established Silhouette Coefficient [24]. However, this only tells us about the quality of the clusters configuration, not the quality of the classifications obtained using the cluster configuration.

For learning to rank methodologies, such as those proposed in the context of information retrieval, it is common to use metrics such as Mean Reciprocal Rank (MRR), Mean Average Precision (MAP) and Normalized Discounted Cumulative Gain (NDCG); but these all require a ground truth ranking. The pathology prioritisation problem was conceptualised as a three class problem, $C = high, medium, low$ which could therefore be evaluated using the "standard" accuracy, precision, recall and F1 metrics using the proxy ground truth (not an actual ground truth but the "nearest best thing"). Five-cross validation was used through out. All the experiments were run using a windows 10 desktop machine with a 3.2 GHz Quad-Core IntelCore i5 processor and 24 GB of RAM. For the LSTM, a GPU was used fitted with a NVIDA GeForceRTX 2060 unit.

As noted earlier, the application focus for the work presented in this paper was Urea and Electrolytes (U&E) pathology testing. For the evaluation U&E data was provided by Arrowe Park Hospital in Merseyside in the UK. Further detail concerning this data set is provided in Subsect. 6.1. The evaluation results are then presented and discussed in Subsect. 6.2.

6.1 Evaluation Data Set

A formalism for U&E data was presented in Sect. 3. The data set D provided by Arrowe Park Hospital comprised records for 3,734 patient records with five U&E task results (time series) per patient. To derive the proxy ground truth class label for each record $P_j \in D$ reference was made to the outcome event(s) associated with each patient. As noted earlier, three outcome events were considered: (i) Emergency Patient (EP), an In-Patient (IP) or an Out Patient (OP). These were correlated to the priority descriptor class labels: "high", "medium" and "low". This resulted in 255 patients with high priority, 123 with medium priority and 3,356 with low priority, covering all five tasks. For the LSTM variation of the proxy ground truth based approach, re-sampling of the data was undertaken to give a total 8, 192 time series to address the class imbalanced problem. This was not needed with respect to any of the other three methods considered.

6.2 Results and Discussion

The evaluation results obtained are given in Tables 1 and 2, best results highlighted in bold font. Table 1 gives the precision and recall results obtained, whilst Table 2 gives the accuracy and F1 Score results obtained. Each table includes average values for the five folds and an associated Standard Deviations (SDs).

Table 1. Precision and recall results, best results in bold font

Fold #	Anomaly detection approach				Proxy ground truth classification			
	Point-based		Time series-based		kNN		RNN	
	Precision	Recall	Precision	Recall	Precision	Recall	Precision	Recall
1	0.298	0.254	0.407	0.458	**0.661**	0.617	0.446	**0.755**
2	0.375	0.467	0.375	0.511	**0.703**	0.609	0.585	**0.663**
3	0.361	0.500	0.367	0.444	0.639	0.570	**0.695**	**0.629**
4	0.211	0.287	0.333	0.315	0.517	0.632	**0.693**	**0.663**
5	0.500	0.643	0.367	0.508	0.758	0.523	**0.762**	**0.626**
Average	0.349	0.430	0.370	0.448	**0.656**	0.590	0.636	**0.667**
SD	0.095	0.144	0.024	0.071	0.080	0.039	0.111	0.047

Table 2. Accuracy and F1 score, best results in bold font

Fold #	Anomaly detection approach				Proxy ground truth classification			
	Point-based		Time series-based		kNN		RNN	
	Accuracy	F1 score	Accuracy	F1 score	Accuracy	F1 score	Accuracy	F1 score
1	0.333	0.248	0.421	0.303	0.585	**0.638**	**0.671**	0.561
2	0.273	0.265	0.529	0.306	0.632	**0.653**	**0.642**	0.622
3	0.333	0.361	0.368	0.227	0.576	0.603	**0.622**	**0.660**
4	0.250	0.198	0.429	0.258	0.523	0.569	**0.608**	**0.678**
5	0.500	0.515	0.522	0.290	0.566	0.619	**0.645**	**0.687**
Average	0.338	0.317	0.454	0.629	0.576	0.616	**0.638**	**0.642**
SD	0.087	0.112	0.062	0.030	0.035	0.029	0.024	0.046

From the two tables the first thing that can be observed is that the anomaly-based prioritisation approach performed poorly (regardless of which metric was considered) and which variation, point or time series. The reason why the anomaly detection-based prioritisation approach did not perform well might be because it featured the disadvantages that, given a large number of outliers with similar characteristics these might form there own clusters and no longer be considered to be outliers.

From Table 1 it can be seen that the RNN Proxy Ground Truth-based Supervised Pathology Prioritisation produced consistently the best recall, and in three of the five folds the best precision. From Table 2, it can be seen that the best average F1 scores, the harmonic mean of precision and recall and thus a good overall measure, were obtained using the RNN Proxy Ground Truth-based Supervised Pathology Prioritisation method, with the kNN method also performing well. Hence, in conclusion, it is argued here that the proxy ground truth-based Supervised method is the most appropriate method for addressing the challenge of pathology data prioritisation as defined in this paper.

7 Conclusions

The motivation for the work presented in this paper was the challenge of prioritising pathology data in the absence of any ground truth data. Two approaches were considered: (i) anomaly detection for prioritisation and (ii) proxy ground truth supervised learning for prioritisation. Two variations of both approaches were considered, point-based and time series-based for the first approach; and kNN and RNN-based, for the second. The four variations (methods) were fully described and evaluated using real data. From the results, the RNN proxy ground truth-based supervised pathology prioritisation method was argued to be the most appropriate. For future work the authors intend to investigate: (i) generate artificial evaluation data sets to provide for a more comprehensive evaluation, and (ii) collaborate with clinicians to obtain feed back regarding the prioritisations produced and to test the utility of the best performing mechanism in a real setting.

References

1. Ahmad, B., Jian, W., Ali, Z.A., Tanvir, S., Khan, M.S.A.: Hybrid anomaly detection by using clustering for wireless sensor network. Wirel. Pers. Commun. **106**, 1841–1853 (2019)
2. Ahmeda, M., Mahmooda, A.N., Islamb, M.R.: A survey of anomaly detection techniques in financial domain. Futur. Gener. Comput. Syst. **55**, 278–288 (2016)
3. Baek, S., Kwon, D., Kim, J., Suh, S.C., Kim, H., Kim, I.: Unsupervised labeling for supervised anomaly detection in enterprise and cloud networks. In: Proceedings 4th IEEE International Conference on Cyber Security and Cloud Computing, CSCloud 2017, pp. 205–210 (2017)
4. Bagnall, A., Lines, J., Bostrom, A., Large, J., Keogh, E.: The great time series classification bake off: a review and experimental evaluation of recent algorithmic advances. Data Min. Knowl. Disc. **31**(3), 606–660 (2017)
5. Brawner, K., Boyce, M.W.: Establishing ground truth on pyschophysiological models for training machine learning algorithms: options for ground truth proxies. In: Schmorrow, D.D., Fidopiastis, C.M. (eds.) AC 2017. LNCS (LNAI), vol. 10284, pp. 468–477. Springer, Cham (2017). https://doi.org/10.1007/978-3-319-58628-1_35
6. Campello, R.J.G.B., Moulavi, D., Zimek, A., Sander, J.: Hierarchical density estimates for data clustering, visualization, and outlier detection. ACM Trans. Knowl. Discov. Data **10**(1), 1–51 (2015)
7. Cerrato, D., Jones, R., Gupta, A.: Classification of proxy labeled examples for marketing segment generation. In: Proceedings of the 17th International Conference Knowledge Discovery and Data, KDD 2011, pp. 343–350. ACM SIGKDD (2011)
8. Chandola, V., Banerjee, A., Kumar, V.: Anomaly detection: a survey. ACM Comput. Surv. (CSUR) **41**(3), 1–58 (2009)
9. Fawaz, H.I., Forestier, G., Weber, J., Idoumghar, L., Muller, P.-A.: Deep learning for time series classification: a review. Data Min. Knowl. Disc. **33**, 917–963 (2016)
10. Geler, Z., Kurbalija, V., Radovanović, M., Ivanović, M.: Comparison of different weighting schemes for the kNN classifier on time-series data. Knowl. Inf. Syst. **48**, 331–378 (2016)

11. Harish, B.S., Kuma, S.V.A.: Anomaly based intrusion detection using modified fuzzy clustering. Int. J. Interact. Multimedia Artif. Intell. **4**(6), 54–59 (2017)
12. He, Z., Xu, X., Deng, S.: Discovering cluster-based local outliers. Pattern Recogn. Lett. **24**(9–10), 1641–1650 (2003)
13. Jing, L., Tian, Y.: Self-supervised visual feature learning with deep neural networks: a survey. IEEE Trans. Pattern Anal. Mach. Intell. **43**, 4037–4058 (2020)
14. Khan, K., Rehman, S.U., Aziz, K., Fong, S., Sarasvady, S.: DBSCAN: past, present and future. In The 5th International Conference on the Applications of Digital Information and Web Technologies, ICADIWT 2014, pp. 232–238. IEEE (2014)
15. Kumar, V.: Parallel and distributed computing for cybersecurity. IEEE Distrib. Syst. Online **6**(10), 1–9 (2005)
16. Landauera, M., Skopika, F., Wurzenbergera, M., Rauberb, A.: System log clustering approaches for cyber security applications: a survey. Comput. Secur. **92**, 101739 (2020)
17. Lee, Y.-H., Wei, C.-P., Cheng, T.-H., Yang, C.-T.: Nearest-neighbor-based approach to time-series classification. Decis. Support Syst. **53**(1), 207–217 (2012)
18. Li, L., Das, S., Hansman, R.J., Palacios, R., Srivastava, A.N.: Clustering techniques to detect abnormal flights of unique data patterns. J. Aerosp. Inf. Syst. **12**, 587–598 (2015)
19. Li, Z., Wu, S., Zhou, Y., Li, C.: A combined filtering search for DTW. In: 2017 2nd International Conference on Image, Vision and Computing (ICIVC), pp. 884–888. IEEE (2017)
20. Manning, C.D., Prabhakar, R., Schutza, H.: Introduction to Information Retrieval. Cambridge University Press (2008)
21. Rahmah, N., Sitanggang, I.S.: Determination of optimal epsilon (Eps) value on DBSCAN algorithm to clustering data on peatland hotspots in Sumatra. IOP Conf. Ser. Earth Environ. Sci. **31**, 012012 (2016)
22. Rakthanmanon, T., et al.: Searching and mining trillions of time series subsequences under dynamic time warping. In: Proceedings of the 18th ACM SIGKDD International Conference on Knowledge Discovery and Data Mining, pp. 262–270 (2012)
23. Roohi, A., Faust, K., Djuric, U., Diamandis, P.: Unsupervised machine learning in pathology: the next frontier. Surg. Pathol. Clin. **13**(2), 349–358 (2020)
24. Rousseeuw, P.J.: Silhouettes: a graphical aid to the interpretation and validation of cluster analysis. Comput. Appl. Math. **20**, 53–65 (1987)
25. Sakoe, H., Chiba, S.: Dynamic programming algorithm optimization for spoken word recognition. IEEE Trans. Acoust. Speech Sig. Process. **26**(1), 43–49 (1978)
26. Sander, J., Ester, M., Kriegel, H.-P., Xiaowei, X.: Density-based clustering in spatial databases: the algorithm GDBSCAN and its applications. Data Min. Knowl. Disc. **2**(2), 169–194 (1998)
27. Thudumu, S., Branch, P., Jin, J., Singh, J.: A comprehensive survey of anomaly detection techniques for high dimensional big data. J. Big Data **7**, 42 (2020)
28. Vikram, S., Li, L., Russell, S.: Handwriting and gestures in the air, recognizing on the fly. In: Proceedings of the CHI, vol. 13, pp. 1179–1184 (2013)
29. Wang, X., Mueen, A., Ding, H., Trajcevski, G., Scheuermann, P., Keogh, E.: Experimental comparison of representation methods and distance measures for time series data. Data Min. Knowl. Disc. **26**(2), 275–309 (2013)

30. Yang, A.C., Huang, N.E., Peng, C.-K., Tsai, S.-J.: Do seasons have an influence on the incidence of depression? The use of an internet search engine query data as a proxy of human affect. PLOS ONE **5**, e13728 (2010)
31. Zhou, C., Paffenroth, R.C.: Anomaly detection with robust deep autoencoders. In: Proceedings of the 23rd ACM SIGKDD International Conference on Knowledge Discovery and Data Mining, KDD 2017, pp. 665–674 (2017)

Evolving Large Scale Prediction Models for Vehicle Volume Forecasting in Service Stations

Himadri Sikhar Khargharia[1(✉)], Siddhartha Shakya[1], Russell Ainslie[2], and Gilbert Owusu[2]

[1] 1 EBTIC, Khalifa University, Abu Dhabi, UAE
{himadri.khargharia,sid.shakya}@ku.ac.ae
[2] British Telecom, London, UK
{russell.ainslie,gilbert.owusu}@bt.com

Abstract. Resource Planning and Service Optimization for operational efficiency constitutes a major factor in the service industry. Internally most of it is dependent on the accuracy of the forecasted demand for the service, which is used to proactively plan resources to match expected demand. In this paper, our focus is on a real-world scenario of vehicle volume forecasting in service stations. Previous work has explored a genetic algorithm (GA) to evolve a regression model based on Neural Networks. Our focus here is to extend on this and show that GA based approach can be also used to evolve other popular regression models for this problem that are widely used in machine learning literature. Each of these techniques considers the historical vehicle volume data along with other correlated data, such as weather, and can have its own set of model parameters as well as other parameters related to data filtration, correction, and feature selections. All of these parameters require proper tuning to achieve the best forecasting accuracy. This can be a challenging task, particularly where different prediction models need to be built for different stations and for different periods, potentially resulting in hundreds of models being built. Manual tuning can be time-consuming, and most importantly, sub-optimal. Our results show that GA can be successfully used to automate the optimization of many popular machine learning models for large-scale vehicle volume forecasting, and more importantly can provide better accuracy than traditionally used manual tuning approaches.

Keywords: Forecasting · elasticNet · SVR · KNN regressor · Neural network · Genetic algorithm

1 Introduction

Knowledge of future demand acts as a decisive factor for the service industry which expands across various domains like retail, telecom, banking, utilities, etc. Historical data is utilized in order to estimate the direction of future trends.

© Springer Nature Switzerland AG 2021
M. Bramer and R. Ellis (Eds.): SGAI-AI 2021, LNAI 13101, pp. 224–238, 2021.
https://doi.org/10.1007/978-3-030-91100-3_19

Businesses use this estimation and project demand of goods and services to determine their budget and to plan for anticipated expenses and required human and machine resources.

Customer satisfaction is one of the key factors that measure success in the service industry. Satisfied customers tend to give repeat businesses which leads to an increase in revenue. Customer satisfaction is evaluated based on certain metrics such as turnaround time, service quality, service efficiency, etc. With accurate forecasting, the service providers can effectively plan their resources to attain maximum operational efficiency for greater revenue generation. Usually, some view of demand is available with an existing contract of a certain set of services for a certain period of time. But in the majority of cases, it is forecasted, with historical demand and other correlated factors affecting the expected volumes [5,13,14,16].

In a service station, including retail stores, fueling stations, repair centers, banks, etc., demand is the footfall of the customers. In modern service stations, IoT sensors are deployed to track this footfall. These sensors include wireless magnetometers, wireless ultra-sonic sensors, radar sensors, optical sensors, and CCTV cameras [2,10,26], all of which keep track of customers entering or leaving the premises and thus generates a huge volume of historical data [13,14,16]. This data can be used to forecast future demand by analyzing the pattern of past demand.

The context of this paper, a typical fueling station, consists of various installations, called bays, such as auto car washing, lube counter, oil change, parking area for retail, fueling station, etc. In [13] and [14] experiments for forecasting demand were run across the fueling bay of the service stations using the historical demand data and the correlated weather inputs to train the models. In [13], using the ad-hoc approach of choosing the hyperparameters of the forecasting models, it was observed that for the specific problem of predicting the demand of fueling stations, a neural network-based model gave the best accuracy with the documented set of hyperparameters. In [12] a recurrent neural network approach was presented and shown to perform well for this problem. [14] showed usage of a genetic algorithm (GA) [8] to intelligently determine the optimal set of hyperparameters for the neural network models, including the parameters for data correction and filtering. In this paper, we further extended the work to see if GAs can be used to evolve other forecasting techniques, such as elasticNet [36], SVR [3], KNN regressor [30] along with neural networks [19] to obtain improved accuracy for this problem.

Manual tuning of hyperparameters is time-consuming and sub-optimal, and when we extend it to building separate forecasting models for each station, for each bay, and for each period, the number of total models required increases significantly, making it nearly impossible to manually build these models. This creates a need for intelligent automation of model building. We show how a GA can be used to automate the tuning of numerous models and further extend this approach to four different forecasting techniques. The results show that the accuracy can be improved significantly in comparison to ad-hoc approaches for all the implemented forecasting techniques.

The paper is divided into 5 sections. Section 2 presents a background study of the forecasting techniques investigated and reviews previous approaches used for tuning their parameters. Section 3 describes the proposed GA approach for optimizing vehicle volume forecasting models. It also describes parameters for each technique and other parameters related to data filtration. Section 4 describes experiments comparing the proposed approach with the ad-hoc approach from [13] and presents an analysis of the results. Section 5 concludes the paper.

2   Background

Forecasting is a process of predicting future demand trends by analyzing historical and current trends, along with the use of any other correlated inputs. Multiple mechanisms exist for forecasting these demand trends. Non-linear regression techniques like KNN regressor, ElasticNet, SVR, and neural network are widely used in the forecasting problem space. The success of each of these techniques depends on many factors, including the effectiveness of the input data, the noise, correctly selected features, and chosen model parameters for topology building and training.

KNN regressor [21,30] uses the mean of the label of its nearest neighbour to compute the labels assigned to a query point. Maltamo et al. [18] used K-nearest neighbour regression for basel area diameter distribution of trees prediction. Forecasting of solar power using gradient boosting and K-nearest neighbour regressor is done by Huang and others [9].

SVR is a support vector machine [3] that supports both linear and non-linear regression. In [20,33], Support Vector Regression was used for financial time series forecasting and travel-time prediction.

ElasticNet is a regularized regression method used when there are multiple features that are correlated with one another and both of them are being picked. In [4,23], Elastic Net is used to forecast economic time series and the US real house price index respectively.

Neural networks (NN) [19] are popular models in machine learning and deep learning literature. Neural networks are used in various real-world applications like future trading volume forecasting [11], work demand prediction for service providers along with optimal resource planning allocation [1], building energy prediction models [7] etc. In [15] a neural network is used for stock market price prediction. [27] used Neural Network trained with genetic algorithms for dynamic pricing.

Evolutionary algorithms including GAs have been used in the past to optimize the parameters of prediction models [34]. GA is a well-known class of evolutionary algorithm motivated by natural selection and biological evolution [24] and has been successfully applied in many real-world optimization problems [22,31]. Some noticeable applications of a GA combined with a Neural network are in [6], where a model is presented that predicts the outcome in critically ill patients that decide whether a patient is to be admitted to intensive care. Also, [17] uses neural networks tuned by genetic algorithms to predict the deformation modulus of rock masses.

3   Methodology

The historical data set of 1 years duration from the set of 3 service stations (anonymized to stations 1, 2, and 3) are used to run the experiments. The data set was from a telecom service provider, who maintains the IoT infrastructure for service stations in the region it operates. The data is collected by the sensors which are installed at different bays of these stations. It is a continuous univariate time-series data of the daily vehicle volume for a 1-year duration. Figure 1 shows the vehicle volume of stations 1. Because of space constraints, we do not plot the data for stations 2 and 3.

Figure 1 shows that there is a dip in the vehicle volume for station 1 from April 2019 onwards. Comparing data from station 2 with data from stations 1 and 3, we found that station 2 has a larger volume of incoming vehicles when compared to station 1 and station 3.

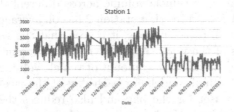

Fig. 1. Vehicle volume by date - Station 1

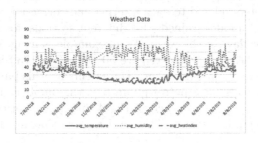

Fig. 2. Weather data

We also consider the weather data as an additional input for prediction as it is likely to have an effect on people's decision to visit the service station. For this, minimum, average, and maximum of the humidity, temperature, and heat index were collected for the whole year. Figure 2 shows the daily average of humidity, temperature and heat index. It can be seen that the humidity is quite high when the temperature decreases and slightly decreases when the temperatures increase. The heat index increases and decreases with the increase and decrease of the temperature.

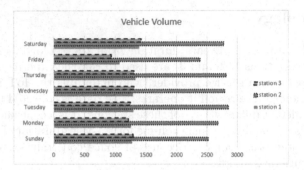

Fig. 3. Day wise average volume

3.1 Model Formulation

Figure 3 shows the average vehicle volume across different days of the week for the three stations. We could see that station 2 has on average double the volume of stations 1 or 3. In all three stations, it is seen that the vehicle volume varies across different days of the week. Also, services in different bays of the station are very different and therefore the amount of vehicle volume is different as well. Hence we create individual models for each day of the week and for each bay. This localizes the dataset for the bay and also reduces the noise that can be introduced if we consider a single prediction model combining all days of the week. The problem of over-fitting is handled by specific algorithms using the internal parameters, e.g. early stoppage in the neural network.

Each of the forecasting techniques investigated has a set of model parameters along with parameters related to data filtering and correction models. They can be different for each model trained - for different stations, for different bays, as well as for different days of the week. As an example, having 50 stations with 5 bays for 7 days of the week would require $50 \times 5 \times 7 = 1750$ individual models to be built and trained. As part of the experiments for this paper, for 3 stations and for one of the bays - the petrol pump bay, the number of models that are run constitutes $7 \times 3 = 21$ for each of the 4 different algorithms KNN, SVR, ElasticNet, and Neural Network. The total models that are being trained are thus 84.

3.2 Parameter Analysis

Generic Parameters: Pre-processing of the data is crucial for the success of any prediction techniques. The data is divided into training and testing set in the ratio of 90% and 10% respectively, repeating multiple times in order to collect multiple samples from it. The parameters related to data filtering and data correction, which are generic across all tested models, need to be optimally set for the model to forecast with higher accuracy and the value can be different for different models based on their internal functions, sensitivity to noise, and their ability to deduct patterns.

These include α the *Outlier Filter* parameter, which is used to reduce noise in the data. The data from the training set which lies outside of $\mu \pm \alpha\sigma$ are considered as outliers. Here, μ is the mean, and σ is the standard deviation of the daily vehicle volumes. Another optimization parameter is the distance correlation value [32]. We filter out any features whose distance correlation is greater than a threshold (β). The correlation filter value ranges from 0 to 1. Next, is the lag in the time series (l) that is to be used as an additional parameter to the model. For example, Input lag for the weather data defines the number of previous day's data that will be used in the feature set to predict the current day's vehicle volume. In other words, it tests whether there is any effect of past temperatures on today's volume in addition to today's temperature. For example, if an input lag of 2 is used, it means mean temperature from the current day as well as mean temperature from yesterday and the day before yesterday will be part of the feature set for predicting today's vehicle volume. *Duration Days (d)* states how many days of the target variable's historical values are part of the input feature set. If the duration days is 7, then the vehicle volume from the past seven days will be part of the feature set. These are also known as autoregressive inputs. *Duration Weeks (w)*, this field states how many target variable data points from previous weeks for any specific day-of-the-week from historical data is being fed as an additional input. If the duration of weeks is 2, then vehicle volume for the past 2 Sundays will be part of the feature set for the prediction model for Sundays, past two Tuesdays for the prediction model for Tuesdays, and so on. Next, we describe algorithm-specific parameters.

KNN Regressor Parameters: KNN regressor is based on learning by comparing given test instances with the training set. The accuracy of a KNN regressor is dependent on the number of neighbours K and the algorithm a for calculating the nearest neighbour e.g. KD-Tree, Ball-Tree, Brute-Force [30].

SVR Parameters: Accuracy of an ϵ-SVR model is dependent on multiple parameters as noted in [21]. C which is a regularization parameter that controls the trade-off between achieving a low training error and a low testing error. Parameter ϵ in the ϵ-SVR model, specifies the epsilon-tube within which no penalty is associated in the training loss function with points predicted within a distance epsilon from the actual value [3,21]. Readily available kernels Kr, as described in [21], are used for the purpose of running the experiments. These include linear, polynomial, rbf, sigmoid kernels.

ElasticNet Parameters: An alternate version of Elastic Net [21,36] i.e. ElasticNetCV [28] is used for our purpose. This is for the fact that ElasticNet parameters α, intercept, *max-iteration* has no upper bound which leads to complexity in modeling the size of bits for an evolutionary algorithm. ElasticNetCV is an estimator that has built-in cross-validation capabilities to automatically select the best hyper-parameters. The advantage of using a cross-validation estimator over the canonical Estimator class along with grid search is that they can take advantage of warm-starting by reusing precomputed results in the previous steps of the cross-validation process. This generally leads to speed improvements [21,28,36]. Parameter CV (cv) which determines the cross-validation splitting strategy and random-state (rs) which selects a random feature to update are needed to be optimized.

Neural Network Parameters: For the purpose of our paper and following [13], we use a feed-forward neural network model with the resilient backpropagation algorithm [25]. We also use the early stopping strategy to avoid overfitting [35]. It subdivides the data from the training set into training and validation sets. This validation set is used to evaluate the accuracy of the model. Once the accuracy of the model stops improving and starts to decrease this indicates overfitting and the training process is stopped. The activation function of the nodes is of sigmoid form [19]. We restrict the neural network model to support a maximum of 6 hidden layers and 12 nodes for each layer. The parameters that have to be optimally set to get the best accuracy from the model are Hidden Layers (h) and the number of nodes $[n_1, n_2, ...n_h]$. The upper bound for the number of nodes was set to 8.

3.3   Ad-Hoc Approach for Improving Prediction Model Accuracy

In this section, we provide detail of an ad-hoc approach from [13], which is compared against the approach proposed in this paper. The ad-hoc approach is an experimental design method where a range was specified for each parameter and a relatively higher step value was used to get the test sequence within the range. Each combination of sequences for each parameter was tested and the best performing settings were recorded. It is noted that not all parameters were tested to all possible ranges and some were kept to a smaller range, in order to limit the possible increase in the number of configurations to be tested. Particularly, most of the parameters related to the additional filtering such as α, β, l, d, and w as described in Sect. 3.2, were kept to a smaller set and were in some cases set to a pre-processed setting. SKLearn, a python based ML library [29] provides readily available implementations and are used in the ad-hoc technique.

3.4   Evolving Prediction Models Using GA

As described before, GAs are a class of population-based optimization algorithms, where a population of strings called chromosomes, representing a solution, is maintained. Using concepts such as crossover and mutation, the recombination of the strings is carried out with the search being guided by the results of the objective function, f, for each string in the population. Strings with higher fitness are given more opportunities to breed. In a discreet search space X and a function $f : X \to \mathbb{R}$. The general problem is $\min_{x \in X} f$. Genetic algorithms allow the separation of the representation of the problem from the actual variables with which it was originally formulated with concepts like genotype (encoded representation of the variable) and phenotype (the set of actual variables). So, if the vector x is represented by a string s of length l, made up of symbols drawn from alphabet A using a mapping $c : A' \mapsto x$ we then need to use a search space $s \subseteq A'$ as some image of A' under c may represent invalid solution.

The optimization problem then becomes $\min_{s \in S} g(s)$ where the function $g(s) = f(c(s))$. Fitness may not necessarily be $f(c(s))$ but $h(f(c(s)))$ where $h : \mathbb{R} \mapsto \mathbb{R}^+$ is a monotonic function used to eliminate the problem of 'negative' fitness [24].

4   Experiment Setup and Analysis of Results

In this section, we compare the prediction accuracy using the ad-hoc approach explained in Sect. 3.3 with the proposed GA approach. Mean Absolute Percentage Error (MAPE) was used as a measure of accuracy. We consider a GA with a population string consisting of 1's and 0's (binary representation). Each parameter of the prediction model as described above is represented by a set of binary bits. The parameter settings for the GA were as follows: the generation allowed was 50, population size was set to twice the size of the bit string solution for each forecasting model, crossover probability was set to 0.6, mutation probability was set to 0.01, 'roulette-wheel' was used as the selection operator, 'one-point crossover' was used as the crossover operator, 'one-bit mutation' was used as the mutation operator. We do not go into the details of these genetic operators, which can be found in [8,24]. All of these GA parameters were set empirically, where multiple experiments were run with many different settings and the one that found the best result was used.

The subsection below describes the solution length for each of the prediction models and the number of bits required to represent each parameter with min and max values defining ranges for each of them. The min and max are used to normalize the binary bits, 2^r, where r is the bit size, to decimal numbers within that range. Table 1 shows for each algorithm, the number of bits used for each parameter with given min and max values, along with the total solution length. Below we discuss this for each of the algorithms.

For KNN regressor Table 1 shows, the solution length is 19 bit. A chromosome, x = {111 100 11 0001 11 10 011} of a KNN model can be decoded to the value of each parameter as 111 (l is 7), 100 (d is 4), 11 (w is 3), 0001 (β is 1/10 = 0.1), 11 (α is 3), 10 (a is 2), 011 (K is 3). The options for nearest neighbour algorithms a are KD-Tree as 1, Ball-Tree as 2 and Brute-Force as 3.

As shown in Table 1 for SVR, the solution length is 24 bits. For example a chromosome, x = {111 100 11 0001 11 1000 01 1000} of an SVR model can be decoded to value of each parameter as 111 (l is 7), 100 (d is 4), 11 (w is 3), 0001 (β is 1/10 = 0.1), 11 (α is 3), 1000 (C is 8/10 = 0.8), 01 (Kr is 1), 1000 (ϵ is 8/10 = 0.8). The options for kernel are linear as 1, polynomial as 2, rbf as 3, sigmoid as 4.

For ElasticNet Table 1 shows, the solution length is 20 bits. For example a chromosome, x = {111 100 11 0001 11 101 011} of an ElasticNet model can be

Table 1. Regressor with solution lengths

Algorithm	Parameters	Bits	Min value	Max value
KNN	KNN $Algo$ (a)	2	1	3
	$Neighbours$ (K)	3	1	8
	$Input$ lag (l)	3	0	7
	$Days$ (d)	3	0	7
	$Weeks$ (w)	2	0	3
	$Correlation$ (β)	4	0.0	1.0
	$Outlier$ (α)	2	0	3
	Total bits	19		
SVR	C (C)	4	0.0	1.0
	$kernel$ (Kr)	2	1	3
	$epsilon$ (ϵ)	4	0.0	1.0
	$Input$ lag (l)	3	0	7
	$Days$ (d)	3	0	7
	$Weeks$ (w)	2	0	3
	$Correlation$ (β)	4	0.0	1.0
	$Outlier$ (α)	2	0	3
	Total bits	24		
ElasticNet	CV (cv)	3	1	5
	$random\text{-}state$ (rs)	3	1	8
	$Input$ lag (l)	3	0	7
	$Days$ (d)	3	0	7
	$Weeks$ (w)	2	0	3
	$Correlation$ (β)	4	0.0	1.0
	$Outlier$ (α)	2	0	3
	Total bits	20		
Neural net	$Hidden$ $layer$ (h)	3	1	6
	$Layer$ 1 - $nodes$ (n_1)	4	1	13
	$Layer$ 2 - $nodes$ (n_2)	4	0	13
	$Layer$ 3 - $nodes$ (n_3)	4	0	13
	$Layer$ 4 - $nodes$ (n_4)	4	0	13
	$Layer$ 5 - $nodes$ (n_5)	4	0	13
	$Layer$ 6 - $nodes$ (n_6)	4	0	13
	$Input$ lag (l)	3	0	7
	$Days$ (d)	3	0	7
	$Weeks$ (w)	2	0	3
	$Correlation$ (β)	3	0.0	1.0
	$Outlier$ (α)	2	0	3
	Total bits	40		

divided as 111 (l is 7), 100 (d is 4), 11 (w is 3), 0001 (β is $1/10 = 0.1$), 11 (α is 3), 101 (cv is 5), 011 (rs is 3)

As shown in Table 1, for Neural Network the solution length is 40 bits. For example a chromosome, x = {010 0111 0101 0000 0000 0000 0000 000 000 01 000 01} of a Neural Network can be divided as 010 (h is 2), 0111 (n1 is 7), 0101 (n2 is 5), 0000 (n3 is 0), 0000 (n4 is 0), 0000 (n5 is 0), 0000 (n6 is 0), 000 (l is 0), 000 (d is 0), 01 (w is 1), 000 (β is 0.0), 01 (α is 1).

We compare the overall accuracy results $(1 - MAPE)$, given by the ad-hoc approach of selecting model parameters to that of the genetic algorithm approach. We do $(1 - MAPE) \times 100$ to get a more readable % representation of the accuracy. For each model, i.e., for each station and for each day of the week, 10 runs of the GA were performed to evolve the model and the average accuracy found was recorded. These averages were then compared against the ad-hoc results as presented in [13]. The results are presented in Table 2 for each of the models.

Table 2. Regressor accuracy % - adhoc approach vs GA

Algorithm	Day	Adhoc - Station 1	Adhoc - Station 2	Adhoc - Station 3	GA - Station 1	GA - Station 2	GA - Station 3
KNN	Friday	93.1	93.2	94.7	97.5	96.7	97.7
	Saturday	95.1	83.4	93.4	99.7	99.6	96.4
	Sunday	89.4	78.5	91.6	97.6	99.7	98.0
	Monday	91.6	80.3	90.6	96.7	97.3	97.5
	Tuesday	93.5	72.1	88.1	90.2	98.6	93.5
	Wednesday	83.5	73.3	92.5	87.9	92.8	94.7
	Thursday	93.0	81.7	95.8	93.6	93.9	98.5
	Average	**91.3**	**80.3**	**92.4**	**95.1**	**96.9**	**96.6**
SVR	Friday	93.8	91.6	94.7	99.8	97.2	97.1
	Saturday	91.1	82.1	93.5	99.2	96.4	96.2
	Sunday	79.4	77.2	91.7	97.6	95.4	98.6
	Monday	88.4	79.0	90.7	95.7	96.2	96.0
	Tuesday	89.7	70.9	88.1	87.5	95.2	97.8
	Wednesday	82.8	72.1	92.6	84.8	95.7	92.2
	Thursday	91.4	80.4	95.8	94.3	97.6	93.8
	Average	**88.1**	**79.0**	**92.4**	**94.2**	**96.3**	**95.9**
ElasticNet	Friday	89.1	86.9	91.4	97.7	94.1	97.1
	Saturday	92.3	77.8	90.1	94.7	98.0	95.4
	Sunday	86.7	73.2	88.4	94.3	96.4	96.9
	Monday	89.3	74.9	87.4	93.3	95.6	93.0
	Tuesday	80.1	67.2	85.0	88.9	96.0	91.5
	Wednesday	83.5	68.3	89.2	87.7	90.5	92.2
	Thursday	92.0	76.2	92.4	94.6	88.8	95.6
	Average	**87.6**	**74.9**	**89.1**	**93.0**	**94.2**	**94.5**
Neural Net	Friday	92.6	85.5	91.0	98.8	97.9	98.4
	Saturday	86.0	86.8	94.9	96.5	97.4	96.4
	Sunday	87.0	78.2	93.7	98.3	98.0	95.9
	Monday	93.8	87.5	97.7	96.8	98.3	98.9
	Tuesday	82.7	89.2	95.6	97.5	95.5	96.2
	Wednesday	74.0	84.4	87.9	92.8	90.6	96.4
	Thursday	90.6	92.6	89.3	97.6	93.5	97.3
	Average	**86.7**	**86.3**	**92.9**	**96.9**	**95.9**	**97.1**

The overall average accuracy of KNN regressor across the three stations for the ad-hoc approach is 88.0% and the genetic algorithm approach is 96.2% (also summarised in Table 3). It is seen that the overall accuracy across all the three stations increased by around 8% when using the genetic algorithm against the ad-hoc approach.

The overall average accuracy of SVR across the three stations using the ad-hoc approach is 86.7% and using the genetic algorithm approach is 95.4% (also summarised in Table 3). It is observed that the overall accuracy across all the three stations increased by around 9% when using the genetic algorithm against the ad-hoc approach for tuning the hyperparameters.

The overall average accuracy of ElasticNet across the three stations for the ad-hoc approach is 83.9% and the genetic algorithm approach is 93.9% (also summarised in Table 3). It is seen that the overall accuracy across all the three stations increased by around 10% when using a genetic algorithm against the ad-hoc approach.

The overall average accuracy of the Neural Network across the three stations for the ad-hoc approach is 88.6% and the genetic algorithm approach is 96.6% (also summarised in Table 3). It is seen that the overall accuracy across all the three stations increased by around 8% when using the genetic algorithm against the ad-hoc approach.

The better results for the GA can be attributed to the fact that the parallel search approach in GA enables searching through a much bigger parameter space than the ad-hoc approach, including parameter space of all 5 filtering and data preparation parameters. The correct setting for parameters such as α and β seem to have an effect on the accuracy which the ad-hoc approach was not able to effectively explore, as the combinations of experimental setups in it were only enough to effectively search through the core model parameters, such as K and a in KNN. This also suggests that each prediction model may work better with different sets of input data, with different levels of noise reduction, and with different period lags, based on the way the model trains and produces the forecasts. And with the GA, the full parameter space was exploited to achieve

Table 3. Overall average accuracy % for 3 stations and for each models - adhoc vs GA

Algorithm	Adhoc approach	GA approach
KNN	88.0	96.2
SVR	86.7	95.4
ElasticNet	83.9	93.9
Neural Network	88.6	96.6
Average	**86.8**	**95.5**

significantly better accuracy. Also, it is important to note that the model training was fully automated and therefore was able to generate numerous prediction models.

4.1 Typical GA Evolution of Model

We find it interesting to show a typical evolution of a prediction model as done by the GA, by plotting the average fitness of the population against the fitness of the best solution in the population (maximum fitness) for a prediction instance (Fig. 4). The fitness here means the calculated accuracy of prediction as the GA generation progresses. We can see that typically, and as expected, the GA starts with lower quality solutions in the population with lower average accuracy. However as generations progress, the population evolves to better solutions, and both average fitness and the best solution fitness increases. By 50 generations the population fully converges. This plotting shows that there is a gain in running the GA, as a typical random solution in the first few generations does not achieve the best settings. The fitness is plotted on a scale of 0 to 1. Analysis of the figure shows that for Saturday for station 3 while using the SVR based prediction model, the final accuracy that was achieved using the ad-hoc approach was 93.5%, while using the GA in generation 0 (using a scale between 0 to 1) the maximum fitness was 0.919 (i.e. 91.9%) which then evolved to 0.962 (i.e. 96.2%) by the end of 50 generations.

4.2 Typical Plot of Actual vs Prediction

Figure 5, shows for the neural network the actual against the predicted value of both the ad-hoc and the genetic algorithm approach plotted for station 2 and for petrol island bay. While using a neural network Station 2 has an average accuracy of 95.9% for the GA approach and 86.3% using the ad-hoc approach. It can be noted that the prediction produced by the GA approach is much closer to the actual in comparison to the ad-hoc approach.

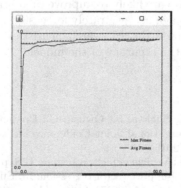

Fig. 4. Evolution of SVR model for Tuesday for Station 3

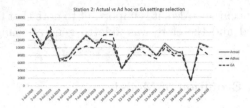

Fig. 5. Actual vs Predicted using adhoc selection and GA selection for station 2 for Neural Network

5   Conclusion

In this paper, our goal was to show that GA can be used to evolve many different prediction models. One of the key objectives was to enhance the accuracy of the prediction models and find the best configuration settings for each neural network, elasticNet, SVR, and KNN regressor based prediction models to predict the visitor demand in service stations. We compared the accuracy of each of the forecasting techniques predictions using settings suggested by the ad-hoc approach from [3] and settings that are found to be optimal by the genetic algorithm. We have seen that the settings selected by the genetic algorithm have much lower MAPE and thus higher accuracy than the settings selected using the ad-hoc approach, with an average improvement of about 8%, 9%, 10% and 8% for KNN regressor, SVR, ElasticNet, and Neural Network respectively. We also saw that KNN and SVR had higher accuracy for station 2 in comparison to the neural network which shows that sometimes other prediction models could outperform the neural network model if trained properly, although neural network had the highest average accuracy for all three stations. The proposed Genetic algorithm approach to evolving the parameters of the prediction models, particularly with neural network is adopted into a prediction framework and is being trialled by our partner telecom. The GA module is triggered every few weeks to rebuild the models and select the optimal parameters, in order to take into account any recent change in the patterns as new historical data becomes available. The results are encouraging and are likely to improve their service offerings, by better management of resources against accurately forecasted demand. Future research would explore other state-of-the-art search heuristics such as multi-objective optimization to improve the accuracy of the model.

References

1. Ainslie, R., McCall, J., Shakya, S., Owusu, G.: Predictive planning with neural networks. In: 2016 International Joint Conference on Neural Networks (IJCNN), pp. 2110–2117. IEEE (2016)
2. Ashraf, A., Baldwin, D.: Vehicle detection system. U.S. patent no. 8,157,219 (2012)
3. Awad, M., Khanna, R.: Support vector regression. In: Efficient Learning Machines, pp. 67–80. Apress, Berkeley, CA (2015). https://doi.org/10.1007/978-1-4302-5990-9_4

4. Bai, J., Ng, S.: Forecasting economic time series using targeted predictors. J. Econometrics **146**(2), 304–317 (2008)
5. Balwani, S.S.V.: Operational efficiency through resource planning optimization and work process improvement. Ph.D. thesis, Massachusetts Institute of Technology (2012)
6. Dybowski, R., Gant, V., Weller, P., Chang, R.: Prediction of outcome in critically ill patients using artificial neural network synthesised by genetic algorithm. Lancet **347**(9009), 1146–1150 (1996)
7. Ekici, B.B., Aksoy, U.T.: Prediction of building energy consumption by using artificial neural networks. Adv. Eng. Softw. **40**(5), 356–362 (2009)
8. Goldberg, D.E., Holland, J.H.: Genetic algorithms and machine learning. Mach. Learn. **3**, 95–99 (1988). https://doi.org/10.1023/A:1022602019183
9. Huang, J., Perry, M.: A semi-empirical approach using gradient boosting and k-nearest neighbors regression for gefcom2014 probabilistic solar power forecasting. Int. J. Forecast. **32**(3), 1081–1086 (2016)
10. Huang, Y.: RFID based parking management system. U.S. patent no. 7,973,641 (2011)
11. Kaastra, I., Boyd, M.S.: Forecasting futures trading volume using neural networks. J. Futures Markets (1986–1998) **15**(18), 953 (1995)
12. Khargharia, H.S., Santana, R., Shakya, S., Ainslie, R., Owusu, G.: Investigating RNNs for vehicle volume forecasting in service stations. In: 2020 IEEE Symposium Series on Computational Intelligence (SSCI), pp. 2625–2632. IEEE (2020)
13. Khargharia, H.S., Shakya, S., Ainslie, R., AlShizawi, S., Owusu, G.: Predicting demand in IoT enabled service stations. In: 2019 IEEE Conference on Cognitive and Computational Aspects of Situation Management (CogSIMA), pp. 81–87. IEEE (2019)
14. Khargharia, H.S., Shakya, S., Ainslie, R., Owusu, G.: Evolving prediction models with genetic algorithm to forecast vehicle volume in a service station (best application paper). In: Bramer, M., Petridis, M. (eds.) SGAI 2019. LNCS (LNAI), vol. 11927, pp. 167–179. Springer, Cham (2019). https://doi.org/10.1007/978-3-030-34885-4_14
15. Lawrence, R.: Using neural networks to forecast stock market prices. University of Manitoba, vol. 333, pp. 2006–2013 (1997)
16. Madanhire, I., Mbohwa, C.: Enterprise resource planning (ERP) in improving operational efficiency: case study. Procedia CIRP **40**, 225–229 (2016)
17. Majdi, A., Beiki, M.: Evolving neural network using a genetic algorithm for predicting the deformation modulus of rock masses. Int. J. Rock Mech. Min. Sci. **47**(2), 246–253 (2010)
18. Maltamo, M., Kangas, A.: Methods based on k-nearest neighbor regression in the prediction of basal area diameter distribution. Can. J. For. Res. **28**(8), 1107–1115 (1998)
19. Mitchell, T.: Machine Learning (1997)
20. Nava, N., Di Matteo, T., Aste, T.: Financial time series forecasting using empirical mode decomposition and support vector regression. Risks **6**(1), 7 (2018)
21. Pedregosa, F., et al.: Scikit-learn: machine learning in Python. J. Mach. Learn. Res. **12**, 2825–2830 (2011)
22. Petrovski, A., Shakya, S., McCall, J.: Optimising cancer chemotherapy using an estimation of distribution algorithm and genetic algorithms. In: Proceedings of the 8th Annual Conference on Genetic and Evolutionary Computation, pp. 413–418 (2006)

23. Plakandaras, V., Gupta, R., Gogas, P., Papadimitriou, T.: Forecasting the us real house price index. Econ. Model. **45**, 259–267 (2015)
24. Reeves, C.R.: Genetic algorithms. In: Handbook of Metaheuristics, pp. 109–139. Springer, Heidelberg (2010)
25. Riedmiller, M., Braun, H.: RPROP-a fast adaptive learning algorithm. In: Proceedings of ISCIS VII (1992)
26. Schmidt, C., B.S.: Parking control device. U.S. patent application no. 13/723,016 (2013)
27. Shakya, S., Kern, M., Owusu, G., Chin, C.M.: Neural network demand models and evolutionary optimisers for dynamic pricing. Knowl.-Based Syst. **29**, 44–53 (2012)
28. SKLearn: Sklearn - elasticnetcv. https://scikit-learn.org/stable/modules/generated/sklearn.linear_model.ElasticNetCV.html#sklearn.linear_model. ElasticNetCV
29. SKLearn: Tuning the hyper-parameters of an estimator. https://scikit-learn.org/stable/modules/grid_search.html#grid-search
30. Song, Y., Liang, J., Lu, J., Zhao, X.: An efficient instance selection algorithm for k nearest neighbor regression. Neurocomputing **251**, 26–34 (2017)
31. Starkey, A., Hagras, H., Shakya, S., Owusu, G.: A genetic algorithm based system for simultaneous optimisation of workforce skills and teams. KI-Künstliche Intelligenz **32**(4), 245–260 (2018)
32. Székely, G.J., Rizzo, M.L.: Brownian distance covariance. Ann. Appl. Stat. **3**(4), 1236–1265 (2009)
33. Wu, C.H., Ho, J.M., Lee, D.T.: Travel-time prediction with support vector regression. IEEE Trans. Intell. Transp. Syst. **5**(4), 276–281 (2004)
34. Yao, X.: Evolving artificial neural networks. Proc. IEEE **87**(9), 1423–1447 (1999)
35. Yao, Y., Rosasco, L., Caponnetto, A.: On early stopping in gradient descent learning. Constr. Approx. **26**(2), 289–315 (2007)
36. Zou, H., Hastie, T.: Regularization and variable selection via the elastic net. J. R. Stat. Soc. Ser. B (Stat. Methodol.) **67**(2), 301–320 (2005)

AI for Medicine

Sequential Association Rule Mining Revisited: A Study Directed at Relational Pattern Mining for Multi-morbidity

Alexandar Vincent-Paulraj, Girvan Burnside, Frans Coenen$^{(\boxtimes)}$,
Munir Pirmohamed, and Lauren Walker

University of Liverpool, Liverpool, UK
coenen@liverpool.ac.uk

Abstract. Sequential rule mining is a well-established data mining technique for binary valued data. Many variations have been proposed, most approaches use the support-confidence-lift framework. Existing approaches make assumptions concerning the definition of what a sequence is. However, this definition is application dependent. In this paper we look at sequential rule mining with respect to multi-morbidity disease prediction which entails a rethink of the definition of what a sequence is, and a consequent rethink of the operation of the support-confidence-lift framework. A novel sequential rule mining algorithm is proposed designed to address the challenge of multi-morbidity disease prediction. The SEquential RElational N-DIsease Pattern (SERENDIP) algorithm.

Keywords: Sequential rule mining · Multi-morbidity disease prediction

1 Introduction

Sequential Association Rule Mining (SARM) is an established extension of Association Rule Mining (ARM). The fundamental foundation of ARM, and by extension SARM, is the *support-confidence-lift* framework, used to distinguish good quality rules from poor quality rules and to limit computational complexity [2,10]. The idea is to identify frequently occurring sequences within a binary valued input data set and to use these frequent item sets to formulate Association Rules (ARs). Frequency in this context is defined in terms of a *support threshold* σ. The value of σ also serves to limit the number of frequent item sets discovered using the "downward-closure property of item sets" principle. Hence many ARM and SARM algorithms operate in what is referred to as an Apriori manner, after the Apriori algorithm described in [1]. The issue that the downward closure property addresses is that there are $2^n - 1$ candidate item sets given a binary valued data set comprised of n items (columns).

© Springer Nature Switzerland AG 2021
M. Bramer and R. Ellis (Eds.): SGAI-AI 2021, LNAI 13101, pp. 241–253, 2021.
https://doi.org/10.1007/978-3-030-91100-3_20

To limit the number of rules generated a confidence threshold λ is also used to prune the rule set so that only "high confidence" rules are retained. However, just because we have high confidence in a rule this does not mean that it is necessarily a good rule. We would like to know the correlation between the antecedent and consequent of the rule. This is typically done using a the *lift* measure. If the lift for a rule is greater than one there exists a positive correlation between the antecedent and consequent, if the lift is less than one there is a negative correlation, and if the lift is equal to one there is no correlation. Typically we are interested in positive correlations.

Traditional approaches to ARM assumes the items are independent of one another, the input simply comprises a bag of items; the order in which items appear in a rule is not important. SARM, however, assumes that there exists an ordering over the items and that we are looking for frequent sequences of items to translate into Sequential ARs (SARs). Traditional approaches to SARM [6–8,16] assume a sequence is any set of items that occur in order, which may be preceded and/or proceeded with other items or be interrupted by other items. An exemplar application domain where this assumption is valid, and that used for reference with respect to the work presented in this paper, is the retail domain. However, this assumption is not valid with respect all application domains where sequential patterns are of interest. One example of the latter is in the context of multi-morbidity disease prediction.

Multimorbidity, the presence of two or more Long-Term health Conditions (LTCs), arises from combinations of physical and mental health conditions that often require the use of daily preventative medicines. People with multimorbidity are major users of health care resources [9,14]. Certain conditions predictably occur together as they share a common aetiology; consequently the behavioural, environmental and genetic risk factors that contribute to one condition are applicable across all [11]. A good example of this is obesity, high blood pressure, diabetes and heart disease. The organisation of care for individuals with these commonly co-occurring disease clusters is relatively well understood and the treatment goals are aligned (i.e. improving one condition will improve the others within the cluster). What is less well understood is how these conditions accumulate over time; an understanding of the order (sequence) of such co-occurring conditions would provide for their better management, and thus outcomes. SARM would seem to provide the answer. However, unlike traditional approaches to SARM, given a sequence of conditions, any preceding conditions are important while at same time any identified sequence should not be interrupted by additional conditions. In this paper we explore what the support-confidence-lift framework means in the context of SARM for multi-morbidity analysis and prediction, and propose a solution, the SEquential RElational N-DIsease Pattern (SERENDIP) algorithm. A feature of this algorithm is the usage of an *occurrence count matrix* to provide efficiency gains. The algorithm has been published at http://serendip.org.uk, where it can be run as a client-server application using users' own data, or using the provided demonstration test data.

The remainder of this paper is structured as follows. Section 2 presents some background to the technical challenge that this paper seeks to address. Section 3 presents a discussion of the support-confidence-lift framework in the context of multi-morbidity disease prediction. Section 4 then presents the proposed SERENDIP algorithm. The evaluation of the proposed approach is presented in Sect. 5. The main findings and conclusions are the presented in Sect. 6, together with some suggestions for future work.

2 Background

Sequential pattern mining has been extensively used to mine patterns from sequence databases, and then to express those patterns as SARS. Typically the well-established support-confidence-lift framework is adopted. Example algorithms include: GSP (Generalised Sequential Patterns) [3], SPADE (Sequential Pattern Discovering using Equivalence classes) [16] and SPAM (Sequential Pattern Mining) [4]. These algorithms use different approaches for candidate generation, and their performance varies with volume of data and computation infrastructure. For example, GSP does not use all the frequent items in a database, it works on time bounds to mine patterns, and tends to be used for generalised pattern mining. The SPAM algorithm stores sequence patterns using a bitmap compression technique (SARM algorithms generate a lot of intermediate data), and significance support counting. SPADE is a depth-first search algorithm which employs vertical formatting to mine patterns. It has been shown to be efficient for the mining of large data sets and support counting. A more recent discussion can be found in [13] where the use of Hadoop-MapReduce is proposed with respect to a retail sequential pattern mining scenario.

What all of the above algorithms have in common is that they assume that it does not matter if a sequences, in the input data, is preceded and/or interrupted by other items, for it to be valid sequence. As noted above, this assumption does not hold with respect to all applications. One example, and that of interest with respect to this paper, is SARM for multi-morbidity disease prediction.

3 The Traditional Versus the Sequential Support-Confidence-Lift Framework

In the traditional approach to ARM the input is a data set $D = \{r_1, r_2, \ldots, r_n\}$ where each record comprises an item set $\{a_1, a_2, \ldots, a_m\}$ taken from a super-set of items A, thus $r_i \subset A$. In shopping basket analysis A is a set of products that might be purchased in a single transaction. In SARM the ordering becomes important. Thus instead of a set we have a list $[a_1, a_2, \ldots, a_m]$ such that (say) product a_i was bought before product a_{i+1}. In both cases the concept of a support count and the downward closure property of item sets still holds, but the way that they are calculated differs. In the traditional approach the support for an item set I, some subset of A, is simply the occurrence count of I in D.

Usually it is more convenient to express this as the probability of A appearing in D (Eq. 1).

$$support_{trad}(I) = \frac{occurrence\ count\ of\ I\ in\ D}{n} \tag{1}$$

The confidence of a rule $X \Rightarrow Y$ would then be calculated using Eq. 2 where $X, Y \in A$ and $X \cap Y = \emptyset$.

$$conf_{trad}(X \Rightarrow Y) = \frac{support_{trad}(\{X \cup Y\})}{support_{trad}(\{X\})} \tag{2}$$

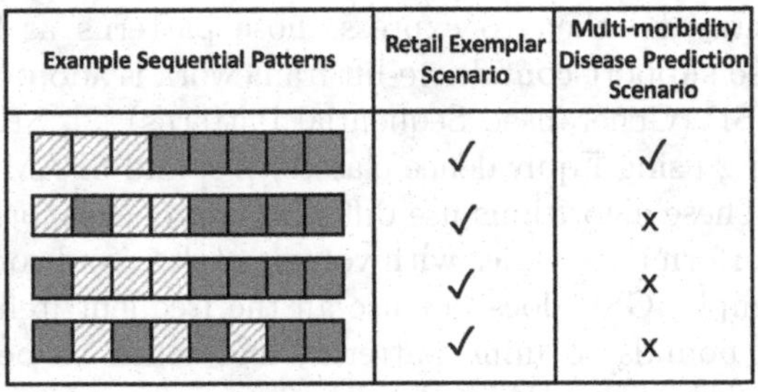

Example Sequential Patterns	Retail Exemplar Scenario	Multi-morbidity Disease Prediction Scenario
	✓	✓
	✓	✗
	✓	✗
	✓	✗

Fig. 1. Distinction between frequent sequential patterns relevant to a retail scenario and a multi-morbidity scenario (sequential patterns indicated by shaded boxes, additional items by filled boxes).

To determine what we mean by support in a sequential setting we first need to establish the nature of the sequential ARs we wish to generate. If we consider the sequential frequent pattern $[a, b, c, d]$, where $\{a, b, c, d\} \in A$, we can identify the rule $[a] \Rightarrow [b]$, if a happens then b will happen next. But is $[a] \Rightarrow [c]$ also a valid rule that can be extracted from this record? What about $[b] \Rightarrow [c]$? Whether these two rules are valid or not depends on whether we are interested purely in the order in which things happen and that, in the case $[a] \Rightarrow [c]$ the fact that b happens between a and c is not important and in the case of $[b] \Rightarrow [c]$ the fact that a precedes b is not important; or that we are interested in the actual sequences and preceding items and intervening items are important. In the case of multi-morbidity disease sequences, the application focus of this paper, any preceding and intervening diseases are important as they may very well have an influence on what happens next. The point is illustrated in Fig. 1 which presents a comparison between the sequential patterns that are relevant in the context of a retail scenario and those that are relevant in the context of a multi-morbidity disease prediction scenario. Thus, in the case of the multi-morbidity application scenario, and given the example frequent sequential pattern $[a, b, c, d]$, we should identify the following valid SARs:

$$[a] \Rightarrow [b]\ \ [a] \Rightarrow [b, c, d]\ [a, b] \Rightarrow [c, d]$$
$$[a] \Rightarrow [b, c]\ \ [a, b] \Rightarrow [c]\ \ [a, b, c] \Rightarrow [d]$$

Thus, in the case of sequential ARM, and given our multi-morbidity application domain where all preceding and intermediate diseases are important, support should be calculated as shown in Eq. 3, where n is the number of records, and confidence is calculated as shown Eq. 4. The notation $X + Y$ indicates the concatenation of sub-sequence Y to the end of sub-sequence X.

$$support_{seq}(X) = \frac{occurrence\ count\ where\ X\ is\ a\ leading\ subsequence}{n(I)} \quad (3)$$

$$conf_{seq}(X \Rightarrow Y) = \frac{support_{seq}(X + Y)}{support_{seq}(X)} \quad (4)$$

If we assume the following trivial data set of sequences D:

$$[a, b, c, d]$$
$$[c, b, d]$$
$$[d, c, a]$$
$$[a, b, d]$$
$$[a, d, c, b]$$

and consider the rule $[a] \Rightarrow [b]$. The sequential support for $[a]$ is $3/5 = 0.6$, and the sequential support for $[a, b]$ is $2/5 = 0.4$. The confidence is then $0.4/0.6 = 0.67$.

Traditionally the lift of a rule is calculated as shown in Eq. 5. In the case of sequential ARM, and given the constraints imposed but our multi-morbidity application domain, lift is calculated as indicated by Eq. 6 where the support of the consequent is calculated as shown in Eq. 7. The variable i is the index of the start of the consequent, calculated as $|X| + 1$ where X is the number of items in X (the antecedent of the rule). Thus, the lift for our sequential example rule $[a] \Rightarrow [b]$ (see above) is $0.67/0.60 = 1.11$.

$$lift_{trad}(X \Rightarrow Y) = \frac{conf_{trad}(X \Rightarrow Y)}{support_{trad}(Y)} \quad (5)$$

$$lift_{seq}(X \Rightarrow Y) = \frac{conf_{seq}(X \Rightarrow Y)}{support\_consequent(Y, i)} \quad (6)$$

$$support\_consequent(Y, i) = \frac{occurrence\ count\ where\ Y\ is\ at\ position\ i}{n} \quad (7)$$

The sequential support-confidence-lift framework as described above, in the context of multi-morbidity disease prediction, requires a rethink of the traditional Apriori approach to ARM and established sequential ARM algorithms such as SPADE [16] where a sequence can be preceded by items not included in the sequence, and that there may be intervening items in the data set that are not included in the sequence. This is considered in the following section, Sect. 4.

Algorithm 1. Sequential ARM for Multi-morbidity $(|A|, D, max, \sigma)$

1: $M = occurrenceCountMatrixGeneration(max, |A|)$ (Algorithm 2)
2: $I_1 = \emptyset$, set to hold frequent one-item patterns
3: **for** $j = 1$ to $j = |A|$ **do**
4:     **if** $M_{1,j} \geq \sigma$ **then**
5:         $I_1 = I_1 \cup [a_j]$, add $a_j \in A$ to the set of frequent one-item sets I_1 so far
6:     **end if**
7: **end for**
8: Add content of I_1 to the set enumeration tree.
9: $C_2 = generateCandiadateItemset(k, I_1, M)$ (Algorithm 3)
10: $k = 2$
11: **while** $C_k \neq \emptyset$ **do**
12:     $I_k = \emptyset$, set to hold frequent k item sets if any
13:     **for** $\forall S_i \in C_k$ **do**
14:         **if** $support(S_i) \geq \sigma$ **then**
15:             $I_k = I_k \cup S_i$
16:         **end if**
17:     **end for**
18:     Add I_k to the set enumeration tree.
19:     $k++$
20:     $C_k = generateCandiadateItemset(k, I_{k-1}, M)$ (Algorithm 3)
21: **end while**
22: Step through the set enumeration tree and generate a set of SARs.

---

4   The SEquential RElational N-DIsease Pattern (SERENDIP) Algorithm

This section presents the proposed SEquential RElational N-DIsease Pattern (SERENDIP) algorithm for multi-morbidity disease prediction where the preceding and intervening items within a given sequence are important; in other words, the proposed algorithm operates using a different definition of a item sequence than that used by established SARM algorithms such as those presented in [3,4,16]. Using the proposed algorithm, the identified frequent item sets are held in a "set enumeration tree" structure where each node holds: (i) a single item set label, (ii) a support value and (iii) a set of links to child nodes (or "null" if there are no child nodes). This offers the advantage of fast look up and efficient storage as oppose to the alternative nested set of arrays approach. The use of set enumeration trees in ARM is well established with respect to existing algorithms (see for example [5]).

The pseudo code for SERENDIP is given in Algorithm 1. The inputs are: (i) the input data set D, (ii) the set of attributes A that feature in D, (iii) the maximum length max of a record in D, and (iv) the support threshold σ. The variables D and A, input data and the associated set of attributes respectively, are assumed to be global variables. We commence, line 1, by generating a $max \times |A|$ "occurrence count matrix" M to hold single item occurrence counts according to the position of the items in each records in D (an item may, of course, not

Algorithm 2. $occurrenceCountMatrixGeneration(max, |A|)$

1: $M = max \times |A|$ matrix with 0 values
2: **for** $k = 1$ to $|D|$ **do**
3:    **for** $i = 1$ to $i = |r_k|$ $(r_k \in D)$ **do**
4:       j = index of attribute $a_i \in r_{k_i}$ w.r.t. A
5:       $M_{i,j} = Mi, j + 1$
6:    **end for**
7: **end for**
8: **return** M

---

exist in a particular record). A value at $m_{i,j} \in M$ is the occurrence count of attribute $a_j \in A$ when at index i in D. The usage of M provides for efficiency gains in that the individual support values need only be calculated once. The pseudo code for generating M is given in Algorithm 2. The inputs are: (i) the maximum length max of a record in D, and (ii) the number of attributes $|A|$ in the set A from which the items in records can be drawn. Note that by definition $max \leq |A|$. The $max \times |A|$ matrix is defined in line 1. We then, line 2, step through the data set D record by record (k is the record index). For each record $r_k \in D$ we then, line 3, step through the record attribute by attribute (i is the location index in a record). For each attribute $a_i \in r_k$ we obtain its index j with respect to the set A (line 4). The index j is the column index in M and i the row index in M. We then, line 5, increment the value in M at row index i and column index j; thus $m_{i,j}$. The occurrence count matrix thus holds information on the frequency of occurrence of individual items according to their position in the individual sequences (records) in D.

Returning to Algorithm 1, the next stage is to identify the frequently occurring one item sets and place these in a set I_1 (lines 2 to 7). The set I_1 is declared on line 2. We then step through the first row in the occurrence count matrix M (this $i = 1$). Each value $m_{1,j}$ is compared against the support threshold σ, and if $m_{1,j} \geq \sigma$ the associate attribute, $a_j \in A$ is added to I_1. Once we have the complete set of frequent one item sets, I_1 these are added as child nodes of the root node in the set enumeration tree (line 8).

Algorithm 3. $generateCandiadateItemset(k, I, M)$

1: $C_k = \emptyset$
2: **for** $\forall X_i \in I$ **do**
3:    **for** $\forall m_{k,j} \in M$ **do**
4:       **if** $m_{k,j} \geq \sigma$ and $a_j \notin X_i$ **then**
5:          $C_k = C_k \cup (X_i + [a_j])$ where $a_j \in A$
6:       **end if**
7:    **end for**
8: **end for**
9: **return** C_k

We are now in a position to generate the two-item candidate set C_2 by stepping through I_1 and, for each items set $X_i \in I_1$, appending the associated attributes from the second row in M ($j = 2$) to X_i if the associated support value at $m_{2,j} \geq \sigma$, and provided that the associated attribute is not already in X_i. The pseudo code for candidate item set generation is given in Algorithm 3. The inputs to the algorithm are: (i) the item set size k for the candidate items we wish to generate ($k = 2$ for two item sets); (ii) the $k - 1$ sequential frequent item sets already discovered, the set I_{k-1}; and (iii) the occurrence count matrix M. Note that k will also be the relevant first index for M, The algorithm commences, line 1, by declaring the empty set C_K in which to hold the candidate sets. We then step through I_{k-1} and for each item set X_i in I_{k-1} we add attributes a_j from A to X_i to form candidate item sets by stepping through row k in M. In each case we create a candidate item set if: (i) a_j is not already in X_i and (ii) the support for a_j in M, $m_{k,j}$, is greater or equal to σ. On completion the algorithm returns the set of candidate k item sets, C_k.

Returning to Algorithm 1, the algorithm next enters into a Apriori style "generate and test" loop (lines 11 to 21), testing the identified candidate item sets against the threshold σ and generating new candidate item sets. The loop continues until no more candidate item sets can be generated. As the loop progresses the set enumeration tree is further populated (line 18).

In the case of the multi-morbidity application domain, we wish to use the sequential ARs for prediction purposes. Thus we are interested in sequential Classification Association Rules (sequential CARs) [12] where the consequent is a single item, the class we wish to predict. In the case of the multi-morbidity application, the class we are interested in is the next disease that a patient can be expected to get. To calculate the lift for a rule $X \Rightarrow Y$ we need the consequent support for X. This can be obtained directly from the occurrence count matrix M generated earlier, and would be the value at $M_{i,j}$ where i is the index of interest ($i = |X| + 1$) and j is the index of $Y \in A$. Note that this assumes the consequent is comprised of a single item as required in the context of sequential CARs, but could easily be adjusted to calculate consequent supports for consequents comprised of more than one item.

These rules can now be used for prediction purposes. Given a query antecedent Q we start at the top of the list looking for matches with the listed rule antecedents. It is possible that we have rules with the same antecedent, but different consequents. The ordering of the rules in the list are therefore important. There are a range of schemes that can be used for rule ranking [15], typically founded on confidence, lift and rule antecedent size. In the case of our multi-morbidity application an exact match is required for a rule to be fired, because of the interplay of diseases, so the size of the rule antecedents is not important. Some applications use subset "matching", where Q is only required to be a subset of a rule antecedent for the rule to be fired, in which case more specific rules, rules whose antecedents have a large number of items, should be listed first. The example rules listed in the following section have been ranked using confidence as the primary ranking and lift as the secondary ranking.

We can also simply fire the first rule we get to, or the top k and use some voting mechanisms should conflicting classes be predicted. Only the first is applicable given that we require exact matching.

Table 1. Statistics analysis of the study population

Gender	Population
Male	45281
Female	54009
Total	99290

Age Band	Population
50-54	6093
55-59	12366
60-64	12687
65-69	13248
70-74	14553
75-79	12877
80+	27466
Total	99290

5   Evaluation

The proposed SERENDIP algorithm was evaluated using a set of multi-morbidity patient records obtained from the Clinical Practice Research Datalink (CPRD)[1]. CPRD is a large electronic health record database that contains anonymised health records of primary health care patients in the United Kingdom. It includes over twenty million patient records of which some five million patients were active at the time of writing. Approval was obtained from the Independent Scientific Advisory Committee (ISAC) in order to use the data for this study (Protocol No. 19159R1). Primary-care patient-level data from a random sample of hundred thousand patients was extracted for the period (1920–2020) for patients aged 50 and over (the age group most likely to be affected by multi-morbidity). Patients were considered eligible for inclusion if they had been registered in a general practice for a minimum of two years and their record indicating diagnosis of two or more recorded Life Threatening Conditions (LTCs). Diagnoses are recorded in CPRD using a coding system. Long-term conditions and associated case definitions were determined by reference to a clinical group with broad generalist and prescribing expertise, including two of the authors. Diagnostic code lists were developed and adapted from previous studies. The code lists are available online[2]. Some statistics concerning the evaluation data are given in Table 1. From the table it can be seen that female patients out number male patients, however this was to be expected given the over 50 age group under consideration.

---

[1] https://www.cprd.com.
[2] http://hammerai.co.uk.

For the evaluation results presented here, $\sigma = 0.00005$ (0.005%) and $\lambda = 0.1$ (10%) were used. A low value for σ was deliberately selected to ensure no relevant sequences were missed. The generated rules were presented to a clinical group for inspection. In total 1261 rules were identified using SERENDIP. Example rules are presented in Tables 2, 3, 4 and 5; the top ten two, three and four-item rules, and the top five five-item rules, according to confidence respectively. Column one gives the rule and column two the support, confidence and lift respectively (calculated as shown in Eqs. 3, 4 and 6).

Table 2. Two disease sequential ARs generated using SERENDIP

Rule	Support	Confidence	Lift
Chronic Constipation $\Rightarrow$ Chronic Pain	0.00329	0.46714	5.03502
Allergic and Chronic Rhinitis and . . . $\Rightarrow$ Asthma	0.00006	0.42857	17.24184
Abdominal Aortic Aneurysm $\Rightarrow$ Lipid Disorder	0.00005	0.38462	5.70573
Stroke CVA and Hypertension $\Rightarrow$ Lipid Disorder	0.00005	0.38462	5.70573
Polycythaemia Vera $\Rightarrow$ Hypertension	0.00005	0.33333	4.33259
Diabetic Eye Disease $\Rightarrow$ Diabetes	0.00028	0.32184	20.41879
Diabetes and Hypertension $\Rightarrow$ Lipid Disorder	0.00007	0.31818	4.72020
Ankylosing Spondylitis $\Rightarrow$ Chronic Pain	0.00041	0.31298	3.37337
Stable Angina $\Rightarrow$ Coronary Heart Disease	0.00020	0.29412	21.11565
Coronary Heart Disease $\Rightarrow$ Lipid Disorder	0.00355	0.29163	4.32633

Table 3. Three disease sequential ARs generated using SERENDIP

Rule	Support	Confidence	Lift
Chronic Constipation, Abdominal Hernia $\Rightarrow$ Chronic Pain	0.00005	0.80000	12.18171
Cancer Solid organ, Chronic Constipation $\Rightarrow$ Chronic Pain	0.00008	0.70000	10.65900
Diverticular Disease, Chronic Constipation $\Rightarrow$ Chronic Pain	0.00014	0.66667	10.15143
Anxiety, Chronic Constipation $\Rightarrow$ Chronic Pain	0.00005	0.66667	10.15143
Cataract, Chronic Constipation $\Rightarrow$ Chronic Pain	0.00005	0.66667	10.15143
Chronic Constipation, Osteoarthritis excluding spine $\Rightarrow$ Chronic Pain	0.00005	0.66667	10.15143
Chronic Constipation, Spondylosis $\Rightarrow$ Chronic Pain	0.00005	0.66667	10.15143
Diabetic eye disease, Hypertension $\Rightarrow$ Diabetes	0.00006	0.62500	30.16532
Gastritis and Duodenitis, Gout $\Rightarrow$ Chronic Pain	0.00006	0.62500	9.51696
Spondylosis, Chronic Constipation $\Rightarrow$ Chronic Pain	0.00006	0.62500	9.51696

From the tables it can be seen that many of the rules feature low support, hence the selection of a low value for σ to ensure no significant rules were missed was appropriate. Some rules feature very high confidence, for example the rule:

Diabetes, Hypertension, Lipid Disorder, Diabetic eye disease $\Rightarrow$ Chronic Kidney Disease

in Table 5 featured a confidence of 1.00000 (100%). The high lift values that feature in the results are also interesting. Recall that a lift greater than one indicates a positive correlation. For example if we consider the rule:

Stable Angina $\Rightarrow$ Coronary Heart Disease

in Table 2, which had a lift of 21.11565 this indicates that as the incidence of "Stable Angina" (chest pain due to poor blood flow through the heart) increases we can expect a significant increase in the incidence of Coronary Heart Disease. Some of the rules had relatively low confidence but even a confidence of 0.25000 (25%), correlated with a lift greater than one, provides a good indicator of a likely follow on condition. Consultation with domain experts indicated that the rules that had been discovered "made sense".

Table 4. Four disease sequential ARs generated using SERENDIP

Rule	Support	Confidence	Lift
Abdominal Hernia, Chronic Sinusitis, Hypertension $\Rightarrow$ Lipid Disorder	0.00006	0.80000	10.42112
Hypertension, Chronic Kidney Disease, Diabetic eye disease $\Rightarrow$ Diabetes	0.00006	0.80000	31.54886
Hypertension, Lipid Disorder, Diabetic eye disease $\Rightarrow$ Diabetes	0.00012	0.72727	28.68078
Diabetes, Diabetic eye disease, Erectile Dysfunction $\Rightarrow$ Hypertension	0.00006	0.66667	8.95264
Psoriasis, Chronic Pain, Thyroid Problem $\Rightarrow$ Hypertension	0.00006	0.66667	8.95264
Chronic Pain, Abdominal Hernia, Chronic Kidney Disease $\Rightarrow$ Hypertension	0.00006	0.57143	7.67369
Lipid Disorder, Chronic Pain, Erectile Dysfunction $\Rightarrow$ Osteoarthritis excluding spine	0.00006	0.57143	14.26342
Chronic Pain, Chronic Constipation, Osteoporosis $\Rightarrow$ Thyroid Problem	0.00007	0.55556	30.39148
Lipid Disorder, Hypertension, Diabetic eye disease $\Rightarrow$ Diabetes	0.00007	0.50000	19.71804
Osteoarthritis excluding spine, Hypertension, Coronary Heart Disease $\Rightarrow$ Lipid Disorder	0.00007	0.50000	6.51320

Table 5. Five disease sequential ARs generated using SERENDIP

Rule	Support	Confidence	Lift
Diabetes, Hypertension, Lipid Disorder, Diabetic eye disease ⇒ Chronic Kidney Disease	0.00005	1.00000	19.33938
Chronic Pain, Obesity, Hypertension, Osteoarthritis excluding spine ⇒ Lipid Disorder	0.00005	0.60000	8.40091
Hypertension, Lipid Disorder, Chronic Pain, Diabetes ⇒ Diabetic eye disease	0.00005	0.42857	33.14166
Chronic Pain, Hypertension, Lipid Disorder, Chronic Kidney Disease ⇒ Diabetes	0.00005	0.33333	11.32475
Chronic Pain, Lipid Disorder, Hypertension, Chronic Kidney Disease ⇒ Osteoarthritis excluding spine	0.00005	0.30000	7.17283

6   Conclusions

This paper has presented the SERENDIP algorithm for SAR extraction, a feature of the algorithm is the usage of an occurrence count matrix M. The motivation for the work was the observation that existing SARM algorithms make certain assumptions about what a sequence is, typically permitting a sequence to be preceded by additional items and/or be interrupted by additional items. This assumption holds with respect to many applications, such as retail analysis and prediction, but those not hold for all applications. One such application, and the focus for the work presented in this paper, is multi-morbidity disease prediction where preceding and intervening conditions are important. In this case existing SARM algorithms are inappropriate because of the assumptions made, and the consequent way in which metrics such as support, confidence and lift are calculated. The proposed SERENDIP algorithm addresses these issues. For future work the authors intend to investigate mechanisms where by the variable interval between multi-morbidity conditions can be included in the SAR extraction process, currently a unit interval is adopted. The SERENDIP algorithm has been published at http://serendip.org.uk as a www service, where it can be run as a client-server application using a user's own data.

References

1. Agarwal, R., Srikant, R.: Fast algorithms for mining association rules. In: Proceedings of 20th International Conference on VLDB, pp. 487–499 (1994)
2. Agrawal, R., Imieliński, T., Swami, A.A.: Mining association rules between sets of items in large databases. In: Proceedings of the 1993 ACM SIGMOD International Conference on Management of Data - SIGMOD 1993, p. 207 (2019)
3. Agrawal, R., Srikant, R.: Mining sequential patterns. In: Proceedings of the Eleventh International Conference on Data Engineering, pp. 3–14 (1995)
4. Ayres, J., Gehrke, J., Yiu, T., Flannick, J.: Sequential pattern mining using a bitmap representation. In: Proceedings of the Eighth ACM SIGKDD International Conference on Knowledge Discovery and Data Mining (KDD 2002), pp. 429–435 (2002)

5. Coenen, F., Leng, P., Ahmed, S.: Data structure for association rule mining: T-trees and p-trees. IEEE Trans. Knowl. Data Eng. **16**, 774–778 (2004)
6. Fournier-Viger, P., Faghihi, U., Nkambou, R., Nguifod, E.M.: CMRules: mining sequential rules common to several sequences. Knowl.-Based Syst. **22**, 63–76 (2012)
7. Fournier-Viger, P., Gueniche, T., Zida, S., Tseng, V.S.: ERMiner: sequential rule mining using equivalence classes. In: Blockeel, H., van Leeuwen, M., Vinciotti, V. (eds.) IDA 2014. LNCS, vol. 8819, pp. 108–119. Springer, Cham (2014). https://doi.org/10.1007/978-3-319-12571-8_10
8. Harms, S.K., Deogun, J.S.: Sequential association rule mining with time lags. J. Intell. Inf. **22**, 7–225 (2004)
9. Head, A., Fleming, K., Kypridemos, C., Schofield, P., O'Flaherty, M.: Dynamics of multimorbidity in England between 2004 and 2019: a descriptive epidemiology study. Eur. J. Public Health **30** (2020)
10. Kaur, M., Kang, S.: Market basket analysis: identify the changing trends of market data using association rule mining. Procedia Comput. Sci. **85**, 78–85 (2016)
11. Navickas, R., Petric, V.-K., Feigl, A.B., Seychell, M.: Multimorbidity: what do we know? What should we do? J. Comorbidity **6**(1), 4–11 (2016)
12. Rudin, C., Letham, B., Salleb-Aouissi, A., Kogan, E., Madigan, D.: Sequential event prediction with association rules. Proc. Mach. Learn. Res. **19**, 615–634 (2011)
13. Verma, N., Singh, J.: A comprehensive review from sequential association computing to hadoop-mapreduce parallel computing in a retail scenario. J. Manag. Anal. **5**(4), 359–392 (2017)
14. Vogeli, C., et al.: Multiple chronic conditions: prevalence, health consequences, and implications for quality, care management, and costs. J. Gen. Intern. Med. **22**(3), 391–395 (2007)
15. Wang, Y.J., Xin, Q., Coenen, F.: Hybrid rule ordering in classification association rule mining. Trans. Mach. Learn. Data Min. Pattern Recogn. **1**, 1–16 (2008)
16. Zaki, M.J.: Spade: an efficient algorithm for mining frequent sequences. Int. J. Mach. Learn. **42**(1–2), 31–60 (2001)

Addressing the Challenge of Data Heterogeneity Using a Homogeneous Feature Vector Representation: A Study Using Time Series and Cardiovascular Disease Classification

Hanadi Aldosari[1]($\boxtimes$), Frans Coenen[1]($\boxtimes$), Gregory Y. H. Lip[2]($\boxtimes$),
and Yalin Zheng[3]($\boxtimes$)

[1] Department of Computer Science, University of Liverpool, Liverpool, UK
{H.A.Aldosari,Coenen}@liverpool.ac.uk
[2] Liverpool Centre for Cardiovascular Science, University of Liverpool, Liverpool, UK
Gregory.Lip@liverpool.ac.uk
[3] Department of Eye and Vision Science, University of Liverpool, Liverpool, UK
yalin.zheng@liverpool.ac.uk

Abstract. An investigation into the use of a unifying Homogeneous Feature Vector Representation (HFVR), to address the challenge of applying machine learning and/or deep learning to heterogeneous data, is presented. To act as a focus, Atrial Fibrillation classification is considered which features both tabular and Electrocardiogram (ECG) time series data. The challenge of constructing HFVRs is the process for selecting features. A mechanism where by this can be achieved, in terms of motifs and discords, with respect to ECG time series data is presented. The presented evaluation demonstrates that more effective AF classification can be achieved using the idea of HFVR than would otherwise be achieved.

Keywords: Unifying homogeneous feature vector representations ·
Time series feature extraction and analysis · Atrial fibrillation
classification

1 Introduction

The sophistication of the global technical infrastructure, and the consequent data acquisition capabilities, are rapidly growing and producing large amounts of data. There is a corresponding interest in strategies and techniques for the automated abstraction of knowledge and analysis of this data. Strategies and techniques that typically employ Machine Learning and Deep Learning (ML/DL).

However, these techniques and strategies still face many challenges. One such challenge, and that of relevance with respect to the work presented in this paper, is that of mixed data formats (types), also known as heterogeneous data. A trivial illustration of this is the distinction between numeric data (for example

M. Bramer and R. Ellis (Eds.): SGAI-AI 2021, LNAI 13101, pp. 254–266, 2021.
https://doi.org/10.1007/978-3-030-91100-3_21

age) and categorical data (for example gender). A more comprehensive example is the distinction between video and free text data. A range of solutions have been proposed, which can be categorised as follows:

1. **Direct Conversion.** Given data sources in several formats convert all the data into one of the formats used, and then apply the ML/DL.
2. **Independent ML/DL Application.** Apply the ML/DL to each format independently and then combine the results.
3. **Unification.** Create a unifying representation that sits over the input formats and then apply the ML/DL to this unified format.

The distinct between the above is illustrated in Fig. 1.

The conversion solution is the most straightforward solution. The solution is based on the observation that numerical values can be converted into categorical values (discretisation) [25], and that categorical values can be converted into numerical values (normalisation) [7,8]. However, the conversion solution assume that given data in two formats it is possible to convert one into the other; this is generally not possible without introducing significant simplification and/or approximation, which in turn may affect the consequent ML/DL.

The independent application of ML/DL solution considers each data format independently; ML/DL is applied with respect to each format, and the "local" results combined to give a "final" global result. For example, given a prediction model generation problem, which has as input data in several formats, build prediction models with respect to each format; and then, given a previously unseen record, apply the models and combine the local predictions to give a global prediction using (say) voting as used in ensemble classification systems [10,14]. This idea has also been incorporated into the concept of "multi-input networks" [23,24] where each format is associated with a different branch of the network. The branches are then brought together at the end so that a single final result will be produced. However, the idea of using multiple ML/DL applications ignores the existence of any relationships that might exit across the data sources, which in turn may have an adverse effect on the quality of the ML/DL.

The idea underpinning the unification solution to the heterogeneous source data problem is that of creating a unifying representation that sits over the heterogeneous data sources. This then serves to capture the relationships that may exist across the data; not the case with the independent ML/DL solution. This idea was promoted in [1] where a Homogeneous Feature Vector Representation (HFVR) was proposed in the context of classification model generation. The intuition was that a feature vector representation is compatible with a wide range of classification model generators. However the main challenge of the HFVR approach is how best to identify the features (attributes) to be included in the HFVR; these should be features that are good discriminators of class. In [1] a Cardiovascular Disease (CVD) scenario was considered that featured time series data, numeric data and categorical data. Motifs were extracted from Electrocardiograms (ECGs) and used to create an HFVR. Reasonable results were obtained. A criticism of the work in [1] is that only one type of time series

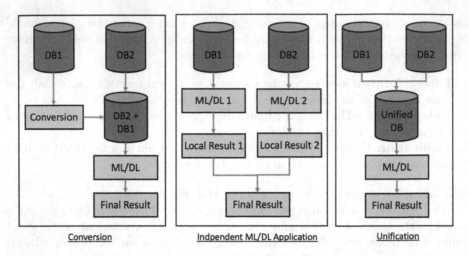

Fig. 1. Distinctions between the potential solutions to the heterogeneous source data ML/DL challenge.

feature was used, motifs (frequently occurring time series sub-sequences). It is argued here that a more sophisticated HFVR would have been produced, and hence better classification results produced, if more than one time series feature type were considered.

In this paper the idea of HFVR is explored further, building on the work presented in [1] also using a CVD scenario, more specifically Atrial Fibrillation (AF) classification, as the application focus for the work. The research hypothesis considered is that for the concept of HFVR to operate effectively much depends on the nature of the features that are included. With respect to some data formats (such as free text, graphs, image, video and time series), this is a non trivial task; with others this is reasonably straight forward (for example numeric or categorical tabular data). The work presented in this paper thus focuses on feature extraction from time series and combining this with numeric and categorical data to form an HFVR. To this end, an HFVR generation approach is presented where by both time series motifs and discords (anomalous time series sub-sequences), coupled with numeric and categorical data, are used to form an HFVR. The reported evaluation indicates that the above hypothesis is correct, and that a more effective prediction system can be built using a more sophisticated set of HFVR features than in earlier work; at least in the context of AF classification.

The remainder of this paper is structured as follows. A review of existing work relevant to this paper is presented, in Sect. 2. The AF application domain used as a focus for the work presented in this paper is presented in Sect. 3 and a number of relevant definitions in Sect. 4. The proposed process for generating an HFVR in the context of AF classification is presented in Sect. 5, and the associated evaluation in Sect. 6. The paper is concluded in Sect. 7 with a summary of the main findings and some suggestions for future work.

2   Previous Work

The domain of interest with respect to this paper is Cardiovascular Disease (CVD) analysis. CVD analysis typically relies on Electrocardiogram (ECG) data coupled with tabular data. ECGs are essentially time series. To build an HFVR that combines time series data with other data formats a feature extraction approach needs to be applied to the time series data.

Feature extraction is well established process in ML/DL used to: (i) reduce the complexity of ML/DL problems and (ii) enhance the effectiveness of the ML/DL models produced [13]. Feature extraction has been applied to time series with respect to many application domains, for example in [4] a time series feature extraction process in the context of a brain-computer interface application was described; and in [2] time series feature extraction was used in the context of signals captured from "rotating machines" (gear boxes). Time series feature extraction has also, as might be expected, been applied to ECG time series data [11]. In this context feature extraction has typically been applied with respect to the global characteristics of ECG time series [18,26]. The global characteristics extracted from ECG data are typically time intervals between key events, and the amplitudes associated with key events with respect to ECG heart beat cycles. A range of techniques have been proposed to achieve this, such as wavelet transform (WT) [5]. There are more than ten global features that can be extracted, some approaches only extract two [21], some four [5], others eight [15]. Intuitively, the more features extracted the better the classification accuracy achieved. However, to reduce the computational overhead associated with ML/DL model generation, while maintaining accuracy, feature selection can be applied subsequent to the feature extraction process [21].

An alternative to extracting global characteristics as features from time series is to extract discriminative time series sub-sequences. One popular form of discriminative time series sub-sequence is the *motif*, defined as a frequently occurring sub-sequence which, it is assumed, is therefore representative of the time series [19]. The advantage offered, compared to the use of global characteristics as features, is that they are easy to identify. The basic idea is to extract all-time series sub-sequences of length w from a "parent" time series, and then select the most frequently occurring. To count the frequency of occurrence we cannot require sub-sequences to match exactly for them to be said to co-occur as very few exact matches occur in practice. Instead a similarity threshold is required applied to a similarity measure of some form. A range of techniques have been proposed to extract motifs from ECG data. In [18] both motifs and global characteristics were extracted from ECG data. Motifs were used with respect to the work presented in [1], which underpins the work presented in this paper.

Motifs are not the only time series sub-sequences that can be used as features. An alternative, and that of significance with respect to this paper, is discords [12]. A discord is a unique sub-sequence within a time series which, it is assumed, is therefore representative of the time series; the counter-argument to the argument for motifs. The work presented in this paper investigates the use of motifs and discords, coupled with numeric and categorical data, to create an HFVR to which ML/DL can be applied.

A variety of mechanisms have been proposed whereby discords and motifs can be discovered. A popular method is the Matrix Profile (MP) technique first proposed in [28]. A MP is a data structure which features two vectors for each time series; a Distance Profile (DP) and Profile Index (PI). The idea is to first extract all sub-sequences from a time series using a sliding window of length w. Then to determine the pairwise distances between the sub-sequences and store these in a matrix. However, the matrix will include redundant information. Only the distances between each sub-sequence and its nearest neighbour will be required (the minimum distance). These distances are therefore stored in a DP and the index of the neighbouring time series in a PI. These two vectors then facilitate the extraction of motifs and discords, of a given length w, in a manner that both avoids approximation and is much more efficient than previously proposed approaches. The Matrix Profile MP idea was used, in the context of ECG time series analysis, in [27]. A number of alternative examples can be found in the literature concerning techniques to extract motifs and discords from ECG data, such as the Multivariate Maximal Time Series technique used in [22]. However, the matrix profile idea is used with respect to the work presented in this paper.

A number of algorithms have been proposed to compute MPs, examples include: the Scalable Time Series Anytime Matrix Profile (STAMP) algorithm [28] and the Scalable Column Independent Matrix Profile (SCRIMP) algorithm [30]. For the work presented in this paper the Correct Matrix Profile (CMP) mechanism, described in [6], was adopted; an extension of the MP technique. The idea here, once the MP has been computed by one of the above algorithms, is to add an Annotation Vector (AV) which contains ranking values of between 0 and 1 effectively changing the shape of the MP so that the motifs and discords are ordered and hence the top-K can be selected.

3   Application Domain

The application focus for the work presented in this paper, as already noted, is CVDs. CVDs are diseases of the heart and blood vessels. According to the World Health Organisation (WHO), 17.9 million people die each year from CVDs, an estimated 31% of all deaths worldwide. The domain of CVD analysis is extensive, therefore the focus of the work presented in this paper is Atrial Fibrillation (AF). AF is a heart condition where the *atria*, the upper two chambers of the heart, contracts in an abnormal manner. Because of the irregular beating of the heart, blood does not flow in a normal manner, and the electrical impulses that control the timing of the heart are disturbed [16]. This can be identified from range of tests including ECG analysis which is widely considered to be the most reliable test for diagnosing AF [3,29]. An ECG indicates the electrical activity of the heart in terms of a summation wave that can be visualised and hence interpreted.

4 Formalism

The following definitions are used with respect to the remainder of this paper. Note that some of the definitions are specific to the CVD AF application focus considered.

Homogeneous Feature Vector Representation (HFVR): A data set $H = \{V_1, V_2, \dots\}$, where each vector $V_i = \{v_1, v_2, \dots\}$ comprises a set of values that correspond to selected features extracted from a heterogeneous data set. When used for model generation, each vector will include an associated class label c drawn from a set of classes C ($V_i = \{v_1, v_2, \dots, c\}$).

Patient Record: A set of records $D = \{R_1, R_2, \dots\}$ where each record R_i comprises information about the patient. In the case of the CVD AF application domain this will include ECG data as well as more general patient data.

Time series: A collection of time series $\mathbf{T} = \{T_1, T_2, \dots\}$, associated with a patient, representing ECG data. Each time series T_j is comprised of a sequence of data values $[t_1, t_2, \dots, t_n]$.

Discords: A discord s is a time series sub-sequence t_j. S is a set of discords extracted from a collection of time series $\mathbf{T}$, $S = \{s_1, s_2, \dots\}$. Not all discords in S will be good discriminators of class, so we prune S to give S' and then S'' (see below).

Motifs: A motif m is a time series sub-sequence t_j. M is a set of motifs extracted from collection of time series $\mathbf{T}$, $M = \{m_1, m_2, \dots\}$. Again, not all the motifs in M will be good discriminators of class, so we prune M to give M' and then M''.

For the evaluation presented later in this paper a binary classification scenario is considered, $C = \{true, false\}$, "has AF" or "does not have AF". To generate the desired HVFR the input time series ECG data was first separated from the rest of the input to form a ECG time series data set $\mathbf{T} = \{T_1, T_2, \dots\}$. Motifs and discords were then extracted from $\mathbf{T}$ and then combined with other data to form the desired HFVR. Each vector in the HFVR, representing a patient, thus comprised $\{S, M, A, c\}$ where A is the additional numeric and categorical patient data, and c is a class label taken from a set of classes C ($c \in C$). For the evaluation presented later in this paper $C = \{AF, \neg AF\}$; hence a binary classification. How the HFVR was generated, with reference to the CVD AF classification application, is discussed in the following section.

5 Homogeneous Feature Vector Representation Generation

This section presents the proposed HFVR generation mechanism. In the context of the CVD AF application the proposed process is as shown in Fig. 2. In more detail, the CVD AF classification application included data from multiple data sources; data from electrocardiograms, blood tests, x-rays and clinical data.

For each data set the features to be included in the HFVR needed to be extracted. In this paper, two data sets were used, ECG time series from which motifs and discords could be extracted and clinical data.

The adopted approach for motif and discords discovery (extraction and selection), as noted earlier (Sect. 2), was the CMP technique described in [6] using the Guided Motif Search (GMS) algorithm presented in [6]. Using the CMP technique, motifs and discord sub-sequences are ranked. The top three motifs and discords were then selected. The proposed process to extract the features and create the desired HFVR was as follows:

1. Divide the input time series data $\mathbf{T} = \{T_1, T_2, \dots\}$ into two D_1 and D_2, where D_1 corresponds to class c_1 and D_2 corresponds to class c_2 (note that we are assuming a binary classification here).
2. Extract the top three motifs for each $T_i \in D_1$ and each $T_i \in D_2$ to give M_1 and M_2 respectively.
3. Extract the top three discords for each $T_i \in D_1$ and each $T_i \in D_2$ to give S_1 and S_2 respectively.
4. Compare the set of motifs within M_1 (M_2) with each other, and select those that occur at least k times to give M_1' (M_2').
5. Compare the set of discords within S_1 (S_2) with each other, and retain those that occur at least k times to give S_1' (S_2').
6. There may be motifs that occur in both M_1' and M_2' that are associated with both class c_1 and c_2, and are therefore not good discriminators of class, prune these to give M''.
7. There may be discords that occur in both S_1' and S_2' that are associated with both class c_1 and c_2 and are therefore not good discriminators of class, prune these to give S''.
8. Use the content of M'' and S'', coupled with data attributes from A (the set of known numeric and categorical patient attributes) to create an HFVR.

For the evaluation presented in Sect. 6 below, to compare discords (motifs), Euclidean distance similarity was used with a similarity threshold σ. If the distance between two discords (motifs) was less than σ they were deemed to match.

6 Evaluation

The evaluation of the proposed approach to HFVR generation, in the context of CVD AF classification, was conducted using the China Physiological Signal Challenge 2018 (CPSC2018) data set[1]. Some detail concerning this data set are presented in Subsect. 6.1. The objectives of the evaluation were:

1. To determine whether the idea of a unifying HFVR did indeed provide real benefits in the context of the CVD AF classification application used as a focus with respect to this paper. In other words, that the use of a combined set of features, facilitated by the HFVR approach, did indeed provide for a more effective classification.

---

[1] http://2019.icbeb.org/Challenge.html.

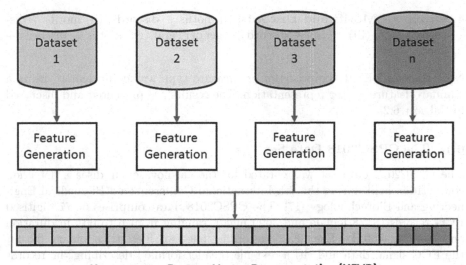

Homogenous Feature Vector Representation (HFVR)

Fig. 2. Schematic of HFVR Generation Process in the context of the CVD AF classification exemplar application domain.

2. To provide evidence that the proposed approach to HFVR generation with respect to time series, using the CMP technique coupled with GMS, produced the desired result.

For the evaluation $\sigma = 0.15$ and $k = 70$ were used for discovering discords, and $\sigma = 0.15$ and $k = 90$ for discovering motifs. These were used because earlier experiments, not reported here for reasons of space, had demonstrated that these were the most appropriate values. The Support Vector Machine (SVM) classification model was used, coupled with the grid search technique to identify best parameters. A range of HFVRs were generated using combinations of features: motifs and discords generated from ECG time series and patient age and gender. The later were chosen because they were exemplars of numeric and categorical data features, and because they had been shown to have an impact on AF (see [20] and [9] respectively). Ten-fold Cross Validation (TCV) was used throughout. The metrics recorded were accuracy, precision, recall and F1; of which F1, the harmonic mean of precision and recall, is a good summarising measure. Experiments were conducted using the following four groupings:

1. **Group 1 - Gender and Age:** (i) gender only, (ii) age only, (iii) age + gender.
2. **Group 2 - Motifs:** (i) motifs only, (ii) motifs + age, (iii) motifs + gender, and (iv) motifs + age + gender.
3. **Group 3 - Discords:** (i) discords only, (ii) discords + age, (iii) discords + gender, and (iv) discords + age + gender.

4. **Group 4 - Motifs and Discords:** (i) motifs + discords, (ii) motifs + discords + age, (iii) motifs + discords + gender, and (iv) motifs + discords + age + gender.

Note that an HFVR comprised of one feature type was equivalent to using a standard feature vector representation. The results are presented and discussed in Subsect. 6.2.

6.1 The CPSC2018 Data Set

The CPSC2018 data set was curated for the cardiovascular disease detection competition held during the 7th International Conference on Biomedical Engineering and Biotechnology [17]. The CPSC2018 data comprises 6,877 digitised ECG records (3178 female and 3699 male), ranging from 6 to 60 s in duration and sampled 500 Hz. Each ECG recording has two files: (i) a binary file for the ECG signal data and (ii) a text file (header format) describing the recording and patient attributes, including age, gender and the diagnosis label (the class attribute c). The class labels were drawn from a set of eight arrhythmia types ($|C| = 8$). However, for the evaluation presented here only AF and Normal rhythm ($\neg$AF) were used. The ECG data was also rationalised so that all records were of fixed length, 5000 points. Each ECG time series was considered in isolation. For the evaluation presented here a total, 600 records were used (300 for each class).

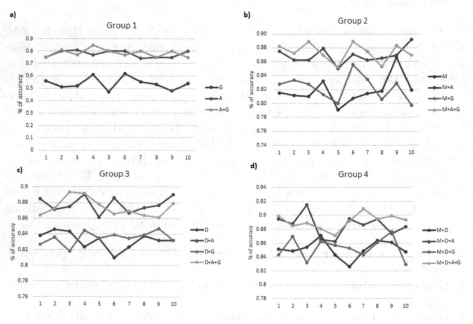

Fig. 3. Comparison of 10-fold cross-validation results: (a) Group 1, (b) Group 2, (c) Group 3, (d) Group 4.

Table 1. Evaluation results for CVD AF binary classification.

HVFR combination	Accuracy %	Precision %	Recall %	F1 %
Group 1 - Gender and Age				
Age (A)	77.60	79.60	77.60	77.70
Gender (G)	53.90	54.90	53.90	54.00
Age + Gender (A+G)	**78.30**	**80.50**	**78.30**	**78.50**
Group 2 - Motifs				
Motifs (M)	79.57	78.51	79.45	78.01
Motifs + Age (M+A)	**86.41**	**87.27**	**86.18**	**86.37**
Motifs + Gender (M+G)	80.17	77.52	82.0	79.22
Motifs + Age + Gender (M+A+G)	85.49	86.22	85.26	85.47
Group 3 - Discords				
Discords (S)	82.63	83.73	82.63	82.73
Discords + Age (S+A)	**87.78**	**88.23**	**87.78**	**87.78**
Discords + Gender (S+G)	82.42	83.80	82.42	82.54
Discords + Age + Gender (S+A+G)	87.50	87.85	87.50	87.50
Group 4 - Motifs and Discords				
Motifs + Discords (M+S)	85.56	85.99	85.56	85.58
Motifs + Discords + Age (M+S+A)	88.51	88.95	88.51	88.52
Motifs + Discords + Gender (M+S+G)	85.62	86.20	85.62	85.64
Motifs + Discords + Age + Gender (M+S+A+G)	**89.16**	**89.42**	**89.16**	**89.16**

6.2 Results

The average accuracy results of each TCV are presented in Fig. 3 for each group. The average accuracy, precision, recall and F1 values are presented in Table 1. Figure 4 presents a graphical representation of the recorded F1 values from Table 1.

From Fig. 4 it can firstly be observed that motifs, discords, age and gender when used on their own do not perform as well as when they are combined; thus supporting the motivation for a unifying representation. From the figure it can also been seen that using discords, without motifs, produces a better result than when using motifs, without discords, illustrating the advantage of using discords (not considered in, for example, [18] or [1]. It is interesting to note that including age does not make a significant difference despite the work presented in [20] that suggests it should do. Overall, the best result was obtained when a unifying HFVR was used that included motifs, discords, age and gender.

Thus, from the foregoing, it can be concluded that the idea of HFVR does indeed provide real benefits in the context of the CVD AF classification application; and, it is argued here, is likely to provide benefits with respect to other classification applications that feature heterogeneous data input. The reported evaluation has also provided empirical evidence that the proposed approach to HFVR generation, with respect to time series, operates well (produces good results).

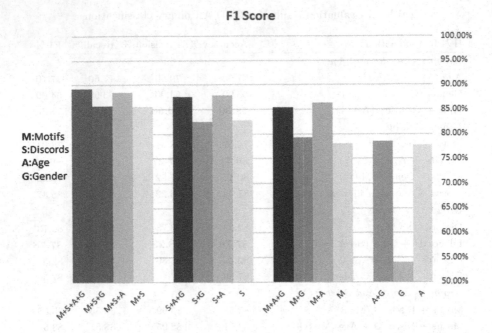

Fig. 4. Bar chart showing comparison of F1 values from Table 1.

7   Conclusion

This paper has reported on an investigation on the use of Homogeneous Feature Vector Representations (HFVRs) as a means allowing ML/DL over input data sets in different formats (heterogeneous data). The fundamental idea was, either directly or indirectly, to extract features from these data sets and incorporate them in to a unifying HFVR. In the case of tabular data, either numeric or categorical, this is a straight forwards process and can be achieved directly. In the case of other forms of data, such as time series data, this first requires the application of a feature extraction and selection process. The investigation was conducted using a CVD classification scenario; more specifically AF binary classification. The input here comprises time series ECG data and tabular data. For the time series data it was suggested that features to be extracted should be motifs and discords. It was further suggested that this be done using the CMP technique coupled with GMS. To support this idea experiments were conducted using four types of feature, motifs, discords, categorical data and numerical data. For the evaluation these four feature types were combined in different groupings. The results indicated that an HFVR made up of all four feature types produced the best results. Thus it was concluded that the idea of HFVR did indeed provide real classification benefits (at least in the context AF classification) and that the proposed approach to HFVR generation, with respect to time series, was a good one. For future work the authors intend to consider the most appropriate way of extracting features from images for inclusion in a unifying HVFR, and to apply the idea to alternative application domains.

References

1. Aldosari, H., Coenen, F., Lip, G., Zheng, Y.: Motif based feature vectors: towards a homogeneous data representation for cardiovascular diseases classification. In: Proceedings of the 23rd International Conference on Big Data Analytics and Knowledge Discovery, DaWaK 2021 (2021)
2. Cabrera, D., et al.: Automatic feature extraction of time-series applied to fault severity assessment of helical gearbox in stationary and non-stationary speed operation. Appl. Soft Comput. **58**, 53–64 (2017)
3. Christov, I., Krasteva, V., I. Simova, T.N., Schmid, R.: Multi-parametric analysis for atrial fibrillation classification in ECG. In: IEEE Computing in Cardiology, CinC 2017, pp. 1–4 (2017)
4. Coyle, D., Prasad, G., McGinnity, T.M.: A time-series prediction approach for feature extraction in a brain-computer interface. IEEE Trans. Neural Syst. Rehabil. Eng. **13**(4), 461–467 (2005)
5. Das, M.K., Ari, S.: ECG beats classification using mixture of features. Int. Sch. Res. Not. **2014**, 178436 (2014)
6. Dau, H.A., Keogh, E.: Matrix profile V: a generic technique to incorporate domain knowledge into motif discovery. In: Proceedings of the 23rd ACM SIGKDD International Conference on Knowledge Discovery and Data Mining, pp. 125–134 (2017)
7. Ding, S., Du, M., Sun, T., Xu, X., Xue, Y.: An entropy-based density peaks clustering algorithm for mixed type data employing fuzzy neighborhood. Knowl. Based Syst. **133**, 294–313 (2017)
8. Golinko, E., Sonderman, T., Zhu, X.: CNFL: categorical to numerical feature learning for clustering and classification. In: 2017 IEEE 2nd International Conference on Data Science in Cyberspace (DSC), pp. 585–594. IEEE (2017)
9. Inoue, H., et al.: Impact of gender on the prognosis of patients with nonvalvular atrial fibrillation. Am. J. Cardiol. **113**(6), 957–962 (2014)
10. Jain, A., Jain, V.: Voting ensemble classifier for sentiment analysis. In: Abraham, A., Castillo, O., Virmani, D. (eds.) Proceedings of 3rd International Conference on Computing Informatics and Networks. LNNS, vol. 167, pp. 255–261. Springer, Singapore (2021). https://doi.org/10.1007/978-981-15-9712-1_22
11. Jovic, A., Bogunovic, N.: Feature extraction for ECG time-series mining based on chaos theory. In: Proceedings of the 29th International Conference on Information Technology Interfaces (2007)
12. Keogh, E.J., Lin, J., Fu, A.: HOT SAX: efficiently finding the most unusual time series subsequence. In: Proceedings of the 5th IEEE International Conference on Data Mining, ICDM 2005, pp. 226–233 (2005)
13. Khalid, S., Khalil, T., Nasreen, S.: A survey of feature selection and feature extraction techniques in machine learning. In: Proceedings of the Science and Information Conference, SAI 2014, pp. 372–378 (2014)
14. Kumar, D., Batra, U.: Breast cancer histopathology image classification using soft voting classifier. In: Abraham, A., Castillo, O., Virmani, D. (eds.) Proceedings of 3rd International Conference on Computing Informatics and Networks. LNNS, vol. 167, pp. 619–631. Springer, Singapore (2021). https://doi.org/10.1007/978-981-15-9712-1_53

15. Li, P., et al.: High-performance personalized heartbeat classification model for long-term ECG signal. IEEE Trans. Biomed. Eng. **64**(1), 78–86 (2016)
16. Lip, G., et al.: Atrial fibrillation. Nat. Rev. Dis. Primers. **31**, 16016 (2016). https://doi.org/10.1038/nrdp.2016.16
17. Liu, F., et al.: An open access database for evaluating the algorithms of electrocardiogram rhythm and morphology abnormality detection. J. Med. Imaging Health Inf. **8**(7), 1368–1373 (2018)
18. Maletzke, A.G., et al.: Time series classification using motifs and characteristics extraction: a case study on ECG databases. In: Proceedings of the 4th International Workshop on Knowledge Discovery, Knowledge Management and Decision Support (2013)
19. Mueen, A., Keogh, E.J., Zhu, Q., Cash, S., Westover, B.: Exact discovery of time series motifs. In: Proceedings of the SIAM International Conference on Data Mining, SDM 2009, pp. 473–484 (2009)
20. Naderi, S., et al.: The impact of age on the epidemiology of atrial fibrillation hospitalizations. Am. J. Med. **127**(2), 158.e1–158.e7 (2014)
21. Nady, S., Moness, M., Massoud, M., Gharieb, R.: Combining continuous wavelet transform and Teager-Kaiser Energy operator for ECG arrhythmia detection. In: 8th Cairo International Biomedical Engineering Conference (CIBEC), pp. 76–79. IEEE (2016)
22. Padmavathi, S., Ramanujam, E.: Naïve Bayes classifier for ECG abnormalities using multivariate maximal time series Motif. Procedia Comput. Sci. **47**, 222–228 (2015)
23. Sánchez-Cauce, R., Pérez-Martín, J., Luque, M.: Multi-input convolutional neural network for breast cancer detection using thermal images and clinical data. Comput. Meth. Program. Biomed. **204**, 106045 (2021)
24. Sun, Y., Zhu, L., Wang, G., Zhao, F.: Multi-input convolutional neural network for flower grading. J. Electr. Comput. Eng. **2017**, 9240407:1–9240407:8 (2017)
25. Ventura, G., Benvenuti, E. (eds.): Advances in Discretization Methods. SSSS, vol. 12. Springer, Cham (2016). https://doi.org/10.1007/978-3-319-41246-7
26. Wang, X., Smith, K., Hyndman, R.: Characteristic-based clustering for time series data. Data Min. Knowl. Disc. **13**, 335–364 (2006). https://doi.org/10.1007/s10618-005-0039-x
27. Wankhedkar, R., Jain, S.K.: Motif discovery and anomaly detection in an ECG using matrix profile. In: Panigrahi, C.R., Pati, B., Mohapatra, P., Buyya, R., Li, K.-C. (eds.) Progress in Advanced Computing and Intelligent Engineering. AISC, vol. 1198, pp. 88–95. Springer, Singapore (2021). https://doi.org/10.1007/978-981-15-6584-7_9
28. Yeh, C.C.M., et al.: Matrix profile I: all pairs similarity joins for time series: a unifying view that includes Motifs, Discords and Shapelets. In: IEEE 16th International Conference on Data Mining (ICDM), pp. 1317–1322. IEEE (2016)
29. Zhao, Z., Särkkä, S., Rad, A.B.: Spectro-temporal ECG analysis for atrial fibrillation. In: Proceedings of the 28th International Workshop on Machine Learning for Signal Processing, MLSP 2018 (2018)
30. Zhu, Y., Yeh, C.C.M., Zimmerman, Z., Kamgar, K., Keogh, E.: Matrix profile XI: SCRIMP++: time series motif discovery at interactive speeds. In: IEEE International Conference on Data Mining (ICDM), pp. 837–846. IEEE (2018)

Context-Aware Support for Cardiac Health Monitoring Using Federated Machine Learning

Godwin Okechukwu Ogbuabor[1](✉), Juan Carlos Augusto[1], Ralph Moseley[1],
and Aléchia van Wyk[2]

[1] Research Group on Development of Intelligent Environments,
Middlesex University London, London, UK
go314@live.mdx.ac.uk, {j.augusto,r.moseley}@mdx.ac.uk
[2] Department of Natural Sciences, Middlesex University London, London, UK
a.vanwy@mdx.ac.uk

Abstract. Context-awareness provides a platform for healthcare professionals to assess the health status of patients in their care using multiple relevant parameters such as heart rate, electrocardiogram (ECG) signals and activity data. It involves the use of digital technologies to monitor the health condition of a patient in an intelligent environment. Feedback gathered from relevant professionals at earlier stages of the project indicates that physical activity recognition is an essential part of cardiac condition monitoring. However, the traditional machine learning method of developing a model for activity recognition suffers two significant challenges; model overfitting and privacy infringements. This research proposes an intelligent and privacy-oriented context-aware decision support system for cardiac health monitoring using the physiological and the activity data of the patient. The system makes use of a federated machine learning approach to develop a model for physical activity recognition. Experimental analysis shows that the federated approach has advantages over the centralized approach in terms of model generalization whilst maintaining the privacy of the user.

Keywords: Cardiac monitoring · Context-awareness · Federated learning

1 Introduction

Cardiac diseases such as arrhythmia, stroke, and coronary heart disease (CHD) has been shown to be managed by monitoring patients' physiological signals in real-time. The symptoms of these diseases are diverse, ranging from minor chest palpitations, chest pain, fainting (syncope) to sudden heart attack, depending on the type and severity of the heart disease [22]. Fortunately, with the most recent advances in ECG monitoring and the help of modern mobile phone technology, monitoring a patient in the remote areas has become easier and more accessible

© Springer Nature Switzerland AG 2021
M. Bramer and R. Ellis (Eds.): SGAI-AI 2021, LNAI 13101, pp. 267–281, 2021.
https://doi.org/10.1007/978-3-030-91100-3_22

[26]. However, it is essential to note that to predict abnormalities, a specific vital sign such as heart rate, ECG signals may not provide sufficient knowledge to assist physicians in decision-making [20]. The combination of the patient's physiological parameters, environmental information, and the physical activity details can go a long way in providing a rich platform, that will enable physicians timely decisions; thereby, offering better environment for healthcare delivery services [25].

Context-awareness is an important part of systems implemented in areas such as Intelligent Environment, Ambient Intelligence, Pervasive and Ubiquitous Computing [3]. The fundamental idea behind context-awareness in healthcare is to develop a proactive and efficient system, that can correlate patient's contextual information and adapt to the changes in the patient's condition and environment [21]. Context-awareness is the ability of a system to use contextual information to provide services that are relevant to the stakeholders based on their preferences and needs while context is "the information which is directly relevant to characterize a situation of interest to the stakeholders of a system" [5]. It plays an essential role in the healthcare delivery decision-making process and assists physicians to properly and timely monitor patients in their care. This research presents a context-aware decision support system for cardiac condition monitoring and management during rehabilitation (mCardiac). The system makes use of federated machine learning approach for activity recognition to maintain users' privacy. Federated learning is a machine learning technique that allows different clients from different locations to collaboratively learn a machine learning model without sending their data to a central server. The formulated scenario below was used to help understand the proposed system in a real working environment.

Scenario: Mike was recently discharged from hospital after suffering from Coronary Heart Disease (CHD). In order to avoid cardiac readmission, his physician, Dr. Charles needs to keep in touch with him regularly. However, Mike lives about 20 mi from the hospital, therefore creating a barrier for a constant visit to the hospital. In order to frequently monitor Mike's health status and offer personalized recommendations, Dr. Charles needs a platform that will generate and correlate Mike's physiological signals and activity details from distance. The proposed system will collect, aggregate and process Mike's contextual information and present it as a decision support tool.

An intelligent analysis of mike's contextual information will assist Dr. Charles in the decision-making process and offer a better platform for healthcare delivery services. It will enable Dr. Charles to understand the daily activity pattern of Mike, the change in daily behavior, change in physiological information, and its effects on the recovering process.

The rest of the work is organized as follows: Works by other researchers is presented in Sect. 2, discussing their strengths and limitations. In Sect. 3, the research presents the context-aware decision support system, discussing the methodology used, federated approach, activity recognition process, and the experimental analysis, while Sect. 4 presents the system evaluation and results of the experimental analysis. Finally, Sect. 5 shows the conclusion of the work and possible future directions.

2 Related Work

Most of the studies on cardiac condition monitoring focus on identifying irregularities in a specific vital sign [17]. This approach might not provide enough information for effective and efficient cardiac condition monitoring. Recently, some researchers proposed context-aware systems for cardiac patient monitoring, however, research in this area requires significant improvements. Li et al. [10] developed a system that records biosignal of the patients and request for context information when there is an abnormality. The patient has to input information about his/her daily life activities. So this system is not fully automatic since it requires user's intervention. The focus of Forkan and Hu [7] was on the older adult, they developed a cloud-based system that extracts health parameters from Fitbit device and ECG sensors. The context information of the patient is sent via social media to the patient's doctor, relative, or friends when there are abnormal changes. They used the Fitbit device to collect the activity details of the user. However, this device could only recognize the steps of the subject and cannot show specific activities performed such as walking, running, and sitting.

Sannino et al. [18], introduced an "intelligent mobile system based on rule decision support system for cardiac patients". The system correlates data from the ECG sensor with physical activities such as walking, running, and body posture. They used the threshold rule to determine the activity of the patient and argued that testing the system with fifteen healthy persons proved the effectiveness of the proposed approach. Kunnath et al. [9] also used the threshold approach to detect different activities (Lying, Standing, Walking, Jogging) for cardiac disease monitoring and claimed a classification accuracy of 94%. Though the approach shown to be effective, however, using a threshold rule to determine the activity of the user might not be the best option because of the wide range of physical activities, coupled with the disparity in how a specific activity is to be performed.

Another similar solution was presented by [13], they combined the ECG signals with physical activities for cardiac disease diagnosis. Miao et al. [13] applied machine learning technique to recognize human activities. Machine learning provides computation methods and learning mechanisms for developing a model to predict a situation based on the ground truth. They recruited seven healthy people who wore ECG sensors on their chest and carried smartphones in their pockets to collect sensor data. Each subject was asked to perform three different activities (Running, Rest and Walking). The sensor data from the seven participants were aggregated, processed, and used to train J48 decision tree algorithms in order to predict the activity of the users when new data without ground truth are fed into the model.

3 Decision Support System for Cardiac Condition Monitoring

Decision Support Systems (DSS) are computer applications developed to assist clinicians in decisions making for patient wellbeing. Such systems range from simple software to complex artificial intelligence applications. The importance of context-aware DSS is revealed by the knowledge gained by the combination of multiple sources of information to provide better insight and understanding of the situation under consideration. A context-aware DSS for cardiac condition monitoring and management during rehabilitation is presented. The system will utilize the patient's contextual information from different sources to provide a useful tool to physicians. This will enable the healthcare professional to make better decisions to avoid cardiac readmission or perhaps death.

This research considers the ECG signals from the Holter monitor, activity data from smartphones, and time of the day as essential sources of information to provide an effective and efficient system for cardiac rehabilitation monitoring. These sources of information are selected based on interviews with the healthcare professionals and the quest to present a real-time, reliable, and energy-efficient system. The system involves data collection from Holter monitor and smartphone sensors, machine learning algorithm training for activity recognition and pattern discovery, and finally, implementation of a decision support tool. During the monitoring process, the subject will be required to carry a smartphone running our mobile app for data collection and a Holter monitor for ECG signals recording. Holter monitor is a portable and continuous monitoring device used to generate and record ECG signals [14]. Some of the modern Holter monitors allow users to wear the device while doing their normal activities. Smartphone is equipped with an accelerometer sensor that generates data regarding the movement of the user.

3.1 Architecture of the Proposed System

The proposed architecture shown in Fig. 1 is made up of the following features: (i) Context acquisition, (ii) Context modeling and storage (iii) Context reasoning and visualization, and (iv) Personalized recommendation. During the monitoring process, the subject will be required to carry a smartphone running the mobile app to collect accelerometer sensor data and a Holter monitor to record ECG signals, this forms the context acquisition unit. Then, at the modeling and storage stage, the acquired contexts will be presented in an efficient and structured format and stored in a database for retrieval; while at the context reasoning and visualization stage, relevant features will be extracted from the context data and analyzed for knowledge discovery. Also at this stage, the outcome of the analysis will be presented as a decision support tool. Finally, healthcare professionals will be able to offer personalized recommendations to the patient based on the contextual analysis. These recommendations could be in the form of text or auditory format regarding the health condition.

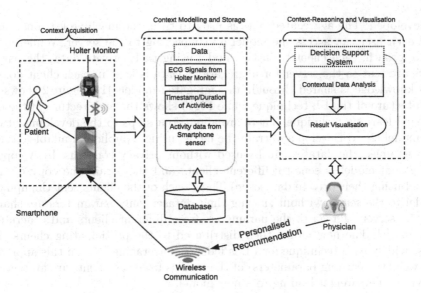

Fig. 1. Proposed context-aware system architecture

3.2 Methodology

The User-Centred Intelligent Environments Development Process (UCIEDP) was adopted for this research [4]. The stakeholders are at the heart of this methodology, hence making it crucial to involve the healthcare professionals at the early stage of this work. As part of the process interview was conducted with a cardiologist and a cardiac rehabilitation nurse to gather user requirements. The outcome of the interview reveals that physical activity recognition is an essential part of cardiac condition monitoring especially during rehabilitation, this leads to the next stage, activity recognition. A mobile application was developed to collect accelerometer sensor data [16], participants recruited for the experiment, and the data used to train machine learning algorithms for activity recognition. Federated machine learning technique was used to develop a model to predict the activity of the user when sensor data without ground truth is fed into the model. Finally, the results of the experiments presented for knowledge discovery and personalized recommendations.

3.3 Federated Learning

Federated learning (FL) is a decentralized model training approach that allows different clients in different locations to collaboratively learn a machine learning model without transferring dataset that may contain private information to a central server [11]. FL has been applied in different domains ranging from healthcare, IoT, transportation, mobile apps, defense [2]. The difference between the centralized approach and the FL approach is that in the centralized approach, the individual dataset is sent to the server where the machine learning model is developed. The aggregated data is used to train the machine learning model and each user can access the model by connecting to the server. While, in the FL approach, each client train the model using their private data, the parameters are sent to the server for aggregation. Data is kept in each client domain and knowledge is shared through an aggregated models [1]. Figure 2 shows the architecture of the FL technique while Fig. 3 shows the architecture of the centralized learning technique. There are about four steps to the development of a FL model [2]. a) Develop and train the model using a publicly available dataset. It is assumed the dataset can be used without privacy concerns. b) A copy of the global model is sent to different clients and they train the copy of their model using their private dataset. c) Then, each of the clients sent the updated model to the server without sharing their dataset, only parameters are shared. d) The server aggregates the parameters from different clients and generates a new model. The new model then distributed to the participating clients. The most widely used technique for FL is federated averaging [12]. In this approach, the weights (learning parameters) of the models from the clients are averaged to provide a new weight leading to a new model.

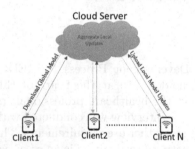

Fig. 2. Federated architecture

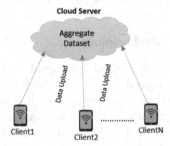

Fig. 3. Central architecture

3.4   Activity Recognition

Recognizing human activities such as walking and running or human-related actions aims to observe and understand what type of activities or routines performed by the subject at time-interval [24]. The work in [19] pointed out that the primary focus of cardiac rehabilitation is on exercise and needs to be automated. The built-in accelerometer sensor in modern Smartphones has made it possible to dynamically detect the activity of the user. To recognize the user's activity, he/she need to carry the mobile phone while doing daily activities. The first phase of the activity recognition is data collection using a mobile app, mobile phone was selected for the research because of its convenient and a large number of the population have smartphone with accelerometer sensor. The mobile app collects the A_x, A_y, A_z axis, and the corresponding timestamps. Secondly, the sensor data are processed and partitioned into equal groups at time-interval representing the segmentation stage. In the third stage, time or frequency domain features are extracted from each group, and finally, the extracted features are used to train machine learning algorithms in order to classify new data without ground truth. Algorithms 1 shows the process of activity recognition using centralized approach. The process starts by aggregating data from different clients $K = k_1, k_2, ...k_n$. The aggregated data is partitioned into windows w and features F_i extracted. The extracted features are used to train machine learning algorithms using the training dataset, $Ftrain$. Finally, the model evaluated using the test dataset, $Ftest$ and the accuracy returned.

Algorithm 1. Activity Recognition Process for Centralized Learning

---

1: **Input:** $D = A_x, A_y, A_z, M_g$
2: **Output:** Predicted Activities
3: Aggregate data D_k from clients $(k_1, k_2, ...k_n)$
4: Partition D_K into sliding windows (w)
5: **for** each w in D_K **do**
6:     Extract features $F_i = f_1, f_2 ....f_j$
7: Split F_i into Train($Ftrain$) and Test($Ftest$) sets
8: Train algorithm with $Ftrain$
9: Predict activity with $Ftest$
10: $results$ = accuracy(Predicted activities)
11: Return $results$

3.5   Experimental Analysis

Samples of accelerometer data from twelve volunteers [15] were used to demonstrate the FL approach. The participants were asked to put the mobile phone running our data collector app in the pocket and perform four activities; sitting, walking, jogging, and standing. However, some of the participants was able to perform only three activities; Sitting, Standing and Walking. The mobile app collects the A_x, A_y, and A_z axis along with the timestamps at a frequency 50 Hz. Figure 4 shows the samples of the dataset collected from one of the participants for sitting and standing activities. The x-axis captures the horizontal movement of the smartphone, y-axis indicates the upward/downward movement of the phone while z-axis shows the forward/backward movement of the mobile device [6].

Activity	X-axis	Y-Axis	Z-axis	Timestamp
Sitting	1.283331	3.091009	9.083879	06/01/2021 10:16:48
Sitting	1.781341	3.03594	9.27542	06/01/2021 10:16:48
Sitting	1.755004	3.141289	9.124581	06/01/2021 10:16:48
Sitting	1.431776	3.122134	8.818114	06/01/2021 10:16:48
Sitting	0.794899	3.541133	8.834874	06/01/2021 10:16:48
Sitting	1.343188	3.526767	7.14691	06/01/2021 10:16:48
Sitting	2.092596	3.462122	7.010437	06/01/2021 10:16:48
Sitting	1.230657	3.447756	8.786988	06/01/2021 10:16:48
Sitting	1.283331	3.677606	8.528407	06/01/2021 10:16:48
Sitting	1.091789	3.668029	8.870789	06/01/2021 10:16:48
Standing	-1.75979	4.575459	6.402291	06/01/2021 10:19:30
Standing	-1.15404	5.339233	9.040782	06/01/2021 10:19:30
Standing	-0.61772	4.73827	9.96976	06/01/2021 10:19:30
Standing	-0.24182	4.223501	8.461368	06/01/2021 10:19:30
Standing	-0.26337	3.972102	7.503657	06/01/2021 10:19:30
Standing	-0.81405	4.16125	8.150111	06/01/2021 10:19:30

Fig. 4. Samples of the dataset

The magnitude of the three axes was computed to handle orientation problems of the smartphones making it four features; A_x, A_y, and A_z and magnitude. The magnitude (m_g) of the total acceleration is computed by the square root of the sum of the squared acceleration of three axes in Eq. (1).

$$M_g = \sqrt{(A_x)^2 + (A_y)^2 + (A_z)^2} \tag{1}$$

Sliding window techniques were used to partition the sensor data into 4 s equal windows and extracted some time-domain features from each segment. For a given time series $[x_1, x_2, x_3, ..., x_n]$, n represents the total number of samples in each window segment, then features were extracted from each window. Table 1 presents the extracted features for the analysis. Each feature represents an input vector used for the algorithm training. The participants were grouped into four different groups, each group having participant(s) that performed the four activities (Sitting, Standing, Walking and Jogging) and assumed each group to be a client hence having four clients for the experiment. The distribution of samples collected from the groups is presented in Table 2.

Table 1. Extracted features for algorithm training

Feature	Equation
Mean	$mean = \frac{1}{n} \sum_{i=1}^{n} x_i$
Variance	$var = \frac{1}{n} \sum_{i=1}^{n} (x_i - mean)^2$
Standard deviation	$std = \sqrt{\frac{1}{n} \sum_{i=1}^{n} (x_i - mean)^2}$
Minimum value	$min = MIN(x_i)$
Maximum value	$max = MAX(x_i)$
Median value	$median = \frac{n+1}{2}$
Standard error of the mean (sem)	$sem = \frac{std}{\sqrt{n}}$

Table 2. Distribution of samples from the users

Activities	Client1	Client2	Client3	Client4
Sitting	21649	32045	19192	14411
Standing	16203	28028	20184	11262
Walking	20470	33160	13821	16200
Jogging	5320	6253	6363	15868

Model Development and Aggregation: Two machine learning algorithms (Support Vector machine and Logistic Regression) were used in demonstrating the FL approach. The regularisation parameter in Support Vector Machine (SVM) and the inverse of the regularisation parameter in Logistic Regression (LR) was used as the learning parameters for the experiment. The regularization parameter shows how much the algorithm will focus to minimize misclassification.

Support Vector Machine: SVM is a supervised machine learning technique that discriminates between two classes by generating a hyperplane that optimally separate the classes. It uses machine learning techniques to maximize classification accuracy while automatically avoiding model overfitting [8]. The algorithm makes use of nonlinear function known as kernels to transform the input data into a multidimensional space [23].

Firstly, a global model was developed using the default parameters provided by Sklearn library in python and dataset from four of the participants. It is assumed that the dataset from the four participants could be used without privacy concerns. Secondly, the optimal value of the learning parameter using each client's dataset was searched. With the help of the gridsearchcv library in python, the optimal parameter was gotten from each client. Figure 5 shows the results of the parameter turning for the four clients. The upper line shows the training score while the lower line indicates the cross-validation scores using 10-fold cross-validation. The optimal parameter for client1 was found at $P_l = 3$, client2 at $P_l = 5$, client3 at $P_l = 1$ and client4 at $P_l = 9$. The optimal parameters were aggregated, the average computed and the result used to update the global model. Evaluating the new model using a new dataset that was not part of the training dataset, gave classification accuracy of 89%.

Logistic Regression: LR is a parametric algorithms in that it summarizes data with a set of parameters of fixed sizes independent of the number of training dataset. The same principle used in SVM was applied here for model development and aggregation. Other parameters were kept constant using Sklearn library in python while searching for the optimal value of the learning parameter (P_l). Figure 6 shows the results of the parameter turning using LR. The optimal parameter for client1 was found at $P_l = 9$, client2 at $P_l = 2$, client3 at $P_l = 8$ and client4 at $P_l = 6$. The parameters were aggregated and the average computed and used to update the global model. The updated model gave

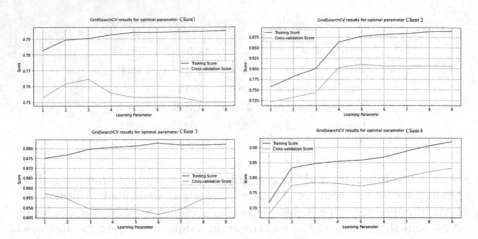

Fig. 5. Results of the learning parameter search using support vector machine

classification accuracy of 81% which is relatively lower than the performance of SVM with 89% accuracy.

The algorithm 2 shows the federated machine learning process for the activity recognition. The algorithms start by developing a global mode m. Then the model distributed to different clients $k = k_1, k_2, \ldots k_n$. Each client extract features $F_i = f_1, f_2 \ldots f_j$ from their dataset. The extracted features was used to obtain the optimal learning parameter P_l using GridSearchCV library. The values of P_l are aggregated from different clients and the average computed and used to update the global model.

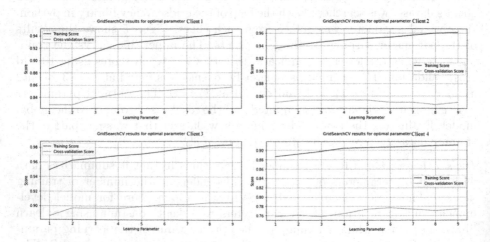

Fig. 6. Results of the learning parameter search using logistic regression

---

Algorithm 2. FederatedAveraging for activity recognition. The K is the number of clients and P_l is the learning parameter

---

1: **Input** $D = A_x, A_z, A_y, M_g$
2: Develop global model m
3: Distribute m to clients K
4: **for** each client in $K = k_1, k_2, \ldots \ldots k_n$ **do**
5:     Partition D_K into sliding windows (w)
6:     **for** each w in D_K **do**
7:         Extract features $F_i = f_1, f_2 \ldots \ldots \ldots f_j$
8:     Search for optimal P_l
9: Aggregate P_l and compute average $avg(P_l)$
10: Update model m

Model Generalization: In centralized learning, each client is required to transfer their dataset to a central server. However, clients might not be happy to send their dataset due to privacy concerns. This often results in developing a model that overfits, hence does not generalize to the population due to insufficient amount of training dataset. Generalization is the ability of a machine learning model to correctly classify data, not in the training dataset. The research investigates the performance of the LR model using each client dataset assuming that some subjects are not happy to send their data due to privacy concerns. Table 3 shows the training and testing score for each client when the new dataset that was not part of the training set is used for validation. It is evident from the results that most of the clients recorded low testing score due to poor model generalization compared to the federated approach which recorded 81% accuracy.

Table 3. Model performance using each client dataset

	Client1 (%)	Client2 (%)	Client3 (%)	Client4 (%)
Train score	88	93	95	89
Test score	64	53	88	58

3.6 Benefits of the Federated Approach

In FL approach, dataset that may contain client sensitive information is not required to be transferred to a central server, only trained models are sent to the server for aggregation. This approach will enable several clients from different locations to participate in the algorithm training, hence better generalization while maintaining clients privacy.

Another advantage of federated learning over centralized learning is that the centralized approach entails that a huge amount of storage capacity is required as well as sophisticated security protocols to avoid violation of the right to data, while in federated learning, only trained model is sent to the server which is not heavy compare to the dataset, and the security required to protect model is not as demanding as for datasets.

4   System Evaluation and Results

To evaluate the system, some of the participants used Holter monitors and smartphone running the mobile app concurrently for data collection. The Holter monitor used is "Lifecard CF" and the mobile app is available in google play store as "MCardiac". The generated raw sensor data were processed and the federated model from SVM used to predict the activities of the user. This model was selected due to better performance. Figure 7, shows the graphical representation of the (a) activity information from smartphones and (b) ECG signals from the Holter monitor, from one of the participants. The information from the Holter

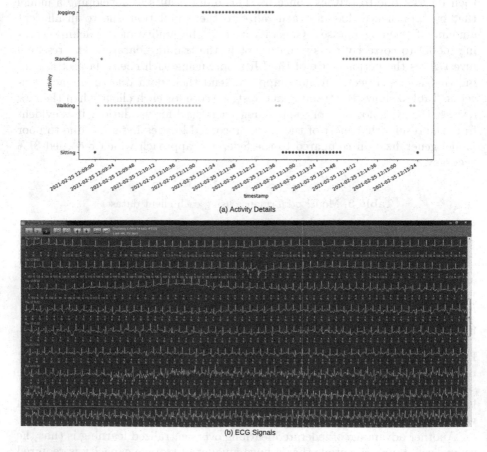

(a) Activity Details

(b) ECG Signals

Fig. 7. System output showing (a) the activity details and (b) the ECG signals

monitor represents the heartbeat at time interval while the information from the smartphone shows the activity of the user at a time interval. The concept is to enable healthcare professionals to understand the activity of the patients when reading the ECG signals. If there are any irregularities in the signals, the health professional can consider the activity of the subject as a guide in decision-making. For instance, if the wave of the ECG signals is high, and the activity of the user is sitting. The physician might consider it as an abnormality, however, if the wave of the ECG signals is high and the activity jogging, he might argue that the increase in the signals wave might be due to the subject doing a rigorous activity. The system will enable the physician to offer the right advice to the patient instead of prescribing unnecessary medications.

5 Conclusion

Health monitoring using contextual information assists health professionals in the decision-making process, which in turn, improves quality of life of the monitored patients. It provides a platform for healthcare professionals to assess the health status of patients in their care using multiple relevant parameters. This paper presented a context-aware decision support system for cardiac condition monitoring during rehabilitation. A federated learning approach was used to develop a model for activity recognition resulting in a better model that maintain users' privacy.

In future, the research will evaluate with real cardiac patients as previous experiment was conducted using healthy volunteers. Pilot to get feedback from the healthcare professionals and update the system is also in progress.

References

1. AbdulRahman, S., Tout, H., Ould-Slimane, H., Mourad, A., Talhi, C., Guizani, M.: A survey on federated learning: the journey from centralized to distributed on-site learning and beyond. IEEE Internet Things J. **8**(7), 5476–5497 (2021)
2. Aledhari, M., Razzak, R., Parizi, R.M., Saeed, F.: Federated learning: a survey on enabling technologies, protocols, and applications. IEEE Access **8**, 140699–140725 (2020)
3. Alegre, U., Augusto, J.C., Clark, T.: Engineering context-aware systems and applications: a survey. J. Syst. Softw. **117**, 55–83 (2016)
4. Augusto, J., Kramer, D., Alegre, U., Covaci, A., Santokhee, A.: The user-centred intelligent environments development process as a guide to co-create smart technology for people with special needs. Univ. Access Inf. Soc. **17**(1), 115–130 (2018)
5. Augusto, J.C., Quinde, M., Oguego, C., Manuel, J.G.: Context-aware systems architecture (CaSa). Cybern. Syst. Anal. (2020)
6. Bayat, A., Pomplun, M., Tran, D.A.: A study on human activity recognition using accelerometer data from smartphones. Procedia Comput. Sc. **34**, 450–457 (2014)
7. Forkan, A.R.M., Hu, W.: A context-aware, predictive and protective approach for wellness monitoring of cardiac patients. In: 2016 Computing in Cardiology Conference (CinC), pp. 369–372. IEEE (2016)

8. Jakkula, V.: Tutorial on support vector machine (SVM). School of EECS, Washington State University, 37 (2006)
9. Kunnath, A.T., Nadarajan, D., Mohan, M., Ramesh, M.V.: Wicard: a context aware wearable wireless sensor for cardiac monitoring. In: 2013 International Conference on Advances in Computing, Communications and Informatics (ICACCI), pp. 1097–1102. IEEE (2013)
10. Li, J.P., Berry, D., Hayes, R.: A mobile ECG monitoring system with context collection. In: Vander Sloten, J., Verdonck, P., Nyssen, M., Haueisen, J. (eds.) 4th European Conference of the International Federation for Medical and Biological Engineering. IFMBE Proceedings, vol. 22, pp. 1222–1225. Springer, Heidelberg (2009). https://doi.org/10.1007/978-3-540-89208-3_292
11. Li, Z., Sharma, V., Mohanty, S.P.: Preserving data privacy via federated learning: challenges and solutions. IEEE Consum. Electron. Mag. **9**(3), 8–16 (2020)
12. McMahan, H.B., Moore, E., Ramage, D., Arcas, B.A.: Federated learning of deep networks using model averaging. arXiv preprint arXiv:1602.05629 (2016)
13. Miao, F., Cheng, Y., He, Y., He, Q., Li, Y.: A wearable context-aware ECG monitoring system integrated with built-in kinematic sensors of the smartphone. Sensors **15**(5), 11465–11484 (2015)
14. Mittal, S., Movsowitz, C., Steinberg, J.S.: Ambulatory external electrocardiographic monitoring: focus on atrial fibrillation. J. Am. Coll. Cardiol. **58**(17), 1741–1749 (2011)
15. Ogbuabor, G.O., Augusto, J.C., Moseley, R.: Physical Activity Recognition Dataset (2021). https://mdx.figshare.com/articles/dataset/Physical_Activity_Recognition_Dataset/14798667
16. Ogbuabor, G.O., Augusto, J.C., Moseley, R., van Wyk, A.: Context-aware approach for cardiac rehabilitation monitoring. In: Intelligent Environments 2020: Workshop Proceedings of the 16th International Conference on Intelligent Environments, vol. 28, p. 167. IOS Press (2020)
17. Ogbuabor, G.O., Augusto, J.C., Moseley, R., van Wyk, A.: Context-aware system for cardiac condition monitoring and management: a survey. Behav. Inf. Technol. 1–18 (2020)
18. Sannino, G., De Pietro, G.: A smart context-aware mobile monitoring system for heart patients. In: 2011 IEEE International Conference on Bioinformatics and Biomedicine Workshops (BIBMW), pp. 655–695. IEEE (2011)
19. Särelä, A., Korhonen, I., Salminen, J., Koskinen, E., Kirkeby, O., Walters, D.: A home-based care model for outpatient cardiac rehabilitation based on mobile technologies. In: 2009 3rd International Conference on Pervasive Computing Technologies for Healthcare, pp. 1–8. IEEE (2009)
20. Shanmathi, N., Jagannath, M.: Computerised decision support system for remote health monitoring: a systematic review. IRBM **39**(5), 359–367 (2018)
21. Varshney, U.: Pervasive Healthcare Computing: EMR/EHR, Wireless and Health Monitoring. Springer, Heidelberg (2009). https://doi.org/10.1007/978-1-4419-0215-3
22. WHO: Cardiovascular diseases (CVDs) (2017). https://www.who.int/news-room/fact-sheets/detail/cardiovascular-diseases-(cvds)
23. Yu, W., Liu, T., Valdez, R., Gwinn, M., Khoury, M.J.: Application of support vector machine modeling for prediction of common diseases: the case of diabetes and pre-diabetes. BMC Med. Inform. Decis. Mak. **10**(1), 1–7 (2010)
24. Yürür, Ö., Liu, C.H., Sheng, Z., Leung, V.C., Moreno, W., Leung, K.K.: Context-awareness for mobile sensing: a survey and future directions. IEEE Commun. Surv. Tutor. **18**(1), 68–93 (2014)

25. Zhang, W., Thurow, K., Stoll, R.: A context-aware mhealth system for online physiological monitoring in remote healthcare. Int. J. Comput. Commun. Control **11**(1), 142–156 (2015)
26. Zimetbaum, P., Goldman, A.: Ambulatory arrhythmia monitoring: choosing the right device. Circulation **122**(16), 1629–1636 (2010)

Using Automated Feature Selection for Building Case-Based Reasoning Systems: An Example from Patient-Reported Outcome Measurements

Deepika Verma[1]($\boxtimes$), Kerstin Bach[1], and Paul Jarle Mork[2]

[1] Department of Computer Science, Norwegian University of Science and Technology, Trondheim, Norway
{deepika.verma,kerstin.bach}@ntnu.no
[2] Department of Public Health and Nursing, Norwegian University of Science and Technology, Trondheim, Norway
paul.mork@ntnu.no

Abstract. Feature selection for case representation is an essential phase of Case-Based Reasoning (CBR) system development. To (semi-)automate the feature selection process can ease the knowledge engineering process. This paper explores the feature importance provided for XGBoost models as basis for creating CBR systems. We use Patient-Reported Outcome Measurements (PROMs) on low back pain from the SELFBACK project in our experiments. PROMs are a valuable source of information that capture physical, emotional as well as social aspects of well-being from the perspective of the patients. Leveraging the analytical capabilities of machine learning methods and data science techniques for exploiting PROMs have the potential of improving decision making. This paper presents a two-fold approach employed on our dataset for feature selection that combines statistical strength with data-driven knowledge modelling in CBR and compares it with permutation feature selection using XGBoost regressor. Furthermore, we compare the performance of the CBR models, built with the selected features, with two machine learning algorithms for predicting different PROMs.

Keywords: Case-based reasoning · Feature selection · Case representation · Patient-reported outcome measurements

1 Introduction

Patient-reported outcome measurements (PROMs)[1] are collected routinely in clinical settings and are designed to capture the patients' perception of their own health through structured questionnaires. By utilising machine learning methods and data science techniques, there is a large potential for PROMs to inform and improve clinical decision making [27]. In the current work, we use PROMs on low

---

[1] https://www.hss.edu/proms.asp.

© Springer Nature Switzerland AG 2021
M. Bramer and R. Ellis (Eds.): SGAI-AI 2021, LNAI 13101, pp. 282–295, 2021.
https://doi.org/10.1007/978-3-030-91100-3_23

back pain (LBP) as an example. Among patients seen in primary care, a specific cause of LBP can rarely be identified and the symptoms are most often diagnosed as being "nonspecific". This also highlights the multi-factorial nature of LBP, i.e., both genetic, physiological, social and psychological factors are likely to contribute to LBP. While an early and thorough assessment of LBP is recommended (for example, to detect cases at high risk of poor outcome) [18], there are currently no clinical decision support systems (CDSS) in use in clinical practice that can assist or improve such detection or predict the likely outcome for a patient.

Case-Based Reasoning (CBR) systems are well suited for the task of CDSS [5] since the PROMs of the patients can be described in a case-base, a knowledge repository that can aid decision making [2]. However, clinical datasets with PROMs usually contain several clinical measures, all of which may not necessarily be required for decision making and it is therefore necessary to be able to select optimal subset of features that can be used for building CBR systems to predict the patient outcomes and facilitate decision making [10].

Retrieval of similar cases is an important phase in CBR systems, which relies on the case representation and similarity measures. Hence, the selection of the most relevant and important features can easen and simplify the development of the entire CBR system. The focus of this paper is the feature selection phase for building CBR systems from PROMs to predict patient outcomes. While the overall method can be applied to other domains, we will present our evaluation using a dataset with PROMs (described in Sect. 3) in this work.

We employ a two-fold approach on our dataset for feature selection that combines statistical strength with data-driven knowledge modelling in CBR and compare it with permutation feature selection using XGBoost regressor. Additionally, we compare the performance of the CBR models, built with the selected features, with two machine learning algorithms for predicting different PROMs.

2   Related Work

PROMs are a valuable source of information and present opportunities for highly sophisticated analysis, but has only been exploited by a few studies in the context of leveraging analytical capabilities of machine learning methods. Rahman et al. [20] used a total of 130 PROMs collected via their pain self-management mobile application ("Manage My Pain"). Using Random Forest, they showed that pain volatility levels at 6 months follow-up could be predicted with a 70% accuracy. In their followup work [19], the authors showed that similar level of accuracy (68%) could be obtained with just 9 features. In another study, Harris et al. [12] used preoperative PROMs to predict whether or not a patient achieves a clinically important improvement in several pain- and function-related outcomes at 1-year post knee arthroplasty. Using several supervised machine learning algorithms, they showed that similar performance can be achieved across different algorithms for the outcomes by varying the number of inputs.

Using the CBR methodology for clinical datasets has already proven useful in decision making [13]. For building robust decision support CBR systems, sufficient description of the problem is necessary. Knowledge about the importance of various features in the dataset plays an important role in problem description for building CBR systems [1]. Xiong and Funk [28] proposed an approach wherein they assessed the feature subset selection based on the performance of CBR models. Later on, the authors proposed a hierarchical approach to select feature subsets for similarity models [29]. They used individual cases to optimise the possibility distributions in the case base and features were selected based on the magnitude of their parameters in the similarity models. Similar to the feature-selection approach proposed by Li et al. [17], we identify optimal feature subsets for our CBR system by iteratively building CBR systems with different feature subsets and evaluating the performance based on the predictions. While Li et al. used mutual information as a preset criterion for selecting feature subsets and evaluating the subsequent CBR systems, we used correlation. In their previous work [16], Li et al. combined feature reduction using rough set with case selection for handling large datasets. Similarly, Zhu et al. [30] selected reduced feature sets through neighborhood rough set algorithm, a method that has been used widely for feature and case selection in CBR [21,22].

3   SELFBACK Dataset

The dataset consists of PROMs collected during the randomised controlled trial (RCT)[2] that tested the effectiveness of the SELFBACK[3] DSS [23].

Care-seeking patients in primary care with non-specific LBP were recruited to the study. Patients were screened for eligibility based on a set of criteria. The eligible patients were invited to participate in the RCT and those who accepted the invite answered a baseline questionnaire. The participating patients were randomized into either intervention group or control group. The intervention group had access to the SELFBACK DSS mobile application and received tailored self-management plans weekly whereas the control group did not. The participants answered questionnaires at different time-points: (1) (only intervention group) at the end of every week: Tailoring questionnaire, and (2) at the end of 6-weeks, 3-months, 6-months and 9-months: Follow-up questionnaire. The questionnaires consist of measures of *pain intensity, pain self-efficacy, physical activity, functional ability, work-ability, sleep quality, fear avoidance* and *mood*. Additionally, the baseline questionnaire included patient sociodemographics (education, employment and family). Table 1 summarises the information collected from the participants at various time-points. We use the Baseline, Follow-up 1 (after 6 weeks) and Follow-up 2 (after 3-months) PROMs in our evaluation. A detailed account of data collection for the RCT can be found in Sandal et al. [23].

From the dataset, six outcomes were selected as target outcomes: Roland Morris Disability Questionnaire (RMDQ, range: [0,24]), Numeric Pain Rating Scale (NPRS, range: [0, 10]), Work-ability index (WAI, range: [0,10]), Pain Self Efficacy Questionnaire (PSEQ, range: [0,60]), Fear Avoidance Belief Questionnaire (FABQ, range: [0,30]) and Global Perceived Effect Scale (GPE, range:

---

[2] https://clinicaltrials.gov/ct2/show/NCT03798288.
[3] http://www.selfback.eu.

Table 1. The SELFBACK dataset created consists of participant characteristics collected at different time points and includes a selection of PROMs.

Descriptive variables		
Patient Characteristics	Sociodemographics	
Primary Outcome Measure		
Roland Morris Disability Questionnaire		
Secondary Outcome Measures		
Pain Self-Efficacy Questionnaire	Fear Avoidance Belief Questionnaire	Pain Intensity
Brief Illness Perception Questionnaire	Saltin-Grimby Physical Activity Level Scale	
Global Perceived Effect		
Other Outcome Measures		
Workability	Health-related Quality of Life	Activity Limitation
Patient Health Questionnaire	Perceived Stress Scale	Sleep
Patient Specific Functional Scale	Paint Duration and frequency	Physical Activity
Exercise		

$[-5, +5]$). The primary outcome, RMDQ, is used to evaluate the effect of the self-management app in the RCT. The other outcomes were chosen to elucidate the variation in LBP symptoms amongst the participants.

The intervention group dataset consists of PROMs from 218 participants while the control group dataset contains PROMs of 158 participants. Each participant is initially described by 47 features. Only the participants who completed at least the first two follow-up questionnaires were included in this work.

4   Feature Engineering for CBR Systems

Feature selection is an important step in the process of developing CBR systems. Reducing the dimensionality of the data enables the algorithm(s) to train faster by removing redundant information, thereby reducing model complexity, risk of overfitting, better generalisation and aiding interpretability of the models [7]. This is especially pertinent for building CBR systems for datasets with a high dimensionality, such as healthcare-oriented datasets, to ensure focus on the relevant attributes and enhance explainability of the models. Nonetheless, the methodology we present can be used for other domains for feature selection since the principle here is determining the best representation of a dataset in order to learn a solution to a given problem. While we use a healthcare domain dataset, the methodology itself has a broader application.

We use both filter and embedded methods in this work to determine reduced sets of predictors for the target outcomes. *Filter methods* use the principal criteria of ranking technique to select the most relevant features. Features are ranked based on statistical scores, correlation in our case, to determine the features' correlation with the outcome variable. This method is computationally efficient and does not rely on learning algorithms which can introduce a biased feature subset due to over-fitting [7]. However, correlation-based feature selection has shortcomings if there is a high degree of mutual correlation in the feature set. *Embedded methods* on the other hand are algorithm-specific, iteratively extracting features which contribute the most to the training of a particular iteration of a model during the training process. Impurity-based feature selection using tree-based algorithms[4] is a commonly used embedded method. Permutation feature importance determines the influence of random permutation of each predictor's values on the model performance while still preserving the distribution of the feature [9].

We experimented with two methodologies for selecting optimal predictors for each target outcome:

1. **Correlation and CBR:** Using a two-step hybrid method that combines statistical strength with data-driven case modelling, we attempted to derive optimal predictors of the target outcomes by computing correlation and iteratively building CBR models using features derived from correlation. Here, similarity measure development and building case representation are important factors in evaluating the performance of the CBR models for each set of features.

2. **Permutation feature importance using XGBoost:** Features are selected by computing permutation feature importance (PFI) with XGBoost (XGB) algorithm based on an evaluation metric.

Both methodologies aim to select optimal feature sets based on the trade-off between model performance and model simplicity, that is, fewer features.

4.1   Feature Selection and CBR System Optimization

To determine the optimal set of predictors for developing CBR systems, we experimented with two methodologies for selecting features: correlation-based and based on the feature importance of a XGBoost model. The features selected by both methodologies were used to build CBR systems for all the outcomes at both follow-up time-points. Additionally, we implemented Support Vector and XGB Regression models to compare and contrast the performance of the CBR systems. Figure 1 illustrates the process of feature selection methods we used.

The modeling of the CBR systems was done with the myCBR workbench [3]. The experiments were run using myCBR Rest API[5] [4] for batch querying the CBR systems and python packages such as Scikit learn [6] and XGBoost [8] (python version 3.6.7) were used for building regression models and Pingouin for

---

[4] https://scikit-learn.org/stable/auto_examples/ensemble/plot_forest_importances. html.

[5] https://github.com/ntnu-ai-lab/mycbr-sdk.

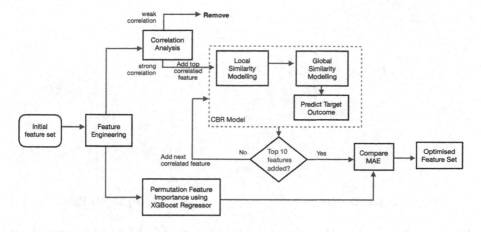

Fig. 1. Flowchart of the feature selection process

the statistical correlation [24]. For each target outcome we created datasets with the baseline data as input features and the PROMs of follow-up 1 and follow-up 2 as target values. These datasets were used to build CBR systems in a data-driven manner and as training data in the other two regression algorithms. In all the CBR models built for various target outcomes in this work, local similarity modelling of the attributes has been done in the same data-driven manner as presented in our previous work [25, 26]. The individual features are weighted equally in the global similarity function. Figure 2 showcases examples of local similarity measure modelling for numerical and categorical (ordinal) attributes (using correlated features of NPRS at follow-up 2 as an example). We urge the reader to refer to the previous work to fully grasp how the local similarity measures have been developed, as it is not possible to include the details in this work. Figure 3 shows the case representation of the same target outcome (NPRS) in myCBR workbench with 10 most correlated features.

To predict the target outcomes for a given participant using CBR model, we exploit the *"similar problems have similar solutions"* principle of CBR. While the query participant has been left out (leave-one-out cross validation), we determine their *n-nearest neighbours* (most similar case) with n in range [1,20] and compute mean of the target value reported by the n-neighbours, which is assigned as prediction for the given participant. The process is repeated for each participant and each target outcome dataset at both follow-up time-points for both the intervention and control group. The mean absolute error (MAE) is used as the metric to evaluate the predictive performance of the models.

4.2 Correlation-Based Feature Selection

Figure 1 shows that we first compute correlation between the baseline features and each target outcome to select features. Since the dataset comprises of both numerical and categorical features, we use Pearson for numerical features and

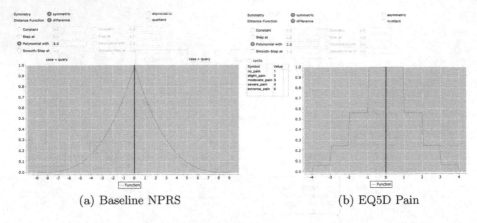

(a) Baseline NPRS   (b) EQ5D Pain

Fig. 2. Modelling of Local similarity measures for numerical (a) and categorical (b) attributes in myCBR workbench.

Instance information		
Name	Patient1	
Attributes		
BIPQ_life	6.0	Special Value: none
BIPQ_pain_continuation	10.0	Special Value: none
BIPQ_symptoms	5.0	Special Value: none
BT_pain_average	3.0	Special Value: none
EQ5D	80.0	Special Value: none
EQ5D_anxiety	not_anxious	Change Special Value: none
EQ5D_pain	slight_pain	Change Special Value: none
Pain_1year	Above30days	Change Special Value: none
Pain_worst	7.0	Special Value: none
RMDQ	7.0	Special Value: none

Fig. 3. Case representation in myCBR for NPRS (at follow-up 2, control group dataset) with 10 most correlated features

one-way ANOVA for categorical features to determine correlation between the baseline features and the target outcomes. Features with absolute correlation greater than the average correlation of the feature set and $p < 0.05$ were selected. For several reasons including simplified process of modelling in myCBR and based on experience from earlier experiments, it was decided to include only the top ten correlated features for building CBR systems. Previous experiments on the intervention group datasets showed that no more than ten features are necessary to predict any of the chosen target outcomes without any loss in the model performance. To build each CBR model, the casebase is populated with cases imported from a csv file in the myCBR workbench. Local similarity measures are developed for each attribute individually. Instead of building a new CBR model for each set of features, we build one model with the ten most correlated features and use ten different global similarity functions to progressively add more features. Once both the local and the global similarity measures are in place, we batch query the casebase using POST calls in the python implementation to generate predictions for the target outcome. The MAE is calculated between the reported outcome and the predictions for the entire dataset.

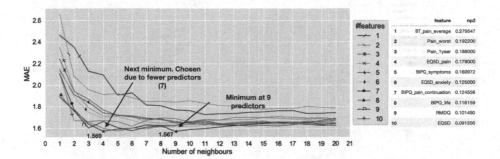

Fig. 4. On the right side of the figure are the top ten correlated features used to build the CBR model for predicting *NPRS* (input: baseline data, target: NPRS at follow-up 2). Features were added progressively one at a time in the given order, starting with the most correlated feature. **np2** (eta-squared) is the squared correlation coefficient. Graph on the left shows the MAE variation with different sets of features in the corresponding CBR model for predicting *NPRS*, with x-axis presenting the n-neighbours used for generating predictions and y-axis presenting the MAE in the predictions for the entire dataset.

Figure 4 gives an example for one target outcome, *NPRS*. It shows the result of the correlation (left) and the MAE when predicting the NPRS using the baseline data (right). We can see that the progressive addition of correlated features improves the prediction by the CBR system already by using the most similar case. Further, we observe that adding neighbors generally reduces the error and for the final model we choose the combination with the lowest MAE.

4.3   Feature Importance Using XGBoost

In this approach, we select features by computing the permutation feature importance using the XGBoost Regressor and compare the MAE of the predictions to determine the optimal feature set. The permutation feature importance is determined by the difference between the modified (permuted) dataset and a baseline model based on the MAE. First, a baseline model with all the features is trained and its MAE is computed. Next, the values of one feature in the dataset are permuted and then the model is re-trained and the MAE is computed for the modified dataset. The process is repeated for all the features in the dataset. The optimal number of features are selected based on the trade-off between model performance and number of features.

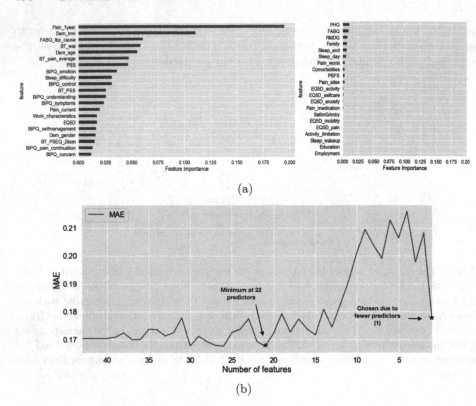

(a)

(b)

Fig. 5. Feature selection using permutation feature importance with XGB for predicting *GPE* (input: baseline data, target: GPE at follow-up 1). **a.** Features ranked by their importance. **b.** Effect of feature permutation on the XGB model: The MAE on the y-axis in this plot is scaled.

Figure 5a shows the feature importance for predicting the GPE and Fig. 5b shows the development of the MAE while adding the features. To select the best configuration, we choose the set with the lowest number of features that has the lowest MAE as shown in Fig. 5b. We favor the lowest number of features to build simpler model that requires minimal data collection and can be better explained. The selected features are then used to build CBR model in exactly the same way as described in the previous section and the prediction results are noted.

5   Experimental Results

To compare the performance of the CBR systems, we implemented two regression algorithms, XGB and Support Vector Regression (SVR) for each corresponding CBR system to predict the target outcomes. The algorithms were selected based on previous experiments with the intervention group data where we evaluated the performance of XGB and SVR along with other algorithms, including

Linear Regression, Passive Aggressive Regression, Stochastic Gradient Descent, AdaBoost, Random Forest, and found SVR and XGB to lead to the best results. For the simplicity of comparison and clarity, it was decided to keep only SVR and XGB for further evaluation. To optimize the hyperparameters, we used grid search [15]. Tables 2 and 3 summarise the results of predicting target outcomes using the CBR models, SVR and XGB for the intervention and control group participants, respectively.

Table 2. Results of Prediction of Target Outcomes using different Feature Selection Methodologies and Regression Methods for the Intervention Group (size of dataset: 218 participants). Numbers in bold letters are lowest MAE. **FU1**: Follow-up 1, **FU2**: Follow-up 2, **n**: number of features

| | | Feature selection methodology | | | | | | |
| | | Correlation+CBR | | | PFI+XGBoost | | | |
Target	Follow-Up	n	CBR	SVR	XGB	n	CBR	SVR	XGB
RMDQ	FU1	4	2.98	3.19	3.32	5	2.78	**2.69**	2.71
	FU2	8	2.90	**2.83**	2.85	4	3.17	3.92	3.02
NPRS	FU1	7	**1.38**	1.45	1.50	3	1.50	1.49	1.52
	FU2	9	1.48	**1.33**	1.38	3	1.46	1.41	1.42
WAI	FU1	5	1.16	1.98	1.98	2	**1.14**	1.96	2.01
	FU2	4	**1.14**	2.16	2.21	1	1.24	2.19	2.24
PSEQ	FU1	1	5.50	16.9	17.0	2	**5.45**	17.2	17.3
	FU2	3	5.95	16.6	16.6	2	**5.95**	16.4	17.1
FABQ	FU1	3	3.87	3.74	3.76	6	3.90	**3.50**	3.67
	FU2	1	3.9	**3.60**	3.84	6	3.83	3.64	3.86
GPE	FU1	1	**1.37**	2.73	2.76	2	1.39	2.82	2.78
	FU2	2	1.54	2.51	2.43	3	**1.49**	2.54	2.46

6   Discussion

A number of inferences can be made based on the results. We see in Fig. 4 that the baseline measurement (listed as *BT_pain_average*) of the associated target outcome *NPRS* is its' first most important predictor. This is a trend observed for all the target outcomes, except *GPE* which does not have an associated baseline measurement (see Fig. 5b). This is an important observation from clinical perspective, since baseline measurements of the associated outcomes have previously been found to be their most important predictor [11,14], and our experiments support these findings.

Selecting optimal features, especially for healthcare datasets, is one of those application domains where no one particular method prevails and one must decide based on application domain knowledge and experience, among others.

Table 3. Results of Prediction of Target Outcomes using different Feature Selection Methodologies and Regression Methods for the Control Group (size of dataset: 158 participants). Numbers in bold letters are lowest MAE. **FU1**: Follow-up 1, **FU2**: Follow-up 2, **n**: number of features

| | | Feature selection methodology | | | | | | |
| | | Correlation+CBR | | | PFI+XGBoost | | | |
Target	Follow-Up	n	CBR	SVR	XGB	n	CBR	SVR	XGB
RMDQ	FU1	2	3.11	2.99	2.97	4	3.07	2.92	**2.75**
	FU2	2	3.11	**2.97**	3.14	3	3.22	2.97	3.14
NPRS	FU1	6	**1.41**	1.77	1.85	2	1.49	1.73	1.85
	FU2	7	1.56	**1.49**	1.7	1	1.72	1.56	1.71
WAI	FU1	1	1.02	1.02	**1.01**	1	1.02	1.02	1.01
	FU2	2	1.14	**1.12**	1.17	1	1.19	1.15	1.18
PSEQ	FU1	7	**6.68**	19.2	19.6	1	7.01	19.4	19.8
	FU2	3	6.23	19.0	19.5	5	**5.94**	19.1	19.3
FABQ	FU1	1	3.47	**3.27**	3.58	1	3.47	3.27	3.58
	FU2	2	3.77	3.69	3.80	2	3.82	**3.58**	3.93
GPE	FU1	7	**1.22**	2.55	2.52	1	1.26	2.61	2.49
	FU2	1	**1.33**	2.65	2.58	2	1.39	2.67	2.56

From the results in Table 2 and 3, we see that the features selected by either of the methodologies give similar results with respect to the error in predictions. There is no clear winner here. However, taking into consideration the time and effort required, XGBoost permutation feature importance methodology requires minima and provides a more streamlined process for selecting optimal feature sets as compared to the two-fold approach, which requires estimating correlation, building several similarity measures and CBR systems for the target outcomes and comparing the MAE for determining optimal feature sets. As for a concrete time comparison, it is not possible since the modelling of local and global similarity measures for building a CBR model requires manual input. On the other hand, this comparison also establishes the utility of the two-fold approach for building tailored CBR systems.

All the three regression methods give fairly similar results when it comes to predicting the outcomes. However, for an outcome with a relatively large range (*PSEQ*) or no baseline measurement of the target outcome (*GPE*), both SVR and XGB fall short in comparison to the results we get from the CBR models. This is similar to our findings in our previous work [25] where we found CBR model built with our data-driven modelling approach to be more sensitive and robust to the data-distribution of individual features, thereby, furthering our premise that both data-driven similarity modelling and CBR are better suited for this task. Moreover, outcomes generated by CBR models are more explainable, which is a pre-requite for any CDSS where explainable systems are preferred over complex ones.

7   Conclusion and Future Work

In this paper, we presented a two-fold approach for feature selection wherein we used the correlation coefficient as a pre-processing step to select ten most correlated features and build the CBR models with progressively more features for predicting PROMs. We examine the performance of the predictions generated using CBR systems to determine optimal feature subsets for the outcomes. Through evaluation and comparison with tree-based feature selection methods (permutation feature importance with XGBoost), it can be concluded that although the presented two-fold approach is feasible and gives results similar to the other approach undertaken, it is however more time and effort intensive and therefore, feature selection using XGBoost permutation feature importance appears to be a more promising option. Predictive performance of the CBR systems is at par with and many a times better than the traditional algorithms such as SVR and XGBoost.

From a clinical perspective, building prognostic models that can provide necessary information to clinicians and patients of possible outcome(s) pertaining to a specific treatment is a necessity to support informed clinical decision making. Access to individualized predictive analytics for different outcomes may be the next step in the management of pain and related symptoms for patients with LBP. The results we get from our dataset confirm the predictive value of baseline measurements of associated target outcomes, similar to other studies such as by Fontana et al. [11] and Huber et al. [14].

In future work, it may be worthwhile to compare performance of the CBR models built with features selected by an expert with the approach presented in this work.

Acknowledgement. The work has been conducted as part of the SELFBACK and Back-UP projects, which have received funding from the European Union's Horizon 2020 research and innovation programme under grant agreement No 689043 and No 777090.

References

1. Aamodt, A., Plaza, E.: Case-based reasoning: Foundational issues, methodological variations, and system approaches. Artif. Intell. Commun. **7**(1), 39–59 (1994)
2. Andritsos, P., Jurisica, I., Glasgow, J.I.: Case-based reasoning for biomedical informatics and medicine. In: Springer Handbook of Bio-/Neuroinformatics, pp. 207–221. Springer (2014)
3. Bach, K., Althoff, K.-D.: Developing case-based reasoning applications using myCBR 3. In: Agudo, B.D., Watson, I. (eds.) ICCBR 2012. LNCS (LNAI), vol. 7466, pp. 17–31. Springer, Heidelberg (2012). https://doi.org/10.1007/978-3-642-32986-9_4
4. Bach, K., Mathisen, B.M., Jaiswal, A.: Demonstrating the mycbr rest api. In: ICCBR Workshops, pp. 144–155 (2019)

5. Bichindaritz, I., Marling, C.: Case-Based Reasoning in the Health Sciences: Foundations and Research Directions. In: Bichindaritz,, I., Vaidya, S., Jain, A., Jain, L.C. (eds.) Computational Intelligence in Healthcare 4. Studies in Computational Intelligence, vol 309. Springer, Heidelberg (2010)
6. Buitinck, L., et al.: API design for machine learning software: experiences from the scikit-learn project. In: ECML PKDD Workshop: Languages for Data Mining and Machine Learning, pp. 108–122 (2013)
7. Chandrashekar, G., Sahin, F.: A survey on feature selection methods. Comput. Electr. Eng. **40**(1), 16–28 (2014)
8. Chen, T., Guestrin, C.: Xgboost: A scalable tree boosting system. In: Proceedings of the 22nd ACM SIGKDD International Conference on Knowledge Discovery and Data Mining, KDD 2016, pp. 785–794. Association for Computing Machinery, New York (2016)
9. Fisher, A., Rudin, C., Dominici, F.: All models are wrong, but many are useful: Learning a variable's importance by studying an entire class of prediction models simultaneously. J. Mach. Learn. Res. **20**(177), 1–81 (2019)
10. Floyd, M.W., Davoust, A., Esfandiari, B.: Considerations for real-time spatially-aware case-based reasoning: a case study in robotic soccer imitation. In: European Conference on Case-Based Reasoning, pp. 195–209. Springer (2008)
11. Fontana, M.A., Lyman, S., Sarker, G.K., Padgett, D.E., MacLean, C.H.: Can machine learning algorithms predict which patients will achieve minimally clinically important differences from total joint arthroplasty? Clin. Orthop. Relat. Res. **477**(6), 1267–1279 (2019)
12. Harris, A.H., Kuo, A.C., Weng, Y., Trickey, A.W., Bowe, T., Giori, N.J.: Can machine learning methods produce accurate and easy-to-use prediction models of 30-day complications and mortality after knee or hip arthroplasty? Clin. Orthop. Relat. Res. **477**(2), 452 (2019)
13. Holt, A., Bichindaritz, I., Schmidt, R., Perner, P.: Medical applications in case-based reasoning. Knowl. Eng. Rev. **20**(3), 289–292 (2005)
14. Huber, M., Kurz, C., Leidl, R.: Predicting patient-reported outcomes following hip and knee replacement surgery using supervised machine learning. BMC Med. Inform. Decis. Mak. **19**(1), 3 (2019)
15. Hutter, F., Kotthoff, L., Vanschoren, J.: Automated Machine Learning. Springer, Cham (2019). https://doi.org/10.1007/978-3-030-05318-5
16. Li, Y., Shiu, S.C.K., Pal, S.K., Liu, J.N.K.: A rough set-based case-based reasoner for text categorization. Int. J. Approximate Reasoning **41**(2), 229–255 (2006)
17. Li, Y.F., Xie, M., Goh, T.: A study of mutual information based feature selection for case based reasoning in software cost estimation. Expert Syst. Appl. **36**(3), 5921–5931 (2009)
18. Lin, I., et al.: What does best practice care for musculoskeletal pain look like? eleven consistent recommendations from high-quality clinical practice guidelines: systematic review. Br. J. Sports Med. **54**(2), 79–86 (2020)
19. Rahman, Q.A., Janmohamed, T., Clarke, H., Ritvo, P., Heffernan, J., Katz, J.: Interpretability and class imbalance in prediction models for pain volatility in manage my pain app users: analysis using feature selection and majority voting methods. JMIR Med. Inf. **7**(4), e15601 (2019)
20. Rahman, Q.A., Janmohamed, T., Pirbaglou, M., Clarke, H., Ritvo, P., Heffernan, J.M., Katz, J.: Defining and predicting pain volatility in users of the manage my pain app: analysis using data mining and machine learning methods. Journal of medical Internet research 20(11), e12001 (2018)

21. Salamó, M., Golobardes, E.: Rough sets reduction techniques for case-based reasoning. In: Aha, D.W., Watson, I. (eds.) ICCBR 2001. LNCS (LNAI), vol. 2080, pp. 467–482. Springer, Heidelberg (2001). https://doi.org/10.1007/3-540-44593-5_33
22. Salamo, M., Lopez-Sanchez, M.: Rough set based approaches to feature selection for case-based reasoning classifiers. Pattern Recogn. Lett. **32**(2), 280–292 (2011)
23. Sandal, L.F., et al.: An app-delivered self-management program for people with low back pain: protocol for the selfback randomized controlled trial. JMIR Res. Protoc **8**(12), e14720 (2019)
24. Vallat, R.: Pingouin: statistics in python. J. Open Source Softw. **3**(31), 1026 (2018). https://doi.org/10.21105/joss.01026
25. Verma, D., Bach, K., Mork, P.J.: Modelling similarity for comparing physical activity profiles - a data-driven approach. In: Cox, M.T., Funk, P., Begum, S. (eds.) CBR Research and Development. Springer, Cham (2018)
26. Verma, D., Bach, K., Mork, P.J.: Similarity measure development for case-based reasoning–a data-driven approach. In: Bach, K., Ruocco, M. (eds.) NAIS 2019. CCIS, vol. 1056, pp. 143–148. Springer, Cham (2019). https://doi.org/10.1007/978-3-030-35664-4_14
27. Wu, A., Kharrazi, H., Boulware, L., Snyder, C.: Measure once, cut twice -adding patient-reported outcome measures to the electronic health record for comparative effectiveness research. J Clin. Epidemiol. **66**, S12–20 (2013)
28. Xiong, N., Funk, P.: Construction of fuzzy knowledge bases incorporating feature selection. Soft. Comput. **10**(9), 796–804 (2006)
29. Xiong, N., Funk, P.: Combined feature selection and similarity modelling in case-based reasoning using hierarchical memetic algorithm. In: IEEE Congress on Evolutionary Computation, pp. 1–6. IEEE (2010)
30. Zhu, G.N., Hu, J., Qi, J., Ma, J., Peng, Y.H.: An integrated feature selection and cluster analysis techniques for case-based reasoning. Eng. Appl. Artif. Intell. **39**, 14–22 (2015)

Advances in Applied AI

A Live-User Evaluation of a Visual Module Recommender and Advisory System for Undergraduate Students

Nina Hagemann[✉], Michael P. O'Mahony, and Barry Smyth

Insight Centre for Data Analytics, University College Dublin, Dublin, Ireland
{nina.hagemann,barry.smyth}@insight-centre.org

Abstract. Modern universities present students with a dizzying array of course and module options, making it difficult for students to make informed decisions about the modules they take and how their choices can help them achieve their educational goals. This is exacerbated when students are uncertain about their goals or when limited information about module options is available, as is all too often the case, leaving many students to follow the choices of their peers. The main contribution of this work is to describe a module recommendation and advisory system to help undergraduate students better understand the options available to them and the implications of their decisions. We describe a system that uses text mining techniques on raw module descriptions to generate rich, interconnected module representations. We demonstrate how these representations can be used as the basis for a visual recommender system and describe the results of a recent live-user evaluation to demonstrate the practical benefits of such a system on different groups of undergraduate students.

Keywords: Academic advising system · User study · Recommender systems · Educational Data Mining

1 Introduction

Today's third-level students often face a bewildering set of choices as they try to navigate their way through their formal studies. As higher education institutions increasingly endeavour to offer students a diverse range of options, deciding what to choose and determining how it might influence their future opportunities can be difficult, especially when students are in the early stages of their studies. Many institutions attempt to support students by providing a wealth of online information combined with in-person advisors, but many students can still feel overwhelmed and under-informed when making their choices. Oftentimes this means that they follow the crowd – choosing the modules that their friends and classmates tend to choose – rather than working to identify a more productive path through the available options that are more relevant to their aims and interests.

© Springer Nature Switzerland AG 2021
M. Bramer and R. Ellis (Eds.): SGAI-AI 2021, LNAI 13101, pp. 299–312, 2021.
https://doi.org/10.1007/978-3-030-91100-3_24

Educational Data Mining (EDM) approaches have been shown to provide valuable insights into educational data by applying a wide variety of techniques and considering different objectives [1]. In this work, we focus on an important challenge in EDM, recommender systems for module recommendations. Today recommender systems have a say in many aspects of our lives, from the books we read and the movies we watch to the places we go and even the people we meet. Therefore, it is natural to consider that similar ideas can be applied to the task of recommending relevant courses to individuals based on their personal interests and learning objectives. In this paper, we present a visual module recommender and advisory system for undergraduate students at University College Dublin (UCD) and discuss the results of a live-user study highlighting the system's utility in helping different types of students make well-informed choices.

The paper is organised as follows. In Sect. 2, we describe the related work in the area of online academic advising. We present the system architecture and technical details of our system and visualisation in Sect. 3. In Sect. 4, we present our user study's design, the research questions considered and the key findings from our study. We conclude this work with a discussion in Sect. 5.

2 Related Work

Educational institutions, especially universities, present a host of exciting challenges in helping staff and students provide an effective and enjoyable learning environment. Therefore, it is not surprising that many have turned their attention to technology-based solutions by drawing on ideas from recommender systems and machine learning.

This is, in part, exemplified by much of the work in the field of AI in education [2,3] and Educational Data Mining [4–6] which have considered a wide range of problems from supporting students in finding the right programme/major [7] to recognising when students may need additional support [8]. Over the last 20 years, a significant body of research has been developed when it comes to modelling students to personalise and adapt a learner's experience [2]. Institutions are interested in modelling student progress and even predicting student performance [9], which can identify struggling students at an early stage [8] and provide opportunities for intervention to reduce dropout rates [10].

In this work, we are interested in yet another challenge and opportunity in the education space by helping students determine what they want from their learning experience (e.g. overall learning goals and career objectives) and the choices they should consider to meet these goals and objectives. Previous work on this topic has explored a variety of approaches [2,3], usually involving some form of user model based on historical module selection and performance (grading) data; for example, the work of [11] relies on collaborative filtering and association rule mining algorithms in order to recommend elective modules based on expected grades. In [12], a recommender based on students' past performance as well as their interests is presented. A collaborative filtering approach is then used to recommend popular modules amongst similar students. A goal-based course recommender that uses recurrent neural networks and historical grade sequences to predict grades and prerequisites is trialled in [13]. While such approaches can be practical, they are not without their shortcomings especially given the often sensitive nature of the information used (e.g. grades and past module choices).

An alternative approach has been to explore content-based methods by using module descriptors as the basis for recommendations. For example, [14] build a *Course2vec* model, a Continuous Bag-of-Word model, that can predict course sequences in many-to-one relationships. In [15] a topic model approach is presented which can recommend courses that fit the students' interests and academic background by using student and course data.

In this work, we focus on supporting the students in making informed decisions by enhancing their understanding of their opportunities within the academic module space, rather than presenting them purely with recommendations. The visual representation we build acts as a natural explanation for module recommendations, something that has previously been stated as a missing piece in many approaches [2]. We support the students in their decision making by giving them the tools to self-explore the available modules, understand their inter-connectivity and importance to subsequent modules and career options. We build a system that is independent of past performance information and solely relies on module content descriptions. We show that we can use standard text mining techniques on these often incomplete and poorly written descriptors to build a system that allows students to gain knowledge about their academic options and ultimately allows them to make more informed decisions based on interests and goals rather than grades and hearsay.

3 System Architecture

For the purpose of this work, we draw on ideas from [16] and [17] to build a visual recommender system using module description data from University College Dublin. The objective of this system is two-fold: (i) to provide students with an interactive visualisation of the modules that are available to them given their programme of study; and (ii) to offer students specific recommendations for modules that fit their experience and goals. In this section, we present an overview of the system and outline the text mining techniques used to represent modules in a suitable way to visualise the resulting information space and generate recommendations.

3.1 System Overview

Figure 1 presents the overall system architecture, comprising of three main components:

1. The *data collection and processing* component is responsible for collecting and preparing the raw module description data. A web scraper collects this data from UCD's module catalog[1]; for this study, we focused on the Bachelor of

---

[1] UCD module catalogue, https://sisweb.ucd.ie/usis/!W_HU_MENU.P_PUBLISH? p_tag=MODSEARCHALL, last accessed 2021/09/08.

Science in Computer Science programme, which comprises 61 modules. Module descriptors are provided by the module coordinators and consist of various information such as title, trimester, stage, description, learning outcome and assessment information. They vary significantly in quality and level of detail provided, making for a challenging text-based recommendation approach. We perform standard preprocessing steps on all module descriptors (i.e. tokenisation, lemmatisation, and stop-word removal) to generate a word frequency vector for each module.

2. The *text analysis* component is responsible for generating module representations that are suitable for recommendations. The module vectors are used to build a Latent Dirichlet Allocation [18] model with five topics. This topic modelling approach allows us to map each module to a dominant topic. Using a cosine similarity metric, we calculate the module-to-module similarity.

3. The *visual recommender* component is responsible for the primary user interface, which presents the end-user with a network-based visualisation of relevant modules alongside a series of specific module recommendations based on their selections.

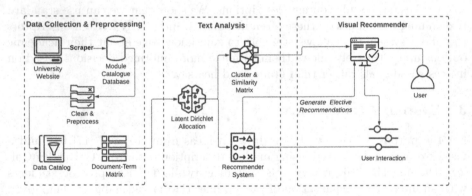

Fig. 1. System architecture diagram.

3.2   Generating Module Representations

To represent the module space adequately, we need to represent the modules based on their affiliation to a topic and the links between modules in subsequent years. To generate the representation for topic affiliation and module-module connectivity, we use two common approaches: cosine similarity and Latent Dirichlet Allocation (LDA). An overview of the approach is shown in Fig. 2. The basis for both techniques lies in the preparation of the scraped module descriptors. We use classic preprocessing steps (i.e. tokenisation, lemmatisation, and stop-word removal) to clean the module descriptors. A term-document matrix is created based on the frequency of each term $t_1, ..., t_n$ in each of the documents $d_1, ..., d_m$. This sparse matrix is then used to create two components for the visualisation:

1. Using the vector representation of the module descriptors we calculate the pairwise *cosine similarity* between each module $d_1, ..., d_m$. While there is potential to use more sophisticated metrics, we have found cosine similarity to perform satisfactorily. The cosine similarity matrix allows us to represent the connectivity between the modules in the students' programme space and establishes the basis for the elective recommender system.

2. We build a *Latent Dirichlet Allocation (LDA)* model, using the vector representation of the module descriptors. A commonly used technique in natural language processing, LDA is based on a generative statistical process that allows us to describe sets of documents by unobserved topics. These latent topics are based on sets of reoccurring terms presented in the term-document matrix. LDA allows us to calculate the distribution for each document $d_1, ..., d_m$, that is each module in the programme space, to the generated latent topics $topic_1, ..., topic_5$. We use these topics to cluster the modules into coherent groups of modules based on their dominant LDA distribution.

With these two module representations, we are able to visualise the programme space and generate recommendations in our visualisation. We present the details of the visualisation and recommender system in the following section.

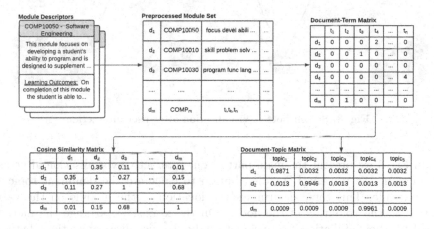

Fig. 2. Module representation for topic detection and module similarity.

3.3 Visualisation and Recommendation

To visualise our system, we developed an interactive visualisation that shows the similarities between modules and the underlying structure of the programme space. The interaction with the visualisation allows the students to actively explore the space, learn about its structure and possible career path/specialisation options.

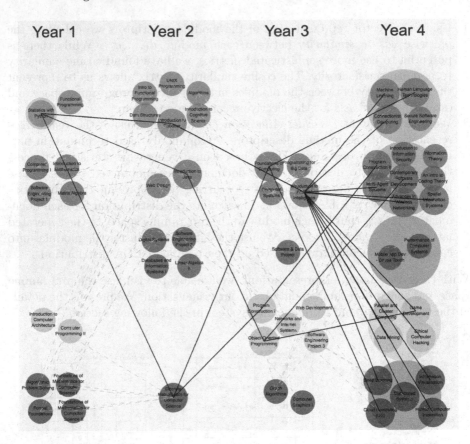

Fig. 3. Screenshots of visualisation after user interaction.

In Fig. 3 we present the main part of our interactive visualisation after user interaction. We use the LDA distribution to calculate the dominant topic for each module. This topic determines the location of the module on the y-axis as well as the colouring of the nodes. On the x-axis, we arrange the modules based on their affiliation to a year of study. To visualise connections between modules in subsequent years, we use the cosine similarity between the modules. The visualisation is implemented using `Plotly`[2] scatter plots and `Plotly Dash`[3] for the interaction functionalities.

Algorithm 1 presents the pseudocode for the recommender system. Initially, the user profile P is empty because the user has not indicated the modules that he/she is interested in. The default visualisation presents a summary visualisation of the modules that are available to them. When the student selects a module, m_i, the visualisation is updated to indicate the links between this

---

[2] Plotly Homepage, https://plotly.com/python/, last accessed 2021/09/08.
[3] Plotly Dash Homepage, https://plotly.com/dash/, last accessed 2021/09/08.

module m_i and the set of related modules, M_c; all of which are added to the user profile, P in line 5–7. If they are already included in the user's profile, then by reselecting the modules, the user is de-activating these modules in the visualisation, and they are removed from P; see lines 9–10.

During each loop, the user is presented with a new set of recommendations based on the current state of their profile. In brief, we recommend the top-10 most similar modules based on their average similarity to the modules in P; this similarity scoring function is provided in line 14 and used in line 15 to identify the top-10 most similar modules, which are then recommender to the user in line 16.

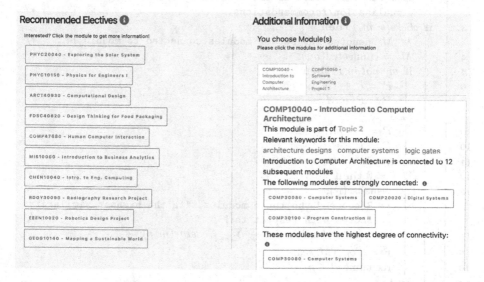

Fig. 4. Screenshot of elective module recommender system and additional information.

The recommended elective modules are presented to the student in the bottom half of the visualisation; see Fig. 4. We further provide additional information about each module that the user has selected. This includes information about the module's topic affiliation, as well as relevant keywords. The keywords are extracted using the *Computer Science Ontology (CSO)* classifier[4], a word embeddings model that extracts relevant concepts [19]. We show strongly connected modules as well as modules with the highest connectivity in the given path. The student can receive further information about the keywords and connected modules by clicking on them.

Additionally, we implemented larger *Topic Bubbles* in the final year, that depict the possible specialisations or career paths. Users can click these larger

---

[4] CSO Homepage, https://cso.kmi.open.ac.uk/cso-classifier/, last accessed 2021/09/08.

nodes and receive slightly different connections, recommendations and additional information. As this functionality is not in focus of this work we will not present it in further detail.

Algorithm 1: Update User Profile, Visualisation, and Recommendations.

Data: M the set of available modules; s student id
Result: Updated User Profile, Visualisation, and Recommendation
```
   /* P is in-session user profile.                                    */
 1 P = ∅;
 2 while session active do
       /* User remains active in the session by interacting with the
          visualisation/recommendations.                              */
 3     if clicks(s, mᵢ) then
           /* M_c denotes the set of modules connected to module mᵢ.  */
 4         M_c = connected(mᵢ);
 5         if mᵢ not in P then
 6             P = P + {mᵢ};
 7             P = P + M_c;
 8         else
 9             P = P - mᵢ;
10             P = P - M_c;
11         end
12         if P ≠ ∅ then
13             visualise(P);
               /* Recommend the top-n modules with the highest similarity
                  scores with respect to P.                            */
14             score(m) = lambda m : 1/|P| Σ_{p∈P} cosine(m,p);
15             R = Top_n(M, score);
16             recommend(R);
17         end
18     end
19 end
```

4   Evaluation

In this section, we describe the results of a live-user study based on the experiences of undergraduate students at University College Dublin who were invited to use the system to inform and reflect on their own module choices. In this paper, we consider two hypotheses:

- H1: Students can benefit from online academic advising tools and are receptive to using such a system.
- H2: Students who feel less informed about their programme structure or have lesser clarity of their career path options can benefit more from online academic advising.

4.1   User Study Design and Research Questions

The browser-based study was designed in three stages. In the first part, students were asked several questions about their background, year of study, career goals, and familiarity with their module options. After completing this questionnaire, participants then used the visual recommender after an introductory explanation of how it worked. Finally, students were asked to complete a second questionnaire to ascertain their experience of using the system and its perceived utility.

The primary aim of the study was to answer several research questions, including: (i) the clarity of their career goals; (ii) their level of familiarity with the modules offered as part of their programme of study; (iii) the quality of their experience when using the module advisor system; (iv) their improvement in knowledge about their programme structure and module options after using the system; and (v) how likely it would be that they use a similar system in the future again? The relevant questions from the accompanying survey are shown in Table 1. Questions *Pre* 1 and 2 were part of the pre-study questionnaire while *Post* 1, 2, and 3 are from the follow-up post-study questionnaire.

BSc Computer Science students (across four years of study) were invited to participate in this study. In total, 45 students completed all three parts fully, and their data form the basis of the results presented in what follows.

4.2   Evaluation Metrics

To evaluate these hypotheses, we consider the responses of participants to the five questions shown in Table 1. In particular, we consider the knowledge gained by students, and the perceived utility of the system, based on the clarity of their career goals and their level of understanding of their programme structure.

Table 1. Selection of questions and answers from pre- and post-study survey.

	Question (Answers)
Pre 1	Which statement best describes your ideas about career goals and specialisations? (clear idea, general idea, unsure, vague idea, no idea)
Pre 2	How familiar are you with your programme structure (i.e. modules in upcoming terms, pre- and co-requisites)? (very familiar, familiar, unsure unfamiliar, very unfamiliar)
Post 1	Would you say your knowledge about the overall programme structure has improved? (high improvement, some improvement, unsure, small improvement, no improvement)
Post 2	Please rate your overall experience using the programme visualisation. (very good, good, unsure, bad, very bad)
Post 3	How likely is it that you would use a system like this to gain knowledge about upcoming modules and module paths? (very likely, likely, unsure, unlikely, very unlikely)

Each of the pre- and post-questionnaire questions is answered using a 5-point Likert scale with lower values corresponding to more positive opinions. To simplify the analysis of each question, we convert the responses to calculate a *Relative Benefit Score (RBS)*, as shown in Eq. 1, which calculates the proportion of positive answers (<3) for each question, Q_i; e.g. $RBS = 0.8$ indicates that 80% of the answers were scored as either a 1 (*very high*) or a 2 (*high*) on the Likert scale.

$$RBS(Q_i, S_i) = \frac{|\{s : s < 3\}|}{|S_i|} \tag{1}$$

where $S_i = \{1, 2, 3, 4, 5\}$, i.e. the set of possible responses to a question.

4.3   Overall Analysis

Figure 5 presents the results of the student feedback on questions 1 and 2 from the pre-questionnaire. They show the percentage of feedback for each of the five response levels and the overall RBS score. For example, we can see how most students (73.3%) indicated that they were either *very familiar* or *familiar* with their programme of study, but just under half of the students (48.9%) indicated that they have a *clear* or *very clear* idea of their career goals.

The relevant results from the post-questionnaire are presented in Fig. 6. They indicate: that most students (71.1%) show either a *high* or *some* level of improvement in their knowledge and understanding of the programme structure as a result of using the system (see Fig. 6(a)); that 82.2% of students found the overall experience to be *good* or *very good* (Fig. 6(b)); and that 66.7% of students would be *likely* or *very likely* to reuse the system again (Fig. 6(c)).

While these results speak to the overall utility of the system from a student perspective—with a large majority of students positively disposed towards the system—they ignore the different perspectives that students may have. For example, do students with different initial levels of knowledge regarding their programme structure and career path benefit differently? Further, are students with a high programme structure familiarity less likely to use an online academic advising system?

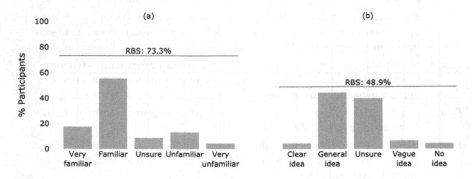

Fig. 5. Answers to question *Pre 1* - initial programme knowledge (a) and *Pre 2* - career path clarity (b).

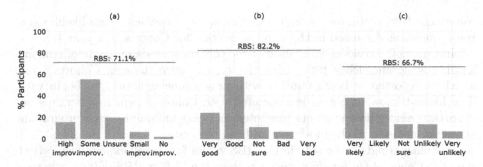

Fig. 6. Answers to question *Post 2* - knowledge gain (a), question *Post 1* - overall experience (b), and question *Post 3* - likeliness of reuse (c).

4.4 Group-Based Analysis

To answer such questions, we next look at a group-based analysis by dividing students into four distinct groups or cohorts, as shown in Fig. 7, based on their level of familiarity with the programme structure and the degree of clarity in their career goals. We can see that most students fall into one of three of these cohorts – Cohort 1 (*familiar/clear*) (20 students), Cohort 3 (*unfamiliar/unclear*) (10 students), or Cohort 4 (*familiar/unclear*) (13 students) – with only two students in Cohort 2 (*unfamiliar/clear*). This is perhaps not surprising as it indicates that students with clear career goals also have a good understanding of their programme structure/module choices. Due to the low numbers of participants in Cohort 2, we will emit those from further evaluation. The bar charts in Fig. 8

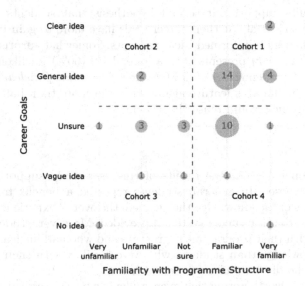

Fig. 7. Cohort definition.

report the RBS scores for the knowledge gain, user experience, and likelihood of reuse questions discussed in the previous section for Cohorts 1, 3, and 4.

In terms of knowledge gain, each of the cohorts shows a majority of students gaining some knowledge from using the system, even those in Cohorts 1 and 4, which reported as being familiar with programme structure, to begin with. The highest knowledge gain is associated with Cohort 3, which is perhaps not surprising since these students presented as being unfamiliar with programme structure and so had the most to gain from the system.

A similar trend can be seen in the RBS values for overall experience: Participants in Cohort 3 (*unfamiliar/unclear*) show the highest RBS of 90%, where as students in Cohort 1 (*familiar/clear*) are again slightly under the overall mean of 82.2% with an RBS of 80% and participants in Cohort 4 (*familiar/unclear*) showing an even lower score of 77%.

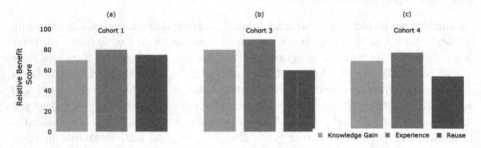

Fig. 8. RBS values for key features for Cohort 1 (a), Cohort 3 (b), and Cohort 4 (c).

These results support our second hypothesis that students who are less informed or less clear about their career goals have more to gain from the advisory system than more informed/clear students. Somewhat surprisingly, Cohort 3 (*unfamiliar/unclear*) presents with a lower RBS (60%) for likeliness of reuse than Cohort 1 (*familiar/clear*) (75%). Cohort 4 (*familiar/unclear*) showing the lowest RBS value for this feature again, with still more than half (54%) of the students saying they would reuse the system.

4.5 Discussion

Overall, we conclude that the results of this user study support both of our principal hypotheses. In general, students reported a benefit from using the system in terms of the knowledge they gained, the overall experience offered, and their likelihood to reuse such a system if provided. Moreover, students that were less familiar with their programme's structure and who had unclear career goals, gain more knowledge than students who were familiar with their programme's structure or who did have clear career goals.

However, it is worth noting that even students who were already familiar with their programme's structure or had clear career goals still benefited in terms of knowledge gain, user experience, and the likelihood of reuse. Going into this study, we felt that these students might not benefit to any significant degree from the recommendations provided if they already knew about the modules on offer and their connections over the years. Nevertheless, the results indicate that these well-informed students also benefited from the recommendations provided.

That being said, it is likely that the system could be fine-tuned or adapted to provide different types of students with different types of advisory feedback. For example, it should be possible to prioritise or emphasise information about programme structure or career opportunities in order to optimise the recommendations and support that each student receives.

5   Conclusion

In this work, we have presented a visual module recommender and advising system for undergraduate students to help them navigate through their many and varied options during their degree programme. The system works by mining information from (often incomplete) noisy module descriptors, and we have demonstrated how meaningful representation of the modules can be generated for use in a recommendation setting. The main contribution of this work is to describe the resulting recommendation system and present the results of a live-user study conducted to evaluate the utility of this system. The results show how a majority of students gained knowledge by using the system, enjoyed the experience, and indicated a high degree of acceptance (given their willingness to reuse the system in the future, if offered). We further assessed these benefits concerning different student cohorts based on differing levels of programme familiarity and career-goal clarity, with beneficial results observed for all cohorts. Thus we conclude that these results establish the validity of the approach taken. Future work may consider more sophisticated text mining techniques as well as ways for optimising recommendations for different types of students.

References

1. Romero, C., Ventura, S.: Educational data mining and learning analytics: an updated survey. Wiley Interdiscip. Rev. Data Min. Knowl. Discov. **10**(12), 1–21 (2020)
2. Iatrellis, O., Kameas, A., Fitsilis, P.: Academic advising systems: a systematic literature review of empirical evidence. Educ. Sci. **7**(4), 90 (2017)
3. Drachsler, H., Verbert, K., Santos, O.C., Manouselis, N.: Panorama of recommender systems to support learning. In: Recommender Systems Handbook, 2nd edn., pp. 421–451 (2015)
4. Du, X., Yang, J., Hung, J.L., Shelton, B.: Educational data mining: a systematic review of research and emerging trends. Inf. Discov. Delivery **48**(4), 225–236 (2020)
5. Guruge, D.B., Kadel, R., Halder, S.J.: The state of the art in methodologies of course recommender systems–a review of recent research. Data **6**(2), 1–30 (2021)
6. Aldowah, H., Al-Samarraie, H., Fauzy, W.M.: Educational data mining and learning analytics for 21st century higher education: a review and synthesis. Telematics Inform. **37**(1), 13–49 (2019)

7. Mostafa, L., Oately, G., Khalifa, N., Rabie, W.: A case based reasoning system for academic advising in Egyptian educational institutions. In: 2nd International Conference on Research in Science, Engineering and Technology, vol. 3, pp. 21–22 (2014)

8. Karypis, G., Elbadrawy, A.: Domain-aware grade prediction and Top-n course recommendation. In: Proceedings of the 10th ACM Conference on Recommender Systems, pp. 183–190 (2016)

9. Polyzou, A., Karypis, G.: Grade prediction with models specific to students and courses. Int. J. Data Sci. Anal. **2**(3–4), 159–171 (2016)

10. Burgos, C., Campanario, M.L., de la Peña, D., Lara, J.A., Lizcano, D., Martínez, M.A.: Data mining for modeling students' performance: a tutoring action plan to prevent academic dropout. Comput. Electr. Eng. **66**, 541–556 (2018)

11. Al-badarenah, A., Alsakran, J.: An automated recommender system for course selection. Int. J. Adv. Comput. Sci. Appl. **7**(3), 166–175 (2016)

12. Bydžovská, H.: Course enrollment recommender system. In: Proceedings of the 9th International Conference on Educational Data Mining, no. 1, pp. 312–317 (2016)

13. Jiang, W., Pardos, Z.A., Wei, Q.: Goal-based course recommendation. In: Proceedings of the 9th International Conference on Learning Analytics & Knowledge, pp. 36–45 (2019)

14. Morsy, S., Karypis, G.: Learning course sequencing for course recommendation (2018)

15. Morsomme, R., Alferez, S.V.: Content-based course recommender system for liberal arts education. International Educational Data Mining Society (2019)

16. Hagemann, N., O'Mahony, M.P., Smyth, B.: Module advisor: guiding students with recommendations. In: International Conference on Intelligent Tutoring Systems, pp. 319–325 (2018)

17. Hagemann, N., O'Mahony, M.P., Smyth, B.: Visualising module dependencies in academic recommendations. In: Proceedings of the 24th International Conference on Intelligent User Interfaces: Companion, pp. 15–17 (2019)

18. Blei, D.M., Ng, A.Y., Jordan, M.I.: Latent Dirichlet allocation. J. Mach. Learn. Res. **3**(4–5), 993–1022 (2003)

19. Salatino, A.A., Osborne, F., Thanapalasingam, T., Motta, E.: The CSO classifier: ontology-driven detection of research topics in scholarly articles. In: Doucet, A., Isaac, A., Golub, K., Aalberg, T., Jatowt, A. (eds.) TPDL 2019. LNCS, vol. 11799, pp. 296–311. Springer, Cham (2019). https://doi.org/10.1007/978-3-030-30760-8_26

AdverseGen: A Practical Tool for Generating Adversarial Examples to Deep Neural Networks Using Black-Box Approaches

Keyuan Zhang[1,2], Kaiyue Wu[1,2], Siyu Chen[1,2], Yunce Zhao[1,2,3],
and Xin Yao[1,2(✉)]

[1] Research Institute of Trustworthy Autonomous System, Southern University
of Science and Technology (SUSTech), Shenzhen, China
`xiny@sustech.edu.cn`
[2] Guangdong Provincial Key Laboratory of Brain-Inspired Intelligent Computation,
Department of Computer Science and Engineering, Southern University of Science
and Technology (SUSTech), Shenzhen, China
[3] University of Technology Sydney, Sydney, Australia

Abstract. Deep neural networks are fragile as they are easily fooled by inputs with deliberate perturbations, which are key concerns in image security issues. Given a trained neural network, we are always curious about whether the neural network has learned the concept that we'd like it to learn. We want to know whether there might be some vulnerabilities of the neural network that could be exploited by hackers. It could be useful if there is a tool that can be used by non-experts to test a trained neural network and try to find its vulnerabilities. In this paper, we introduce a tool named AdverseGen for generating adversarial examples to a trained deep neural network using the black-box approach, i.e., without using any information about the neural network architecture and its gradient information. Our tool provides customized adversarial attacks for both non-professional users and developers. It can be invoked by a graphical user interface or command line mode to launch adversarial attacks. Moreover, this tool supports different attack goals (targeted, non-targeted) and different distance metrics.

Keywords: Adversarial examples · Black-box attack · Deep neural networks

This work was supported by the Research Institute of Trustworthy Autonomous Systems, the Guangdong Provincial Key Laboratory (Grant No. 2020B121201001), the Program for Guangdong Introducing Innovative and Enterpreneurial Teams (Grant No. 2017ZT07X386) and Shenzhen Science and Technology Program (Grant No. KQTD2016112514355531).

M. Bramer and R. Ellis (Eds.): SGAI-AI 2021, LNAI 13101, pp. 313–326, 2021.
https://doi.org/10.1007/978-3-030-91100-3_25

1   Introduction

Deep Neural Networks (DNNs) has demonstrated advanced performance in a myriad of machine learning tasks such as image classification, speech recognition and natural language processing. However, lots of study have revealed the robustness problem of DNNs. In the domain of image classification, Szegedy et al. [19] first discovered that DNNs are vulnerable to minor crafted perturbations, which are called adversarial perturbations. Kurakin et al. [13] conducted experiments in the physical world and showed that many adversarial examples are misclassified even when perceived through the camera. Moreover, Adversarial examples are of value in the adversarial training. Goodfellow et al. [6] demonstrate the improvement of robustness using adversarial examples to train the model. Mixing adversarial examples with the clean data is the basis of many adversarial training methods. Consequently, it is of increasing importance to develop a comprehensive toolbox to integrate the state-of-the-art adversarial attacks so that users can systematically experiment with adversarial algorithms and gain keen insights into the robustness of deep neural networks.

So far, there are some existing libraries to study the robustness of DNNs. Foolbox [17] is one of the earliest toolboxes to run adversarial attacks against deep neural networks. It is built on top of EagerPy[1] and works natively with models in PyTorch, TensorFlow, and JAX. Although it provides compatibility for algorithms in different machine learning frameworks, it is difficult to adapt it to the library by rewriting the algorithms with EagerPy. Advertorch [4], cleverhans [16], Deep Robust [14] and Torchattacks [12] are recent adversarial attack platforms that provide service for adversarial attacks, defenses, training and robustness benchmarking. Comprehensive as all the above libraries are, they only provide an API for running the program. Therefore, beginners and other non-professional users may find it hard to utilize them to evaluate the DNNs by generating adversarial examples. First, users need to provide the label of image to be attacked, but it can be hard if they do not know which dataset the image comes from, determining the mapping from labels to images. Second, it's hard for users to learn the purpose or the hyper-parameters of algorithms, let alone select the proper attack method. Also, most of tools focuses on gradient-based attacks rather than black-box adversarial attacks. Some new algorithms are not included in existing tools, which may apply new criteria to evaluate adversarial examples, or assess the robustness of deep neural networks from different perspectives.

Compared with above adversarial attack libraries, AdverseGen[2] has new functionalities that others don't. First, it can be invoked by a graphical user interface (GUI). Users are able to upload an image, select appropriate attack parameters based on their requirement in the GUI and craft an adversarial example without the need of professional knowledge in DNNs. Second, this tool integrates more comprehensive black-box adversarial attacks. For example, we

---

[1] https://eagerpy.jonasrauber.de/.
[2] https://github.com/Pikayue11/AdverseGen/.

incorporate an attack algorithm utilizing a new metric called SSIM [20] to evaluate the similarity between an original image and its adversarial example. To
sum up, AdverseGen has the following new features:

- A **graphical user interface** that allows users to craft adversarial examples
  and evaluate deep neural networks without professional knowledge.
- A comprehensive integration of state-of-art **black-box** adversarial attacks.

The rest of paper is organized as follows. Section 2 introduces preliminary
concepts in adversarial learning. Section 3 gives an overview of our tool from the
perspectives of GUI and back-end design and the ways to implement a "test".
Section 4 explains the methodology and implementation details of attack algorithms in the toolbox. Section 5 concludes the paper and points out the future
work.

2 Background

Our tool is aimed to find adversarial examples by adding imperceptibly small
perturbations to an original correctly classified image so that they are classified
wrongly (i.e., to another class or even a specific different class) [19]. According to this informal definition, an adversarial example typically has at least two
properties: 1) it is misclassified by deep neural networks and 2) modified with
imperceptible perturbation. They can be formalized as the following two constraints:

$$F_m(x) \neq F_m(x_0) \tag{1}$$
$$D_i(x_0, x) \leq L_i \tag{2}$$

where x_0 and x denote the original correctly classified image and a perturbed
image. F_m is the prediction function of DNN model m whose input is images
and output is the classes of corresponding images. $D_i(x_0, x)$ is the i-th kinds of
distance between the original image and its adversarial example. L_i is a positive number representing the upper bound of the i-th distance. If x can satisfy
these two formulae, then it is called the adversarial example of x_0. Formula 1
represents the misclassified property and formula 2 represents the perturbation
should be imperceptible. Note that the distance can be calculated in l_p-norm,
such as l_0-norm, l_2-norm (i.e., Euclidean distance) and l_∞-norm, or evaluated
as the similarity between images like SSIM [20].

To generate adversarial examples that satisfy these two constraints, many
efforts have been made on adversarial attacks from different perspectives such
as attack's goal, attack's visibility, attack's required information of query on the
DNNs and so on.

According to the goal of attack, attack methods can be categorized as **Targeted Attack** and **Non-targeted Attack**. Our tool supports both targeted
and non-targeted attack.

- **Targeted Attack**: Given a DNN model F, an image x with ground truth label $y \in Y$, the goal of targeted attack is to induce F to give a special label $t \in Y$ $(t \neq y)$ to the adversarial example x'.
- **Non-targeted Attack**: If there's no specific $t \in Y$ given, the attack succeeded if the adversarial example is classified as any wrong label.

According to the attack's visibility, attack methods can be divided into **White-box Attack** [19] and **Black-box Attack** [2,10,15].

- **White-box Attack**: White-box attack has access to all the information about the DNNs, including its architecture, learnt weights, parameters used to tune the model, etc. With such information, the usual strategy of attack is to derive adversarial examples from the distribution of weights.
- **Black-box Attack**: Black-box attack can only query the DNNs and get the results, such as labels, or confidence possibility. There is no other model information available.

We only focus on black-box attacks in our tool because: 1) they're more practical than white-box attacks in the real-world scenarios. For some DNNs built on robots or embedded systems, it is hard to get the inner information of them. 2) black-box attack is also an important way to evaluate the robustness of DNN models in addition to white-box attack. For example, It does not require the gradient information and can apply to non-differentiable models.

3   System Design

One of the major objectives for our tool is the ease of use by non-specialists in deep neural networks so that they could use the tool as a preliminary test of a DNN's robustness without any knowledge of the DNN except for its input and output. The tool could also be used to generate adversarial examples used in adversarial training. To meet the above objectives, our tool has incorporated a comprehensive set of black-box attack methods, more than other existing tools, in addition to a user-friendly GUI. Our tool also allows for easy inclusion of new attack methods.

3.1   Graphic User Interface

To make our tool user-friendly, we develop our GUI by PySimpleGUI [3], a python GUI plugin. The procedure of generating adversarial examples can be mainly divided into three phases: before attack, during attack and after attack, which is illustrated in Fig. 1.

---

[3] https://github.com/PySimpleGUI/PySimpleGUI

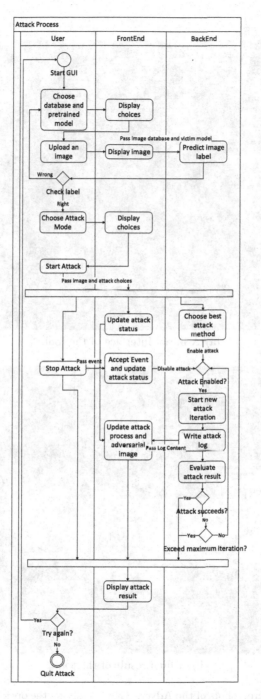

Fig. 1. Procedure of our tool for generating adversarial examples. It shows users' interaction with the program and the activities of front end and back end.

(a) A initial interface of the tool.

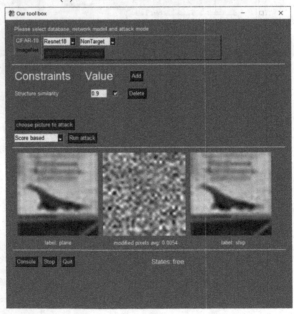

(b) A final result of the tool.

Fig. 2. Example screenshots of the AdverseGen. (a) shows the options users can choose before the attack and (b) shows the result after the attack.

Before Attack. The main task before attack is to help users configure following attack parameters: the victim model (i.e., the deep neural network to be attacked), dataset the victim model is trained on, attack goals (i.e., targeted or non-targeted attack), constraints and the original image. The GUI in this phase is depicted in Fig. 2(a).

Users can select the dataset based on the size of image they want to upload. After choosing the dataset, the victim model list will be updated in line with it. Then, if users want to launch targeted attack, they can choose the target class label in two ways, either by picking one in the choice box or uploading an image whose label predicted by the victim model will be the target class label. The latter approach is more suitable in the case when the selected dataset has a myriad of classes such as ImageNet (about 1000 classes). After that, users can add or delete constraints on adversarial examples, including l_0-norm distance, l_2-norm distance, l_∞-norm distance, and $SSIM$. When users upload the original image, the victim model will tell them its predicted label because users may not be sure about its corresponding class in the dataset. Finally, if all attack parameters are configured and confirmed, users can click `Run attack` button to start the attack.

When choose the distance constraints on adversarial examples, it is possible for users to choose multiple constraints. Some attack algorithms also support multiple constraints. However, a potential problem is that there may be no matched algorithm for some composition of constraints. So in the GUI, when users select one constraint, the program will search the matched algorithms and update available constraints. For example, if users first choose to limit the number of modified pixels (L_0-norm) and there is no algorithm that can confine both L_0-norm and $SSIM$ at the same time, then $SSIM$ will be disabled.

During Attack. During the attack, two main threads are working simultaneously: one is to run attack methods in the back-end, and the other is to update inner process of attack in the front-end (GUI) including the current image crafted by attack and the perturbation vector. Also, more details of the current result are displayed in the console window including the distance to the original image and its label information. In this phase, users are able to stop the attack or clear the message in the console.

After Attack. Figure 2(b) shows the final output after an attack. The image found by the attack algorithm and its label predicted by the victim model are displayed on the right. The perturbation vector, which is magnified for visualization, and the average value of modification are displayed in the middle. Users can know if the attack succeeds by checking information in the console.

Besides, we also provide some warning messages to better guide the usage of this tool. For instance, if users press button "Check image" without uploading a image, console will display a piece of warning message. Moreover, if users want to launch another attack when the current attack is running, a warning message will stop you from doing so.

3.2 Back-End

When design the architecture of the back-end, We refer to the system design of Foolbox [17]. Our back-end design is depicted in Fig. 3. There are three main classes in back-end: Model, Attacks and Log classes. Model is an abstract base class that represents the victim model to be attacked. Attacks is also an abstract base class that defines a process of performing an attack and judging the result. Log is the class that we add to record the attack process. All these three classes are invoked by Attacker class, which is an instance of the back-end. Similar to the Foolbox [17], we encapsulate distance metrics and attack goals as Distances and Criteria classes respectively to strengthen the extensibility of our tool.

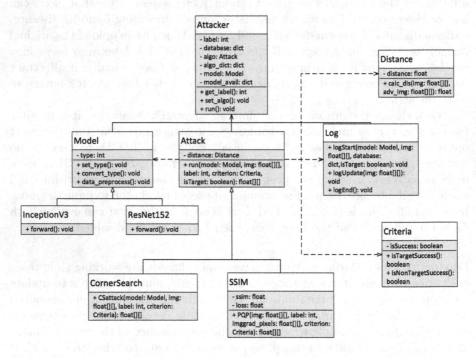

Fig. 3. Class hierarchy diagram of back-end. Attacker is the instance invoked by front-end to execute launch black-box adversarial attack based on user's option. It uses Model and Attack class to load the victim model and attack algorithm which relies on Distance and Criteria classes for attack evaluation, Log class for documenting attack process. Several concrete classes inherit these two abstract classes to represent specific models and attack algorithms. Note that the diagram only shows a fraction of concrete models and attack algorithms.

Attacker. The GUI creates an attacker instance and transfers the information selected by users to the attacker. There are three main functions of Attacker: First, it contains database and model information and can provide images' labels for the GUI. Second, it selects an appropriate algorithm based on the constraints supplied by the GUI. Third, attacker initializes a Log instance and transfer it to the attacking method to store and display midterm results.

Log. Log is to record the process of an attack. A Log class instance will be transferred to the concrete attack method. Every a few iteration (decided by attack method itself), the attack method will invoke the update function of Log class. It will output the inner information of images and then save them into a log file. These information is for professional user to study the process of the attack. Besides, Log will also update and save current perturbation vector and adversarial example as images for the front-end to display.

Models. Models create a bridge between the concrete DNN models and attack methods. To deal with the compatibility problem, it provides an function call for attack methods to get the result of model and the function can detect the inputs' type and change to the type consistent with the models. The Models need only provide the prediction result because the black-box attack algorithms do not need other information like gradient.

For convenience, we pre-load some Pytorch[4] models trained on CIFAR-10 or Imagenet into our tool, so that users can choose these model directly. Users can also add their own models: Firstly, the model class should be callable. Secondly, in the `models.model_importer.py`, users need to define the init function of the models, which encapsulates the model according to the framework the model uses. Finally, add the name of model to the dictionary in the `attacker` so that it can be found in the GUI.

Attacks. It is similar to `foolbox.attacks` in Foolbox [17]. Attacks is to call the concrete attack methods and test whether the result generated by the methods satisfies all the constraints. In the Foolbox, the constraints only contain one distance, but in our tool, it is allowed for users to select multiple distance constraints. So we extend the `Attacks` class and now it can test if the result satisfies multiple distance constraints.

Criteria. It is similar to the `foolbox.criteria` in Foolbox [17]. Criterion is used to define if the result attacks the model successfully. We choose the non-targeted and targeted attack as two criteria. Some modification is added to adapt to our architecture.

Distances. It is similar to the `foolbox.distances` in Foolbox [17]. Distance is used to calculate the distance between a original image and its perturbed image. On top of the common distance implemented in Foolbox, we also add the SSIM [20] metrics.

---

[4] http://pytorch.org.

We have chosen several typical criteria for users to choose: l_0, l_2, l_∞-norm and $SSIM$. These criteria are related to different problem characteristics. l_2 and l_∞ are two common norm values to compare the similarity of images. l_2-norm measures the Euclidean distance and l_∞-norm measures the maximum difference of pixels. l_0-norm is also one of the important metrics to measure how many pixels are modified. This is also an intriguing way to study the decision boudary of the DNNs [18]. Besides the normal norm value, there are some metrics that study the pictures of images. $SSIM$ is one of them, which measures the structure similarity of two images.

3.3   Test Implementation

Users can run the Main.py program to activate the GUI and then select the data set, victim model that the AdverseGen provided and upload an image to attack. For target attack, user should additionally upload an image to be served as the target label. Then the AdverseGen shows users the label of images the model predicted. If the label is wrong, it means images are already misclassified and users can change another image. After uesrs clicking 'Run' button, the attack begins. Three images displayed on the screen as shown in Fig. 2(b) indicate the original image, the difference between two images and the perturbed image. The consequence of the attack will be demonstrated on the console and the adversarial example will be saved in the result folder.

3.4   Summary

In this section, we have introduced the design of the GUI and the back-end. For the GUI, we considered the possible problems users might face when they choose algorithms and configurations in the command-line mode. Therefore, the goal of GUI is to help users describe their requirements (victim model, attack goal, constraints and original clean image) without knowing the information of the dataset, algorithms, etc. In the back-end, in addition to the features one would expect from such a tool, we have one feature which supports users to select multiple constraints.

4   Implemented Attack Methods

We have implemented five different black-box attack methods in our tool, with possible extension by including more attack methods, as indicated in Sect. 4.6. We choose these algorithms based on their success rate, the quality of adversarial exampels and the efficiency to perform attacks. To make our tool comprehensive, we try to find more algorithms that cover more metrics. We will introduce the concept of the algorithms we choose and the reason why we select these algorithms in the following part.

4.1   CornerSearch Attack

Among l_0 norm attack methods, we choose CornerSearch [3] for two reasons. First of all, the performance of the algorithm is very competitive or better than other state-of-the-art black-box l_0 methods since Croce and Hein [3] made a quantified comparison among them. The outcome of CornerSearch either has less perturbed pixels with nearly the same success rate or owns similar pixels but higher success rate. Secondly, CornerSearch tries to reduce the perceptibility of the adversarial example by limiting the perturbing area in the region of high variation and also banning perturbation along axis-aligned edges. The source code of the algorithm is from github[5].

4.2   Simple Black-Box Adversarial Attacks

We choose Simple Black-box Adversarial Attacks (SimBA) [9] from novel l_2 norm score-based attacks with following reasons. First and foremost, the algorithm is simple but perhaps a surprisingly strong baseline for black-box adversarial attacks. From a set Q of orthonormal vectors, the algorithm randomly draws a single vector q to perturb the original sample x as $x + q\epsilon$ or $x - q\epsilon$ where ϵ represents step size and can be controlled by the adversary. The idea behind this is to perturb images in a particular direction and check if it decreases classification accuracy of the victim model. Also, inspired by the research of Guo et al. [8], authors employed the discrete cosine transform (DCT) mapping signals into lower dimension space in order to generate low-frequency noises. Secondly, the algorithm has already shown its potential over other state-of-the-art black-box adversarial attack algorithms. Its experiment result indicates that their algorithm has achieved similar success rate with dramatically fewer average number of queries and less l_2 distance. Furthermore, the attack algorithm can outperform others even more by integrating other techniques. Yang et al. [21], for instance, utilized model-guided query coordinate selection, spatial data prior stemmed from the work of Ilyas et al. [11] and introduced transferability-based attack to further enhance the attack performance.

Simple Black-box Adversarial Attacks implemented by Yang et al. [21] is used by us.

4.3   Patch-Wise Attack

Patch-wise black-box adversarial attack [5] is the state-of-the-art l_∞-norm score-based attack that tries to launch transfer-based attack based on the surrogate model. We choose this algorithm for its high success rate. Compared with other adversarial attack methods crafting pixel-wise noises, Patch-wise Attack attempts to generate patch-wise noise so as to enhance the transferability without sacrificing the performance of surrogate model. Also, it introduced an amplification factor ϵ that adaptively adjusts the step size of each iteration to avoid

---

[5] https://github.com/fra31/sparse-imperceivable-attacks.

from being caught into the local optima during iterations. The experiment result in the work is rosy as well. Contrast to the current state-of-the-art attacks, their attack methods improve the success rate by 9.2% for defense models and 3.7% for normally trained models on average.

The Patch-Wise Attack implemented by Gao et al. [5] is used by us[6].

4.4 Perceptual Quality-Preserving Attack

We choose perceptual quality-preserving (PQP) [7] because it evaluates the similarity by SSIM and achieves a relatively high success rate. PQP fully utilizes the SSIM index. It first chooses candidate pixels with smaller SSIM, then keep modifying more pixels until it exceeds the preset threshold of SSIM. The source code is from github[7].

4.5 HopSkipJumpAttack

We select this algorithm for two reasons: firstly it is a decision-based attack [1], secondly it is effective, hyperparameter-free and query-efficient while its idea is clear and simple. HopSkipJump is an iterative attack method. For each iteration, it first uses Binary Search to reach the decision boundary, then uses Monte Carlo estimate to approximate the direction of the gradient. HopSkipJump can minimize l_2 and l_∞-norm for both targeted and untargeted attacks. The source code is from Foolbox[8].

4.6 Incorporating a New Algorithm into Our Tool

There are three main steps to incorporate a new algorithm into our tool. Firstly, the victim model is defined by Models class, which only accepts the image intensity from 0 to 1 and returns the confidence possibility vector of input images. So the related codes of the algorithm should be modified if it is required to query the victim model. Secondly, add a class to encapsulate the algorithm. This class should inherit one base class defined in Attacks and implement a method called run where the algorithm is called. Method run only needs to return the image perturbed the algorithm. The type of input images and output images are all Numpy. Thirdly, change the algorithms' selection strategy in the Attacker to define under what conditions the algorithm should be used. The third modification is not needed if the algorithm will not be used in the GUI.

5   Conclusion

We have developed AdverseGen as a tool to generate black-box adversarial examples on deep neural networks. It integrates state-of-the-art black-box adversarial

---

[6] https://github.com/qilong-zhang/Patch-wise-iterative-attack.
[7] https://github.com/dgragnaniello/PQP.
[8] https://github.com/bethgelab/foolbox/blob/master/foolbox/attacks/.

attack algorithms, which are more practical than white-box adversarial attacks algorithms for non-specialists to use. Our tool is equipped with a user-friendly GUI and command-line panel. It could be used to evaluate preliminarily the robustness of a DNN. It could also be used to generate adversarial examples used in adversarial training. Currently, the adversarial examples generated by our tool is only to fool one specific DNN model. In the future, the generalisation ability of the adversarial examples can be improved so that one adversarial example could fool many models at the same time. Other evaluation metrics like average query times and success rate can also be added to evaluate the DNN models. These metrics can show the performance of attack algorithms more comprehensively and reflect, at least partially, how robust the DNN is.

References

1. Brendel, W., Rauber, J., Bethge, M.: Decision-based adversarial attacks: reliable attacks against black-box machine learning models. In: International Conference on Learning Representations, pp. 1–12 (2018)
2. Chen, P.Y., Zhang, H., Sharma, Y., Yi, J., Hsieh, C.J.: Zoo: zeroth order optimization based black-box attacks to deep neural networks without training substitute models. In: Proceedings of the 10th ACM Workshop on Artificial Intelligence and Security, pp. 15–26 (2017)
3. Croce, F., Hein, M.: Sparse and imperceivable adversarial attacks. In: 2019 IEEE/CVF International Conference on Computer Vision (ICCV), pp. 4724–4732 (2019)
4. Ding, G.W., Wang, L., Jin, X.: Advertorch v0. 1: an adversarial robustness toolbox based on pytorch. arXiv preprint arXiv:1902.07623 (2019)
5. Gao, L., Zhang, Q., Song, J., Liu, X., Shen, H.T.: Patch-wise attack for fooling deep neural network. In: Vedaldi, A., Bischof, H., Brox, T., Frahm, J.-M. (eds.) ECCV 2020. LNCS, vol. 12373, pp. 307–322. Springer, Cham (2020). https://doi.org/10.1007/978-3-030-58604-1_19
6. Goodfellow, I.J., Shlens, J., Szegedy, C.: Explaining and harnessing adversarial examples. In: International Conference on Learning Representations (ICLR) (2015)
7. Gragnaniello, D., Marra, F., Verdoliva, L., Poggi, G.: Perceptual quality-preserving black-box attack against deep learning image classifiers. Pattern Recogn. Lett. **147**, 142–149 (2021)
8. Guo, C., Frank, J.S., Weinberge, K.Q.: Low frequency adversarial perturbation. In: Adams, R.P., Gogate, V. (eds.) Proceedings of The 35th Uncertainty in Artificial Intelligence Conference. Proceedings of Machine Learning Research, vol. 115, pp. 1127–1137. PMLR, 22–25 Jul 2020
9. Guo, C., Gardner, J., You, Y., Wilson, A.G., Weinberger, K.: Simple black-box adversarial attacks. In: International Conference on Machine Learning, pp. 2484–2493. PMLR (2019)
10. Hayes, J., Danezis, G.: Learning universal adversarial perturbations with generative models. In: 2018 IEEE Security and Privacy Workshops (SPW), pp. 43–49. IEEE (2018)
11. Ilyas, A., Engstrom, L., Madry, A.: Prior convictions: black-box adversarial attacks with bandits and priors. In: International Conference on Learning Representations (ICLR), pp. 1–25 (2018)

12. Kim, H.: Torchattacks: a pytorch repository for adversarial attacks. arXiv preprint arXiv:2010.01950 (2020)
13. Kurakin, A., Goodfellow, I., Bengio, S.: Adversarial examples in the physical world. In: 5th International Conference on Learning Representations (ICLR) (2017)
14. Li, Y., Jin, W., Xu, H., Tang, J.: Deeprobust: a platform for adversarial attacks and defenses. In: Proceedings of the AAAI Conference on Artificial Intelligence, vol. 35(18), pp. 16078–16080 (2021)
15. Liu, Y., Chen, X., Liu, C., Song, D.: Delving into transferable adversarial examples and black-box attacks. In: Proceedings of 5th International Conference on Learning Representations (ICLR), pp. 1–14 (2017)
16. Papernot, N., et al.: Technical report on the cleverhans v2.1.0 adversarial examples library. arXiv preprint arXiv:1610.00768 (2018)
17. Rauber, J., Brendel, W., Bethge, M.: Foolbox: a python toolbox to benchmark the robustness of machine learning models. arXiv preprint arXiv:1707.04131 (2017)
18. Su, J., Vargas, D.V., Sakurai, K.: One pixel attack for fooling deep neural networks. IEEE Trans. Evol. Comput. 23(5), 828–841 (2019). https://doi.org/10.1109/TEVC.2019.2890858
19. Szegedy, C., et al.: Intriguing properties of neural networks. In: International Conference on Learning Representations (ICLR), pp. 1–10 (2014)
20. Wang, Z., Bovik, A., Sheikh, H., Simoncelli, E.: Image quality assessment: from error visibility to structural similarity. IEEE Trans. Image Process. 13(4), 600–612 (2004)
21. Yang, J., Jiang, Y., Huang, X., Ni, B., Zhao, C.: Learning black-box attackers with transferable priors and query feedback. In: Advances in Neural Information Processing Systems, vol. 33, pp. 12288–12299 (2020)

Adaptive Maneuver Planning for Autonomous Vehicles Using Behavior Tree on Apollo Platform

Mais Jamal[1(✉)] and Aleksandr Panov[1,2]

[1] Moscow Institute of Physics and Technology, 141701 Dolgoprudny, Russia
mayssjamal@phystech.edu, panov.ai@mipt.ru
[2] Federal Research Center "Computer Science and Control" of the Russian Academy
of Sciences, 117312 Moscow, Russia

Abstract. In safety-critical systems such as autonomous driving systems, behavior planning is a significant challenge. The presence of numerous dynamic obstacles makes the driving environment unpredictable. The planning algorithm should be safe, reactive, and adaptable to environmental changes. The paper presents an adaptive maneuver planning algorithm based on an evolving behavior tree created with genetic programming. In addition, we make a technical contribution to the Baidu Apollo autonomous driving platform, allowing the platform to test and develop overtaking maneuver planning algorithms.

Keywords: Maneuver planning · Behavior trees · Apollo auto ·
Self-driving cars · Genetic programming

1 Introduction

In automated driving systems, maneuver planning is a significant challenge. In an unpredictable planning environment, the planner must make the best safe decision. A bad decision endangers not only the passengers' lives, but also the lives of pedestrians and passengers in other nearby vehicles.

Behaviour planners [12,13] and finite state machines (FSM) [11,19,22] are an early approach for intelligent vehicle maneuver planning and decision-making. The possible scenarios are implemented by hand to define its states and transitions between the states, and the rules are based on human experience. However, in complex control systems, such as automated driving systems, there are many rules and traffic situations, making it difficult to implement all world scenarios in the form of finite state machines. Later approaches [2,10,16,17] are based on probabilistic methods for dealing with uncertainty in decision effects, such as Markov Decision Processes (MDPs), as well as uncertainty in environmental observations, such as Partially Observable Markov Decision Processes (POMDPs). Such methods rely on maximizing the future possible rewards of actions to find the optimal policy. Because this process examines all possible

© Springer Nature Switzerland AG 2021
M. Bramer and R. Ellis (Eds.): SGAI-AI 2021, LNAI 13101, pp. 327–340, 2021.
https://doi.org/10.1007/978-3-030-91100-3_26

actions, it requires a significant computational load and is difficult to apply in vehicle behavior planning. A compromise in the number of the states is usually employed to reduce the calculations.

Behavior trees (BT) are another approach that has previously been used in AI games and, more recently, in robotics. BTs are a modular execution processes that switches between a finite set of tasks. A task can be any program or subroutine and it can be either a conditional task or an action task. The control flow nodes define the switching rules between the tasks. Control flow nodes can be either a sequence, which executes all of its children and returns success only if all of its children succeed, or a selector node (fallback node), which executes all of its children and returns success if one of its children succeeds.

Because of their flexibility, reactivity, and modularity, BTs are effective tools for autonomous agent maneuver planning. They are preferred over the FSMs when the number of transitions between the states is significant. As the size of the behavior tree rises proportionally to the complexity of the planning system, several attempts [4,5,14,20] have been made to learn a part or all of its structure from the environment rather than manually constructing the entire tree. The learning approach adapts the behavior tree to the needs of an autonomous vehicle's maneuver planning.

In this paper, we present an adaptive maneuver planning approach based on a learning behavior tree. As an example of maneuver planning, we consider the overtaking maneuver decision-making. We use genetic programming (GP) to learn the entire structure of the BT. The structure is denoted by the character string x. The problem is viewed as an optimization problem, with the GP algorithm searching in the genotype space G for the string $x*$ denoting a behavior tree program for which a fitness function f is optimized:

$$f(x) \rightarrow max : find\, \vec{x}^{*}\, so\, that\, \forall \vec{x} \in G : f(\vec{x}) \leq f(\vec{x}^{*}) = f^{*} \qquad (1)$$

The programming language $L = \{F, T\}$ of GP includes two sets: the function set F and the terminal set T. F includes all the possible functions in the program of a BT (control flow nodes). T includes all the possible conditions and actions.

In GP, the genotype space G includes strings representing all BT programs that can be constructed from elements of the programming language L. $P(t) \subset G$ denotes the population's state at time t. The GP's run-time is defined in terms of generations. N individuals $\vec{x_1}(t), \vec{x_2}(t), ..., \vec{x_n}(t)$ make up the population. The GP population evolves from the initial state $P(t = 0)$ by selecting μ parents $(P_p(t))$ for variation and then performing a *variation operation* to them to produce λ-offspring from each parent. The set of offspring is denoted by $P_c(t)$. The variation operation can be either a Crossover or a Mutation. After evaluating the fitness of the new offspring, it is combined with the population to form the new set $P_a(t)$. The new generation $P(t + 1)$ is a subset of $P_a(t)$. Over generations, the GP algorithm seeks for x values that maximize the fitness function f.

To conduct the experiments, we use the Baidu Apollo (open source) autonomous driving platform [1]. The platform has multiple subsystems that give the essential information to the planning subsystem regarding routing, localization, perception, and prediction of surrounding objects. Because of its structure, as well as its high concurrency and low latency, the platform provides an accurate simulator suitable for developing and testing planning algorithms for autonomous vehicles.

The decision-making process for overtaking maneuvers on the Apollo platform is integrated with motion planning in the planning subsystem. The planning subsystem receives as input: the HD map , ego vehicle location and speed, the surrounding objects, their estimated 3D shape, speed, and a prediction of their future trajectory and heading. In the presence of a slowly moving obstacle in front of the ego vehicle for an extended period of time, the candidates include paths from neighbor lanes to allow lane change if necessary. Then, for each candidate lane, the Piecewise-jerk optimizer [21] is used to optimize the path, followed by optimizing the speed profile of the optimized path. Finally, a trajectory decider will use a cost function to determine which lane to take. With the appearance of dynamic obstacles, the path-speed approach does not guarantee the optimal solution. In response to this limitation, the EM planner is designed to select a lane-change maneuver rather than overtaking (nudging) for high-speed dynamic obstacles.

We have integrated our overtaking planning method, as well as a technical contribution that allows for overtaking high-speed dynamic obstacles, into the Apollo platform.

The remainder of this paper is divided into five sections. Section 2 discusses some recent related works. Section 3 presents the proposed approach of adaptive planning using an evolving behavior tree and describes the simulation environment of Apollo. Section 4 presents the preparation for experiments in Apollo, as well as the experimental results, and analysis. Finally, Sect. 5 concludes with a discussion of future work.

2   Related Work

The works [2,3,8] used probabilistic methods of MDPs, POMDPs, or a combination of them with other methods to plan the autonomous vehicle's maneuver. [2] developed a driver assistance maneuver planning framework based on MDP that learns the policy using reinforcement learning (RL) by performing actions and getting a reward. The researchers attempted to compromise the significant computational load by combining offline and online planning. However, the framework still has unresolved issues with computational complexity as the number of objects in the surrounding environment grows. [18] developed an online POMDP algorithm to plan lane changes, which are a part of overtaking maneuvers. The computational complexity was reduced by the proposed algorithm. Because direct state transitions from a lane change left to a lane change right were not considered, the model had only eight states. The algorithm was tested in real-world traffic, but the execution required the driver to confirm the lane changes. [15] modeled the problem of intersection planning as an MDP that learns the policy with RL using what is known as Hierarchical

Options (HOMDP). Their results showed an improvement in performance and success rate over POMDP.

Other works like [9,16] depend on non standard methods for planning and decision-making of lane change maneuver for autonomous vehicles. [9] proposed a behavior planner that selects the appropriate maneuver by creating and evaluating a set of all existing gaps between close dynamic vehicles. A neural network was trained to predict future success based on prior experience and was involved in the evaluation process. The results indicated a high success rate for a lane change. However, the algorithm assumes that other vehicles behind the autonomous one will brake within cautious limits, allowing to change into relatively small gaps. As a result, in high-traffic situations, the algorithm will fail to complete the lane change. On the other hand, [16] proposed a behavior planner to decide whether to stay in the lane or switch to the right/left lane. The proposed planner's model is a state-action spaced deep Q-network that learns through reinforcement learning. The results indicated a relatively high success rate.

Although probabilistic methods and RL [6,7] have shown good results, they are not reproducible and computationally expensive, necessitating some compromise with the complexity of the planning system. When evolved through genetic programming, behavior trees, on the other hand, are adaptive and reactive. The GP searches for the best fit structure in the space of all possible tree structures without interference from the expert, which may lead to creative solutions. As a result, in this study, we use a behavior tree to plan the overtaking maneuver and genetic programming to find the best-fit structure of the tree.

3   Method

The structure of the overtaking maneuver's behavior tree is learned via genetic programming. The BT determines whether the ego car will overtake the moving vehicle (dynamic obstacle) in front of it from the right or left side, or if it will keep the current lane. The scenario includes several variables: the speed of the front obstacle, the number of dynamic obstacles on both the right and left lanes, their speed and their initial location.

In the Apollo platform, a technical solution for overtaking dynamic obstacles was developed and implemented with the genetic programming to evaluate the individuals (behavior tree structures) in the population.

3.1   Behavior Tree Primitives

The phenotype is the program version of the genotype. To evaluate the fitness of the BT individual, a mapping between genotype and phenotype is required. A set of all the BT's action, condition, and control nodes defines the phenotypic primitives. *KeepLane*, *SwitchToLeft*, and *SwitchToRight* are the possible actions. A Control node might be a sequence or a selector node. Each neighbor lane is split into three zones with varying lengths of s to reflect occupancy status (Fig. 1).

$s(t)$ indicates the safe following-distance and is dependent on the autonomous vehicle's current speed. The "three-second rule" is used to define it:

$$s(t) = \tau * v(t) \tag{2}$$

where $\tau = 3\ s$. There are two states for each zone: $\{free, occupied\}$. Furthermore, the speed of an occupant obstacle (km/h) is treated as a range and is expressed in six conditions: $[1, 10], [11, 20], [21, 30], [31, 40], [41, 50], [51, 60]$. Table 1 contains the whole list of conditions, actions, and descriptions.

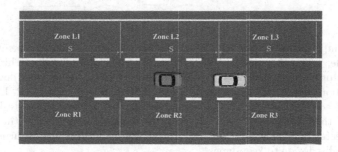

Fig. 1. The zones of the two adjacent lanes. The left lane is divided into three zones L1, L2, and L3. The right lane is also divided into R1, R2, and R3 zones. Each zone has a variable length of s.

The state of the BT can be one of three: SUCCESS, FAIL, or RUNNING. When an action is called for, the RUNNING status is activated. If the tree state is RUNNING for an extended period of time without the action being performed, the status is considered as a FAIL. Adding the RUNNING state to the tree's characteristics, not only excludes the trees that lead to an inapplicable actions, but it also maintains the tree's reactivity when the environmental conditions change during the action.

Characters representing actions and conditions (Table 1) form the terminal set $T = \{c, d, e, f, g, h, i, j, k, l, m, n, o, p, q, r, s, t, u, v, w, x, y, z, X, Y, Z\}$, which maps the behavior tree program (phenotype) to the genotype alphabet. The sequence node is represented by the symbol '&' with two parentheses containing the sub-trees under the sequence node. Similarly, the selector node is represented by the symbol '/' with two parentheses. The function set F is the set of two control functions:$\{\&, /\}$. For instance, the overtaking behavior tree that decides to overtake only when one of the adjacent lanes is clear of obstacles (Fig. 2) is represented by the following string: '/(&(cegY)&(ikmZ)X)'.

3.2 Genetic Programming

To find the optimal structure of the behavior tree, we use a GP execution scheme similar to the one described in [5]. However, for the planning optimization problem, we chose better-fitting parameters (Table 2). The binary tournament selection method is used to select μ parents for variation. This method selects two

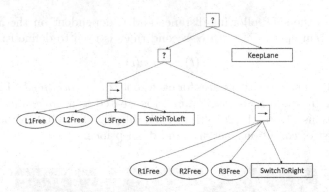

Fig. 2. A simple behavior tree for the overtaking maneuver. The tree begins with the selector node, which checks the SUCCESS state of its children nodes. This causes the second selector node to check its children. The first child (sequence node) evaluates the three conditions of the left lane's zones state; if three free zones L1, L2, L3 exist, the decision is made to switch to the left lane, and the tree returns the state RUNNING. If one of the three conditions is not satisfied, the sequence node returns the state FAIL and the selector node continues to check the second child; if it also returns FAIL, the tree will finally decide to keep lane.

random individuals and the one with the higher fitness value is chosen and added to the parents' set. Tournament selection allows individuals with poor performance to maintain their genotype, resulting in better exploration of the genotype space and less likelihood of being stuck in a local maximum. λ-offspring are created by performing either a crossover operation or a mutation operation on the selected parents with a probability (Algorithm 1). The variation operations are as follows:

Crossover Operation. This operation takes two individuals P_1, P_2 from the selected parents $P_p(t)$ and performs a sub-tree swapping to create two new offspring C_1, C_2.

Mutation Operation. This operation allows an individual to vary in one of three ways with probabilities: addition, mutation, or deletion. In addition, a random element from the programming language L is added to the tree. In mutation, a random element from L is mutated to another element in L. In deletion, a terminal element (condition or action) gets removed from the tree.

The mutation percent is set at 60% to improve the discovery of the searching space and to avoid the rapid growth in the depth of the tree caused by the crossover operation. 70% of the mutation operations are mutation or addition to explore all the possible actions and conditions while searching for the optimal solution. Following variation, all offspring $(P_c(t))$ are evaluated and combined with the population $P(t)$ to form $P_a(t)$. Afterwards, e individuals with the highest fitness values are selected from $P_a(t)$ to survive to the next generation (Elitist selection), and the rest of the generation$(N - e)$ is chosen by the binary tournament selection without repeating any individual. All previously surviving

Table 1. Primitives of the behavior tree. The possible actions and conditions, their description and the alphabet representing them.

Alphabet	Actions	Description
Y	SwitchToLeft	Switch from the current lane to the left lane
Z	SwitchToRight	Switch from the current lane to the right lane
X	KeepLane	Keep going on the current lane

Alphabet	Conditions	Description
c	L1Free	Is Zone L1 free? (Fig. 1)
d	L1Occ	Is Zone L1 occupied? (Fig. 1)
e	L2Free	Is Zone L2 free? (Fig. 1)
f	L2Occ	Is Zone L2 occupied? (Fig. 1)
g	L3Free	Is Zone L3 free? (Fig. 1)
h	L3Occ	Is Zone L3 occupied? (Fig. 1)
i	R1Free	Is Zone R1 free? (Fig. 1)
j	R1Occ	Is Zone R1 occupied? (Fig. 1)
k	R2Free	Is Zone R2 free? (Fig. 1)
l	R2Occ	Is Zone R2 occupied? (Fig. 1)
m	R3Free	Is Zone R3 free? (Fig. 1)
n	R3Occ	Is Zone R3 occupied? (Fig. 1)
o	ObsSpeed1–10	Is the speed of occupant obstacle in range [1,10] km/h?
p	ObsSpeed11–20	Is the speed of occupant obstacle in range [11,20] km/h?
q	ObsSpeed21–30	Is the speed of occupant obstacle in range [21,30] km/h?
r	ObsSpeed31–40	Is the speed of occupant obstacle in range [31,40] km/h?
s	ObsSpeed41–50	Is the speed of occupant obstacle in range [41,50] km/h?
t	ObsSpeedMore50	Is the speed of occupant obstacle more than 50 km/h?
u	EgoSpeed1–10	Is the speed of the Ego vehicle in range [1,10] km/h?
v	EgoSpeed11–20	Is the speed of the Ego vehicle in range [11,20] km/h?
w	EgoSpeed21–30	Is the speed of the Ego vehicle in range [21,30] km/h?
x	EgoSpeed31–40	Is the speed of the Ego vehicle in range [31,40] km/h?
y	EgoSpeed41–50	Is the speed of the Ego vehicle in range [41,50] km/h?
z	EgoSpeedMore50	Is the speed of the Ego vehicle more than 50 km/h?

Table 2. Parameters of genetic programming.

Parameters of GP	
Population size (N)	20
Parents number (μ)	10
Parents selection method	Binary Tournament
Offspring number (λ)	4
Max depth	6
Crossover percent	40%
Mutation percent	60%
Mutation/addition percent	40%
Mutation/deletion percent	30%
Mutation/mutation percent	30%
Elitist selection percent	10%

individuals are evaluated again on the new scenario in the next iteration of GP. The following equation combines the previous fitness value associated with the survived individuals with the new fitness value calculated on the new iteration's scenario:

$$f(\overrightarrow{x}(t)) = \alpha * f(\overrightarrow{x}(t-1)) + (1-\alpha) * f(\overrightarrow{x}(t)) \tag{3}$$

where $\alpha = 1/2$. In this manner, a BT program's fitness will be defined as an integration of its fitness over scenarios.

Each individual's (BT) fitness in the scenario is determined by two factors: reaching the goal without colliding, and the time it takes to reach the goal following this BT program. If the individual (BT) caused a collision, a negative fitness value will be assigned to it. If the goal is reached without a collision, the fitness is defined as the difference between the time spent following the action $KeepLane\ T^{a_0}$ and the time spent following the tree's output action T^{a_x}:

$$f(x) = T^{a_0} - T^{a_x} \tag{4}$$

As a result, the BT that results to an overtaking and reaching the goal faster without colliding will be assigned a high fitness value. The BT that leads to the $KeepLane$ action will be assigned a fitness value close to zero.

3.3 Implementation in Apollo

The Apollo planning module includes two essential planners, *Public Road Planner*, which handles lane follow, junction, and U-sharp turn scenarios, and *Open Space Planner*, which handles parking scenarios. Every planner initializes a *scenario manager* and updates it every planning cycle. The *scenario manager* specifies the current scenario, processes it, and executes a series of predefined tasks for each scenario. Tasks can either be deciders or optimizers.

To demonstrate the planning process in Apollo, we consider the planning of a lane-follow scenario in which the planner can make an overtaking decision. The planning process begins with the *Lane Change Decider*, which determines if the road has additional lane available for change if necessary. *Path Lane Borrow Decider* then checks for the existence of a front static long-term blocking obstacle, making the decision to overtake if it is there. The optimal path profile in Frenet is then found using the Jerk path optimizer, followed by the optimal speed profile in Frenet using the Jerk speed optimizer.

The *Path Lane Borrow Decider* in Apollo is designed to make overtaking decisions exclusively for static front obstacles and obstacles with very slow speeds. The proposed behavior tree method is implemented in a BT decider, which is added to the tasks of the Lane-follow scenario in Apollo before the *Path Lane Borrow Decider*. All the primitive conditions and actions of the BT are programmed in the decider as functions. The decider begins by decoding the tree string generated by the GP from the genotype space to the phenotypic space. The decider then runs a recursive tree execution function to perform the behavior tree tasks based on the control flow nodes. For the behavior tree evaluation process, an extra collision check function and a goal-reaching function were also developed.

4 Experiment

4.1 Simulation in Apollo

The source code of Apollo is the pre-version of the Baidu Apollo Open Platform 6. The source code was modified and a decider of the behavior tree was added to the tasks to allow testing of the overtaking maneuver, performance of the behavior tree, and evaluation of it on each planning cycle. To run experiments locally we used an Intel Core i7-9700 CPU:8×3 GHz computer with 32 GB RAM, and NVIDIA GeForce RTX 2080 Ti video card. The behavior tree decider runs with a frequency of $\approx$10 Hz frequency. The algorithm simulates a random overtaking scenario to evaluate the individuals (BTs) during the GP.

Algorithm 1. Genetic Programming

$INPUT : N, MaxGenerations, e(ElitesNumber),$
$Crossover - Percent.$
$OUTPUT : \overrightarrow{x}^{*} so\ that\ \forall \overrightarrow{x} \in G : f(\overrightarrow{x}) \leq f(\overrightarrow{x}^{*}) = f^{*}$
$t = 0$
$initialize : P(t = 0) = \{\overrightarrow{x_1}(0), \overrightarrow{x_2}(0), ..., \overrightarrow{x_n}(0)\} \in G$
while $t < MaxGenerations$ **do**
   $evaluate : P(t) : \{f(\overrightarrow{x_1}(t)), f(\overrightarrow{x_2}(t)), ..., f(\overrightarrow{x_n}(t))\}$
   $P_p(t) = TournamentSelection(\mu, P(t))$
   $P_c(t) = \emptyset$
   for $i = 1, 2, ..., \mu$ **do**
     $rand = RandNumber(1 - 100)$
     $P_1 = P_p^i(t)$
     if $rand \leq Crossover - Percent$ **then**
       for $k = 1, ..., \lambda/2$ **do**
         $P_2 = RandSelect(P_p(t))$
         $C_1, C_2 = CrossoverOperation(P_1, P_2)$
         $P_c(t) = P_c(t) \cup C_1 \cup C_2$
       end for
     else
       for $k = 1, ..., \lambda$ **do**
         $C = MutationOperation(P_1)$
         $P_c(t) = P_c(t) \cup C$
       end for
     end if
   end for
   $evaluate : P_c(t) : \{f(\overrightarrow{x_{c1}}(t)), f(\overrightarrow{x_{c2}}(t)), ..., f(\overrightarrow{x_{cn}}(t))\}$
   $P_a(t) = P_c(t) \cup P(t)$
   $P(t + 1) = ElitistSelection(e, P_a(t))$
   $P(t + 1) = P(t + 1) \cup TournamentSelect(N - e, P_a(t))$
   $t \leftarrow t + 1$
end while

The overtaking scenario includes three lanes on a forward highway road, with the ego vehicle always in the middle lane (Fig. 3). A front obstacle with a starting distance of 20 m exists. The speed of the front obstacles is assigned at random between 2.7 and 5.5 m/s. There are also 5 obstacles placed at random on the neighboring lanes. The neighboring obstacles move at random speeds (between 2.7 and 6.5 m/s). The experiments are run in Apollo's SimControl mode, and the obstacles data is published at a rate 10 Hz on the Perception channel. Starting from the autonomous agent's initial location, the distance to the goal is 200 m.

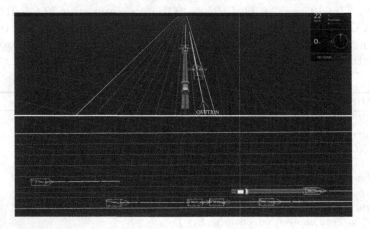

Fig. 3. A random overtaking scenario. The ego vehicle is surrounded by five random dynamic obstacles and one in the front.

4.2   Experiment Result and Analysis

Running 50 generations of the GP algorithm took nearly 48 h, which is considered very time-consuming. When compared to the time required for each experiment to evaluate a BT individual, the time required for creating offspring and decoding the BT's string is relatively short and may be neglected. Each evaluation experiment can last between 10 and 70 s, depending on the tree's output action and validity. The results of running the GP algorithm for the first 50 generations, starting with a random first population $P(0)$, are shown in Fig. 4. A behavior tree can either be successful or unsuccessful. A tree is considered successful if it achieves its goal without colliding with any of the surrounding obstacles, regardless of the type of output action (KeepLane, SwitchToLeft, SwitchToRight). $S(t) \subseteq P(t)$ denotes the set of successful BTs, $O(t) \subseteq S(t)$ denotes the set of successful BTs with an overtake output action. While a tree is considered an unsuccessful tree in the following cases: the BT output action resulted in a collision, the action run-time has exceeded a predefined maximum limit and the action has not yet been performed, or the BT's execution has ended and no action is running.

$U(t) \subseteq P(t)$ denote the set of unsuccessful BTs and $P(t) = S(t) \cup U(t)$. The results in Fig. 4 show that the number of successful trees increases over generations, while the number of unsuccessful trees decreases significantly. It can be seen that the evolving population has found its way to generate behavior trees with an overtaking action that has been successful in some scenarios. Starting with a random population may cause the searching problem to take longer, but such an algorithm should never end in a local maximum, because the mutation feature and the selection method spread the searching process.

Table 3. A comparison between GP with prior and GP with random $P(0)$.

t	GP with prior			GP with random		
	$S(t)\%$	$O(t)\%$	$L(t)\%$	$S(t)\%$	$O(t)\%$	$L(t)\%$
1	80	0	0	5	0	5
5	100	0	5	75	0	20
10	100	0	15	95	0	60
15	95	5	40	95	0	15
20	100	75	35	100	0	60
25	100	90	75	100	0	60
30	100	75	95	100	0	50

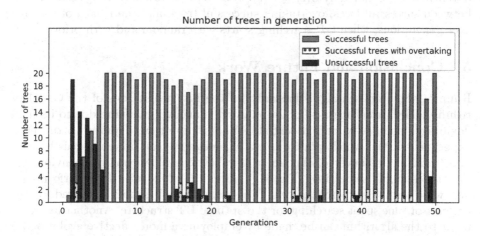

Fig. 4. A bar graph of successful and unsuccessful trees over generations from the first generation to the 50th. The initial population is a randomly generated population.

Figure 5 shows the results of running the GP algorithm for the first 30 generations, starting from an initial population that contains one simple effective behavior tree (Fig. 2). Results show that the genetic algorithm is dynamically converging to the optimum fitness value. The algorithm optimizes the fitness function over generations, by evolving the trees that output an overtaking action

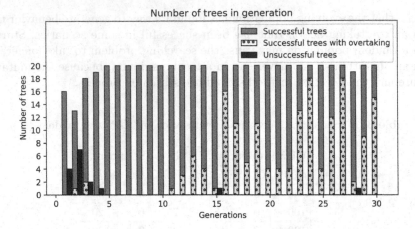

Number of trees in generation

Fig. 5. A bar graph of the number of successful and unsuccessful trees over generations from the first generation to the 30th. The initial population contains one simple effective behavior tree.

to reach the goal faster, and also keeps the size of the tree reasonable due to the constraint of maximum depth of the behavior tree.

The set of BT individuals with a length of l bigger than 40 symbols (including parentheses) is denoted by $L(t) \subseteq P(t)$. Table 3 presents a percentage comparison between successful trees, overtaking successful trees, and the length of the tree over generations, when GP searching starts with random and with prior.

5   Conclusion and Future Work

Running the proposed algorithm only for the first generations of the GP algorithm yielded promising results for adaptive maneuver planning due to its high flexibility, modularity, and potential. Although the time required to run each experiment in the Apollo platform is a challenge, we can overcome this by running multiple instances of Apollo in parallel to evaluate many behavior tree structures at the same time (Fig. 6). This can be done with high-performance hardware such as supercomputers. This solution will significantly reduce the amount of time spent searching for the optimal BT structure. Another improvement to the algorithm can be made by employing a more effective evolutionary

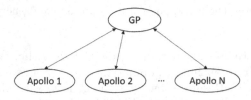

Fig. 6. Multi-instance architecture of GP

algorithm, expanding the environmental conditions, and including information from Apollo's Prediction module.

Acknowledgements. The reported study was supported by RFBR, research Project No. 18-29-22027.

References

1. Baidu Apollo team: Apollo: Open Source Autonomous Driving, howpublished. https://github.com/apolloauto/apollo, note = Accessed 11 Feb 2019
2. Brechtel, S., Gindele, T., Dillmann, R.: Probabilistic mdp-behavior planning for cars. In: 2011 14th International IEEE Conference on Intelligent Transportation Systems (ITSC), pp. 1537–1542. IEEE (2011)
3. Brechtel, S., Gindele, T., Dillmann, R.: Probabilistic decision-making under uncertainty for autonomous driving using continuous pomdps. In: 17th International IEEE Conference on Intelligent Transportation Systems (ITSC), pp. 392–399 (2014). https://doi.org/10.1109/ITSC.2014.6957722
4. Fu, Y., Qin, L., Yin, Q.: A reinforcement learning behavior tree framework for game AI. In: 2016 International Conference on Economics, Social Science, Arts, Education and Management Engineering, pp. 573–579. Atlantis Press (2016)
5. Iovino, M., Styrud, J., Falco, P., Smith, C.: Learning behavior trees with genetic programming in unpredictable environments. arXiv preprint arXiv:2011.03252 (2020)
6. Ivanov, D., Panov, A.I.: Application of reinforcement learning in open space planner for apollo auto. In: Kovalev, S., Tarassov, V., Snasel, V., Sukhanov, A. (eds.) IITI 2021. LNNS, vol. 330, pp. 35–43. Springer, Cham (2022). https://doi.org/10.1007/978-3-030-87178-9_4
7. Kiselev, G., Panov, A.: Q-learning of spatial actions for hierarchical planner of cognitive agents. In: Ronzhin, A., Rigoll, G., Meshcheryakov, R. (eds.) ICR 2020. LNCS (LNAI), vol. 12336, pp. 160–169. Springer, Cham (2020). https://doi.org/10.1007/978-3-030-60337-3_16
8. Martinson, M., Skrynnik, A., Panov, A.I.: Navigating autonomous vehicle at the road intersection simulator with reinforcement learning. In: Kuznetsov, S.O., Panov, A.I., Yakovlev, K.S. (eds.) RCAI 2020. LNCS (LNAI), vol. 12412, pp. 71–84. Springer, Cham (2020). https://doi.org/10.1007/978-3-030-59535-7_6
9. Menéndez-Romero, C., Winkler, F., Dornhege, C., Burgard, W.: Maneuver planning for highly automated vehicles. In: 2017 IEEE Intelligent Vehicles Symposium (IV), pp. 1458–1464. IEEE (2017)
10. Mirchevska, B., Pek, C., Werling, M., Althoff, M., Boedecker, J.: High-level decision making for safe and reasonable autonomous lane changing using reinforcement learning. In: 2018 21st International Conference on Intelligent Transportation Systems (ITSC), pp. 2156–2162. IEEE (2018)
11. Montemerlo, M., et al.: Junior: the stanford entry in the urban challenge. J. Field Robot. **25**(9), 569–597 (2008)
12. Osipov, G.S., Panov, A.I.: Rational behaviour planning of cognitive semiotic agent in dynamic environment. Sci. Tech. Inf. Process. **48**(6) (2021, In press)
13. Panov, A.I.: Goal setting and behavior planning for cognitive agents. Sci. Tech. Inf. Process. **46**(6), 404–415 (2019). https://doi.org/10.3103/S0147688219060066

14. Pereira, R.d.P., Engel, P.M.: A framework for constrained and adaptive behavior-based agents. arXiv preprint arXiv:1506.02312 (2015)
15. Qiao, Z., Muelling, K., Dolan, J., Palanisamy, P., Mudalige, P.: Pomdp and hierarchical options MDP with continuous actions for autonomous driving at intersections. In: 2018 21st International Conference on Intelligent Transportation Systems (ITSC), pp. 2377–2382. IEEE (2018)
16. Rezaee, K., Yadmellat, P., Nosrati, M.S., Abolfathi, E.A., Elmahgiubi, M., Luo, J.: Multi-lane cruising using hierarchical planning and reinforcement learning. In: 2019 IEEE Intelligent Transportation Systems Conference (ITSC), pp. 1800–1806. IEEE (2019)
17. Ulbrich, S., Maurer, M.: Probabilistic online pomdp decision making for lane changes in fully automated driving. In: 16th International IEEE Conference on Intelligent Transportation Systems (ITSC 2013), pp. 2063–2067. IEEE (2013)
18. Ulbrich, S., Maurer, M.: Probabilistic online pomdp decision making for lane changes in fully automated driving. In: 16th International IEEE Conference on Intelligent Transportation Systems (ITSC 2013), pp. 2063–2067 (2013). https://doi.org/10.1109/ITSC.2013.6728533
19. Urmson, C., et al.: Autonomous driving in urban environments: boss and the urban challenge. J. Field Robot. 25(8), 425–466 (2008)
20. Zhang, Q., Yao, J., Yin, Q., Zha, Y.: Learning behavior trees for autonomous agents with hybrid constraints evolution. Appl. Sci. 8(7), 1077 (2018)
21. Zhang, Y., Sun, H., Zhou, J., Pan, J., Hu, J., Miao, J.: Optimal vehicle path planning using quadratic optimization for baidu apollo open platform. In: 2020 IEEE Intelligent Vehicles Symposium (IV), pp. 978–984 (2020). https://doi.org/10.1109/IV47402.2020.9304787
22. Ziegler, J., et al.: Making bertha drive–an autonomous journey on a historic route. IEEE Intell. Transp. Syst. Mag. 6(2), 8–20 (2014)

Behavioural User Identification from Clickstream Data for Business Improvement

Gaurav Misra, Matteo Migliavacca, and Fernando E. B. Otero[✉]

School of Computing, University of Kent, Canterbury, UK
{G.Misra,M.Migliavacca,F.E.B.Otero}@kent.ac.uk

Abstract. One of the key elements for businesses to succeed is to get to know their customers. Traditionally this task has been performed through user studies, however, over the last few years clickstream analysis has been proposed as a potential way of conducting automated behavioural studies at scale. In this paper, we explore the use of a recently-proposed unsupervised data-mining technique to identify common behavioural patterns from a clickstream and use them to automatically group users into clusters. In particular, our goal is to validate the potential of behavioural user identification with respect to a key business-level objective. We consider to which extent it is possible to link overall user in-application behaviour to the completion of a particular business-relevant action. Identifying behavior patterns resulting in such business-relevant actions can enable businesses to make changes to their interface, target relevant user groups or trigger actionable insights, all with the objective of maximizing the likelihood of preferable user actions. We analyzed a realworld dataset from a mobile application deployed on both the iOS and Android platforms for this experiment.

1 Introduction

The growing amount of data collected by online services, in particular mobile apps, presents a unique opportunity to understand how users interact with services. The analysis of these data could potentially help to identify frequent, unexpected and desired (or undesired) user behaviours, which in turn can be used to increase user experience and engagement. This insight may also be leveraged by businesses to personalize their product for certain behavior profiles, with the objective of steering users towards monetizable actions. Traditionally, user studies have been employed to understand how users interact with services. However, one significant drawback of employing user studies to analyse online services is the need to establish the questions in advance, potentially limiting the ability to characterise unexpected and undesired behaviour. Such studies also suffer from several biases (e.g., sampling, self-selection bias), which ends up leading to a situation where the business tends to capture data from only a subset of their users (or behavior profiles), limiting their reach and therefore making the findings less generalizable and actionable.

© Springer Nature Switzerland AG 2021
M. Bramer and R. Ellis (Eds.): SGAI-AI 2021, LNAI 13101, pp. 341–354, 2021.
https://doi.org/10.1007/978-3-030-91100-3_27

Recently, the analysis of actual user actions has emerged as an alternative to user studies, in order to learn about user behavior. The ability to collect and analyze usage data from websites and apps has enabled researchers to create data mining techniques which can leverage this data to identify behavior patterns prevalent among users. Wang et al. [12, 13] proposed one such technique by using clickstream information to detect and model user behaviour. A *clickstream* is a sequence of timestamped actions performed by a user while interacting with an online system. Thus, the sequence of actions defines the user behaviour on the system, and the analysis of these sequences can lead to the identification of common patterns of user behaviour—i.e., common sequence of actions performed by users. To this end, they first create a graph to capture the similarity between user clickstreams, and then apply clustering to group users according to their behavioural patterns. Clustering is an unsupervised task, which consists of finding a finite set of categories (clusters) to describe the data [4, 14]. Clusters are created based on the similarity of features' values—in this case, the frequency of users' action patterns—and, as a result, similar users are grouped together. A clustering algorithm aims at grouping the users into clusters so that the similarity of users in a cluster is maximised and the similarity of users from different clusters is minimised.

The analysis of users' clickstreams addresses the limitation of user studies—in relation to both the design of questions and scale of users—since user behaviour is automatically detected based on how users interact with the system. Authors in [12, 13] employed a clickstream user behavioural model to detect malicious users. The rationale is to cluster users based on their clickstream to differentiate the behaviour of normal and malicious users. They further extended their technique to model user behaviours as hierarchical clickstream clusters, using an iterative feature pruning clustering (IFPC) algorithm. User behaviour is represented as a tree of clusters, where high-level clusters are formed based on the most important features and sub-clusters at lower levels of the hierarchy are formed based on less important features. The feature set that characterises each cluster can then be used to understand the behaviour of users of the cluster. They presented three case studies showing advantages of the iterative feature pruning algorithm in identifying *inactive*, *hostile* and *malicious* user behaviours in two real-world online social networks. Other researchers have successfully used clickstream data to detect malicious social bots [6, 10], model user engagement [5] and identify e-commerce item access patterns [15].

In this paper, we apply the IFPC algorithm to analyse clickstream data from a real-world mobile application available for both iOS and Android platforms. We use this technique as it provides a view of the most dominant behavior patterns within clusters, which in our case, is demonstrated by the sequence of events that are invoked by user actions. Another advantage of using IFPC is that it has been proven to be able to analyze previously unknown behavior patterns, due to its non-reliance on prior knowledge of labels [13]. Our aim is to evaluate its performance in identifying patterns in the user behaviour that are linked to a particular action on the system. Understanding such behavior is key for the business to gain a better understanding of their users, and what makes them perform actions of interest for the business. This action could be one which leads to direct monetary benefit for the business (e.g., user making an in-app purchase) or fulfills other key business outcomes (e.g., engagement with a newly released feature). Such insight about favourable user behavior can then be used to improve user experience by optimising the application interface, or create additional triggers, to ultimately identify and encourage similar user behavior in order to improve engagement/completion of this desired action.

The rest of the paper is organised as follows. Section 2 presents the details of the iterative feature pruning clustering algorithm. Section 3 provides details of the case study presented in this paper. The results and discussion are presented in Sect. 4, while conclusions and future research directions are presented in Sect. 5.

2 Method

Overview. We now describe the IFPC technique proposed in [13] in more detail, and in particular its open-source implementation[1], which we adopted to perform our experiments. At a high level, the technique obtains clusters by partitioning a similarity graph where nodes are users and weighted edges represent the similarity in activity between users. The partitioning is recursive: after the graph is partitioned into clusters, a new similarity graph is constructed for each cluster, and partitioned again until the quality of the resulting clusters drops below a minimum threshold. At each step, features that lead to the creation of a cluster are removed when creating the new similarity graph for users in that cluster, allowing the clustering to highlight finer differences in behaviour. Next, we explain how the user activity is captured by a set of features, which are used to compute the similarity graph, and how this is partitioned to obtain clusters.

Clickstream Model. The starting point is the clickstream of each user, composed by all click events e_i from that user, ordered by timestamp t_i. For each event, the model captures both the event type $T_i \in \mathcal{T}$ and a time gap until the next event $G_i = b(t_{i+1} - t_i) \in \mathcal{G} = \{1, 2, \ldots, 5\}$; b is a bucketing function used to make gaps discrete using *less than 1 s, 1 s - 1 min, 1 min - 1 h, 1 h - 1 day* and *more than 1 day* as thresholds for the five buckets. The user clickstream is then converted into a sequence $S = (s_1, s_2, \ldots, s_{2n-1})$ where s alternates event types $\mathcal{T}$ and time gaps $\mathcal{G}$. A simplified model where S is only composed of event types is also considered in our study, as proposed in [12].

Features. Sequences are turned into features by counting the frequency of each sub-sequence of length $k \leq k_{\max}$ (k-grams). The value for feature $f = (s_j, s_{j+1}, \ldots, s_{j+k-1})$ is then c_f, the count of occurrences of f in S. Conceptually a sequence, and thus a user's activity, is characterised by a feature vector c counting occurrences of each possible k-gram in $\bigcup_{k=1}^{k_{\max}} (\mathcal{T} \cup \mathcal{G})^k$, however in practice the feature vectors are sparse enough that is convenient to store features as a map between occurring k-grams and their count. We fixed $k_{\max}$ at

---

[1] https://github.com/xychang/RecursiveHierarchicalClustering.

5 as in [13], with longer sub-sequences becoming unlikely to be repeated across users and thus not contributing substantially to the clustering quality.

Similarity Graph. The similarity between two clickstreams is then computed as the normalised polar distance between their feature vectors:

$$d(S_i, S_j) = \frac{2}{\pi} \arccos \frac{c_i \cdot c_j}{\|c_i\| \|c_j\|} .$$

The distance d is small when the two clickstreams are similar (e.g. S_i is a repetition of S_j) and maximum $d = 1$ in the extreme case of all k-grams of S_i and S_j being disjoint.

Iterative Clustering with Feature Pruning. After a similarity graph is constructed, divisive hierarchical clustering is used to partition the similarity graph into a set of clusters $C = \{C_1, \ldots, C_{n_0}\}$. The number of clusters obtained is controlled by the *modularity* metric which compares the density of intra-cluster edges with the density of cross-cluster edges: clustering stops when the modularity reach the maximum.

As the top-level set of clusters C is obtained, the most relevant features that led to the formation of each C_i are determined by using a simple elbow method based on the χ^2 score to compare users in C_i with users outside it. These features explain the salient characteristics of C_i in C, and thus can be used to interpret each cluster. These feature are then removed from the set of feature for C_i and a new similarity graph is computed from the remaining features. The process is then repeated, performing divisive clustering again on the new similarity graph for C_i resulting in a new cluster set $C_i = \{C_{i1}, C_{i2}, \ldots, C_{in_i}\}$. The process stops when every cluster can not be split further by the divisive clustering procedure.

3 Case Study

The IFPC technique has been previously applied to event streams generated by users of social media to identify malicious, unexpected or low engagement [12,13]. In this paper, we wanted to analyze whether this technique is useful in analyzing and interpreting user behaviour with respect to a specific business key performance indicator (KPI). With this objective in mind, we obtained a labeled dataset of user generated events from Company X^2 which provides a financial management mobile app to its users on both iOS and Android platforms. The company appropriately anonymized the dataset, in accordance with their terms of use and privacy policies, before providing access to the researchers for the purpose of this experiment.

The main objective of this research was to explore how the IFPC technique applied to user clickstreams [13] may benefit the company in understanding how users interact with their mobile application, and identifying certain behaviour patterns which lead to specific actions of interest.

---

[2] Name withheld due to confidentiality.

3.1   Data

For this research, we obtained a dataset of event streams generated by 1000 users who interacted with the mobile application during the period of 15th January 2020 to 28th July 2020. After pre-processing, where we removed any users who had just logged-in and logged-out of the application and had not performed any other tasks, we were left with a dataset composed by **956** unique users. In addition to providing the data, the company also helped us in categorizing the various event types into the following categories:

- **Signup** - This category represents all the events triggered when a user creates an account on their first use of the application.
- **Profile** - Events that are triggered when users go into the profile section of the application to edit information they provided during the signing up process.
- **Connect Bank** - The users can connect their bank accounts through the application. This enables them to benefit from the company's transaction categorization and get better insight into their spending patterns.
- **View Transactions** - Events in this category are triggered when users view their bank transactions, visible after connecting a bank account via the application.
- **Categorize Transactions** - Users may also choose to manually categorize a particular transaction into a certain category, if it wasn't automatically categorized by the application, or if the user wants to modify the category a transaction belongs to.
- **Insights** - The application provides timely and topical insights about users' financial behaviour.
- **Notifications** - These are generated as a "call-to-action" for the users. An example scenario is when a user needs to re-authenticate with the application if an access token has expired.
- **Financial Actions** - This category consists of events which are generated when the user takes a particular action in the application (e.g. saving money by selecting personalized product offerings).

The dataset provided to us by the company also contained labels assigned to all the users. Any user who performed a "Financial Action" at least once during the period for which the data was collected, was labeled as class '1' (considered as *converted user*) and others were labeled as class '0'. Out of the **956** total users in our dataset, **345 (36.1%)** of the users were converted users.

Table 1. Breakdown of events by category.

Event category	No. of events
Sign Up (SU)	3005
Profile (P)	1845
Connect Bank (CB)	6317
View Transactions (VT)	7928
Categorize Transactions (CT)	258
Insights (I)	1979
Notifications (N)	796
Total Events	**22128**

Table 1 shows the distribution of events for each category in the dataset used for the experiment. It is important to note here that when preparing the data, we truncated the clickstreams of the users who performed a financial action (and hence were assigned class label of '1') up to the point they performed the action for the first time. As a result, we excluded a large number of events triggered by them in their subsequent interactions with the application. This was done deliberately as we wanted to cluster based on user actions in other areas of the application and see whether it is a good predictor of a financial action.

3.2   Feature Extraction

Once we had the event streams for the users, the next step was to extract the features to be used for clustering as explained earlier in Sect. 2. Similar to [13], we created k-grams up to $k_{\max} = 5$ and computed their occurrence count for each stream. We tried two variations of modeling the event data into k-grams, namely:

- **Excluding time gaps:** We created k-grams from the sequence of events, ignoring the time intervals between them. As an example the stream ABAC is encoded by the following features: $\{A \to 2, B \to 1, C \to 1, AB \to 1, BA \to 1, AC \to 1, ABA \to 1, BAC \to 1, ABAC \to 1\}$

- **Including time gaps:** In this variation, we considered time gaps between consecutive events, following the same discretisation of the intervals as [13], *i.e., less than 1*s, *1*s–*1*min, *1*min–*1*h, *1*h–*1 day* and *more than 1 day.*

3.3   Evaluation Metrics

We explained earlier in Sect. 2 that the clustering algorithm optimizes for modularity when finding the optimum clustering configuration [1]. Each of the clusters produced by the algorithm is associated with a certain behavioural pattern that characterise users in their interaction with the application. Our aim is to identify to which extent the identified patterns are related to certain business outcomes (e.g. user conversion) which are represented by class labels. Therefore, we used the following well established *external criteria* to evaluate the clustering [9],

Purity

Purity is a simple and transparent external criterion to measure cluster quality when the clustered data is labeled [11]. In our case, the two classes—i.e., whether a user performed a financial action (converted) or not—are the ground truth labels. Given a set of clusters where each data point (user) is labeled, purity is computed by labelling each cluster with the class (i.e., '0' or '1') which is the most frequent in that cluster, and then the accuracy of this assignment is measured by counting the number of correctly assigned points and dividing by the total number of points [7]. More generally, purity (p) is calculated as:

$$p = \frac{1}{N} \sum_k \max_j |c_k \cap y_j| \tag{1}$$

where,
$C = \{c_1, c_2, ..., c_k\}$ is the set of clusters,
$Y = \{y_1, y_2, ..., y_j\}$ is the set of class labels, and
$N = $ the total number of points.

To interpret Eq. 1, consider c_k as the set of users in cluster k and y_j as the set of users belonging to class j. Therefore, for any given values of k and j, $|c_k \cap y_j|$ represents those users in cluster k who belong to class j. The value of purity lies between 0 and 1, where a value of 0 indicates bad clustering and a value of 1 indicates perfectly pure clusters. It is important to note that high purity, as well as the other metrics, is easier to achieve with a large number of clusters. For example, in the most trivial case, if each point is assigned to its own cluster, so we have N clusters, the purity score will be 1. As mentioned earlier the number of clusters is determined according to an internal quality metric (modularity).

Homogeneity

A clustering is defined as being perfectly *homogeneous* (denoted by homogeneity value equal to '1') if all its clusters contain only data points belonging to a single class [8]. In other words, the class distribution within each cluster should be skewed to a single class (*zero entropy*). The homogeneity score of a particular clustering can be calculated based on the conditional entropy of the class distribution given the proposed clustering [8]. In the perfectly homogeneous case, this value, $H(Y|C)$ is 0, where Y is the set of classes and C is the set of clusters (refer to Eq. 1). In the degenerate case, when we have a single class across all points in the dataset, i.e. $H(Y) = 0$, we have perfect homogeneity. For other cases, where there are more than one class, homogeneity (h) can be calculated as follows:

$$h = 1 - \frac{H(Y|C)}{H(Y)} \tag{2}$$

where, C and Y represent the set of clusters and class labels respectively (see Eq. 1). Conditional entropy $H(Y|C)$ is calculated as follows:

$$H(Y|C) = -\sum_{k=1}^{K}\sum_{j=1}^{J} \frac{n_{kj}}{N} \log_2 \frac{n_{kj}}{\sum_{j=1}^{J} n_{kj}} \qquad (3)$$

where, n_{kj} is the number of points in cluster c_k which belong to class y_j.

Classification Metrics

The two metrics discussed so far in this section do not discriminate between the cluster labels, and treat any "misclassification", i.e., assigning a point to a cluster where it is in the minority, equally. However, for our use cases, it is important to understand those incorrect classifications in terms of their types: "false positive" (a class '0' point is assigned to a majority class '1' cluster) or "false negative" (a class '1' point is assigned to a majority class '0' cluster). To achieve this, each cluster is assigned the class label to which the majority (more than 50%) of its points (users) belong. For clusters which have equal number of users belonging to each class, we assign it the positive class label (class '1'). It is worth noting that fully homogeneous clusters will not have any incorrect classifications. We define the following scenarios, in order to use classification metrics to evaluate our clustering:

- **True Positive (TP)**: user labeled as class '1' is assigned to a majority class '1' cluster.
- **True Negative (TN)**: user labeled as class '0' is assigned to a majority class '0' cluster.
- **False Positive (FP)**: user labeled as class '0' is assigned to a majority class '1' cluster.
- **False Negative (FN)**: user labeled as class '1' is assigned to a majority class '0' cluster.

From these values, we can calculate the Precision $(\frac{TP}{TP+FP})$, Recall $(\frac{TP}{TP+FN})$ and F_1 score $(2 \times \frac{\text{Precision} \times \text{Recall}}{\text{Precision} + \text{Recall}})$.

4 Results

In this section, we evaluate the clusters produced by the IFPC technique (Sect. 2) using the external evaluation metrics (Sect. 3.3) that represents whether IFPC is effective in identifying user behaviour which leads to performing a financial action through the app.

Table 2. Events per user.

Class	Users	Events	Events per user
0	611	14478	23.7
1	345	7650	22.2
Total	**956**	**22128**	**23.1**

Our dataset for this experiment consisted of **956** users with a combined total of 22128 events (Table 2). As we can see from Table 2, we had 611 users who did not perform a financial action using the app whereas there were 345 users who did so. Interestingly, the average number of events triggered by both these sets of users is very similar. Therefore, it seems that users interact with the app to a similar extent before deciding whether they want to perform a financial actions (class '1') or not (class '0'). This indicates that the length or scale of user engagement rarely determines whether they will perform this action, and therefore the actual behaviour is important.

4.1 Purity

Table 3 shows the purity scores for the clustering for this experiment. We see that both clustering configurations produce reasonably high values of overall purity. In both cases, the purity value is well above 0.5, which means that most users were placed in clusters where the majority of users had the same class. We see that including time gaps produces a lower number of clusters (50) as compared to when excluding time gaps (63), and the overall purity score for this configuration (0.687) is also slightly lower (0.700 when excluding time gaps).

In addition to calculating the purity of clusters, we were interested in analyzing the nature of clusters with a higher purity score. Figure 1 shows a plot of cluster purity (in %) *vs* the size of the clusters (number of users present in the cluster). Ideally, clusters in the top right corner of the plots—i.e., large clusters having very high purity—are beneficial, as that would enable us to definitively identify behaviour patterns which can be attributed most accurately to each class. We can see from the figure that most such clusters are majority class '0' clusters. For both configurations, the few clusters which are majority '1' class and also have a reasonably high purity score, are very small in size (below 20 users). On the other hand, there are one or two very large clusters which are almost entirely made up of class '0' users (i.e., purity score close to 100%). While such clusters do not contribute in identifying which user profiles are likely to perform a financial action through the app, they nevertheless inform the company as to what action patterns associated with these clusters are very unlikely to result in a financial action in the future.

Table 3. Purity and Homogeneity of clustering.

	Clusters	Purity	Homogeneity
No gaps	63	0.700	0.188
With gaps	50	0.687	0.150

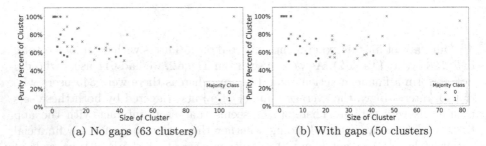

(a) No gaps (63 clusters)   (b) With gaps (50 clusters)

Fig. 1. Comparison between purity and cluster size

4.2   Homogeneity

Table 3 shows that the homogeneity scores for both configurations is quite low. This is expected by looking at purity values as well as Fig. 1, which show that there are many clusters which contain a mix of both classes, and therefore are not homogeneous. Clustering user event streams excluding time gaps produces slightly higher values of homogeneity (0.183) when compared to including time gaps (0.142).

4.3   Classification

Table 4 shows the results of assigning the majority class label to each cluster. We can see that in both configurations, a higher number of clusters were assigned '0' as the majority class label, i.e., more than 50% of users in these clusters had never performed a financial action.

As explained in Sect. 3.3, we use the classification metrics by the majority class label to each cluster generated by the algorithm. Then, we consider how many correct classifications would be made, if the majority label was assigned to each user in each cluster.

To better contextualize the results in this section, we also utilized two well-known classification algorithms, namely *Decision Tree (DT)* [2] and *Random Forests (RF)* [3] with the data—these were used with their default parameters. The feature vectors used by these algorithms are the same k-grams constructed as described in Sect. 2, however IFPC is not used to cluster the users according to the similarity graph, and the algorithms operate directly on the (labelled) k-gram frequency vectors. The comparison with baseline classification algorithms helps us better understand the performance of the IFPC clustering.

Table 4. Label assignments for clusters.

	No. of clusters (majority class)		
	0	1	**Total**
No gaps	40	23	63
With gaps	33	17	50

Table 5. Results for classification metrics.

		Metrics							
		TP	FP	TN	FN	Accuracy	F_1	Precision	Recall
No gaps	**IFPC**	140	82	529	205	**70.0%**	**49.4%**	**63.1%**	40.6%
	DT	112	113	498	233	63.8%	39.3%	49.8%	32.5%
	RF	151	122	489	194	66.9%	48.9%	55.3%	**43.8%**
With gaps	**IFPC**	112	66	545	233	**68.7%**	42.8%	**62.9%**	32.5%
	DT	176	185	426	169	63.0%	**49.9%**	48.8%	**51.0%**
	RF	156	125	486	189	67.2%	49.8%	55.5%	45.2%

Table 5 summarises the classification performance for both configurations. The results show that IFPC produces higher accuracy than Decision Tree and Random Forests in both configurations. Comparing the two configurations, it seems that IFPC performs better without including time gaps in the clickstreams while both the other classification algorithms (in particular Random Forests) seem to perform slightly better when time gaps are included. It is also evident from looking at the results that IFPC has better precision than the other algorithms. This is due to the significantly lower number of false positives (FP) seen for IFPC in comparison to the other algorithms. On the other hand, Random Forests has a better recall than IFPC when excluding time gaps and both Decision Tree and Random Forests outperform IFPC in terms of recall when considering time gaps. Overall, looking at the results for IFPC, it indicates that using clickstream data without time gaps produces better performance, which is in line with results seen for purity and homogeneity as well (Table 3).

For the business, the implication of the performance of IFPC seems to be that it is better than other classifiers at not making false positive errors, therefore, using this technique, the business is less likely to mistakenly identify unfavourable behavior as favourable (low false positives), with the risk of missing out on some favourable user behavior (higher false negatives).

4.4   Action Patterns

The IFPC technique produces action patterns (sequence of k-grams) for each identified cluster. These are the most relevant features that contributed to the formation of a cluster at a specific iteration (see Sect. 2 for details). Such action patterns are interesting for the business to understand and link to particular actions—i.e., for this experiment, a user performing a financial action through the app. To briefly illustrate this, we selected one majority '0' class and one majority '1' class cluster from each configuration.

Looking at Table 6, we see that cluster number 24, when clustering with time gaps, has 79 total users and has only 5.1% of its users labeled as class '1'. The characteristic action pattern shown in the last column illustrates that the users in this cluster did not go beyond the signup flow (SU) of the app. for cluster 46, which is majority class '1' cluster (56.1% users were labeled as class '1'), we find that the users were more engaged with the "view transaction" functionality (VT) of the app. As this is one of the core functionalities of the app, it can be concluded that these users spent more time exploring the app when compared to those in cluster 24.

Considering the clustering without time gaps, we present results from cluster 14 and cluster 49 in Table 6. We can see that cluster 14 is characterized by multiple action patterns and include engagement with "Insights" (I) and "Notifications" (N). However, considering that this is a majority '0' cluster, it indicates that these features of the app did not direct all users towards taking a financial action. Such information can be a useful method of evaluating the effectiveness of certain features (such as notifications and insights) if they are released with clear objectives. This depth of analysis is impossible by just looking at front-end analytics of event streams which generally analyze sequence of events but fail to capture behavior patterns such as these.

Table 6. Action patterns associated with clusters

Configuration	Cluster ID	Size	Majority Class	Class '1' User Percentage	Action Patterns
With Gaps	24	79	0	5.1%	SU 1H / SU 1H SU / SU 1M SU 1H
	46	41	1	56.1%	VT 1H VT 1M / VT 1H / VT 1H VT
No Gaps	14	35	0	37.1%	I / N / I I VT VT VT / I VT
	49	38	1	55.3%	VT / CB VT

Symbols for time gaps:
- 1S : Gap < 1s
- 1M : Gap ∈ [1s, 1min)
- 1H : Gap ∈ [1min, 1hour)

Symbols for events:
- SU ⟶ Signup
- VT ⟶ View Transactions
- I ⟶ Insights
- N ⟶ Notifications
- CB ⟶ Connect Bank

4.5   Discussion

The results presented show that iterative feature pruning clustering does a good job in identifying user behaviours which lead to a financial action in our experiment. We already observed that the difference in levels of engagement, measured as average events per user, between the two classes (i.e., users who converted *vs* those who didn't) was minimal (Table 2) and therefore being able to identify different behaviour patterns using the clustering technique can be beneficial. We find that precision, in particular, is better than recall when using classification metrics, which enables the company to be selective in nudging users who have favorable behaviour profiles with targeted insights and notifications which may lead to user conversion. When comparing the results against classification algorithms, we observed that both precision and accuracy are higher when using IFPC. On the other hand it would be possible to increase the recall performance at the expense of precision and accuracy, by lowering the labelling threshold for class '1' clusters (below the 50% threshold used in our experiment). This would result in identifying more users belonging to the positive class (who can potentially perform an important action), while still maintaining some "targeting" power. While this technique does indeed provide the company with a deeper understanding of user activity in the app, the overall results, including purity and homogeneity of the clusters, indicate that using iterative feature pruning clustering will still leave margins for improvement for predicting user activity on its own, and should rather be used to augment other intelligent systems which rely on other sources of user data (such as information exchanged by users through the platform).

We also observed that modeling the data with or without time gaps has a negligible effect on the clustering. The results produced with these differing models of clickstreams results in very similar clustering which indicates that the algorithm is more sensitive towards the sequence of events rather than the time gaps between them.

5   Conclusions and Future Work

In this paper, we applied the iterative feature pruning clustering (IFPC) algorithm to analyze a real-world dataset of clickstreams from a mobile application. The aim of the research was to explore whether clustering technique can enable businesses to identify different behaviour profiles among their users or not, which may lead to specific actions of interest for the business. Our results show that the clustering is effective in identifying user behaviour that leads to a specific action (e.g., financial action)—the measurements of purity, homogeneity and accuracy are better than a random assignment (50% mark). The method used for experimentation in this paper is agnostic to the target action of interest and may be used in the future to identify behavioural patterns leading to other actions by the company. Hence, the company can potentially use this technique to identify relevant user behaviours and encourage users to trigger any number of actions which may be critical to business outcomes.

A limitation of this research is the amount of data that was available to us for the experimentation. A natural next step would be to consider the impact of larger datasets on the performance of behavioural identification in terms of number of users, event granularity and length of the observation period.

References

1. Blondel, V.D., Guillaume, J.L., Lambiotte, R., Lefebvre, E.: Fast unfolding of communities in large networks. J. Stat. Mech. Theory Exp. **2008**(10), P10008 (2008)
2. Breiman, L., Friedman, J., Stone, C., Olshen, R.: Classification and Regression Trees. Chapman and Hall (1984)
3. Breiman, L.: Random Forests. Mach. Learn. **45**, 5–32 (2001)
4. Larose, D.T.: Discovering Knowledge in Data. Wiley (2005)
5. Liu, Y., Shi, X., Pierce, L., Ren, X.: Characterizing and forecasting user engagement with in-app action graph: a case study of snapchat. In: Proceedings of ACM SIGKDD 2019, pp. 2023–2031. ACM (2019)
6. Luceri, L., Giordano, S., Ferrara, E.: Detecting troll behavior via inverse reinforcement learning: A case study of russian trolls in the 2016 us election. In: Proceedings of International AAAI Conference on Web and Social Media 14(1), pp. 417–427 (2020)
7. Manning, C.D., Raghavan, P., Schutze, H.: Flat Clustering, chap. 16, pp. 356–359. Cambridge University Press (2008)
8. Rosenberg, A., Hirschberg, J.: V-measure: a conditional entropy-based external cluster evaluation measure. In: Proceedings of EMNLP-CoNLL, pp. 410–420 (2007)
9. Schütze, H., Manning, C.D., Raghavan, P.: Introduction to information retrieval, vol. 39. Cambridge University Press Cambridge (2008)
10. Shi, P., Zhang, Z., Choo, K.K.R.: Detecting malicious social bots based on clickstream sequences. IEEE Access **7**, 28855–28862 (2019)
11. Solomonoff, A., Mielke, A., Schmidt, M., Gish, H.: Clustering speakers by their voices. In: Proceedings of the 1998 IEEE International Conference on Acoustics, Speech and Signal Processing, ICASSP 1998 (Cat. No. 98CH36181), vol. 2, pp. 757–760. IEEE (1998)
12. Wang, G., Zhang, X., Tang, S., Wilson, C., Zheng, H., Zhao, B.Y.: Clickstream user behavior models. ACM Trans. Web (TWEB) **11**(4), 1–37 (2017)
13. Wang, G., Zhang, X., Tang, S., Zheng, H., Zhao, B.Y.: Unsupervised clickstream clustering for user behavior analysis. In: Proceedings of the 2016 CHI Conference on Human Factors in Computing Systems, pp. 225–236 (2016)
14. Witten, H., Frank, E.: Data Mining: Practical Machine Learning Tools and Techniques. Morgan Kaufmann, 2nd edn. (2005)
15. Xylogiannopoulos, K., Karampelas, P., Alhajj, R.: Clickstream analytics: an experimental analysis of the Amazon users' simulated monthly traffic. In: IEEE/ACM International Conference on Advances in Social Networks Analysis and Mining (ASONAM), pp. 841–848. IEEE (2018)

Short Application Stream Papers

AI Enabled Bio Waste Contamination-Scanner

Frederic Stahl[1,2(✉)], Oliver Ferdinand[1], Lars Nolle[1,3], Alexandra Pehlken[5], and Oliver Zielinski[1,4]

[1] German Research Center for Artificial Intelligence (DFKI), Marine Perception, Marie-Curie-Straße 1, 26129 Oldenburg, Germany
{Frederic_Theodor.Stahl,Oliver.Ferdinand,Lars.Nolle, Oliver.Zielinski}@dfki.de
[2] Department of Computer Science, University of Reading, Whiteknights, PO Box 225, Reading RG6 6AY, UK
F.T.Stahl@reading.ac.uk
[3] Department of Engineering Science, Jade University of Applied Sciences, Friedrich-Paffrath-Str. 101, 26389 Wilhelmshaven, Germany
lars.nolle@jade-hs.de
[4] Institute for Chemistry and Biology of the Marine Environment, Carl von Ossietzky University of Oldenburg, Marine Sensor Systems Group, Schleusenstraße 1, 26382 Wilhelmshaven, Germany
oliver.zielinski@uol.de
[5] OFFIS-Institut für Informatik Oldenburg, 26121 Oldenburg, Germany
Alexandra.Pehlken@offis.de

Abstract. In Germany Bio waste is collected in separate garbage bins from households in the municipalities (e.g. garden waste, kitchen waste, etc.) and composted. The end result is humus, which is finally fed back into agriculture and closes the organic materials cycle. Waste must be inspected for non-biological contaminants prior to composting, as these can compromise the composting process and damage screening equipment at the recycling facility. Undetected contaminants affect the quality of the humus and can lead to contaminants re-entering the food chain through agriculture. The paper presents a feasibility study of an automatic bio waste Contamination-Scanner aiming to catch contamination early in the recycling process. Image data of bio waste contamination has been collected from a recycling facility. These images were used to design, train and evaluate two Convolutional Neural Networks (CNNs) aimed at detecting contaminants during bio waste collection. One CNN was trained on RGB and the other on greyscale images. The results show an initial surface scan can detect contamination with an accuracy of up to 86% and could form part of a holistic detector attached to bin lorries.

Keywords: CNNs · Contamination detection · Bio waste recycling

M. Bramer and R. Ellis (Eds.): SGAI-AI 2021, LNAI 13101, pp. 357–363, 2021.
https://doi.org/10.1007/978-3-030-91100-3_28

1 Introduction

Contamination of bio waste with inorganic material such as plastic is a major challenge in the bio waste recycling industry, since excessive contamination can break filtering machinery (personal communication with RETERRA GmbH). Also filtering machines are not 100% accurate, the higher the contamination the more contaminants remain in the compost. Contaminants in bio waste significantly reduces the purity of the final product (see Fig. 1) and can lead to contamination of soils and groundwater with microplastics. Microplastics in soils can lead to a reduction of soil density and the release of additives having negative impact on germination, agriculture and ultimately the food chain. If it were possible to automatically detect plastic materials in bio waste bins during collection, composting contaminated bio waste could be avoided. This paper investigates if it is possible to develop an intelligent Contamination-Scanner for the use during bio waste bin collection.

Fig. 1. Bio waste heavily contaminated with impurities (left image) and resulting compost contaminated with plastic (right image)

The scanner opens two possibilities to tackle the contamination problem: (a) avoidance of contaminated bio waste collection, and (b) to reach out to specific clients or neighbourhoods to raise awareness of the environmental implications of incorrect bio waste separation to improve behaviours. The paper contributes a CNN architecture for the Contamination-Scanner, a trained implementation of this architecture on bio waste images, and (3) an evaluation on real data. The use of CNNs is motivated by recent works utilising CNNs to assess the proportion of recyclables in residual waste [5] and to detect plastic contamination in aquatic environments [1,8]. The current limitation is that contaminants must be visible on the surface of the collected waste bin. If successful the study may be extended to different types of sensors to also capture contamination deeper inside the bins. The paper introduces the Contamination-Scanner methodology in Sect. 2, provides an experimental evaluation in Sect. 3 and conclusions are discussed in Sect. 4.

2 Contamination-Scanner Methodology

2.1 Data Preparation and Augmentation

The image data was obtained at a bio waste recycling facility near the town of Bohmte (Germany) part of RETERRA Nord GmbH. At the time of data collection the case study was not planned, hence the images were casually taken from different angles, different lighting conditions and distances. This is expected to negatively affect the detection performance results of the methodology. The images were cut into tile sizes of $100 \times 100 \times 3$ pixels. Experiments with larger tile sizes of up to $200 \times 200 \times 3$ and $300 \times 300 \times 3$ have been conducted. However, the detection performance was considerably lower, with around 50%–60% accuracy, and hence these tile sizes have been omitted in the experimental evaluation. In other works detecting plastic debris from vegetation a $100 \times 100 \times 3$ tile size has also been proven successful [4], although these pictures are different since they were taken from drones at larger distances. The tiles were manually labelled in two classes whether they contain contamination or not. This resulted in a total number of 2227 tiles (84%) not containing contaminants and 426 tiles (16%) containing contaminants. From these tiles three random samples without replacement were taken for training, validation and testing. Each sample contained 142 tiles for each of the two classes. Please note an equal number of tiles per class was desired to avoid bias of training and evaluation towards non-contaminated tiles as they are over-represented. CNNs typically need a large number of training instances to achieve good results, thus augmentation was applied to the training data only. Here the tiles were flipped randomly horizontally and vertically and also randomly rotated by a 90-degree angle. The probability of a flip, rotation or a combination of these was 75%. This resulted in 852 training tiles for each class, thus 1704 training tiles in total. Data augmentation is a common technique to decreases the overfitting on image processing tasks [6].

2.2   Network Architecture

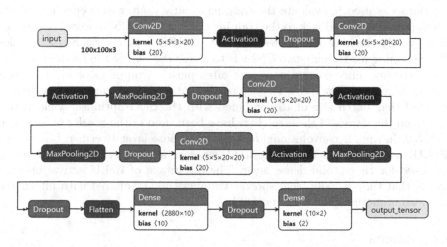

Fig. 2. Contamination-Scanner architecture

The architecture that yielded the best results has been empirically determined and is illustrated in Fig. 2. It consists of four 2D convolutional layers with 20 5×5 kernels. These layers work well on image data by preserving some of the pixel's locality [2,3]. 2×2 max pooling and dropout layers with a dropout rate of 0.2 were included in positions indicated in Fig. 2. Dropouts in neural networks are known to mitigate overfitting and non-optimal co-adaptation, minimizing generalization uncertainties [2,7]. The network is completed by a fully connected dense neural network layer with 10 units followed by a fully connected output layer comprising 2 units, since there are two classes (whether there is contamination or not). Various alternative architectures with different numbers of convolutional and dense layers and also larger dens layers and variations and different levels of dropouts have been experimented with in this study. However, the here presented architecture yielded the highest accuracy and reproducible results. A larger number of dense and larger dense layers appeared detrimental to the stability of the validation accuracy.

3   Experimental Evaluation

This Section presents the preliminary experimental evaluation including experimental setup in Sect. 3.1 and Dicussion of Results in Sect. 3.2.

3.1   Experimental Setup

The data tiles were separated into a training, validation and test dataset, each comprising 142 image tiles for each class. The training data was augmented as described in Sect. 2.2 resulting in 852 training tiles for each class, thus 1704 training tiles in total. Validation and test data were not augmented. The training and validation data were used to train the network and tune hyperparameters. The test data was used to evaluate the training accuracy, after each epoch, however, it was not used as feedback to the training process. Two CNNs were trained, one on greyscale versions of the tiles and one on RGB colour versions of the tiles. The reasoning for training two CNNs is to assess the bias of the method towards bright colours, since contaminants are often plastic wrappings or bin bags containing bright colours. With respect to the batch size an empirical evaluation revealed that batch size of 15 combined with the SDG optimiser yielded best results on the data and these settings have been used in the results presented in Sect. 3.2. In the 2D convolutional and the first dense layer Rectified Linear Unit (ReLU) activation functions were used, whereas a softmax activation function was used for the second dense layer. The advantage of ReLU activation function is that they usually yield shorter training time compared with alternative activation functions like tanh units [2].

3.2   Results

The experiments using the RGB and the grayscale images were repeated 10 times each. The configuration with the highest validation accuracy of each of the

10 models was used for calculating the accuracy of the test images. Hereby the RGB trained Contamination-Scanner achieved an average validation accuracy of 0.89 and a test accuracy of 0.86. The greyscale trained Contamination-Scanner achieved an average validation accuracy of 0.73 and a test accuracy of 0.71. The results of a typical training run with the RGB version of the Contamination-Scanner are illustrated in Fig. 3(a). The model loss is decreasing until 52 epochs and then the model starts to overfit, validation accuracy is also increasing up to epoch 52 to 0.89. The measured test accuracy on unseen test data is 0.84 indicating a small amount of overfitting.

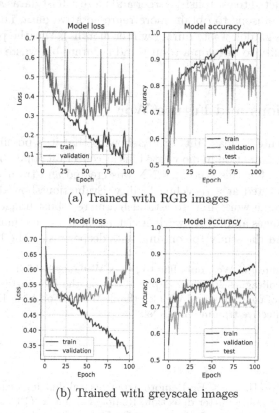

(a) Trained with RGB images

(b) Trained with greyscale images

Fig. 3. Contamination-Scanner trained with RGB and greyscale images

The results with the greyscale version of the Contamination-Scanner are illustrated in Fig. 3(b). The model loss is decreasing until 40 epochs and then the model starts to overfit, validation accuracy is also increasing up to 0.78 at epoch 40. The measured test accuracy on unseen data is slightly lower at 0.73 indicating a small amount of overfitting. Overall, it was observed that training with greyscale images is starting to overfit sooner than for RGB tiles at about 40 epochs and achieves a lower accuracy on test data. Also the training with RGB tiles results in larger fluctuations on the validation and test accuracies compared with training on greyscale tiles. The tiles have thus been examined qualitatively. It was found that contaminants are often plastic bin bags and/or have bright colours. It was also found that a large portion of non-contaminated tiles contain garden waste which often has brown or green colours. Therefore, it is possible that RGB trained networks are to some extent biased towards bright and green colours, which is indicated by the accuracy difference of 0.11 compared with greyscale images. Nevertheless, if some bias towards colours achieves a higher accuracy in identifying contaminants, it is not inconceivable to use RGB images or a combination of RGB and greyscale images. However, more research would need to be conducted to establish a larger and more robust dataset. I.e., collection during different seasons to obtain more representative data, i.e., it is expected that there is less garden waste during winter months). Yet, the presented results show the feasibility to develop a robust and accurate bio waste Contamination-Scanner.

4   Conclusions and Future Work

The paper presented a feasibility study showing that it is possible to automatically detect contamination in bio waste bins at collection point through RGB and greyscale images. For this study a CNN was created and trained on image tiles of bio waste collected at a recycling facility. Evaluation showed an accuracy of up to 84%. Ongoing work aims to establish a more robust image dataset reflecting seasonal changes and future work envisions the use of bio matter penetrating sensors to extend the study to contaminants deeper inside the bins.

Acknowledgemenets. We would like to thank Wolfgang Schöning from RETERRA GmbH and his colleagues for their explanations on the bio waste recycling process and the impacts of contaminants. We also thank Mattis Wolf from DFKI for valuable pointers to the effective training of CNNs.

References

1. Freitas, S., Silva, H., Silva, E.: Remote hyperspectral imaging acquisition and characterization for marine litter detection. Remote Sensing **13**(13), 2536 (2021)
2. Krizhevsky, A., Sutskever, I., Hinton, G.E.: Imagenet classification with deep convolutional neural networks. Adv. Neural. Inf. Process. Syst. **25**, 1097–1105 (2012)
3. LeCun, Y., Bengio, Y., Hinton, G.: Deep learning. Nature **521**(7553), 436–444 (2015)
4. Martin, C., Parkes, S., Zhang, Q., Zhang, X., McCabe, M.F., Duarte, C.M.: Use of unmanned aerial vehicles for efficient beach litter monitoring. Mar. Pollut. Bull. **131**, 662–673 (2018)
5. Mittermayr, R., Klünsner, S.: Smart waste. In: Sihn-Weber, A., Fischler, F. (eds.) CSR und Klimawandel. MCSR, pp. 425–437. Springer, Heidelberg (2020). https://doi.org/10.1007/978-3-662-59748-4_30
6. Shorten, C., Khoshgoftaar, T.M.: A survey on image data augmentation for deep learning. J. Big Data **6**(1), 1–48 (2019)

7. Srivastava, N., Hinton, G., Krizhevsky, A., Sutskever, I., Salakhutdinov, R.: Dropout: a simple way to prevent neural networks from overfitting. J. Mach. Learn. Res. **15**(1), 1929–1958 (2014)
8. Wolf, M., et al.: Machine learning for aquatic plastic litter detection, classification and quantification (Aplastic-Q). Environ. Res. Lett. **15**(11), 114042 (2020)

Parkinson's Disease Tremor Severity Classification - A Comparison Between ON and OFF Medication State

Ghayth AlMahadin[1]([⊠]) [iD], Ahmad Lotfi[1] [iD], Marie Mc Carthy[2] [iD], and Philip Breedon[1] [iD]

[1] Nottingham Trent University, Nottingham, UK
ghayth.almahadin2016@my.ntu.ac.uk
[2] ICON PLC., Dublin, Ireland

Abstract. Tremor is one of the cardinal symptoms of Parkinson's disease. Currently, tremor severity is scored based on the Movement Disorders Society's Unified Parkinson's Disease Rating Scale, MDS-UPDRS, which is subjective and unreliable. Therefore, several studies have tried to measure tremor objectively using machine learning techniques. However, a limited number of studies have explored or compared medication state (ON or OFF) effect on objective measurement of tremor severity. Also, few studies have compared different types of wearable devices for tremor measurement. In this study, the medication state effect on tremor measurement is explored using different machine learning algorithms utilising different datasets that have been collected from different sensors. The results showed that the objective measurement of tremor severity is higher when patients are on medication using the Pebble smartwatch. The highest accuracy achieved was when patients were on medication and obtained 80% accuracy using Random Forest classifier, while the highest accuracy achieved when patients were off medication was 77% using Random Forest and Artificial Neural Network based on Multi-Layer Perceptron.

Keywords: Machine learning · Parkinson's disease · Medication state · Random forest · Support vector machine · Parkinson's disease rating scale

1 Introduction

The four cardinal motor symptoms or features of Parkinson's disease (PD) are often abbreviated as TRAP are Tremor, Rigidity, Akinesia (or bradykinesia), and Postural instability [15].

Tremor is the most common and easily recognised symptom of PD and presents in 70%–90% of PD patients [18]. PD patients show different types of tremor: rest and action tremors [15]. Rest tremor (RT) describes unilateral involuntary, rhythmic and oscillatory movements in relaxed limb. RT occurs at a frequency between 4–6 Hz [18]. The action tremor has two types: Kinetic tremor

© Springer Nature Switzerland AG 2021
M. Bramer and R. Ellis (Eds.): SGAI-AI 2021, LNAI 13101, pp. 364–370, 2021.
https://doi.org/10.1007/978-3-030-91100-3_29

(KT) and postural tremor (PT) [13]. KT is a type of tremor presents during voluntary hand movements such as typing or writing, and occurs at a frequency between 6–9 Hz. PT occurs when a person maintains a position against gravity, such as stretching arms, and occurs at a frequency between 9–12 Hz [13].

Currently, Parkinson's tremor severity is scored based on the Movement Disorders Society's Unified Parkinson's Disease Rating Scale (MDS-UPDRS) from 0 to 4 with 0: normal, 1: slight, 2: mild, 3: moderate, and 4: severe [8]. However, The MDS-UPDRS is subjective and lengthy process [5]. Therefore, researchers have tried to quantify tremor severity objectively using Machine Learning (ML) algorithms with signal processing techniques [3].

An extensive review of the literature showed that many studies have explored many aspects of tremor measurements such as medication response and motor fluctuations. For example, in [14], the authors explored medication dose affect on motor symptoms. In [2], the authors investigated the medication wearing-off effect. In [19], the tremor severity were quantified under two conditions, while patients were on medication and off medication and showed that the correlation with clinical score is higher when patients were on-medication.

This study have investigated medication state effects on tremor severity classification using different machine learning algorithms by utilising data were collected using different sensors while patients were performing various scripted tasks. The main goal of this study is to identify the best medication state to measure tremor either ON or OFF or both.

2   Materials and Methods

The dataset processed and analysed to identify medication state on tremor severity estimation. The sub-datasets were passed independently through three main phases: 1) Signal processing, 2) Features extraction, 3) classification. Each step is described in detail in the following sections.

2.1   Datasets

The datasets used in this study was taken from Levodopa response trial wearable data from the Michael J. Fox Foundation for Parkinson's research (MJFF) [1]. The data were collected from 30 PD patients using two wearable devices that contain a triaxial accelerometer, a GENEActiv[1] wearable device on the wrist of the most affected hand and a Pebble Smartwatch[2] on the wrist of the least affected hand. Data were collected over four days. On the first day of data collection, patients Patients arrived to the lab on their regular medication (On medication) and performed scripted Activities of Daily Living (ADL) and task from Part III of the MDS-UPDRS. Tremor severities were scored by a clinician from 0 to 4. The same procedures on the first day are carried out on the fourth day again,

---

[1] https://www.activinsights.com/products/geneactiv/.
[2] https://www.fitbit.com/global/uk/products/smartwatches.

but the patients were off medication for twelve hours. Table 1 shows the number of instances from each class (tremor severity) that have been extracted from the collected data for day 1 and day 4 from used sensors (GENEActiv, Pebble).

Table 1. Tremor severity distribution on Day 1 (On Medication) and Day 4 (Off Medication).

Tremor severity	Day 1 (On medication)		Day 4 (Off medication)	
	GENEActiv	Pebble	GENEActiv	Pebble
0	18843	19389	16860	17215
1	5845	4491	6534	4421
2	2185	1357	2921	1112
3	845	117	676	103
4	43	11	53	59

2.2   Signal Processing

The signals were recorded through tri-axial accelerometers composed of three orthogonal accelerations a_x, a_y, and a_z . In order to extract meaningful information from the recorded signals, a prepossessing steps is performed. The first step is to eliminate sensor orientation dependency by calculating the vector magnitude of these accelerations. The second step is to eliminate unwanted signals by passing the signals through three band-pass filters with cut-off frequencies 3–6 Hz for RT and 6–9 Hz for PT and 9–12 Hz for KT. The filtered signals were segmented using Fixed-length sliding windows with 50% overlap to isolate the tremor region. The three band-pass filters produced three filtered signals (one signal for each band). The filtered signals were segmented using sliding windows of four seconds length with 50% overlap.

2.3   Features Extraction

Guided by previous work, various features are extracted from each window in the time and frequency domains that showed high correlation with tremor severity [9,13,17].

The features are calculated from three frequency bands, 3–6 Hz for RT, 6–9 Hz for PT, and 9–12 Hz for KT. Table 2 shows the extracted features, where 13 features are calculated in the time and the frequency domain, 7 features in the frequency domain and one feature in the time domain, the total calculated features are $((13 * 2) + 7 + 1 = 34)$. These features are calculated for 3 bands to form a 102 features vector $(34 * 3)$.

Table 2. Extracted features in the time and frequency domains.

Time and Frequency	Frequency	Time
Above mean	Amplitude	Number of peaks
Below mean	Centre frequency	
Autocorrelation	Frequency dispersion (SF50)	
Energy	Fundamental frequency (F0)	
Sample entropy	SF50 − F0	
Kurtosis	Maximum power spectral density	
Skewness	Mean power spectral density	
Standard deviation		
Maximum		
Mean		
Median		
Sum of changes		
Complexity-invariant distance		

2.4   Classification

Three classifiers are considered for classification; Artificial Neural Network based on Multi-Layer Perceptron (ANN-MLP) [16], Random Forest (RF) [6] and Support Vector Machine (SVM) [11].

The ANN-MLP is a multi-layer feed-forward ANN consists of input layer, one or more hidden layers and an output layer. The layers in ANN-MLP are fully connected; this means each node is connected to all the nodes in the previous layer with different weights. The data flows through the layers in one direction from the input layer through the hidden layers to the output layer. ANN-MLP utilises the backpropagation technique to minimise mean squared error between neural network predictions and the actual output by sending the error back through the network and readjust nodes weights.

In this study, an ANN-MLP with 102 nodes in the input layer corresponds to the number of extracted features, 180, 180, 100 nodes in each of the three hidden layers respectively based on prior explorative testing, and 5 nodes in the output layer match to the five tremor severities. A rectified linear unit (ReLU) activation function used in the hidden layers due to it is high convergence performance [10] and softmax activation function in the output layer to predict tremor severities probabilities [7].

RF is an ensemble supervised classification algorithm consists of a set of decision trees. Each tree in the random forest trained from different subsets of the same training set and gives a classification vote. The final classification is based on the majority votes across all the trees in the forest. Guided by previous work, in this study the RF classifier was built with 100 trees [12], and Gini impurity as decision trees split criteria [4]. Other RF parameters were set as the following: The maximum number of features were set to 10, the minimum number of samples required to be at a leaf node was set to 1, the minimum number of samples required to split an internal node was set to 2.

SVM is a supervised classification algorithm that transforms the original feature space into a higher-dimensional space and then finds support vectors to maximize the separation between classes. It used kernel function such as Radial Basis Function (RBF) to form an optimal hyperplane (decision boundary) or hyperplanes in high-dimensional feature space that separates the instances corresponding to different classes. In this study a SVM was built with RBF kernel with coefficient 0.1 , regularization parameter was set to 1, and without limit on iterations.

3   Results and Discussions

The section will discuss the effect of medication state on tremor severity estimation and compare GENEActiv sensor's accuracy with Pebble Smartwatch. Figure 1 shows the accuracy of three classifiers ANN-MLP, RF and SVM used to estimate tremor severity. The classifiers were evaluated with data have been collected using two sensors, GENEActiv and Pebble smartwatch under two conditions: on medication and off medication.

The initial objective of the project was to identify medication state effects on tremor severity estimation. It is clear that the accuracy is higher when patients were on medication with all classifiers and with both sensors. This finding was also reported by Zajki-Zechmeister et al. [19].

Overall, the performance of all classifier with the Pebble smartwatch is higher than the GENEActiv sensor. The best performance is achieved using the RF classifier when patients were on medication using the Pebble smartwatch and obtained 80% accuracy. On the other hand, the worst performance is achieved using the SVM classifiers when patients were off medication and obtained 63% accuracy.

Closer inspection of the figure shows that the RF classifier achieved higher accuracy than other classifiers with both sensors when patients were on medication and obtained 80% with the pebble smartwatch and 71% with the GENE-Active sensor. On the other hand, the ANN-MLP achieved higher accuracy with both sensors when patients were off medication with 66% with the GENEActive sensor and 77% with the pebble smartwatch.

These findings suggest that medication state and type of sensor affect tremor severity objective measurement. In this study, particularly with the dataset used in this work tremor estimation is better when patients were on medication using the pebble smartwatch. However, with a small sample size, caution must be applied, as the findings might not be applicable to all clinical settings and experiments setups, and this need to be validated with different datasets.

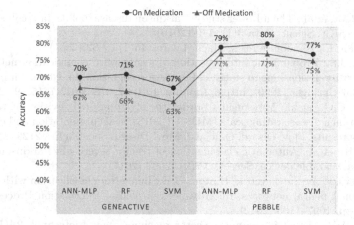

Fig. 1. Classification accuracy of three classifiers (ANN-MLP, RF, SVM) with two sensors (GENEActiv, Pebble smartwatch) under two conditions (On and Off medication).

4   Conclusion and Future Work

The present research aimed to explore medication state effect and type of sensor on tremor severity objective measurement. This study has shown that tremor quantification is better when patients are on medication. Also, it compared different classifiers with two different sensors and found that the Pebble smartwatch with the RF classifier is the best approach to evaluate tremor severity when patients are on medication and achieved 80% accuracy. On the other hand, the ANN-MLP and RF achieved the highest accuracy with the Pebble smartwatch when patients were off medication and obtained 77% accuracy.

These results must be interpreted with caution because of sample size and experiment setup. Therefore, for future studies, it is suggested to evaluate these classifiers and sensors with larger and different datasets that have been collected under two conditions of medication state: on and off. In addition the Pebbles is always used in the least affect hand which need more investigation. Also, the results show that different classifiers achieved different results with different sensors.

References

1. Levodopa response study dataset. https://www.michaeljfox.org/news/levodopa-response-study. Accessed 1 Sept 2021
2. Aghanavesi, S., et al.: A multiple motion sensors index for motor state quantification in Parkinson's disease. Comput. Meth. Programs Biomed. **189**, 105309 (2020)
3. Belić, M., et al.: Artificial intelligence for assisting diagnostics and assessment of Parkinson's disease-a review. Clin. Neurol. Neurosurg. **184**, 105442 (2019)
4. Berk, R.A.: Classification and regression trees (cart). In: Statistical Learning from a Regression Perspective, pp. 1–65. Springer (2008). https://doi.org/10.1007/978-0-387-77501-2

5. Bot, B.M., et al.: The mPower study, Parkinson disease mobile data collected using ResearchKit. Scient. Data **3**(1), 1–9 (2016)
6. Breiman, L.: Random forests. Mach. Learn. **45**(1), 5–32 (2001)
7. Bridle, J.S.: Probabilistic interpretation of feedforward classification network outputs, with relationships to statistical pattern recognition. In: Neurocomputing, pp. 227–236. Springer (1990). https://doi.org/10.1007/978-3-642-76153-9_28
8. Goetz, C.G., et al.: Movement disorder society-sponsored revision of the unified Parkinson's disease rating scale (MDS-UPDRS): scale presentation and clinimetric testing results. Mov. Disord. Official J. Mov. Disord. Soc. **23**(15), 2129–2170 (2008)
9. Jeon, H., et al.: Automatic classification of tremor severity in Parkinson's disease using a wearable device. Sensors **17**(9), 2067 (2017)
10. Krizhevsky, A., Sutskever, I., Hinton, G.E.: ImageNet classification with deep convolutional neural networks. In: Advances in Neural Information Processing Systems, pp. 1097–1105 (2012)
11. Noble, W.S.: What is a support vector machine? Nat. Biotechnol. **24**(12), 1565–1567 (2006)
12. Oshiro, T.M., Perez, P.S., Baranauskas, J.A.: How many trees in a random forest? In: Perner, P. (ed.) MLDM 2012. LNCS (LNAI), vol. 7376, pp. 154–168. Springer, Heidelberg (2012). https://doi.org/10.1007/978-3-642-31537-4_13
13. Pierleoni, P., Palma, L., Belli, A., Pernini, L.: A real-time system to aid clinical classification and quantification of tremor in Parkinson's disease. In: IEEE-EMBS International Conference on Biomedical and Health Informatics (BHI), pp. 113–116. IEEE (2014)
14. Santiago, A., et al.: Qualitative evaluation of the personal KinetiGraphTM movement recording system in a Parkinson's clinic. J. Parkinson's Dis. **9**(1), 207–219 (2019)
15. Shahed, J., Jankovic, J.: Motor symptoms in Parkinson's disease. Handb. Clin. Neurol. **83**, 329–342 (2007)
16. Svozil, D., Kvasnicka, V., Pospichal, J.: Introduction to multi-layer feed-forward neural networks. Chemom. Intell. Lab. Syst. **39**(1), 43–62 (1997)
17. Thorp, J.E., Adamczyk, P.G., Ploeg, H.L., Pickett, K.A.: Monitoring motor symptoms during activities of daily living in individuals with Parkinson's disease. Front. Neurol. **9**, 1036 (2018)
18. Weintraub, D., Comella, C.L., Horn, S.: Parkinson's disease-part 1: pathophysiology, symptoms, burden, diagnosis, and assessment. Am. J. Manage. Care **14**(2 Suppl), S40–S48 (2008)
19. Zajki-Zechmeister, T., et al.: Quantification of tremor severity with a mobile tremor pen. Heliyon **6**(8), e04702 (2020)

Towards Publishing Ontology-Based Data Quality Metadata of Open Data

Iker Esnaola-Gonzalez(✉)

TEKNIKER, Basque Research and Technology Alliance (BRTA),
Iñaki Goenaga 5, 20600 Eibar, Spain
iker.esnaola@tekniker.es

Abstract. Although more and more Open Data is available nowadays, this is not translated into an increase of value-added products and services based on this data. To overcome this issue, communicating the quality level of a specific data set is essential. This article presents a service to help Open Data publishers generating the data quality metadata (DQM) for data sets in an automatic manner, for a variety of file formats, and represented with ontological terms to improve its interoperability. Such a service is expected to contribute to fostering the FAIRness of data.

Keywords: Data quality metadata · Open data · Ontologies

1 Introduction

According to the Open Knowledge Foundation[1], knowledge is open if anyone is able to freely access, use, modify, and share it for any purpose, being subject only, at most, to measures that preserve its provenance and openness. Furthermore, the openness of knowledge or data can drive potential innovation, transparency and economic benefits and this is why governments, organisations and researchers, among others, are contributing to the Open Data movement [6]. However, although more and more Open Data is available nowadays, this is not translated into an increase of value-added products and services based on Open Data [5]. Therefore, it can be concluded that legal and technical openness of data sets is not enough to create a prolific reuse ecosystem.

One of the main barriers may be attributed to failures in providing high quality data, as this affects its reuse [2]. There are techniques and methods that deal with different data quality problems, but if the actual problems of the actual datasets are not known, potential Open Data reusers need to make an thorough analysis of the data to be reused first, which can end up being very resource-consuming. This article presents a service to help Open Data publishers generating the data quality metadata (DQM) for data sets in an automatic manner, for a variety of file formats, and represented with ontological terms to

---

[1] https://okfn.org.

© Springer Nature Switzerland AG 2021
M. Bramer and R. Ellis (Eds.): SGAI-AI 2021, LNAI 13101, pp. 371–376, 2021.
https://doi.org/10.1007/978-3-030-91100-3_30

improve its interoperability. Such a service is expected to contribute to fostering the FAIRness of data.

The rest of the article is structured as follows. Section 2 motivates the need ofthe presented service and Sect. 3 describes the proposed approach. Section 4 showcases the application of the approach in a real-world scenario and finally, conclusions are presented in Sect. 5.

2   Motivating the Need of Data Quality Metadata

Literature suggests that communicating the quality level of a specific data set is essential [4], specially with a view to increasing such data set's reusability potential. That is, if data consumers are informed about a given data set's high-quality, it is probable that they will be more eager to reuse it compared with another data set with no quality-related information.

Let us consider the following scenario to motivate the need of publishing DQM. 50 weather stations are deployed across the Basque Country (Spain) and a public body is in charge of publishing their measurements. Each weather station is composed of different IoT devices measuring a total of 8 weather parameters with a periodicity of 10 min. So, at the end of the day, a total of 57,600 data items have to be published, and over 1,720,000 data items by the end of the month.

Manually checking that all the collected data items are correct, can end up being an arduous task. Furthermore, the associated metadata has to be understandable by different potential users, applications and services to increase its reusability. And since data sets may also be published in different file formats, the DQM needs to be able to be generated from a variety of them. Therefore, all this evidence reinforces the need of a service that helps data publishers generating DQM automatically and with the less human intervention possible, in an interoperable format following ontologies but avoiding the problems that may derive from a lack of technical skills and understanding of ontologies from the data publishers, and from a wide variety of machine-processable files formats, including proprietary as well as non-proprietary ones.

3   The Approach

This article proposes a service that, given a file containing time series data, generates its corresponding DQM. The service involves minimum human intervention, admits a wide range of file formats as input, and represents metadata with ontologies accepted and well-known by the community to improve its interoperability.

The process followed by the proposed service is as follows. First, the data publisher chooses the file from which the DQM will be generated. Then, the content of the file is analysed and its quality metrics are evaluated automatically. Afterwards, the obtained quality metrics, which are in plain text, are automatically translated and converted into RDF triples which represent the data quality information with adequate ontology terms. Finally, these triples are materialised in an RDF file. Figure 1 summarises this process which, with a minimal human intervention, generates the original file's corresponding DQM.

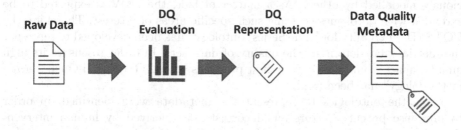

Raw Data   **DQ Evaluation**   **DQ Representation**   **Data Quality Metadata**

Fig. 1. DQM generation workflow.

3.1 Data Quality Evaluation

After reading the content of the original file, the data quality metrics need to be calculated. This is done by leveraging the functionalities of the DQTS (Data Quality for Time Series), a tool developed in R to measure and evaluate certain data quality dimensions and metrics of time series, including completeness and timeliness. These data quality metrics are Strings, and therefore, they are not compliant with the interoperability needs previously identified.

3.2 Data Quality Representation

In order to make the output of the DQTS interoperable, this information needs to be annotated with adequate ontological terms. And to select these ontological terms, an analysis of existing ontological resources was performed, aiming at reusing an existing ontology, as recommended by the Data on the Web Best Practices[2]. After assessing and comparing ontologies based on the criteria defined by [3], the Data Quality Vocabulary (DQV)[3] [1] was selected for being the most appropriate one.

The DQV provides a metadata model for expressing data quality. One of the main reasons for selecting DQV is that it reuses standard W3C vocabularies such as SKOS[4], the RDF Data Cube vocabulary[5] or the PROV Ontology (PROV-O[6]). Furthermore, it is based on DCAT[7], just like the DCAT-AP does, which is the standard ontology used by the official European Open Data portals.

---

[2] https://www.w3.org/TR/dwbp/.
[3] https://www.w3.org/TR/vocab-dqv.
[4] http://www.w3.org/TR/skos-reference.
[5] http://www.w3.org/TR/vocab-data-cube.
[6] http://www.w3.org/TR/prov-o.
[7] https://www.w3.org/TR/vocab-dcat.

However, there are some concepts that are not covered either by the DQV or other existing ontologies, namely, the concepts referring to the time series data quality metrics. This fact is not exceptional at all in the Semantic Web community, as there are very specific knowledge areas that have not been previously modelled by others. As a matter of fact, the DQV is expected to be extended with ontologies covering such specific areas of interest. Therefore, the DQTS (Data Quality for Time Series) ontology[8] has been developed to represent the metrics that determine the quality of data sets. In order to ensure its high quality, apart from following the best practices, the LOT (Linked Open Terms) methodology[9] has been used.

Once the ontologies to represent the metadata were identified, in order to minimise potential errors and inconsistencies derived by human intervention, a specific service has been developed for performing the semantic annotation and the creation of the corresponding RDF file. This service is based on Apache Jena[10], a Java framework for building Semantic Web and Linked Data applications.

4   In Use: Generating Open Data DQM

The feasibility of the proposed approach has been tested in a real-world use case. Namely, an Excel file containing air quality measurements retrieved from the Open Data portal of the Basque Government[11] has been used. This data set contains air quality data hourly registered by a station during January 2021. Each registry measures twelve different qualities, including ammonia and ozone concentration levels. Figure 2 shows an excerpt of the Excel file.

1	Date	Hour	CO (mg/m3)	CO 8h (mg/m3)	NO (µg/m3)	NO2 (µg/m3)	NOX (µg/m3)
41	27/01/2021	09:00	0,29	0,31	21	48	79
42	27/01/2021	08:00	0,26	0,32	3	29	33
43	27/01/2021	07:00	0,37	0,33	28	40	82
44	27/01/2021	06:00	0,36	0,33	19	31	60

Fig. 2. Excerpt of the Excel file containing air quality information registered by the weather station.

This Excel file is used as input for the service to generate its associated DQM. In a first step, the Excel file is analysed and its data quality metrics are automatically calculated, as summarised in Table 1.

After this information about the actual quality of the data is obtained, it is automatically annotated with previously selected ontologies. An excerpt of

---

[8] https://w3id.org/dqts.
[9] https://lot.linkeddata.es/.
[10] https://jena.apache.org.
[11] https://opendata.euskadi.eus.

Table 1. Data quality metrics of the use case Excel file.

Data quality metric	Value
Starting time	01/01/2021 1:00:00
End time	29/01/2021 00:00:00
Completeness	98%
Time uniqueness	100%
Timeliness	100%

the resulting RDF triples describing the Excel file's data quality are shown in Listing 1.1.

```
PREFIX dcat: <http://www.w3.org/ns/dcat#>
PREFIX dcterms: <http://purl.org/dc/terms/>
PREFIX dqv: <http://www.w3.org/ns/dqv#>
PREFIX dqts: <http://www.w3id.org/dqts#>
PREFIX ode: <http://opendata.euskadi.eus/>

ode:airQuality2021_barakaldo a dcat:Dataset ;
    dcat:distribution ode:airQuality2021_barakaldo_xlsx .

ode:airQuality2021_barakaldo_xlsx a dcat:distribution ;
    dcterms:title "XLSX distribution of the air quality
        data set for Barakaldo".

:completeness a dqts:CompletenessMetric.

:measurement1 a dqv:QualityMeasurement;
    dqv:computedOn ode:airQuality2021_barakaldo_xlsx;
    dqv:isMeasurementOf :completeness;
    dqv:value "98"^^xsd:decimal.
```

Listing 1.1. Excerpt of RDF triples describing the data quality of the Excel file.

Finally, these triples are materialised into an RDF file, thus storing the DQM associated to the original Excel file. Summarising, thanks to this process, the Open Data portal can now publish the DQM associated to the air quality measurements registered by a weather station. Likewise, this is expected to increase this Open Data's reusability.

5   Conclusions

Data Quality is one of the main issues in nowadays plentiful Open Data and if its full potential is aimed to be unlocked, it is necessary to ensure its high quality. To do so, both Open Data publishers and reusers would benefit from having an associated DQM to their target data sets.

In this article a service that generates DQM with a minimum human intervention, works for different file formats, and is interoperable thanks to its representation according to standardised ontologies is presented. This service is expected, on the one hand, to help Open Data providers to increase their data sets' reusability, and on the other, to ease the exploitation of this Open Data for the development of value-added products and services.

5.1 Future Work

In order to further test the usability and validity of the presented service, author envisions to contact regional and state Open Data portal managers and present them the service, as this feedback would help improving the service. Once these improvements are made, the release of the code is envisioned as a contribution to the Open Data community.

Furthermore, the presented service is envisioned to be enhanced in future iterations, including functionalities to (semi-)automatically improve the quality issues and deficiencies identified in the data sets. Likewise, FAIRness assessment tools will be used for its evaluation and further improvements.

Acknowledgments. This work is partly supported by the project 3KIA (KK-2020/00049), funded by the SPRI-Basque Government through the ELKARTEK program and the REACT project which have received funding from the European Union's Horizon 2020 research and innovation programme under grant agreement no. 824395.

References

1. Albertoni, R., Issac, A.: Introducing the data quality vocabulary (DQV). Semant. Web **12**(1), 81–97 (2021). https://doi.org/10.3233/SW-200382
2. Detlor, B., Hupfer, M.E., Ruhi, U., Zhao, L.: Information quality and community municipal portal use. Gov. Inf. Q. **30**(1), 23–32 (2013)
3. Esnaola-Gonzalez, I., Bermúdez, J., Fernandez, I., Arnaiz, A.: Ontologies for observations and actuations in buildings: a survey. Semant. Web **11**(4), 593–621 (2020). https://doi.org/10.3233/SW-200378
4. Moges, H.T., Van Vlasselaer, V., Lemahieu, W., Baesens, B.: Determining the use of data quality metadata (DQM) for decision making purposes and its impact on decision outcomes-an exploratory study. Dec. Supp. Syst. **83**, 32–46 (2016). https://doi.org/10.1016/j.dss.2015.12.006
5. Rhind, D.: What is the Value of Open Data? (2014). https://www.nationalarchives.gov.uk/documents/meetings/20140128-appsi-what-is-the-value-of-open-data.pdf
6. Sadiq, S., Indulska, M.: Open data: quality over quantity. Int. J. Inf. Manage. **37**(3), 150–154 (2017). https://doi.org/10.1016/j.ijinfomgt.2017.01.003

Towards a Brain Controller Interface for Generating Simple Berlin School Style Music with Interactive Genetic Algorithms

C. James-Reynolds[✉] ⓘ and E. Currie ⓘ

Middlesex University, London, UK
C.James-Reynolds@mdx.ac.uk

Abstract. A novel approach to generating music is presented using two interactive Genetic Algorithms with electroencephalogram inputs from two subjects as their fitness functions. Many interactive Genetic Algorithm approaches for generating music employ constrained solution spaces that only utilise notes from a given scale. Our work incorporates the use of mutation to extend the solution space through the inclusion of accidental notes. A thresholding approach is adopted, that allows riffs to be repeated until fitness drops, together with a 'kill switch' to ensure unpleasant sounding riffs are removed from the population. The development is ongoing, with more testing and calibration required to ensure that there are no timing errors in communication between the microcontroller boards and to identify the most appropriate threshold and mutation ranges, in addition to determining the most appropriate mixes for the users to hear.

Keywords: Interactive genetic algorithm · Electro-encephalograph · Music generation

1 Background

1.1 Literature Review

Direct Brain to Music interfaces have been built [1] but it is not yet possible to map brain output in the form of electroencephalogram (EEG) data for example to create music that can be performed by a synthesiser as it is imagined. A simple interface of this type would map energy in frequency bands from the EEG data to Musical Instrument Digital Interface (MIDI) data for example. Of course it is possible to have an intermediary system that can do this. The human body with its appendages can do this with years of training. Technology allows us to create user interfaces that make it easier to create meaningful music by restricting the user to specific scales, rhythms and patterns; for example the Korg Kaossillator [2] does this. Alternative approaches have made use of evolutionary algorithms [3–5]. These are not Direct Brain to Music interfaces, but users can evaluate outputs and adopt the role of a fitness function.

Genetic Algorithms (GAs) are a form of search or hill climbing algorithm based on Darwinian evolution theory. They were popularized by Holland [6]. We typically

© Springer Nature Switzerland AG 2021
M. Bramer and R. Ellis (Eds.): SGAI-AI 2021, LNAI 13101, pp. 377–382, 2021.
https://doi.org/10.1007/978-3-030-91100-3_31

start off with a random population of solutions where each solution is considered as an individual. The parameters that define the solution are the alleles. We then evaluate the individuals for fitness by using a fitness function. Individuals that have the best fitness are then selected to be parents on the basis of that fitness. Different selection strategies can be used such as ranking and roulette wheel approaches. Parents are then used to create offspring using a crossover function that combines alleles. The process repeats until an optimal solution is generated. To avoid the possibility that the original population did not have sufficient diversity to find an optimal solution, for each of the offspring, random mutations may be applied with a given probability [7].

Interactive GAs differ from tradition GAs in that the fitness function is based on human interaction, typically by a human consciously rating the output. Ratings can also be obtained subconsciously by measuring the subject's response to the output using sensors such as EEG [5, 8–10].

iGAs such as GenJam [3] have used crowd sourced input as their fitness function to produce musical scores. This project explores the use of two individual subconscious human inputs using EEG, into two iGAs. One iGA generates lead riffs and the other iGA generates bass riffs. These are outputted together as a single coherent piece of music for rating by the listeners. A threshold function is implemented to keep riffs (We use the definition from [11]) playing by pausing the playing of the next pattern while mindfulness [12] levels remain high and these resume when the mindfulness levels falls below a specific threshold. Typically many iGA strategies allow for a reduced solution space to facilitate the greater probability of producing musically pleasant riffs. This may take the form of using a specific key and scale type to ensure that note sequences are not "unpleasant" sounding. In order to achieve the benefits of this approach and the greater probability of creating genuinely interesting patterns facilitated by a larger solution space, the introduction of accidental notes via mutation is allowed to increase the solution space.

A more restricted solution space could produce solutions similar to those of Mozart's dice game [13, 14], which uses the idea of throwing dice to generate a piece of music from pre-selected patterns that fit together. This works with music where some simple structural rules can be applied such as Electronic Dance Music.

1.2   Motivation

The work described in this paper is based on previous work involving the use of an iGA to generate Mondrian-style paintings [9] and visual effects to assist with achieving mindfulness [10]. The fitness function of these iGAs was computed from real-time EEG readings from the subject, thus quantifying the subject's subconscious responses to the successive 'paintings' and patterns with which they were presented by the iGA. From these works, two issues were identified that needed further exploration. Firstly it was noticed that when EEG readings were used as a fitness function for an iGA, the human subject would often produce a high rating for mindfulness for a while as the algorithm converged on a satisfactory solution (one for which the subject might choose to stop the algorithm), but after a time the rating would drop, possibly indicating that the subject was bored, distracted or that the image no longer held the same appeal.

This is easy to understand in terms of music. A short riff may be catchy and interesting to listen to, but if it is played for a long period of time, it might become boring or even irritating. The introduction of a threshold value for the fitness function that would cause the iGA to pause when it found a good enough solution, store that solution and then to continue when the rating dropped below the threshold. We also considered some of the issues caused by restricting the solution space to a limited set of solutions. For example, in [9] the solution space was limited to values obtained through analysis of a number of Mondrian's works and teasing out a simplified version of their common defining characteristics. The software then embodied these rules, leading to the production of creations with limited variability. Boden discussed this issue in her work on creativity and AI [15].

However, utilising unrestrained solution spaces can also cause interesting issues to arise. For example, in a previous iGA project [16], we found that allowing a wide range of variables in an interactive synthesiser created sounds that were fit solutions inasmuch as they encouraged mindfulness, but were not musically useful. By using a compromise it is hoped to allow the solution space to grow over time if selection permits; this is achieved by enabling mutation to select values (accidental notes) that are outside the initial solution space. This might also produce some unpleasant results and undesired results could be terminated early.

Music is often the result of collaboration and musicians will often "jam" together in order to develop riffs and songs. In order to achieve this, we employ two EEG headsets with two users; one responsible for the lead line and the other responsible for the bass line.

The prototype is being developed on the Arduino platform [17], as this is low cost and standalone.

2 Implementation

Two Mindwave EEG headsets are used [18] to send data to two Bluesmirf Silver Bluetooth [19] modules connected to Arduinos. The headsets provide data as a range from 0 to 100 for different frequency bands, The code parses the data and allows for EEG bands identified by the manufacturer as attention and meditation to be selected via a pushbutton and a corresponding LED displays the selection. The parameters available in the implementation are attention, meditation and an average of the two which is taken to represent mindfulness [20]. In order to facilitate testing and modification of the code, a software based serial link using pins 10 and 11 of the Arduino as Tx and Rx respectively are used to send the data to the Arduinos running the iGA.

The individual solutions generated by the iGA algorithms running on each of the two Arduinos differ in the number of notes in their patterns and in their octaves. This allows one of the iGAs to produce a bassline and the other a lead line. The patterns are also adjusted accordingly.

The iGA has four seeded patterns as the starting parents and these are sent to the MIDI Master Board over I2C. Each parent consists of the following parameters:

• Notes – currently a one octave range (C to C), the bassline is two octaves lower than the lead line, Notes are 7 bit integers.

• Key – for both riffs
• Pattern – Eight patterns with 16 slots are available for the lead line. The bass line has eight patterns with 8 slots allowing timing changes
• Delay Time – delay times are in fractions of the tempo
• Delay Amount – the level of the delay (currently not implemented)

The MIDI Master Board plays a pattern for 4 bars (this is easily adjustable for more or less bars) and if the threshold has been met will continue to play for another 4 bars or until the threshold falls. The tempo of the music is manually controlled by a potentiometer and allows a range of 80 to 140 Beats Per Minute. The MIDI output is sent to two MIDI channels on a synthesiser (Currently using a Roland MU50 to test) and also to an effects unit to create the delay effect. The next sequence is then sent to the MIDI Master Board. At the end of each sequence the current EEG data is stored as a rating value by the IGA Boards. Button switches connected to the iGA Arduinos and the MIDI Master Board allows riffs to be killed off if they are unpleasant, much in the way that musicians jamming might try something and then not repeat it if it does not sound pleasant.

The iGA can use either a roulette or tournament method for selecting candidates for creating the next generation and this can be changed in the code. Offspring are created using a single point crossover and have a chance of mutation for all their values, the mutation probability can be determined in real-time with a potentiometer, currently allowing between 0 and 10%.

One of the challenges in designing the hardware is the communication between different boards. The I2C protocol used does allow for boards to switch between Master and Slave, but this was considered to be overly complex, as only one board at a time can be Master and the EEG Boards and iGA Boards run in parallel. Use of I2C between MIDI Master and Slave iGA boards is appropriate as the communication can always be initiated by the Master which will request data when it is ready to play. A simple serial communication between the EEG boards and their associated iGA boards allows for communication between the slaves and is accomplished using a software serial port. The prototype wired for testing the communication is shown in Fig. 1.

Overall structure of iGA algorithm (simplified):
Initial seeded population sent from iGA boards to MIDI board
(A)For each individual ():
    MIDI board plays individual for x number of times (currently 4)
    Rating is taken from EEG board as an average of meditation and attention and stored
  If rating exceeds threshold for satisfactory solution, repeat from (A)
Ratings of all individuals are used to create roulette wheel
Roulette wheel runs to select parent pairs
Crossover and mutation (approx. 5% used currently) applied to create offspring
Repeat from (A).

An example of an output on the 6th generation is C, C (Oct), A, G, D$^{\#}$, E, F, F where the D# is from a mutation and works musically. Fine tuning of mutation rate and thresholds for each user can be modified on the fly by means of potentiometers.

Fig. 1. The prototype for testing communication on the bass line.

3 Limitations and Future Work

The main purpose of the research was to explore the use of thresholding to provide novel and interesting solutions, with the potential of extending the solution space through mutation. The use of the crude EEG headset is a limitation and it might be possible to get much better results with more sophisticated EEG equipment.

From a musical perspective electronic music in this style often evolves quite subtly over time and may revisit earlier riffs. This can be achieved by making the riffs chosen for initial seeding more similar to each other, which leads to the generation of more subtle sequences of changes by the algorithm. It might be possible revisit riffs by allowing "good" riffs to be saved to memory and reintroduced to the population.

It is difficult to be certain whether the current approach is optimal. It might be better to have a single iGA for both the lead and bass riffs and this could also be extended to include rhythm [21]. However, the advantage of having separate users responsible for different instruments is that they can make their own decisions about when to remove an individual from the population or keep it for future use.

Currently the main developmental issues are around the timing and communication between boards. Having delays between notes is not a problem if all the delays are equal. When one note is slightly out of time it disrupts the flow of the sequence.

References

1. Miranda, E.R., Brouse, A.: Interfacing the brain directly with musical systems: on developing systems for making music with brain signals. Leonardo **38**(4), 331–336 (2005)
2. https://www.korg.com/uk/products/dj/kaossilator2s/. Accessed 7 July 2021
3. Biles, J.A.: GenJam: a genetic algorithm for generation jazz solos. In: Proceedings of Computer Music Conference (ICMC 94), pp. 131–137 (1994)
4. Miranda, E.R.: Brain-computer music interface for generative music. In: Virtual Reality, p. 8 (2006)

5. 'Vox Populi: Evolutionary Computation for Music Evolution.pdf (no date)
6. Holland, J.H.: Adaptation in Natural and Artificial Systems. University of Michigan Press, Ann Arbor (1975)
7. Melanie, M.: An Introduction to Genetic Algorithms. The MIT Press, Cambridge, Massachusetts, London, England, Fifth printing (1999)
8. James-Reynolds, C., Currie, E.: EEuGene: employing electroencephalograph signals in the rating strategy of a hardware-based interactive genetic algorithm. In: Bramer, M., Petridis, M. (eds.) Research and Development in Intelligent Systems XXXIII, pp. 343–353. Springer, Cham (2016). https://doi.org/10.1007/978-3-319-47175-4_25
9. Němečková, I., James-Reynolds, C., Currie, E.: Evolutionary art with an EEG fitness function. In: Bramer, M., Petridis, M. (eds.) Artificial Intelligence XXXVI, SGAI 2019. Lecture Notes in Computer Science, vol. 11927. Springer, Cham (2019). https://doi.org/10.1007/978-3-030-348
10. James-Reynolds, C., Currie, E.: Mindfulness mirror. In: Bramer, M., Petridis, M. (eds.) SGAI 2019. LNCS (LNAI), vol. 11927, pp. 456–461. Springer, Cham (2019). https://doi.org/10.1007/978-3-030-34885-4_36
11. Salomoni, M., Carter, J.: GenMuse: an evolutionary creativity enhancement tool. In: Bramer, M., Petridis, M. (eds.) SGAI 2019. LNCS (LNAI), vol. 11927, pp. 229–240. Springer, Cham (2019). https://doi.org/10.1007/978-3-030-34885-4_18
12. Bishop, S.R.: Mindfulness: a Proposed Operational Definition. Clin. Psychol. Sci. Pract. **11**(3), 230–234 (2004); Health Module
13. Hedges, S.A.: Dice music in the eighteenth century. Music Lett. **59**(2), 180–187 (1978)
14. Noguchi, H.: Mozart: Musical game in C K.516f (1996). http://www.asahi-net.or.jp/~rb5hngc/e/k516f.htm
15. Boden, M.A.: Creativity and artificial intelligence. Artif. Intell. **103**, 347–356 (1998)
16. James-Reynolds, C., Currie, E.: Eugene: a generic interactive genetic algorithm controller. In: AI-2015, The Thirty-fifth SGAI International Conference, 15–17 Dec 2015. Cambridge (2015)
17. Arduino. https://www.arduino.cc/. Accessed 7 July 2021
18. NeuroSky: NeuroSky Brainwave Starter Kit (2018). http://developer.neurosky.com/docs/doku.php?id=mindwave_mobile_and_arduino. Accessed 19 July 2021
19. Bluesmirf. https://www.sparkfun.com/products/retired/12577. Accessed 16 July 2021
20. Lomas, T., Ivtzan, I., Fu, C.H.Y.: A systematic review of the neurophysiology of mindfulness on EEG oscillations. Neurosci. Biobehav. Rev. **57**, 401–410 (2015). https://doi.org/10.1016/j.neubiorev.2015.09.018
21. Horowitz, M.D.: Generating rhythms with genetic algorithms. In: Proceedings of the AAAI National Conference on Artificial intelligence, Menlo Park (1994)

Author Index

Printed in the United States
by Baker & Taylor Publisher Services